An Age of Accountability

New Directions in the History of Education

Series editor, Benjamin Justice

The New Directions in the History of Education series seeks to publish innovative books that push the traditional boundaries of the history of education. Topics may include social movements in education; the history of cultural representations of schools and schooling; the role of public schools in the social production of space; and the perspectives and experiences of African Americans, Latinx Americans, women, queer folk, and others. The series will take a broad, inclusive look at American education in formal settings, from prekindergarten to higher education, as well as in out-of-school and informal settings. We also invite historical scholarship that informs and challenges popular conceptions of educational policy and policy making and that addresses questions of social justice, equality, democracy, and the formation of popular knowledge.

Dionne Danns, *Crossing Segregated Boundaries: Remembering Chicago School Desegregation*

Sharon S. Lee, *An Unseen Unheard Minority: Asian American Students at the University of Illinois*

Margaret A. Nash and Karen Graves, *Mad River, Marjorie Rowland, and the Quest for LGBTQ Teachers' Rights*

Diana D'Amico Pawlewicz, *Blaming Teachers: Professionalization Policies and the Failure of Reform in American History*

John L. Rury, *An Age of Accountability: How Standardized Testing Came to Dominate American Schools and Compromise Education*

Kyle P. Steele, *Making a Mass Institution: Indianapolis and the American High School*

An Age of Accountability

How Standardized Testing Came to
Dominate American Schools and
Compromise Education

JOHN L. RURY

Rutgers University Press

New Brunswick, Camden and Newark, New Jersey

London and Oxford

Rutgers University Press is a department of Rutgers, The State University of New Jersey, one of the leading public research universities in the nation. By publishing worldwide, it furthers the University's mission of dedication to excellence in teaching, scholarship, research, and clinical care.

Library of Congress Cataloging-in-Publication Data

Names: Rury, John L., 1951– author.
Title: An age of accountability : how standardized testing came to dominate American
  schools and compromise education / John L. Rury.
Description: New Brunswick, New Jersey : Rutgers University Press, 2023. |
  Series: New directions in the history of education | Includes bibliographical
  references and index.
Identifiers: LCCN 2023007455 | ISBN 9781978832275 (paperback) | ISBN 9781978832282
  (hardcover) | ISBN 9781978832299 (epub) | ISBN 9781978832312 (pdf)
Subjects: LCSH: Education—Standards—United States—History. | Educational
  accountability—United States—History. | School improvement programs—
  United States—History. | Academic achievement—United States—History.
Classification: LCC LB3060.83 R87 2023 | DDC 379.1/580973—dc23/eng/20230324
LC record available at https://lccn.loc.gov/2023007455

A British Cataloging-in-Publication record for this book is available from the British Library.

References to internet websites (URLs) were accurate at the time of writing. Neither the author nor Rutgers University Press is responsible for URLs that may have expired or changed since the manuscript was prepared.

♾ The paper used in this publication meets the requirements of the American National Standard for Information Sciences—Permanence of Paper for Printed Library Materials, ANSI Z39.48-1992.

rutgersuniversitypress.org

To America's educators, who have endured so much in the wake of accountability and yet persevered in service to their students and the nation's future

Contents

Abbreviations

ACT	American College Testing
AERA	American Educational Research Association
AYP	Adequate Yearly Progress
CAP	Cooperative Accountability Project
CAT	California Achievement Test
CATS	Commonwealth Accountability Testing System
CEEB	College Entrance Examination Board
CEO	Chief Executive Officer
CLAS	California Learning Assessment System
CPS	Chicago Public Schools
CTBS	California Test of Basic Skills
DIF	Differential Item Functioning
DoDEA	Department of Defense
ECS	Education Commission of the States
ESEA	Elementary and Secondary Education Act
ESSA	Every Students Succeeds Act
ETS	Educational Testing Service
GED	General Educational Development test
IQ	Intelligence Quotient
ITBS	Iowa Test of Basic Skills
KERA	Kentucky Education Reform Act
KIRIS	Kentucky Instructional Results Information System

MCT	Minimum Competency Testing
NAACP	National Association for the Advancement of Colored People
NAEP	National Assessment of Educational Progress
NAGB	National Assessment Governing Board
NCEST	National Council on Educational Standards and Testing
NCLB	No Child Left Behind
NCME	National Council on Measurement in Education
NCTM	National Council of Teachers of Mathematics
NCTPP	National Commission on Testing and Public Policy
NEGP	National Educational Goals Panel
NESAC	National Education Standards and Assessment Council
NGA	National Governors' Association
PARCC	Partnership for Assessment of Readiness for College and Careers
PISA	Programme for International Student Assessment
PTA	Parent Teacher Association
RAND	Research and Development (Corporation)
SAT	Scholastic Aptitude Test/Scholastic Assessment Test
SSATII	State Student Assessment Test II (Florida)
STEM	Science, Technology, Engineering, and Mathematics
TAAS	Texas Assessment of Academic Skills
TIMSS	Trends in International Mathematics and Science Study
UCLA	University of California at Los Angeles
USCCR	U.S. Commission on Civil Rights

An Age of Accountability

Introduction

School Accountability and Standardized Testing in American History

The observation that standardized testing is out of hand in American education has become a familiar refrain. In the past fifty years the use of such assessments has increased markedly, and now represents a focal point in many thousands of schools. Much of the public may associate such tests with the 2001 "No Child Left Behind" legislation, but it actually began much earlier. It also preceded the well-known 1983 report, *A Nation at Risk*, often credited with inspiring school accountability. The roots of today's "high stakes" assessments extend back to the 1960s and the advent of expanded federal and state-level responsibility in public schooling.[1]

Accountability is a term that denotes responsibility, the necessity of justifying actions or decisions, and an answerable party. It has a long history in education, dating at least from the nineteenth century. Beginning with the advent of state-sponsored school systems to train virtuous and responsible citizens, and perhaps prepare them for work, critics wanted to know how well they functioned. This was certainly the case in Europe, and many other parts of the world.[2] In the United States education remained a largely local concern and accountability there took a somewhat different course. In larger school districts, mostly in big cities, it often accompanied rapid growth, when budgets swelled dramatically. This inevitably raised questions about resources being used prudently and effectively. Similar questions prompted accountability measures in years to follow.[3]

These matters were political to one degree or another, often addressing productivity, integrity, and goals: What was the appropriate cost for schools and who should pay? Was corruption and waste a danger? And what were the most valuable purposes schools should serve? Other questions focused on the competence of educators. Their work could be rather ambiguous, especially regarding outcomes, and critics suggested it often was ineffective or even toxic. Some argued that teachers were lazy or cruel, failing to respect students or deliver useful lessons. Educators usually had one set of answers to such questions; political leaders frequently had others. Much debate has revolved around which of these perspectives would prevail. Struggles also occurred between communities over educational goals and resources, especially regarding minority groups. But accountability commonly involved conflicts between those situated inside and outside of education systems, especially in more recent times, when school efficacy became a compelling political question.[4]

In the past half century the politics of education has taken a distinct form, which Lorraine McDonnell has described as a "hortatory" policy orientation, exhorting goals or objectives to mobilize or shape public opinion. From a somewhat more practical standpoint, accountability policies have hinged decisively on using test scores to leverage school improvement.[5] In this respect they became more than hortatory, usually entailing an implicit theory that public dissatisfaction with test results could compel educators to make changes or face the wrath of disgruntled constituents. Accountability policies could have other effects too, such as raising real estate values with high assessment scores. In this manner test results could cast a bright light on an educational marketplace, creating winners and losers in popular opinion and the quest for status.[6]

At the national level, and in many states, hortatory politics focused on academic achievement, often in response to disappointing assessment outcomes and public discontent with schools. In this respect it reflected a human capital agenda, represented in arguments that certain academic abilities were essential to success in economies driven by technological advancement. Human capital theory had emerged during the 1960s, holding that skills and knowledge were a driving force in economic growth. It was a perspective that appealed to business leaders and others worried about regional and national development, especially after 1980. To the extent that it gained political traction, however, this agenda rarely improved school performance, although it did help to rally popular support for additional testing. As education became an ever larger public concern, the human capital agenda gained wider influence. And standardized assessment became the prevailing mechanism for documenting its progress.[7]

Yet other historical developments contributed to the contemporary rise of test-based accountability. As mentioned above, rising public expenditures often led to calls for greater oversight of institutions and their budgets. In 1965

Senator Robert Kennedy suggested requiring reports on the use of Title 1 funds when the historic Elementary and Secondary Education Act was debated in Congress. And as academically trained economists gained more influence in federal agencies, similar expectations for linking programmatic budgets to observable outcomes became more widespread. During the long postwar era, local and state funding for education grew more than sixfold, prompting worries about how these dollars were being spent. The increase was due partly to rising enrollments, but per-pupil costs grew too. By 1980 state education expenditures exceeded either local or federal contributions, a dramatic change from largely local funding fifty years earlier. These developments helped to set the stage for enhanced accountability measures at the state level, which is where they then appeared.[8]

At the same time, opinion polls suggested that Americans were growing more concerned about problems in the schools. Newspaper headlines featured student protests over a range of issues, including racial conflict linked to school desegregation, greater teenage personal freedom, and disciplinary policies. Some reports focused on recent graduates' lack of skills, suggesting that standards had declined with the "baby boom" generation. And some parents worried that desegregation posed a threat to academic and disciplinary norms, fueling "white flight" from big city education systems. The term "social promotion" assumed negative connotations, reflecting public concerns that students were graduating without expected skills, knowledge, and self-control. Such concerns also contributed to calls for greater accountability.[9]

Eventually test scores themselves became grist for the mill, as widely publicized declines in college entry exam results contributed to public apprehension about the quality of education offered by American schools more generally. This was especially important in the 1970s, when many began feeling anxious about the country's global status and future prospects. International test results likewise became a factor, especially during the years when American students scored well below peers in certain other countries. These events became an additional source of commentary, contributing directly to the human capital policy agenda thereafter. Enabling American students to excel in such assessments became a major hortatory talking point in the 1980s for national and state leaders, who argued that test-based accountability was essential to achieving that goal.[10]

Finally, a generation of political leaders embraced the idea that markets represented the most efficacious means of improving institutions. This was symptomatic of what Gary Gerstle has described as a neoliberal political order, emerging in the closing decades of the twentieth century. Economists were influential then too, but figures from both major political parties—including Lamar Alexander, George W. Bush, Bill Clinton, and Richard Riley—eagerly embraced this perspective, with particular emphasis on education. They largely agreed that assessment could foster school reform, making American students more competitive in a global marketplace where human capital dictated economic success. After failed attempts at establishing national tests to boost academic performance, this impulse culminated in the bipartisan 2001 No Child Left Behind (NCLB) legislation, the product of a historic coalition of business and civil rights organizations that resulted in a broad (if disjointed) national assessment program. It was a remarkable turn in federal policy and put testing at the very center of the nation's education system.[11]

NCLB may have been partially sold on human capital grounds, making American students more productive, but it also reflected the application of market principles to education policy. As suggested earlier, assessment was critical to creating competition among schools, helping families make choices between institutions. And this became yet another function of accountability. As long as test scores signaled districts and schools for families to patronize, market pressures were supposed to incentivize educators to improve performance. And the key was a comprehensive and reliable testing regime widely considered legitimate and fair. Whether this was actually accomplished, on the other hand, was another question.[12]

Given its recent genesis, in that case, test-based accountability in education has remained a fundamentally political issue in contemporary American history. At its core, questions about competence, the cost of schooling, and the aims of education continued to be important. But hortatory politics played an outsized role too, especially in light of popular sentiment that American schools were underperforming. Politicians largely succeeded in mobilizing opinion to support accountability policies, but they also often ignored difficulties in standardized testing. Contemporary psychometric assessments represented a peculiar form of technology, developed in response to widely perceived problems. While much of the public has viewed such tests as valid measures of achievement, however, contemporary assessments have also produced a number of problems. There has been significant evidence of narrowing instruction, curricula altered to boost test scores, and even outright cheating. And research has indicated that such problems mounted as standardized assessment became more pervasive. It is thus hardly an exaggeration to suggest that widespread testing has compromised more reasonable and comprehensive goals in many American schools, even though most policy makers—and the public at large—continued to endorse it.[13] The process by which this came about is the focal point of this book.

Standardized Testing in the United States: A Capsule History

As suggested above, accountability became an important school policy question in the nineteenth century, as leaders sought to exert control over institutions. One of the earliest instances occurred in the mid-1840s, when Horace Mann and allies on the Boston School Committee challenged the teachers in some better-known local institutions. They administered an exam to students, and results seemed to show that many of the schoolmasters were ineffective, resulting in some being dismissed and others reassigned. Following this, such assessments eventually became widespread, at least in the larger cities and other districts where questions about the schools often arose.[14]

Early versions of such tests were fairly simple by today's standards, often requiring students to fill in blanks or match answers to questions from a list of choices. They also might have asked for short definitions, corrections of misspelled words, or even summaries of reading excerpts. They could be graded relatively easily, offering a rudimentary snapshot of academic skills. Their chief use was for promotion from one grade to another, especially in the upper reaches of urban systems, and entry to secondary schools. One understandable effect was heightened student stress and anxiety, and failure rates that led to older youth remaining in lower grades. "Testing mania" became a public concern, leading to reforms that curtailed such assessment in favor of classroom tests written by educators. These were considered progressive reforms, providing educators greater latitude in shaping assessment to align closely to instruction, and to assess student interests and strengths.[15]

A new era of assessment began in 1904, when French psychologists Alfred Binet and Theodore Simon unveiled a series of tests to determine the educability of children. While Binet and Simon did not believe such instruments measured a single construct that could be labeled "intelligence," others did adopt various versions of the scale for that purpose. In particular, Stanford University educational psychologist Lewis Terman launched a line of inquiry with lasting effects both in education and society at large. In 1916 he published the first version of the so-called Stanford–Binet test of intelligence (or "mental age"), which became widely influential. Two versions of a similar test were administered to more than a million army draftees a year later, following U.S. entry into World War I. This was the first large-scale use of a standardized mental assessment, with a lasting impact.[16]

Firmly believing that group differences in the resulting scores were linked to inherent cognitive ability, psychologists interpreted the army testing results as confirmation of such distinctions. In particular, they treated the performance of minority groups as evidence of mental inferiority. These views were widely disseminated, conforming with long-standing stereotypes and bolstering policies of racially segregated and unequal schooling. Tests based generally on the Stanford–Binet scale were soon employed widely in schools and other settings to decide appropriate courses for students, given presumed differences in intellectual capacity. Such assessments legitimized educational and social inequality, linking both to supposedly scientific findings in the emerging field of psychometrics.[17]

Just before Terman's intelligence test was published, Frederick Kelly at the Kansas Normal School in Emporia administered the first standardized test including multiple-choice items. Designed to measure ability as a function of speed and accuracy, it was closer to a modern achievement exam than Terman's IQ test, focused on a single skill domain. Kelly and other test builders published similar assessments for a range of subjects, often used to compare school systems and even to judge teacher performance.[18]

With respect to higher education, the era's best known assessment product was the Scholastic Aptitude Test, or SAT, a standardized college admissions exam. Its development was sponsored by the College Entrance Examination Board (known today as the College Board), founded in 1899 to propose college admission requirements. The SAT was somewhat similar to the army test, but broader in orientation and including questions deemed relevant to college-level work. It was first administered in 1926, hailed as a more democratic means of choosing applicants than simply recruiting from select secondary schools, as leading universities had previously done.[19]

Despite widespread prejudices regarding mental abilities, tests such as the SAT eventually helped identify a wide range of potential college students. African Americans and certain other minority groups were generally excluded from most institutions, despite growing college enrollments, often with test score differences as a rationale.[20] Subsequent research demonstrated that much of the racial difference in IQ scores was linked to long-standing inequalities in education and standards of living, especially in the South.[21] And starting with James Coleman in the 1960s, sociologists clearly showed that family background factors played a major part in test score variation of all types. Remarkably, this point often was overlooked in debates over test-based accountability, certainly in the past but in more recent times too. There can be little doubt that such factors perform critical but often unappreciated roles in determining who succeeds and fails on tests of all kinds.[22]

The word "aptitude" in the SAT was a telling remnant of its historic connection to the army intelligence testing program (it was later changed to "assessment"), but also pointed to changing conceptions of performance in psychometrics. As the field grew in scope and technical sophistication, statistical analysis of test data revealed patterns that were labeled traits, constructs, and abilities, along with error. Psychometric theory held that assessment data could reveal latent attributes and capabilities that otherwise might be unrecognized, especially if tests could be devised to minimize inaccuracy regarding stated goals. The concepts of reliability (consistency of measurement) and validity (approximation of veracity) became familiar touchstones for evaluating test score data. In the end, psychometricians aimed to measure qualities of mind, with aptitude—or specific abilities—being especially important both to educators and the general public.[23]

At about the same time that the SAT became more widely used, so-called achievement tests began to appear in American schools. Among the best known was the Iowa Test of Basic Skills, or ITBS, a standardized assessment intended to help elementary educators identify student strengths and weakness and improve instruction. First developed in 1935, the ITBS was norm referenced, ranking individual performance on a scale developed with a nationally representative sample of peers. It featured math problems, reading exercises, and questions about vocabulary, science, civics, and other subjects in elementary curricula. Created at the University of Iowa for use in the state's public schools, it eventually found a national market. For the most part, however, the ITBS and its high school counterpart, the Iowa Test of Educational Development, was *not* intended for use in accountability programs.[24]

Given these developments, it did not take long for American schools to become beset by standardized testing of one sort of another. Students were regularly assessed with the ITBS or one of its many competitors, along with similar exams at the secondary level, and many took the SAT or the ACT (American College Testing, also developed at the University of Iowa) for college admission. While the latter carried high stakes in evaluating youth for higher education, the others were intended to help teachers identify learning problems their students faced. It took decades for standardized in-school assessments be adapted to accountability purposes, and the appearance of a changing political environment that demanded answers to widespread concerns about the quality of education.[25]

Problems with Test-Based Accountability

By the time Americans entered the postwar era, standardized testing had become a familiar feature of school life. But it still was not widely used systematically for accountability. Most American schools prior to the 1960s were controlled and funded locally, so there was little pressure from other sources to account for resources or assess instruction. Yet the potential dangers of testing for accountability were clearly recognized. Leading psychometricians acknowledged the difficulties such measures could entail. Indeed, as E. F. Lindquist, director of the Iowa Testing Program, observed in 1951, the use of tests for these purposes threatened to compromise the educational process being scrutinized: "The widespread and continued use of a test will, in itself, tend to reduce the correlation between the test series and the criterion series for the population involved. Because of the nature and potency of the rewards and penalties associated in actual practice with high and low achievement test scores of students, the behavior measured by a widely used test tends in itself to become the real objective of instruction, to the neglect of the (different) behavior with which the ultimate objective is concerned."[26]

In 1976 the prominent statistician and psychologist Donald T. Campbell published an essay entitled "Assessing the Impact of Planned Social Change," in which he made an observation quite similar to Lindquist's. It has since become known as Campbell's Law, a widely cited caution against the use of tests for high-stake accountability when assessments have material consequences for individuals and organizations delivering instruction. "Achievement tests may well be valuable indicators of general school achievement under conditions of normal teaching aimed at general competence. But when test scores become the goal of the teaching process, they both lose their value as indicators of educational status and distort the educational process in undesirable ways."[27]

The implications of both Lindquist's and Campbell's observations were sobering for test-based accountability as an education policy option. When substantial rewards and sanctions are linked to assessment results, as in most accountability systems, there is a very strong tendency for test scores to become the focal point of instruction rather than simply a source of information about it. While this was principally a question of potential danger when Lindquist and Campbell wrote, it would become a much bigger problem in years to follow.[28]

In everyday classroom practice, of course, testing always has been integral to accountability, whether holding students responsible for homework or conscientious attention to readings and lectures. This mainly was a matter of teachers routinely assessing students for what they were expected to learn. Such exams also were useful for providing feedback to students and teachers alike, helping them to identify points of weakness in mastering relevant information and skills. But all assessments work best when they challenge students to gain a comprehensive command of relevant material, even if only a sampling of it can be included in a test. Preparing for a such an exam, after all, can help students to think about topics in new ways, to discover new information, distinctions, and interactions that may not be evident otherwise. To perform effectively, however, most assessments require that students do not know questions in advance, as it could constrain their preparation and foreclose such insights. Student performance under these conditions is generally a poor reflection of what they actually know about a particular topic or knowledge domain. In fact, when students gain access to test questions in advance, it is generally described as "cheating."[29]

A related if somewhat different condition also worried both Lindquist and Campbell. Even the most comprehensive assessments only can cover a sampling of the material addressed in a given grade level, class, or other locus of instruction. It is thus important that students do *not* know which topics and skills such examinations will cover. If they only learn such tested material, after all, their education will be incomplete, and the test would be a poor indicator of the curriculum they were supposed to master. The same is true if teachers only focus instruction on tested topics; their students are shortchanged then too. This is one of the principal challenges of test-based accountability, and Lindquist's remarks more than seventy years ago, along with Campbell's Law, suggest it has long been known within the measurement field. The greater the role of assessment in evaluating educators and institutions, the more such behavior is likely, even if motivated by concerns about students. As Daniel Koretz has argued, these conditions threaten to make test-based accountability a "charade."[30]

Campbell and other critics of test-based accountability have suggested that quantitative measures of student achievement should be augmented by qualitative assessment to avoid these pitfalls. Just how this can be best accomplished, however, has been subject to debate.[31] Part of testing's appeal, after all, is its relatively low cost and seeming objectivity. Historically, authors of norm-referenced assessments claimed that they largely were impervious to test preparation, apart from a general orientation. Along with being inexpensive, this seemed to make them ideal for a new age of standardized exams in education, but not for accountability. The shift to so-called criterion-referenced testing for accountability purposes posed a different set of problems. These assessments were supposed to reflect what students had been taught, and as such they were subject to the testing vagaries that Lindquist, Koretz, and other critical observers had identified. There was also the difficult question of how to establish cut scores to identify proficiency on such exams. These were challenges that advocates of testing for accountability purposes faced almost from the beginning, even if they often failed to acknowledge them.[32]

But these were hardly the only problems with test-based accountability. Even if these psychometric limitations were less a conundrum, its very premise as widely practiced also was problematic on sociological grounds. Social scientists have long understood that test scores are far more sensitive to variation in family background and peer effects than to institutions or teachers. This meant that the test scores that typically were used to assess schools in NCLB and similar accountability regimes were at best a very limited and possibly distorted representation of institutional performance. Accountability advocates have argued that factors such as family background and peers should *not* be considered mitigating conditions in evaluating schools and educators. But this viewpoint represented a failure to acknowledge the realities of working in low income or largely impoverished settings. Pointing out the effect of such circumstances was not just "making excuses" for seemingly poor performance. Unlike more affluent and better educated parents, households in these communities often lacked the resources to carefully "cultivate" children for success in school. The results have contributed to what sociologist Annette Lareau has described as "unequal childhoods," which routinely prepare students for quite different pathways in academic achievement. Simply put, the disheartening test scores that schools serving low income and poor communities often report are more likely the consequence of these factors than the effort and ability of educators who staff them.[33]

As a consequence of widening residential segregation along socioeconomic lines, not all schools faced quite the same challenge in meeting assessment expectations. Faced with preparing students for accountability exams, institutions serving impoverished communities often devote far more time to test preparation than other schools. The consequences can mean curricula and instruction hewed decisively to tested topics and skills, instead of otherwise meaningful and engaging education. This is where the admonitions of Lindquist and Campbell likely have greatest resonance. Years of research have demonstrated that low income students have borne the brunt of narrowly focused instruction in the wake of NCLB and other test-based accountability regimes. And studies suggest that such teaching is far less effective in stimulating deeper mastery than helping students to learn through inquiry and discovery. In this regard, it is possible to say that these policies contributed to greater inequality in American education, at least regarding well-rounded and appealing school experiences.[34]

Economists have voiced yet another set of concerns, suggesting that the academic skills measured by standardized tests may not even be the most important aspects of schooling. Achievement exams, after all, focus on just one dimension of school experiences, the academic curriculum. The best known critic in this respect has been James Heckman, a Nobel laureate at the University of Chicago. In studying the economic effects of the General Educational Development test, or GED, Heckman found that individuals who passed that exam, an achievement test to certify high school skills and knowledge, did little better in the labor market than high school dropouts. The reason for this, he has argued, is that while individuals who take the GED may have good academic skills, they often lack character traits that employers value. These include respect for others, punctuality, cooperativeness, honesty, loyalty, and following organizational rules, among other attributes.[35]

It turns out that formal schooling cultivates many of these qualities in students, at least partly out of necessity in serving large numbers of them in rather confined spaces with many goals to accomplish. Perhaps most significantly, successful teachers cultivate responsible behavior and respect for others for orderly and effective delivery of instruction. Heckman suggested that early development of these attributes was especially important.[36] He and other economists have argued that such so-called noncognitive character traits, which achievement tests measure only indirectly at best, are the principal contributions of schools to the economy, and perhaps society at large.[37] Heckman and Tim Kautz also cited Lindquist to corroborate the limits of achievement testing, drawing from the same 1951 essay quoted earlier: "In general, satisfactory tests have thus far been developed only for objectives concerned with the student's *intellectual* development, or with his purely *rational* behavior. Objectives concerned with his nonrational behavior, or his emotional behavior, or objectives concerned with such things as artistic abilities, artistic and aesthetic values and tastes, moral values, attitudes toward social institutions and practices, habits relating to personal hygiene and physical fitness, managerial or executive ability, etc., have been seriously neglected in educational measurement" (emphasis in original).[38]

Heckman and his collaborators have suggested that the widely purported relevance of achievement tests to economic development is largely a "myth." They argue that test-based accountability has contributed to higher dropout rates and more difficult labor-force transitions for many thousands of youth. High school exit exams, an approach to accountability practiced for nearly fifty years, appeared to lead students to leave school prematurely, many thinking the GED a better option.[39] This was a serious indictment of hortatory policy stances premised on the belief that higher achievement was essential to economic growth and prosperity. If the principal contribution of schooling is the development of desirable character traits, adopting requirements that drive students away from schools can hardly be judged positively.

Test-based accountability, it turns out, has become associated with a variety of problems, both within the schools and in their larger social and political contexts. But the politics of educational reform hinged so decisively on psychometric assessment that policy makers were disinclined to question it, and public opinion largely viewed it favorably for many years. Added to this, many measurement practitioners proved quite willing to embrace various accountability tasks despite these issues.[40] Looking at how this approach to educational reform developed can be quite helpful in understanding it, and the many debates regarding its pitfalls over the years. To do this, of course, requires some historical perspective, which is the chief objective of this book. A necessary first step is one of considering how standardized testing itself became associated with accountability, which was hardly inherent in its development.

Test-Based Accountability in Recent History: A Synopsis of the Book

The chapters that follow provide a historical account of test-based accountability in the United States. Focusing on the period between 1970 and 2020, they identify major stages in the evolution of accountability policies and politics at local, state, and national levels. Roughly chronological in organization, the book is also organized thematically. While not an omnibus history, it does offer a guide to key developments both in education policy and in measurement technology. It is not a pleasant or happy tale, but one that held profound implications for millions of students and the educators who served them.

As suggested earlier, accountability became an important policy objective during the latter 1960s and 1970s, when state and federal governments began providing substantial streams of revenue to public schools. Some date it from Robert Kennedy's 1965 recommendation that states monitor these programs and issue reports to Washington. The accounting that resulted varied considerably and focused inconsistently on educational outcomes. Few state-level points of comparison existed, although assessments such as the SAT and ACT offered an incomplete picture of significant differences. Starting in 1970, the National Assessment of Educational Progress offered a profile of academic achievement for different age groups, but not state-level statistics until 1992. In the meantime, state expenditures on education also began to increase, especially in the South, as governors and legislatures sought to improve school performance, usually with an eye to economic development. This often included higher pay for teachers and new facilities, but also entailed demands for greater accountability. Additional funding typically proved politically feasible when linked to accountability measures of one kind or another. This was especially true when business interests played a role in economic development plans, and taxation also became an issue.[41]

The first stage in the rise of test-based accountability began in the South and eventually extended to other parts of the country. It is addressed in chapter 1. The focal point was basic skills assessment, typically under the umbrella term "minimum competency testing" (or MCT), and was aimed at students rather than teachers or schools. MCT was intended to address an apparently widespread perception that school standards were slipping, and that high school graduates lacked essential skills and knowledge. Many such concerns likely were linked to school desegregation, and racialized fears of declining standards with greater integration. The hortatory message at the time was that such assessments would cause students and educators to take achievement more seriously, and thus resolve problems of poor performance. These tests generally were not norm referenced in the manner of the Iowa tests, but rather were "criterion referenced." This typically meant they were intended for particular curricula or programs of study, although distinctions between the two types of tests often blurred in practice. Many states eventually adopted high school exit exams, which students had to pass in order to graduate. One result, not surprisingly, was higher dropout rates, especially among minority youth. MCT-based accountability programs ultimately proved very controversial and did little to improve the overall performance of schools. Racial and ethnic achievement gaps did begin to close at this time, but most observers did not credit MCT-based accountability for these gains.[42]

The disparate impact of MCT accountability programs on racial minority groups, and African Americans in particular, led to legal challenges in Florida,

Texas, and elsewhere during the 1980s and 1990s. These cases turned decisively on the question of how well such assessments reflected the curricula that students had been taught. They also hinged somewhat on the question of cultural bias in test questions and other aspects of these assessments, a long-standing concern of African Americans and other groups. These questions are explored in the book's second chapter, which extends discussion of them into the 1990s. After a rather protracted process of litigation and related investigations, federal courts upheld the authority of states to conduct assessments for accountability purposes, utilizing MCTs for secondary graduation requirements. Subsequent research, however, challenged the premise that such examinations improved achievement generally or even helped to close racial and ethnic gaps in test scores or graduation rates, eventually leading many states to drop or relax such requirements. Continuing investigation revealed a range of factors potentially impacting minority performance on assessments, including differential item functioning and so-called stereotype threat. Eventually, civil rights organizations also shifted their stance on testing, supporting accountability as a means of monitoring how well schools served minority students.[43]

MCT remained the predominant form of test-based accountability for nearly two decades, but it ultimately was replaced by standards-based reform, which entailed the development of more sophisticated assessments and higher expectations regarding achievement. The latter tests emerged in the wake of a so-called excellence movement in education, often attributed to the influence of *A Nation at Risk*, a widely publicized critique of American schools issued by a federal commission in 1983. Together with a well-documented decline in SAT scores during the 1970s and the lackluster performance of American students on international assessments, this report helped to heighten public concerns about education. These developments took the better part of the 1980s decade to unfold, and are described in chapter 3. *A Nation at Risk* represented hortatory politics taken to an extreme, highlighting education as a national issue. But other factors also encouraged new approaches to test-based accountability, and once again much of the action occurred in the states. Kentucky, Maryland, California, Vermont, and a number of other states emerged as leaders in experimenting with new accountability measures. New exam formats and so-called authentic assessment also became a focal point of reform. By the latter 1990s, it was possible to say that much of the country had moved beyond MCT, and most new state tests assessed the performance of schools rather than students. This was a critically important shift, and paved the way for historic developments at the federal level in the following decade.[44]

At the same time that state accountability systems were changing, Washington roiled with debates over national testing proposals. This was partly spurred by the international assessments mentioned earlier. The articulation of national educational goals became a controversial response, a paradigmatic instance of hortatory policy deployment. This era is the focal point of chapter 4. It began with President George H. W. Bush's proposal for a national testing program with coordinated state assessments in 1990, which failed to find much support in Congress. Six years later the Clinton administration proposed a "voluntary national test" in mathematics and English that met a firewall of Republican opposition, although a pilot version was eventually authorized. Both incidents were instructive, revealing deep-seated opposition to national assessments both from right and left wings of the political spectrum. Republicans were wary of federal intrusion into education, a responsibility traditionally assigned to states. And African Americans and other minority groups worried that a national test would highlight achievement gaps without providing resources to address them. By the time of George W. Bush's election in 2000, it was clear that the idea of a nationwide test like those utilized in other countries was not a politically viable option for the United States.[45]

These developments set the stage for the NCLB legislation passed in George W. Bush's first year as president, and described in chapter 5. NCLB was similar in some respects to the testing program proposed by his father, requiring states to assess their students annually but allowing them to choose the tests to accomplish it. The principal difference was that NCLB required testing in most elementary grades and expected results to improve with time. It also stipulated that scores for key subgroups be reported, for racial and ethnic minority students in particular, and that their achievement should also improve. The stated goal was universal proficiency by the year 2014, and a special version of the National Assessment of Educational Progress (NAEP) was designated as an audit test to ensure that state assessments were sufficiently demanding and thorough. Altogether, it was an ambitious reform program guided largely by an expansive hortatory political framework. As such it represented a culmination of test-based accountability proposals at both state and national levels. At stake were federal funds for Title 1 and other programs, resources that nearly all states viewed as indispensable. Schools that did not meet improvement targets were subject to sanctions, including dismissal of staff and state takeover of administration to effect changes. It was a bold policy intervention, premised on the assumption that annual assessments and required improvement could compel educators to make American students competitive with the best of their global peers.[46]

Despite its commendable goals, however, NCLB ultimately proved a disappointment. While it did appear to increase achievement in elementary mathematics somewhat, overall there was little improvement in NAEP scores over the next fifteen years. Accountability requirements soon proved unpopular with educators, especially in schools that struggled to meet test score improvement expectations. These generally were institutions serving low income and minority students, which often had difficulty keeping students in school and focused on instructional goals. Staff turnover often was a problem too. NCLB testing expectations also proved difficult in affluent communities that served poor and minority students, as achievement gaps persisted. The Obama administration, while initially quite critical of NCLB, kept most testing provisions in place following 2008, but also offered states waivers from annual improvement guidelines. Under the leadership of Arne Duncan, its Department of Education sponsored a "race to the top" competition with economic recovery funds, while continuing to emphasize standardized assessment for accountability. Under Obama and Duncan, the competitive logic of marketplaces remained a keystone of educational reform, a central tenet of neoliberal policy doctrine. Even if the most draconian features of NCLB were softened somewhat, federal commitment to test-based accountability remained intact throughout the era.[47]

In late 2015 the Obama administration managed to pass the Every Student Succeeds Act (ESSA), which provided states greater discretion in meeting federal accountability expectations, but also kept test-based accountability requirements largely in place. This reflected the continued significance of business interests and civil rights organizations, the right–left coalition that helped to bring NCLB to fruition. It also was testimony to how thoroughly accountability had become engrained, despite growing public skepticism about testing, as no other policy regime was generally considered worthy of serious consideration. The idea that educators and schools must be held accountable through standardized assessment, despite all the problems that it entailed, had become an article of conventional wisdom among policy makers. Put another way, the nation's educators continued to be considered untrustworthy and the human capital agenda remained inviolate. The fact that this was a policy initiative sponsored by a Democratic administration was evidence of how deeply rooted such focal points had become, despite a historic alignment between the national party and major teacher unions and other professional education organizations. This was confirmation that an "age of accountability" had clearly dawned in the history of American education, and when it was likely to end remained far from clear.[48]

The Limitations and Future of Test-Based Accountability

The theory of change embedded in almost all test-based accountability programs held that assessment with stipulated consequences could lead to major improvements in schools, particularly regarding academic achievement. Judging from a variety of indicators, however, the results almost always have been disappointing. Even though there often were some gains, typically at the outset, they generally did not persist. This was certainly the case with NCLB, arguably the culmination of many state and local test-based accountability regimes reflecting this logic. While there were gains in elementary grades at the outset, as reflected in NAEP scores, the performance of high school students, which should have reflected any cumulative improvement, did not change appreciably. When 2014 rolled around, NCLB's accountability regime had fallen far short of its goal of raising most (or even many) American students to proficiency levels more competitive with students elsewhere. If international exams such as Trends in International Mathematics and Science Study (TIMSS) and the Programme for International Student Assessment (PISA) were interpreted broadly as audit assessments, NCLB did not appear to contribute much change at all. While accountability of some form may have been a necessary component of educational reform, the test-based variety apparently was not sufficient to effect significant improvement in the outcomes it was intended to address.[49]

Another selling point of the NCLB legislation, of course, was its requirement that the scores of certain subgroups be reported, with the expectation that they improve as well. The theory in this case held that such advances eventually would reduce or eliminate achievement gaps, which narrowed dramatically during the 1970s and 1980s, but they more or less held steady subsequently. It was these provisions that led civil rights organizations to support the 2001 legislation, and to endorse ESSA as well. But in this regard, test-based accountability also turned out to be disappointing. By and large, achievement gaps evident on NAEP remained stable, especially at the secondary level where any enduring impact should have been evident. And as indicated above, many schools that served large numbers of poor and minority students responded to NCLB by focusing instruction resolutely on test preparation. This was hardly an approach aimed at establishing equity in learning experiences, or conceptions of achievement that extended beyond state and local accountability systems. As a consequence, not only did the achievement gap remain a problem, but millions of youth also received an education compromised by the troubling questions that Lindquist, Campbell, and other observers had identified decades earlier.[50]

Such has been the legacy of accountability in the recent history of American education. For virtually a half century, the quest to hold schools and educators accountable for academic achievement has relied almost exclusively on standardized assessment of one form or another. This was accomplished politically by proclaiming lofty goals of attaining universal proficiency and closing achievement gaps, which repeatedly failed to materialize. But even after these very clear disappointments, no other policy framework has emerged to challenge its hegemony. The American public today has little confidence in institutions to improve the quality of goods and services they provide, especially in the public sector. This attitude extends far beyond schools but impacts public education systems especially profoundly. As a consequence, many Americans continue to believe that accountability remains a vital necessity, even if educators and policy scholars disagree. And the technology of standardized testing remains the most legitimate and fiscally tolerable means of performing that task, despite its many limitations.[51] That remains one of the most troubling dilemmas facing American schools at present, and it is hardly clear just what sort of historical circumstances are likely to change it.

1

The Origins of
Test-Based Accountability

Assessing Minimum
Competencies in the 1970s

In 1975 Ralph Turlington, Florida's newly elected commissioner of education, addressed a regional conference of educators and state political leaders about a growing accountability movement. Noting a dramatic increase in his state's school population and rapidly rising costs, he declared that "the public is demanding that those of us in education be held accountable for the way in which we use our resources and for the quality of our product." The conference was held in Tampa, one of two sponsored by the Cooperative Accountability Project (CAP), a consortium of state-level agencies created several years earlier to consider policy changes. It represented a budding movement for information on just how well the nation's children were being educated. Noting that many educators opposed systematic assessments, Turlington asserted that critics "would like a testing system which would analyze data and print out a list of those to be punished."[1]

At the time of the CAP's founding, the accountability movement was well underway in the United States. Another speaker at the Tampa meeting reported that more than thirty states had passed or considered legislation to enact some form of accountability for public education.[2] Florida was the first to establish a comprehensive statewide testing system as a cornerstone of its accountability policy framework, and Turlington became an influential spokesman for the advantages of standardized assessment. The Florida accountability system, and its assessments in particular, certainly did not lack critics. But Turlington was an astute political strategist and conducted an ongoing campaign to promote standardized testing as key to the future of public education. Within just a few years, states across the country adopted new testing systems, some quite similar to Florida's. This marked the beginnings of a standardized assessment regime that would ultimately find expression at the federal level in No Child Left Behind.[3]

An age of accountability in the United States thus began in earnest when many states started using standardized assessments in public schools during the 1970s, an outgrowth of calls for greater answerability. These developments provoked considerable controversy, much of it focused on the use of such tests on a large scale. And points raised by critics at this time resonated for decades to come.

Accountability's Origins

As suggested in the introduction, the roots of educational accountability in contemporary times can be traced to 1965 and passage of the Elementary and Secondary Education Act. Observing that Title I of that legislation called for a large outlay of federal funds across the country, Robert Kennedy insisted that measures be added to ensure that such resources be used appropriately. Because the bill was already in conference, however, only "some rather vague language about evaluation" was added, as political scientist Lorraine McDonnell later observed. Most of the resulting assessment efforts were made at the local level, with great variation in scope and quality. This was hardly the sort of accountability that later advocates of comprehensive assessment would abide, although more systematic evaluations of Title I programs had been conducted by 1980.[4]

Perhaps a more important precedent was the Planning-Programming-Budgeting System developed under Robert McNamara at the Defense Department earlier in the decade, which became more widely influential with the advent of expanded funding on social programs during the Johnson administration. Economists hired to conduct evaluations in agencies responsible for these initiatives focused on programmatic goals and estimating the cost effectiveness of expenditures. Spearheaded by organizations such as the RAND Corporation (a spin-off of the Defense Department), the Urban Institute, and Abt Associates, and prompted by rising expenditures, this sort of analysis was conducted for a wide array of programs in the mid- to latter sixties. By the end of the decade RAND was becoming more heavily involved in evaluation of education programs by a variety of means, including the use of test scores to specify goals and measure outcomes.[5]

The idea of employing test results to evaluate schools also had been inspired a bit earlier by the 1966 Equality of Educational Opportunity report by James

Coleman, and later by the launch of the NAEP in 1969. Coleman, of course, had challenged conventional wisdom by highlighting the influence of family background factors in shaping achievement, but his use of test data to identify sources of variation in achievement also was a methodological milestone. NAEP followed within a few years, providing the first of many periodic snapshots of student performance on a standardized assessment regime administered to national samples of students.[6] Both of these developments featured the use of test data to evaluate schools, similar to approaches taken by RAND and other evaluation organizations.

Like Turlington, many observers also suggested that public demand for information about school performance was a factor in calls for accountability, but evidence on the point was mixed. Survey data from the time suggest that most Americans believed institutions should be evaluated with test data, and many were concerned about discipline and order in the schools. Yet they also felt that additional resources could improve achievement and that alternative schools could benefit many students. Most found that their own institutions were effective, but they also responded that educators should be accountable for "the progress of students." As one observer noted, parents did "not appear to have much specific representation on the panels currently arguing the case of accountability." While popular support for such measures may indeed have been widespread, there was somewhat inconsistent evidence of it in the early seventies. Things changed in subsequent years, however, when public concern about declining SAT scores and international assessments took hold.[7]

When accountability first appeared as a compelling issue in education, it usually was in the recommendations of policy analysts and leaders. Dozens of articles and books addressed the topic, starting in 1969.[8] For instance, an essay by Harvard University's David K. Cohen was titled "Social Accounting in Education: Reflections on Supply and Demand." Cohen lamented the unwillingness of schools and districts to share systematic data about their performance, but also the public's lack of interest in such information. Following the lead of Coleman and RAND evaluators, he urged greater attention to educational outcomes, along with fostering market mechanisms such as vouchers to spur interest in school performance. While hardly original, such prescriptions were signs of the time.[9]

Within a matter of months, meetings on accountability were convened by the National School Boards Association, the American Management Association, the Educational Testing Service (ETS), the Education Commission of the States, and a number of other organizations.[10] The national education publication *Phi Delta Kappan* also featured articles on the topic, signaling its rising significance. Most such pieces endorsed the idea of accountability, focusing on how best to go about it. They covered a wide range of topics, including oversight of educators and applying business management techniques to schools.[11]

Others addressed methodological challenges in measuring the impact of teachers and achieving uniformity in outcomes.[12]

Perhaps the biggest concern, however, was "social promotion," the idea that standards of behavior and academic rigor in schools had declined dramatically. As one author suggested, educators had abdicated responsibility for student performance, especially in city schools. "Social promotion is virtually a universal practice," he declared. "In urban high schools the student who merely sleeps through it all is rewarded with a passing grade by his grateful teacher."[13] Comments such as these suggested that the problem lay both with students and educators.

These sentiments paralleled popular worries about discipline troubles, contributing to calls for change. In 1970 ETS sponsored conferences on accountability in Washington, DC, and Hollywood, CA, with participants from a range of backgrounds. They included academic leaders, public school superintendents, and Albert Shanker, president of the American Federation of Teachers. The result was a lively dialogue, extending from scholarly musings about accountability as a concept, to more practical concerns about its implementation and outright rejection of its underlying premises. There also was skepticism about whether standardized tests could address the depth of learning that many educators aspired to.[14] But policy makers were moving forward with accountability, regardless of what skeptics believed. This was evident in a range of published commentary, most of which held that accountability in education had become largely inevitable, or as one commentator put it, a "watchword for the 70's." This observation turned out to be prophetic, as did a somewhat narrowly focused article titled "Moving Toward Educational Accountability: Florida's Program," which reported on the state's evolving assessment plans.[15]

Testing under Siege

Standardized assessment has a long history in the United States and had become a familiar feature of public schooling by the postwar era. It turned into a highly contentious issue, however, just as accountability was beginning to gain national attention. Much of the controversy revolved around intelligence (IQ) tests and the question of race, particularly the substantial gap in the scores of white and Black students. In 1969 the graduate student editors of the *Harvard Educational Review* published an article by Berkeley educational psychologist Arthur Jensen that argued these group disparities were likely due to genetic differences between races. Titled "How Much Can We Boost IQ and Scholastic Achievement?" it suggested that remedial education for African American students was largely ineffective because of alleged incapacity to learn and reason. It prompted an almost immediate outcry from a variety of sources.[16]

While Jensen argued that schools could do a better job of addressing racial achievement differences, it was his views regarding group disparities in IQ that became a source of controversy. Psychometric arguments to this effect had long been a staple of racist depictions of African Americans, dating from the initial IQ tests more than a half century earlier. Coming in the midst of the civil rights movement, this viewpoint was widely interpreted as a challenge to the very premise of Black social and civil equality. It also was questioned on empirical and methodological grounds by a wide range of scholars, and Jensen himself became an object of vilification on Berkeley's campus. It did not help that soon afterwards Harvard psychologist Richard Herrnstein and Stanford engineering professor William Shockley endorsed similar positions that also were widely pilloried. In the eyes of many critics, it was tantamount to a resurrection of racist stereotypes from the nineteenth century. To the extent that standardized tests of one sort or another were implicated, the very idea of such formalized assessment became a point of controversy. After all, if instruments designed for identifying differences in academic performance could be used to question the principle of democratic equality, perhaps they too ought to be contested.[17]

One consequence of this turmoil was a series of resolutions by various groups to ban or limit the use of standardized assessments, on the assumption that they could make invidious distinctions between people, or were social or culturally biased. Calls for such restrictions came from the National Education Association, various civil rights groups, and the Black Psychologists section of the American Psychological Association.[18] The uproar over the Jensen article and protests against Shockley and other proponents of IQ on campuses also affected public concerns about the issue. This placed a new degree of pressure on the testing industry. Rather suddenly, the very legitimacy of certain forms of standardized assessment was coming sharply under attack.[19]

An answer to the dilemma of such disagreeable tests was so-called criterion-based assessments, instruments that examined how well students knew particular knowledge domains or had mastered academic skills. As University of California at Los Angeles's (UCLA) James Popham argued, such tests were different from the norm-referenced variety, which compared students to one another on a common scale. IQ tests were the classic form of a norm-refenced instrument, reflected in the familiar bell curve that characterized a normal distribution of scores, but most other standardized achievement tests did so too. This was true of widely used assessments produced by the Iowa Testing Service and most commercial publishers, as well as the ETS.[20] Popham and other proponents of criterion-based tests, on the other hand, suggested that these assessments measured what students knew about a particular subject or academic field, based on a specific curriculum, not unlike exams taken in class, and did not lend themselves to potentially invidious comparisons.[21] The difference from classroom tests was that these assessments were standardized for a particular school, district, or—eventually—a state and its general curricular framework. This often meant that they offered something more than just an indication of how much math, history, or science students happened to learn in class. It also made them a potent instrument of large-scale evaluation, a form of testing well suited to the newly dawning age of accountability.

The appealing simplicity of criterion-based testing was certainly understandable, especially in light of the IQ controversies. As advocates such as Popham pointed out, however, an important caveat was the requirement that test items hew closely to the curricular domains being tested.[22] In that regard he provided guidance for conducting item analysis and identifying flawed questions for removal or correction. He (and Ted Husek) anticipated some of the many challenges facing such instruments, including how to assess reliability and validity, as well as the appropriate interpretation of individual and group scores. A particularly thorny question was how to set cut-off scores to distinguish students who had succeeded from those who had not. And when such assessments were utilized by policy makers to make decisions about student success and institutional accomplishment, these issues became critically important. Yet Popham remained steadfast in his belief that this type of test had an important "role to play."[23]

The form of criterion-referenced assessment that came into widespread use during the early to mid-1970s was known as "minimum competency testing" (MCT). One reason that it gained traction was the seemingly straightforward proposition that if curricular goals were clear, taught to, and tested, it would be possible to determine whether students were minimally competent or better. Specific behavioral objectives, determined by educators themselves or identified by others, were key to the endeavor. Educators could use the test results to determine if their approaches to a particular curriculum were successful, whether individual students needed help, or if instructional practices required attention. At the same time, institutions could be evaluated for how much students were learning, presumably a function of how well they were being taught and how hard they studied. This appeared to be precisely the sort of appraisal that accountability advocates such as Cohen had called for.[24]

But as Popham, Husek, and others had anticipated, establishing criteria for determining who to be judged capable proved a very sticky wicket. The issue was highlighted by Gene Glass, then at the University of Colorado, who argued that all such judgments were unavoidably arbitrary, to one degree or another, and could not be made in a strictly scientific manner. He noted that the original formulation of criterion-based testing conceived of competence as a continuous rather than a dichotomous measure, making identification of criteria for failure potentially problematic. He also wondered how reliable and valid test items could be devised to represent various levels of competence in a given domain. Glass appraised the various approaches used at the time to set standards, noting that many were in fact normative (comparing students or setting standards based on national norms). Having educators or policy makers set a passing score based on beliefs about what students should know or how many succeeded, he argued, was hardly scientific.[25]

Popham did not directly react to these points, except to suggest that public opinion did constitute a general set of standards, and that perhaps more rigorous approaches to identifying competence could be devised later. He worried that Glass could discourage further development of MCT, but subsequent events proved such concerns unwarranted. Other observers suggested that a middle ground could be found, with reasonable standards identified by educators and subject experts carefully built into assessments.[26] In the end, however, policy makers committed to accountability cared little about such technical and methodological concerns. As long as some psychometricians were willing to construct such tests and attest their value, they enthusiastically embraced them as a cornerstone of accountability.[27] But the issues that Glass had raised remained a source of disagreement among assessment professionals for years to follow.

Beyond meaningful cut scores or standards, there was also the matter of general test validity in these assessments. When high stakes were attached to such instruments, after all, it created a powerful incentive to focus instruction on material included on them. As mentioned in the book's introduction, this issue had been raised by E. F. Lindquist decades earlier, and by Donald Campbell in the 1970s.[28] It undermined the legitimacy of such tests, as they were supposed to be a sampling of knowledge and skills represented in a curriculum. When students were instructed principally on items or topics included on tests, the larger purpose of these instruments could be compromised.[29] Beyond that, there was the fundamental question of how well various test items assessed the knowledge and skills that students normally were taught across many schools. Glass raised the latter point regarding the Florida testing program launched in 1977, and it was explored in somewhat greater depth a year later by Walt Haney and George Madaus, both at Boston College. The question of whether MCT exams were linked in any meaningful manner to the curriculum offered in schools was directly tied to their validity.[30]

Yet another set of questions concerned the distinction between norm- and criterion-referenced tests, as some observers suggested that the differences were not as great as many MCT proponents suggested. Both included items scaled to measure varying levels of knowledge and skills, typically producing one form or another of a normal distribution with relatively few high and low achievers. In other words, each was inherently comparative, even if the scores on criterion-based assessments were not necessarily dictated by group norms. The key was whether the latter instruments met high standards of so-called content validity. Studies in the 1970s indicated that many failed to do this, focusing on broad objectives rather than specific behavioral or academic domains. The result were tests that often functioned much like norm referenced assessments. As suggested in the introduction, student performance on most standardized exams was naturally affected by a range of factors outside of schooling: family background in particular. And the closer that tests came to simply measuring broad performance profiles, the more such influences were likely to come into play. Children from low income and poverty backgrounds, after all, were often ill prepared to compete with those from more affluent circumstances on such general assessments, regardless of their motivation and effort or how well they were taught. This could make the presumption that such tests were valid indicators of student responsibility or school effectiveness inherently problematic.[31] Altogether, a host of concerns were registered by scholars in education and psychometrics about these tests, yet their general use spread rapidly in years to follow.

Criterion-based assessments soon became the foundation of testing for accountability across the United States. Supporters of these tests held fast to the proposition that educators and policy makers could distinguish between students (and eventually teachers) who met minimum levels of competency. Acknowledging that "educational tests have shortcomings," Popham also maintained that "the use of these tests is preferable to other less objective methods of categorizing students."[32] But the appeal of criterion-based testing hinged on confidence that a single assessment could pinpoint competency in specific curricular domains, which also turned out to be its Achilles' heel. Without widely agreed upon standards of competence, after all, it could be difficult to accept the proposition that a single test would identify students who met this potentially complex specification and those who did not. In particular, lacking a valid and reliable cut score, MCT could not function effectively as an instrument of accountability.[33] This was a question that would gain salience in the years to come, especially as such tests swept the nation.

A Movement Begins in Florida

By most accounts, test-based accountability was launched for the first time on a statewide basis in Florida, under the leadership of Ralph Turlington.[34] Becoming the state's commissioner of education after a long legislative career, Turlington was an enthusiastic proponent of testing to hold both schools and students to higher standards. As an experienced political operative he worked assiduously to address criticisms of the state's accountability program.[35] He was particularly adept at marshaling assistance in the press and broadcast media, which he believed to be crucial to political support both for accountability and the state's public schools.

Accountability in Florida can be dated to 1971, when newly elected Democratic governor Reuben Askew asked the legislature to increase funding for public schools. Responding in part to court cases that challenged unequal funding based on property taxes, Askew aimed to create greater equity in education. Following the recommendations of a "blue ribbon" Citizens Committee, he orchestrated a comprehensive reform of school funding that required statewide tax increases. As in other states, however, additional funding was accompanied with calls for greater accountability, and the Citizen's Committee recommended a focus on school outcomes. Along with enhanced funding, consequently, the legislature passed an Educational Accountability Act, which led to a series of tests being developed with assistance from the Center for the Study of Evaluation at UCLA. Following input from a range of educators, the new assessment battery was designed to report percentages of students achieving statewide objectives in grades two, four, seven, and ten. Individual and school-level results were not to be publicly reported, but for the first time in American history, all of the districts in a state were required to assess students on exams designed for accountability purposes.[36]

In 1976 Florida's Accountability Act was amended to require a test of functional literacy and basic skills to receive a high school diploma, beginning with the class of 1979. Concerned about "media stories" from South Florida, legislators were quoted as declaring "we don't want any more social promotion."[37] A former speaker of the state House of Representatives who was elected commissioner in 1974, Turlington was an eager advocate of testing. The instrument created to perform this role, with assistance from the ETS, was labeled the Functional Literacy Test, and later changed to the State Student Assessment Test II (or SSAT II). Based partly on a test of adult education, it required students to demonstrate ability in "real world" problems, linked at least conceptually to basic competencies believed to be required to function effectively in modern life. The test was assessed for construct validity by ascertaining skills necessary for basic adult reading abilities, and was judged similar to other widely used reading tests. But it was not initially evaluated with respect to curricula utilized in the schools.[38] A passing rate of 70 percent correct answers was established, apparently because it normally represented a passing grade for most subjects in schools. This was hardly a scientifically informed standard of success, and a state official admitted it to be "somewhat subjective" but necessary for "political credibility in the state." Of course it did little to address the concerns that critics expressed about such exams. A poll conducted by the *Miami Herald* in 1978 found that most respondents thought the test far too difficult to declare those who failed "functionally illiterate." As things turned out, the cut scores did indeed pose a problem for many students.[39]

Creating a single statewide assessment as a condition for high school diplomas was a bold step, especially since Turlington and other officials expected a quarter or even a third of students to fail upon its first administration in 1977.[40] But Turlington wielded hortatory politics enthusiastically, linking accountability to improved school performance and better results on national tests like the SAT.

"This school year," he declared, "may well be one of the most critical in recent Florida education history," suggesting that it would bring "new and increased emphasis on what takes place in the classroom."[41] The clear implication, of course, was that insufficient attention had been given to instruction in the past.

Turlington also worked assiduously to normalize standardized testing, and to foster public confidence in such assessments as objective and fair. He reached out to journalists from across the state to gain "favorable press coverage."[42] Turlington invited thirty-seven reporters and editors to take the exam themselves, so that they could see what high schoolers were being asked to do. All but one passed, but most found that the test was not easy, even if they agreed that it represented skills and knowledge that high school graduates ought to have. Turlington also lobbied for funding remedial education, as students who failed the test at first could take it again twice. State officials thus framed the test as appropriately difficult yet reasonably administered. Students who failed the test in all attempts, however, would receive a certificate of attendance upon completing grade twelve, a credential of very ambiguous standing.[43]

If state officials expected many students to fail the first test, the results were considerably worse than anticipated. While passing rates on the "communications" portion were better than expected, nearly 40 percent failed the math section, including more than three-quarters of Black students. Just 8 percent failed the communications portion overall, but that included 25 percent of African Americans. Since this was the first such statewide assessment, the failure rates in math became national news. The *New York Times* reported a 42 percent passing rate in Dade County, while the *Washington Post* focused on the types of problems that gave students trouble. At the same time, Turlington's outreach to Florida journalists paid off, as editorials from across the state registered broad approval of the assessment program and the test, despite the relatively poor results.[44]

As suggested in the *Washington Post*, one reason for the low math passage rate was the types of problems featured. Most required "real world" calculations, such as figuring interest rates, waiting times for trains, or sales taxes on purchases. As Popham had suggested, however, criterion-referenced assessments were supposed to stick closely to the curriculum that test takers had studied, and it was hardly clear that the Florida test met that expectation, at least initially. The *Post* reported that teachers complained about the test tripping up good students unfamiliar with such applied problems. "There are algebra students who haven't worked with decimals or per cents for a long time," declared on state official, and "some kids have never figured a sales tax." Insofar as this was true, and failure rates suggested these issues were pervasive, it indicated a potential problem of validity in Florida's assessment program.[45]

This view was corroborated by a panel of experts and educators that visited Florida in 1978 at the request of the National Education Association and its

Florida branch, to evaluate the accountability program. Chaired by renowned assessment scholar Ralph Tyler, the visitors were critical of both the way the Florida MCT program was conducted and the test itself. But they especially took issue with the decision to require the test with knowledge that large numbers of students were likely to fail. "It appears," their report declared, "as if the current class of eleventh-graders who are black and poor were sacrificed for the purpose of rapid implementation of the Accountability Act." In particular, it continued, "it is evident that there was little active concern for the appropriateness of the testing program for a large segment of the school population (the black and poor)." It was a forceful indictment, but drew little response from Turlington and his administration, except to note that the test came from a legislative mandate and students who failed could retake it.[46]

Given these developments, it appeared that the mathematics assessment may have been a particularly poor measure of the curriculum that many Florida students had been taught. But Turlington and other state education officials, along with most of the press, were unwilling to acknowledge that possibility. They had staked their professional standing on the principle of accountability that the test represented. While Turlington allowed that it "is not perfect" he also declared it to be "an excellent product." In the end he stressed the dangers of failure: "What are the opportunities for a student who cannot read or do simple arithmetic? The handicap is not the absence of a diploma, the handicap is the absence of the skills." Given this stance, questioning the technical merits of the assessment was simply not politically acceptable.[47]

Assessment results on the SSAT II did improve in the years to follow, perhaps because of compensatory instruction, students becoming more serious about school, and teachers focusing on test content to better address it. A survey of educators indicated that these were important factors impacting scores in the years following the exam's initial administration.[48] Passing rates went up to 78 percent in math within a couple years, where they stayed through the early 1980s. African American mathematics passing rates barely made it past 50 percent on the first try, however, marking a substantial racial achievement gap.[49] A significantly enhanced remedial education program enabled many to eventually succeed, but overall secondary graduation rates dropped considerably. While Florida reported a graduation rate of 70.12 percent in 1976, by 1979 it had dropped to 62.8 percent. That year the Department of Education reported that more than 5,000 seniors had failed to pass the test after remediation (more than 5 percent), fully two-thirds African American. Seven years later the overall graduation rate had improved somewhat but still remained more than 6 percent lower than in the mid-1970s.[50]

Failure on the SSAT II was hardly the only reason for lower graduation rates, but it also may have affected them indirectly. Some students dropped out rather than face the test, while others opted to sit for the GED or simply moved out of the state. A study of Hillsborough County (including Tampa) found such effects were pronounced for African Americans. In these respects, accountability in Florida had a discernable racial impact. In other regards, it was hardly clear that this form of accountability raised achievement as Turlington and other officials had hoped. As the author noted, "the number of students who withdrew to attend adult high school and evening or business school represented a large increase in 1977–78 and 1978–79 over the 1976–77 school year."[51] As fewer students remained in school to take the SSAT II, it also became a less effective indicator of improvements in overall achievement.

There also was evidence that the new testing regime had an adverse impact on instruction in many schools. Another study found that half of Florida teachers surveyed in two counties reported "teaching to the test" in preparing students to take the assessment. Teachers also noted that less instructional time was given to other subjects as a consequence, and more than two-thirds believed that students did not retain skills gained in test preparation. These observations, of course, suggested serious potential threats to the instrument's validity as a sampling of skills and knowledge that students were supposed to learn. And there was the added concern that students from economically deprived backgrounds would need additional preparation, even if tests were better aligned with curricular content.[52] Such evidence suggested that the state's MCT assessment program actually may have lowered the quality of education in some of its public schools.

These were precisely the types of problems that testing authorities such as Donald Campbell and E. F. Lindquist had warned about. And if students were hastily taught material likely to be on the test, they were unlikely to retain it as a result.[53] This was not the sort of improvement in overall achievement that Turlington had predicted. The drop in high school graduation rates, especially among many of the state's most vulnerable students, was little short of an educational calamity. For many white Floridians, however, the fact that African American students bore the brunt of these changes may have made them more politically acceptable.[54]

Diffusion Effect: MCT Becomes a National Phenomenon

Florida's accountability program was the opening bell of a race to adopt similar measures across the country. Accountability became fashionable in state education agencies, and legislators often saw it as a means to link schools to larger policy goals. Not all such policy initiatives featured graduation requirements, and many did not have a common statewide assessment, but all sought to provide measures of how well schools imparted basic academic skills. Some states, of course, had long used readily available assessments that were intended for diagnostic purposes in the schools, with the ITBS and the California

Achievement Test (CAT) being perhaps the best known. These were norm-refenced instruments that found use throughout the country and were not intended for use in accountability regimes. And some states, such as New York, offered high school exams that could lead to an enhanced diploma, but were not required for graduation. Florida's innovation was not the use of tests for ascertaining knowledge and skills, but rather for making all students take them and demanding certain scores for a diploma.[55]

Just as Florida began its statewide accountability program, MCT received national endorsement when secretary of health education and welfare Joseph Califano Jr. advocated the idea of basic skills testing. "I believe every state should have a program for developing and measuring basic skills that includes competency testing," he declared in 1978. "But the individual states and the districts should decide how to make use of competency testing in their programs."[56] At about the same time, Arizona, New Mexico, and California passed legislation calling for a more localized approach than Florida's. In New Mexico, school districts were asked to use assessment data in planning. In Arizona and California districts were required to conduct their own assessments, using state guidelines for a degree of consistency.[57] But Florida's approach to accountability was especially influential in the South, where tests as graduation requirements were adopted most widely. North Carolina was another early example, as Governor James B. Hunt made greater accountability and MCT a focal point, and other states in the region followed suit.[58]

Tellingly, the North Carolina testing program was proposed in 1977, the year of the first Functional Literacy Test administration in Florida. After initial development, pilot studies, and adjustments, the state's MCT exams were administered in 1978. The failure rate was not as acute as Florida's, particularly for African American students, partly because cut scores were selected less arbitrarily and the mathematics passing score was lower than the one for reading (64 percent vs. 72 percent). Additionally, tests were more carefully developed, with panels of educators to review items and standards. Responding to African American critics of the MCT program, Hunt also invested heavily in remedial test preparation programming. But even if Black students' passing rates were somewhat higher, results in North Carolina, along with other Southern states, generally mirrored those in Florida. African American students were more than twice as likely to fail in North Carolina, and benefited less from remediation, so that racial disparities in graduation continued to be evident. There was also evidence of increasing dropout rates there and teaching to the test. Broadly similar outcomes were reported for Virginia and Maryland, two other states with politically mandated minimum competency programs.[59]

By 1980 more than thirty-five states had instituted some form of test-based accountability, and others were preparing to do so. There was wide variation, however, in the tests that were utilized and their implications for districts, schools, and students. The Florida model of making an MCT a graduation requirement reportedly was adopted or planned in a dozen states in 1979, half of them in the South. The others, including New York, Utah, and California, also were supposed to raise standards and combat social promotion. But they were outliers in their respective regions and did not appear to encounter comparable problems of widespread failure, even if racial disparities existed.[60] Other states approached accountability in collaboration with local districts, setting goals and issuing standards for discussion and implementation.[61] But southern states generally took a different path; over the next six years, seven of nine states to require testing for graduation were located there. The result eventually was that nearly all the region enacted such measures, along with a number of other states.[62]

In a revealing analysis of such graduation testing requirements conducted decades later, sociologists John Robert Warren and Rachel B. Kulick found that states with "less favorable economic conditions" were more likely to adopt them, presumably to improve levels of human capital for investment and job growth. They also found that states with higher numbers of minority students, particularly African Americans and Hispanics, were more likely to enact such requirements. They speculated that desegregation controversies may have prompted such steps, perhaps out of concern for greater equity in educational outcomes. But they also note the possibility that popular concerns about educational standards may have linked desegregation with social promotion and discipline problems. These questions were especially controversial in the South, where rapid desegregation occurred during the 1970s and was widely opposed by whites, a point that Warren and Kulick acknowledged.[63]

In North Carolina and elsewhere in the region, the National Association for the Advancement of Colored People (NAACP) and other African American organizations argued that test-based graduation requirements were racially discriminatory, as Black students had long been systematically excluded from higher standards of instruction. But more moderate Black leaders argued that testing was useful for gauging just how well African American students were being taught. At the same time, lingering white resentment also was a political reality across the region. Even if leaders such as Hunt and Turlington believed that these accountability measures helped to foster greater equity, many of their constituents likely had little objection to African American failure rates. Both Blacks and whites thus helped to make MCT-style accountability viable politically, even if for quite different reasons.[64]

Leaders across the South highlighted economic development and improved educational outcomes, and the region had just undergone a protracted and difficult process of desegregation. Concerns about relatively low educational standards often focused on African American students, who had historically been denied access to equitable institutional settings. Schools in these states served many more Blacks than institutions elsewhere. Given this, it was hardly surprising that leaders such as Turlington and Hunt emphasized improving African American academic performance. They also proved generally successful in gaining support for testing from at least a fraction of the Black community leadership, including Black educators. This was a crucially important political consideration, as African Americans were well organized and could issue serious challenges to accountability measures. Such actions occurred in a number of states, but they were most impactful in Florida. The relevant federal case, *Debra P. v. Turlington* (discussed in chapter 2), clearly demonstrated the scale of the potential pitfalls that test-based accountability faced in the region.[65]

If some southern leaders were furtively interested in pushing Black students out of their institutions, evidence from Florida, North Carolina, and other southern states suggests they also may have been successful. Extant documentation suggests that tens of thousands of these students were denied diplomas or dropped out of school because of the region's accountability policies. Turlington astutely focused his public remarks on improving African American test scores, which often occurred following remediation. But their initial passing rates remained low, barely exceeding 50 percent in mathematics. Many did eventually succeed after taking remedial classes that replaced other courses in the curriculum, but it is an open question whether this reflected meaningful educational experiences or narrowly "teaching to the test." Warren and Kulick concluded that the MCT movement generally, and high school exit exams in particular, did little to improve overall achievement as reflected in NAEP and other measures, and they lowered graduation rates, especially for minority students. Other studies have corroborated these findings.[66] It was hardly the sort of legacy that Turlington, Hunt, and other proponents of testing for school accountability had forecast.

A Great Debate about Testing Policy

As MCT became widespread it also grew more controversial. The national attention given to it by the *New York Times* and the *Washington Post* helped to inspire broader coverage in states where accountability policies were debated. There were a number of reasons for this, but a few stood out as especially salient. Among the most prominent was test-based graduation requirements, a particularly contentious topic given events in Florida and other southern states. But there were other issues too, including the potential for labeling students and persistent racial test score disparities, which became the source of legal challenges to accountability. These issues played out conspicuously in the press and other forums. It also drew the interest of educational researchers, reflected in a commentary both critical and supportive of assessment policies.[67]

The rising discord eventually gained attention in Washington, DC, leading to a publicly staged "adversary evaluation hearing." Sponsored by the National Institute of Education, then the chief federal educational research agency, it featured debate between leading assessment experts. Recorded segments were aired in a series of public television broadcasts. Intended "to provide a public forum for clarifying some of the most salient issues concerning minimum competency testing," it presented a rare opportunity to voice conflicting views of MCT programs at a key point in their development. It also highlighted themes that would prove quite enduring, as standardized assessment became an ever larger question facing educators.[68]

The debate occurred in July 1981 and lasted three days. It was moderated by Barbara Jordan, a prominent African American leader and former congresswoman from Texas. Shirley Chisolm, the first Black woman elected to Congress and a presidential candidate, also participated, along with a wide range of other public figures and assessment experts. Pro and con teams were assembled, and debate was conducted in the manner of a trial, including cross-examination. It provided a remarkably useful if contentious inventory of issues related to testing and accountability.[69]

W. James Popham served as the leader of the team favoring MCT. He asserted that the public had demanded MCT, focusing on the question of social promotion, and he responded to worries about labeling children by claiming that the quality of education was a bigger issue. "There is another concern which I have that troubles me even more," he declared, "and that is to falsely deceive youngsters into thinking they possess basic skills which, in fact, they do not. In other words, awarding them diplomas which are essentially meaningless."[70] This view, of course, implied that other functions of education were unimportant, and that MCT could be an accurate accounting of skills and knowledge. As critics were quick to point out, it also suggested that even for students scoring just below cut points, perhaps due to imperfect test reliability, high school had been pointless.

The team in favor of MCT argued that MCT programs would have positive effects on students, on the curriculum and teaching, and on popular perceptions of schooling. Popham also suggested that such tests would enable students to develop more positive self-concepts. His team argued that MCTs could help define goals to inform instruction. Such tests additionally were supposed to boost public confidence in promotion practices and student success.[71] *Washington Post* African American columnist William Raspberry, who spoke as a witness, highlighted the loss of public trust in the schools. "People have become increasingly aware that schools are not doing what we expect them to do," he declared. "We keep hearing about children who are graduating from high schools who are awarded diplomas, who are illiterate or nearly so."[72] The use of MCTs, their supporters argued, could resolve such concerns substantially.

Regarding the impact of MCT assessment on students, Popham asked Florida's Ralph Turlington to testify about African American students. "I have talked to many black students," Turlington responded, "and the greatest complaint that they have made is that we have not had the expectations of black students that we should." He cited the case of predominately Black Ribault High School in Duvall County, where only 20 percent passed the math test in 1977 but 84 percent did several years later. "We need to be very positive," he asserted, "and the evidence we have had in Florida is that you can make significant improvement in educational achievement in a relatively modest period of time."[73] Raspberry concurred, adding that "if these opponents to the entire notion of minimum competency really believe that children are capable of learning, capable of acquiring the skills, they would insist on some kind of testing to make sure that they had acquired the skills so you would know whether the schools were doing what they were supposed to do."[74]

But not all gains on test scores represented greater achievement, as MCT opponents were quick to point out. Under cross-examination by George Madaus, Michael Priddy, director for research, planning, and evaluation for the Guilford County School system in North Carolina, acknowledged that higher pass rates were not necessarily due to students mastering relevant skills. Sometimes tests were amended to be less challenging. As Popham himself had reported at the time, "it is apparent that . . . the new and revised test questions, are easier."[75] Political pressure to alter MCT exams also could result in higher scores, regardless of how much students had learned.

Madaus served as leader for the team opposed to MCT. The opposition focused much of its attention on the use of MCT as a sole determinant of students' fates, particularly as a single criterion for promotion at certain grade levels or requirement for graduation. But it also considered the effect of MCT on teachers and the curriculum, and its impact on the public's view of the quality of education.[76]

The opposition argued that the widely reported perception of declining basic skills was a misconception, and its members offered evidence that such skills had been improving before the advent of MCTs. They also addressed the inappropriate use of using norm-referenced assessments, such as the SAT, to gauge basic skills. Rather than improving skills, Madaus suggested that the form of MCT being debated was probably most appropriate for identifying students needing help, perhaps as a diagnostic or prescriptive tool. But he worried that such tests did not provide enough information about *why* a student failed, but instead only specific objectives that possibly were improperly addressed.[77]

Assessment scholar Robert Linn questioned whether a relatively brief paper-and-pencil test, largely comprising multiple-choice questions, had the capacity to predict competency as an adult.[78] The opposition also cast doubt on the ability of such exams to accurately assess a wide range of academic tasks. One witness demonstrated that it was entirely possible for a student to pass or fail an MCT assessment simply by luck of the draw, given the limited number of questions, imperfect correspondence to statewide curricula, and a rigid cut score.[79] Witnesses also testified that measurement errors could disproportionately harm certain students, an issue possibly related to questions of item bias.[80]

Potential test bias became a significant focal point of the hearing. One example cited the word "interstate" on an exam. Two of the possible answer options included "between cities within a state" and a second option "between states." The question intended students to look at the Latin prefix, but witness Robert Calfee noted "In fact, if you are a California student and you drive from Sacramento to Los Angeles on Interstate 5, your life skills are perfectly well served by thinking it means 'between cities within a state.'"[81] Robert Linn described the effect of including or excluding biased questions on white and Black students. In one example, when eight suspect questions were removed, 3,000 more Black students passed a communication test.[82] Opposition witnesses offered considerable evidence that questions of underlying forms of bias in testing were far from settled.

There also was evidence of racially motivated use of MCT assessments. Professor Melvin Hall of Sangamon State University in Illinois testified that racial bias may have encouraged some districts to implement an MCT requirement. He cited a district that went from serving an 8 percent minority students population to 65 percent in nine years. "Both district staff and parents," Hall reported, "indicated that the minimum competency exam was attractive because it would guard the academic standards of the district." When asked if Black student scores were the major concern, his answer was yes.[83] This was a rarely reported instance of candor, and it occurred outside of the South, but it may have represented the sentiments of many white educators and community members. It was an example of how African American students were viewed as a threat to academic standards, perhaps a reason that MCT programs were more likely to be enacted in states with larger Black populations.[84]

Perhaps the most telling point made by the opposition, however, was how arbitrary passing (or cut) scores could harm students, especially those facing graduation test requirements. Robert Linn demonstrated how a minor change to the cut score could significantly impact the number of students who pass or fail in a particular state. "In fact," he stated, "you would reduce [failure] by lowering the cutting score by three points [and] it would change [passing] for black students about 6 percent, which would amount to roughly 13,000 students."[85] If clear and reasonable standards for cut scores were not developed, setting them was too often a largely arbitrary task, as appeared to occur in Florida. The impact for African American students could be quite adverse indeed.

In the end it is doubtful that many people changed their minds as a result of the National Institute of Education hearing proceedings in 1981, as public attitudes about testing remained firmly in favor of it. There is little evidence that opposition experts and other witnesses against the use of MCT assessments made an impact on policy. Supporters of these assessments leaned heavily on the argument that American schools were in need of greater accountability, that the public no longer had confidence in them, and that tests of this sort could restore their credibility. This appeared to be as much or more a political argument than an educational one, however. Their basic point on the latter account was that raising standards and holding students accountable could improve instruction and incentivize students to be more serious. But little systematic evidence was offered on such assertions. The opposition focused on the limitations of testing in performing the accountability functions that policy makers asked of it.[86] Its team members questioned whether statements about "meaningless" diplomas were warranted when many students likely failed because of test error, bias, or missing just a few questions beyond the cut score. Supporters of testing had few answers to such points, except that students had multiple opportunities to pass the exams and that scores did improve with time. Whether higher scores were solid evidence of improved achievement, however, was another question altogether.

Conclusion

It is commonplace today to suggest that the contemporary accountability movement began with *A Nation at Risk*, but the events described herein place its origins more than a decade earlier.[87] The fact that MCT approaches to accountability proved so widespread by the 1980s, suggests that the Florida experience was a decisive precedent. Ralph Turlington was determined to make test-based accountability work and his success helped to make it a viable option for other states. Another key historical figure in this account was W. James Popham, who became a keen advocate of criterion-based testing, and MCT in particular, as well as a champion of the Florida accountability regime. Even if his opponents cast considerable doubt on such pronouncements, assertions about the loss of standards played well in the court of public opinion, which generally supported testing for accountability purposes.[88] The image of illiterate graduates, the products of social promotion, was a card played repeatedly by proponents of test-based accountability. It was hortatory politics at its most impactful register.

As it turned out, on the other hand, the opposition had raised points that could not be easily dismissed.[89] And it eventually appeared that they were mainly correct: MCT did not produce the dramatic transformation that its proponents had predicted, starting with Turlington but extending to Harold Hunt in North Carolina and other reform leaders at the time. In an article summarizing years of research on these tests and their impact, sociologists John Robert Warren and Eric Grodsky concluded that MCT accountability requirements rarely produced positive outcomes for students. "Exit exams harm students who fail them," they concluded, "and don't benefit students who pass them." They also found that "exit exams have a greater [negative] impact on graduation rates in states that are more racially/ethnically diverse and have higher rates of poverty." This, of course, included most states in the South, including Florida.[90] It is particularly damning evidence that the political decision to implement such measures injured many thousands of students, most of them non-white and likely poor.

If there is a lesson to be drawn from this series of historical events, it concerns the willingness of political figures to ignore critical feedback from assessment scholars concerned with the integrity of schools and the fates of children attending them. And they were not the only ones objecting to such policies. In 1982 a report from the National Research Council concluded that "the major impact of minimum competency testing will be on students who fail them," noting that many would suffer "damage to . . . self-esteem that must accompany being classified as 'incompetent' or 'functionally illiterate,'" and likely would have trouble finding employment.[91] Questions raised by critics of MCT would continue to be salient for years to come, and many of the same individuals would continue to ask them. In the 1990s additional voices raised questions about the next generation of accountability tests, the so-called standards-based assessment regimes that emerged then. In the end, even James Popham became somewhat critical of the use of standardized testing for such purposes.[92] But they too have largely been ignored by the political leaders who gave shape to subsequent events in the development of test-based accountability. In this regard, events in Florida and elsewhere during the 1970s were a disturbing portent for a troubled era in American educational history.[93]

2

Standardized
Testing and Race

Continuity and Change,
1975–2000

In 1981, Yale psychologist Edmund W. Gordon and graduate student Molidawn D. Terrell published an essay in the *American Psychologist* titled "The
Changed Social Context of Testing." Gordon was a leading African American
scholar and the article described how race and standardized testing were linked
in American history. It mentioned the army IQ test and racist contentions
about the inferiority of Black students, arguing that such assertions had helped
maintain unjust status distinctions. But Gordon and Terrell also suggested that
times had changed and those tests were no longer appropriate for an age of
greater social and cultural diversity. "Rather than serving as a vehicle for sorting persons according to ability," they wrote, "assessment should be used as an
aid to pedagogical and/or rehabilitative intervention." In other words, the challenge of the day was achieving greater equity by using tests to inform and
guide education.[1] While considerable skepticism about standardized assessment
remained evident in Black communities, the more pragmatic position that Gordon and Terrell had articulated also was taking root.

These changes did not occur overnight, of course. In the 1970s there was still
widespread concern about the inequitable legacy of standardized assessment
among African Americans. In the years to follow, however, these attitudes
began to change, as extensive advocacy and criterion-based testing tempered

Black skepticism. Many were persuaded that such tests could be utilized to document just how well the schools were serving their children. As suggested elsewhere, however, these assessments became controversial when linked to graduation requirements, and federal trials focused on the disparate racial impact of such policies. But eventually most of the nation's major civil rights organizations chose to support standards-based assessments in order to identify racial achievement gaps.[2]

At the same time, the assessment industry wrestled with questions about the fairness of its tests. In the wake of controversy over Arthur Jensen and like-minded figures, charges of systematic prejudice in testing resonated more significantly.[3] The result was a significant endeavor to develop methods of identifying potential bias in standardized assessments, and a related campaign to assure the public that tests were impartial and fair to all groups that took them. Despite these efforts, however, such concerns continue to find voice, fueled by persistent racial disparities in assessment results.[4]

Yet another important development was the discovery of psychological factors affecting minority group performance on standardized tests. Labeled "stereo-type threat" by psychologist Claude Steele this appeared to reflect a high degree of negative self-consciousness on high-stakes exams. It was not identified until the mid-1990s and thus was not fully recognized during testing debates in prior decades, even though it likely contributed to racial differences in scores.[5]

Finally, debates over racial test score disparities resumed during the 1990s with publication of *The Bell Curve*, a controversial book by Richard Herrnstein and Charles Murray. Their argument regarding IQ as a determinant of status and well-being was vigorously contested, and stimulated new research on "achievement gaps" and progress in closing them. It marked the dawn of a new era in educational policy discourse, with race and inequality again taking center stage.[6]

Challenging the Testing Establishment

Led by the NAACP, African Americans took the lead in contesting the fairness and validity of standardized assessments. In the wake of the controversy over IQ, a flurry of activity focused on cultural bias and other ways that racial disparities could appear in testing. These events had an immediate and lasting impact on the assessment industry and its role at all levels of the education system.

At its 1972 convention, the NAACP passed resolutions calling for a moratorium on standardized testing. In particular, the group called for a halt to them "whenever such tests have not been corrected for cultural bias" and called upon its leaders "to use all administrative and legal remedies to prevent the violation of students' constitutional rights through the misuse of tests." The 1974 convention also called upon the Association of Black Psychologists to work with the College Entrance Examination Board (CEEB) and the ETS "to develop standardized tests which have been corrected for cultural bias and which fairly measure the amount of knowledge retained by students regardless of . . . individual background."[7]

The latter meeting led to a special invitational conference the following year and publication of a report a year later. Both featured a variety of participants, including Black and white academics and representatives from ETS and other testing organizations. Additional groups issued calls for curbing standardized assessment, but the NAACP offered the most comprehensive and discerning examination of questions facing the testing industry. It also gained attention in the press, underscoring wider interest in these issues.[8]

The prologue to the 1975 meeting, the "Conference on Minority Testing," highlighted the principal problems, starting with issues to be considered. They included "ability grouping practiced by whole education systems which results in racial isolation, the enforcement of stereotypes, the labeling of children, and in the reinforcements of feelings of inferiority which can lead to third class education."[9] It reflected the growing frustration that many felt regarding the use of standardized assessments.[10] These complaints came just as Black students had made significant advances in educational attainment, moving into middle-class status at a rapid rate. Low performance on standardized tests represented a serious impediment to further progress, however, threatening the prospects of African American youth. These concerns, along with bigoted pronouncements issued by Richard Herrnstein, William Shockley, and their supporters, made test scores a compelling civil rights issue.[11] The testing industry made a rather amorphous target, however, and much of the public had difficulty appreciating the depth of these grievances.

The conference convened a number of task forces to address a range of questions. They included scholars from the education disciplines, measurement experts and administrators from the CEEB, ETS, school districts, and community organizations, along with NAACP leaders and staff. Topical focal points included development of a minority code on testing, the psychometric integrity of tests, social and public policy related to testing, and the use and misuse of tests.[12] The result was a comprehensive and insightful analysis of testing as a civil rights question.

Major Concerns about Standardized Testing

All of this activity represented a significant moment for large-scale assessment in the United States. The outcome was a telling critique of long-standing testing practices, highlighting issues that had been widespread concerns for minority groups. The involvement of ETS and CEEB leaders made it especially significant. For the first time, prominent members of the testing industry were engaged in dialogue with civil rights leaders and minority scholars, to address ways that standardized tests may function in a discriminatory fashion. The results were summarized in the report of the Task Force on the Code of Testing, which was revealing, if not necessarily revolutionary, in scope.[13]

In general terms, the issue perhaps most readily grasped was test bias. Commonplace examples featured items that called for knowledge especially familiar to white, middle-class students. One was described by former City College of New York president Buel Gallagher.[14] In a test administered in Harlem, one question asked to choose the best definition of a *lark*. The answer choices were a dog, an automobile, a bird, or a kind of cheese. No students answered the question, reporting that the choices did not include a cigarette. They did not see birds described this way in their daily lives, and did not learn about them in school, but they did see ads for the cigarettes. This was offered as an example of a culturally biased question, penalizing African American students.

In recommendations to address the problems identified, task force reports suggested a range of responses. The first concerned the administration of assessments. Research suggested that the race, gender, and other characteristics of individuals overseeing tests could have a slight but telling impact on performance, especially for Black and other minority students. The authors suggested that "proctors should be hired to reflect the ethnic makeup of the testing candidates," and "must be sensitive to the needs, questions, anxieties of all candidates."[15] This spoke to questions of student comfort and security, which could affect their ability to focus on tests effectively. This was an early acknowledgment of psychological factors potentially inhibiting minority students, an issue that would gain additional salience two decades later.

Conferees also expressed concerns about norms for many tests, especially those that claimed to represent national or state populations. They asked that criteria used in building tests be made quite clear, adding "it is imperative that the norms reflect the pluralistic characteristics of the different ethnic groups that make up the testing population."[16] "Test development," the authors concluded, "must consider the different cognitive structures and styles of different groups."[17] They also called for "culturally appropriate and content-valid criterion referenced procedures to be investigated," along with assessments that could consider creativity, motivation, persistence, and "other personality measures."[18] These concerns reflected perceptions that many assessments reflected modes of communication and problem solving most commonly found in the white middle class.

Regarding achievement tests, especially those focused on particular objectives of instruction, conferees called for fairness in teaching. Such exams, they asserted, should be administered only when students "have been taught in ways they can reasonably be expected to have learned the information contained in the examination." Beyond that, they called upon the testing industry to "assist school systems and other users in better understanding the content and constraints of the examinations, and in helping them understand how to make optimal use of the results."[19] These matters had particular relevance regarding state accountability systems then taking shape, and eventually would become germane in litigation concerning them.

Following its meeting, the NAACP published a "Fair Testing Code" that encapsulated the main points of the task force reports. It also called upon test makers to "develop and publish standards of competence for those who administer, score and/or interpret tests," and to "state with clarity . . . the specific uses for which the test is designed, the specific limitations of the instrument and a full explanation as to how the results should be interpreted." Finally, it called for "an independent research and development corporation to identify critical problems in assessment as they relate to minority groups," and "a national monitoring body, with the power to enforce through sanctions, to assure proper assessment and policy [regarding] assessment tools."[20]

Altogether, this body of work represented the most sweeping analysis of the American testing industry in its time, particularly regarding its impact on racial and ethnic minority groups. Its challenge to test purveyors was both pointed and comprehensive. While it did produce some tangible results, however, many of the issues it addressed remained pertinent for years to follow. ETS and CEEB participated in the conference, but other test producers were less visible. As a consequence, certain changes were made—especially regarding the question of bias in testing—but serious, consequential oversight of the industry never materialized. In this respect the 1975 conference, and its many participants, failed to achieve its principal mandate.[21]

Rooting Out Bias

The NAACP conference's most tangible impact likely concerned potential bias in test questions. As suggested earlier, this was perhaps the most palpable complaint against standardized tests. It also addressed issues of cultural differences that conferees had raised. These and related issues became a focal point of research, particularly for the ETS. For its part, the NAACP turned to programs for helping Black students get higher scores on the SAT and other tests.[22]

Bias can be a tricky question in the measurement field and goes well beyond considerations of race.[23] The term has been associated generally with validity (accurate measurement of knowledge and skills). Bias was possible if test items did not accurately represent intended knowledge and skill domains, and favored the knowledge of a particular group. It occurred, for example, when standardized exams were written historically by educated, middle-class white men and were administered to students from many backgrounds. When test takers from similar backgrounds had an advantage on such assessments, disparities in results often were attributed to this sort of validity problem.[24]

This was a larger dilemma on norm-referenced tests not tied to particular curricula or instructional goals. As suggested earlier, such tests historically set standards by utilizing the distribution of scores from a larger population sample. Furthermore, the possibility of bias also existed if the sample did not have a representative array of subgroups. And the way items were written could be a factor too. Most such tests aimed to assess general knowledge or aptitude, but understanding of particular words could vary depending upon local circumstances. If a test used terms that students had not learned, it could mistakenly score their aptitude lower, a problem called *construct validity bias*. This could have been the case in the example offered by Dr. Gallagher in 1976.

Defenders of norm-referenced assessments, and IQ tests in particular, argued that bias of this sort did not contribute substantially to racial or ethnic differences in scoring. A pivotal work on the topic was written by none other than Arthur Jensen, who established empirically in 1980 that this form of bias made only a modest contribution to such variation in outcomes. But Jensen's work did not demonstrate that bias in assessment was nonexistent. Shortly afterwards, a panel convened by the National Academy of Sciences found no evidence of substantial bias against racial or ethnic minority groups on exams such as the SAT and the ACT, a development given considerable publicity.[25] But these tests were quite different from the criterion-based assessments that most states used for accountability purposes.

Not everyone believed that standardized tests were altogether free of systematic bias, however. The extent that it did contribute to differences in outcomes remained a point of contention within the field. In particular, some rejected the very conceptualization of cognitive ability or aptitude that Jensen and similarly minded scholars utilized. Edmund W. Gordon and Tresmaine J. Rubain, for instance, argued that "conceptions of intelligence reflected in existing standardized tests are quite narrow and culturally encapsulated," concluding that "we thus distort the meaning of intelligence by our failure to appreciate its different manifestations and sources of expression."[26] In other words, existing tests potentially excluded the knowledge and skills of most people outside of the educated middle- and upper-class strata of American society. This was a potentially insidious form of prejudice that could render the very premise of ability testing problematic. Jensen's work on bias did not address these questions, but rather assumed that general intelligence was a well-established concept.

These debates, of course, concerned norm-referenced assessments of ability and not criterion-based exams. In the latter instruments, test questions were supposed to hew closely to material that was taught, as Popham and others pointed out. If students did not answer a question correctly, it presumably was either due to failure to learn the relevant knowledge or skill, or a failure to teach it. Exclusion of material that was taught, or including material that was not taught, was sometimes called "content-validity bias." If the public schools in

Harlem taught students effectively about the lark as a bird, many likely would have correctly answered the question. Including it on an exam would have been fine, and students' answers would be at least partly a function of learning from instruction. What then was called content validity regarding criterion-based assessments, in that case, concerned whether and how well relevant material was taught.

Gordon and Rubain suggested that this type of test had "the potential to be useful to the minority test taker, as it permitted "the development of programs and instructional procedures matched to the particular individual's need." But they also added that it was "the responsibility of the modern test designer to begin to produce methods of evaluation that are relevant to the minority test taker, and to satisfy the requirements for them to be useful."[27] This was salient advice, and evaluating achievement tests for various forms of bias soon became a preoccupation of the testing industry.

Following the uproar about Jensen's 1969 article, measurement experts began to explore questions of bias in ability testing and college entrance exams. One of the first papers addressing this appeared in 1972, by William Angoff of ETS. He proposed a scatterplot approach to finding items deviating from observable response patterns, to locate possible bias against subgroups.[28] It was an early example of what became known as differential item functioning, or DIF, which developed into a widely used family of methods to identify test items that subgroup members were likely to answer incorrectly. The most efficacious approaches flowered in the next decade and were designed to statistically control for individual proficiency and find group variation net of such controls.[29] This was a response to Gordon and other critics who called for tests better attuned to minority students, and to women as well.

One sign of this was a flurry of research at ETS focused on minority group test performance during the 1970s, mostly documented in technical reports.[30] Other organizations looked into it as well. But it took time for DIF to emerge as a coherent area of inquiry and development. Taking ETS as an example, during the 1970s much of its attention was focused on educational inequality to understand test score differences. It funded an Institute for Urban and Minority Education at Teachers College, Columbia University, which studied problems faced by urban, low income youth. In 1976 its support shifted to an Office for Minority Education at ETS, which worked with school districts and other organizations on equity questions. In 1979 ETS created a "Social Learning Lab" to "investigate psychological processes affecting minority children." Other research efforts focused on unequal funding for schools, and gender stereotypes in education and assessment.[31]

Despite all of this activity, an ETS study in 1979 found that test questions depicted many more men than women, contributing to lower scores for women. This led to sensitivity reviews of ETS assessments, to eliminate such imbalances and other forms of "stereotypic content." It was a telling episode, suggesting that the organization had devoted more attention to problems in the schools than its own products. DIF eventually became a major focal point at ETS, and eventually a routine step in the development of its assessments.[32] To the extent that this record is revealing of national trends, events in the 1970s, including the NAACP conference and the points that Gordon and other critics had raised, may have had a palpable effect. But it took time for testing organizations to critically assess their own practices, and an influential court case in 1984 alleging discrimination in a licensing exam also likely was a factor.[33]

Progress proved slow. Statistical procedures to identify bias in test questions developed incrementally and with a good deal of uncertainty. In a review of different approaches published in 1981, Lorrie Shepard, Gregory Camilli, and Marilyn Averill found considerable congruence in procedures to identify biased test items, but they also noted that considerable ambiguity regarding the extent of bias remained.[34] At ETS, interest in DIF resulted in an approach developed by Neil Dorans and Paul Holland in 1982.[35] The key in all such procedures was finding variability on items among test takers of equivalent overall proficiency that was manifest along racial, ethnic, or gender lines. This did not necessarily indicate bias, but it did help identify questions where some degree of unfairness may have existed. It was not until 1987, however, and development of the Mantel–Haenszel approach to estimating DIF, that ETS decided to employ such procedures for screening of all assessments with large enough samples of questions.[36] This was a critical step for the nation's preeminent testing organization, but also for the industry as a whole.[37] The fact that it came more than a decade after the landmark NAACP meeting and the rise in DIF research during the 1970s, was testimony to the rather measured pace of change in the field.

DIF methods were hardly a cure-all for attacking bias in testing, however. While DIF could help identify potentially problematic items, it could not settle the question of bias completely. And it did not address the larger issue of knowledge and skills that standardized tests did not measure well. As many measurement scholars noted, DIF procedures did not always produce consistent findings. And beyond that, while it could detect potential bias in purely statistical terms, it was not always possible to explain why or how it occurred. That unavoidably involved a question of judgment, since identifying bias of one kind or another often was a matter of interpretation, as the Gordon–Rubain critique of "narrow" tests suggested. Consequently, the assessment industry turned to other sources of insight. This typically took the form of panels convened to examine items selected for evidence of bias to consider that possibility further. This approach also arose during the 1970s, largely separate from DIF procedures. It typically focused on problems of cultural variation in the interpretation of test items, with attention to racial and ethnic differences in responses. A question that often arose, however, was whether it was effective in identifying biased items, as there was considerable variability on that score too.[38] There also were issues regarding who should serve on such panels, and how heavily their viewpoints should be weighed.

In light of the controversies about bias in testing, a consensus soon suggested that such questions should not be left wholly to assessment experts. The industry response was to convene panels with significant representation from minority groups, so that insights regarding related cultural differences in language, everyday knowledge, and commonplace experiences could be considered. As Lorrie Shepard wrote in 1980, "minority review panels . . . serve important political and social justice goals. For these purposes, it is more appropriate that members of the panel represent constituencies pertinent to the use of the test rather than experts on the trait measured by the test." In short, bias was not simply a technical matter. Beyond that, Shepard also endorsed the idea that "appropriate numerical representation of minorities in test development activities is insufficient unless it is accompanied by meaningful minority participation and input."[39] Given the discord surrounding the question of bias in testing, it was considered important that panels of relevant minority group members review potentially problematic test items for evidence of unfairness.

Interpretive review procedures of this sort eventually became widespread, although little consensus appeared to exist about how to conduct them. Questions of their appropriate size and composition, for instance, received little attention in the professional literature. Approaches reportedly varied substantially, with some organizations convening panels of educators and others inviting participants from all walks of life. And occasionally such panels proved reluctant to label particular test items as culturally biased or otherwise inappropriate. Too often their reviews differed substantially from the results of DIF analyses; questions that panel members deemed problematic did not always prove difficult to minority students, while others did.[40]

The authority granted to these reviews varied as well, as problematic items for minority students were not always excluded, especially if other items seemed difficult for white students. In the end, review panels did not provide a comprehensive solution to the problem of bias in testing.[41] While the impact of this approach to addressing questions of bias was hardly revolutionary, it did provide the industry with answers to charges of prejudice. The testing industry may have taken years to respond to charges of bias, but the significance of such investments of time and resources eventually became clear.

Testing on Trial: Florida, Texas, and Beyond

Given racially disproportionate failure on competency exams in the South, particularly regarding high school graduation, legal challenges soon began to percolate there. Florida witnessed the first federal court case about these tests, and it concerned the SSAT II in 1979. The plaintiffs were students who had failed the test, represented by a local NAACP chapter, a Tampa legal clinic, and attorneys from the Center for Law and Education in Cambridge, Massachusetts.[42] The case began in the Middle District of Florida, before Judge George C. Carr, and subsequently was heard on appeal by a judicial panel for the U.S. Fifth Circuit. It then was remanded to the district, where Judge Carr ruled in favor of the state.[43]

A second major case occurred in Texas, starting in 1999. It concerned many of the same issues, began with student plaintiffs, and also took place in a federal district court, but other circumstances were different. The precedent set in Florida and developments in the testing industry made it harder to impugn the validity of a criterion-based test, as procedures for responsibly conducting such assessments had been well established by then. The case was brought on somewhat different legal grounds by lawyers from the Equal Employment Opportunity Commission and the Mexican American Legal Defense Fund, among other attorneys representing the plaintiffs. It was argued before Judge Edward C. Prado in San Antonio, who also ruled for the defense, representing the Texas Educational Agency.[44]

There were other cases too, such as *Green v. Hunt* in North Carolina, which was summarily dismissed in 1979. *Anderson v. Banks* in Georgia was argued 1982, concerned testing in a single school district, and was guided by the trial in Florida.[45] Yet another case occurred in Louisiana in 1994, *Rankins v. State Board of Elementary and Secondary Education*, and also was settled in favor of the defendants.[46] Other suits against MCT requirements, including tests for grade promotion, also failed to alter school policies. These included *Sandlin v. Johnson* in 1980, *Bester v. Tuscaloosa City Bd. of Education* in 1984, and *Erik v. By And Through Catherine V. V. Causby* in 1997. By and large, federal courts proved unwilling to amend accountability decisions made by public education authorities.[47]

Testing, Content Validity, and Discrimination in the 1980s

The Florida case was titled *Debra P. et al. v. Turlington* and concerned the fairness of a test that lacked content validity with respect to curricula in Florida public schools. As noted earlier, the Florida legislature had authorized a test of "functional literacy," which was evaluated for construct validity by faculty members at Florida State University. It was not appraised, however, for congruence with instruction in institutions across the state. This proved to be a question with a decisive bearing on the case.

Given how the exam was rushed into place, under conditions of considerable confidentiality, teachers had little opportunity to adjust their instruction to it and cut scores were established rather arbitrarily. Florida schools were formally segregated until 1972, with unequal resources for Black and white institutions, and this was conceivably linked to disparities in test scores. The plaintiffs argued that Turlington and other state officials realized that significant racial disparities in passing were likely and proceeded with the test's administration, representing a failure to equally protect the property right that a secondary diploma represented. This charge made the case a potential violation of the equal protection clause of the U.S. Constitution's fourteenth amendment.[48]

The case went through several steps, which have been described elsewhere, along with its Texas counterpart.[49] Judge Carr initially ruled that the test requirement, while perhaps not intentionally prejudicial, did potentially penalize African American students unfairly. He reasoned that while the state may have had an interest in such a graduation requirement, the conditions out of its rollout and the state's history of racially unequal schooling made its equitability suspect. Carr assigned the latter point particular significance declaring that "punishing the victims of past discrimination for deficits created by an inferior educational environment neither constitutes a remedy nor creates better educational opportunities." He thus found the requirement a violation of both the Constitution's equal protection and due process clauses and enjoined its administration until 1983, to provide an opportunity to better prepare students equitably for the test.[50]

Upon appeal, the Fifth Circuit judges affirmed Carr's decision but remanded the case to the district court for findings on two key issues: whether the test covered material actually taught in the schools, or content validity, and the extent of "the role and vestiges of past discrimination" on African American students. This occurred in 1981 and set the scene for the decisive stage of the case.

Following this, Judge Carr decided to schedule hearings for each issue separately. Regarding the test's validity, the defense submitted a study conducted by IOX Assessment Associates, a firm headed by W. James Popham, an expert witness for the state. It featured several components, including a survey of teachers regarding instruction in the twenty-four skill areas addressed on the exam, and a survey of administrators in sixty-seven districts regarding teacher professional development and instructional materials. The study included a cover letter from Turlington emphasizing its importance, which may have influenced survey responses. The study also included site visits for follow-up interviews and to "verify the accuracy of district reports." Finally, a survey of students inquired about material taught to prepare for the exam.[51] Altogether, the IOX team gathered a substantial body of data, which the court ruled as admissible in conjunction with expert testimony for the defense.

Unsurprisingly, Popham argued that the study supported the content validity of the exam. Most teachers indicated that skills measured on the test were addressed in their classrooms, and district leaders reported that they provided relevant support and appropriate instructional materials. Robert Gangné, a prominent psychologist at Florida State University, also testified that the study provided credible evidence that the exam was a valid indicator of material that had been taught. A third defense witness, Dr. Donald Henderson, stated that districts were supportive of teachers and extended assistance to students who failed the test.[52] At the center of this testimony was the proposition that such data represented credible evidence that the test was both a reasonable and a valid measure of what students were taught.

In testimony for the plaintiffs, on the other hand, Robert Linn and Robert Calfee questioned whether survey data of this sort was an accurate reflection of what actually occurred in classrooms. Linn noted that the teacher questionnaire seemed to invite positive reactions and Calfee found considerable variation in responses, especially regarding math skills, generally corresponding to student performance. Instead of supporting the defense, he suggested that the data might also have supported the plaintiffs' position. The resulting rebuttal of the state's argument stated that the evidence was not "clear and convincing," largely representing indirect information about what students had been taught that also could indicate inequities in instruction.[53]

In making his ruling, Judge Carr noted that witnesses on each side (and plaintiff attorneys) had participated in the National Institute of Education sponsored debate, and trial arguments echoed disputes that occurred then. But he decided against the "clear and convincing" standard of evidence that the plaintiffs had advocated, ruling that a "preponderance of evidence" was sufficient to support the "compelling interest of the state" in raising expectations in the public schools. While acknowledging that some teachers may not fulfill their duties properly, and their students may have been tested unfairly, he stated that it was not the duty of the court to thus monitor or question the education system. "The elimination of racial discrimination in public schools is a large task," he declared, "and one that should not be retarded by efforts beyond the jurisdiction of school authorities." On the question of "vestiges of discrimination," Carr found that there was "no causal link between the disproportionate failure rate and the present effects of past school segregation."[54] The court therefore decided for the state, and students who failed the exam in 1983, or all retesting opportunities, would receive a certificate of attendance rather than a diploma.

As a matter of policy, *Debra P. v. Turlington* was significant on a number of counts. It established a firm precedent for MCT as a high school graduation requirement, regardless of racially disproportionate failure rates.[55] In this respect it opened the door to similar requirements elsewhere, especially in the South, where such disparities could be especially impactful. But the case also held implications for test builders and policy makers, as content validity became such an important an issue. Additionally, instruction proved to be an especially decisive factor, a consideration referred to as "instructional validity" in the trial. As Popham and others had suggested years earlier, criterion-referenced tests of this sort were ultimately judged on compliance with curricular and instructional standards, even if such terms were not yet widely used.[56] Given that the Florida test was not initially designed for a particular curriculum, it was quite fortuitous for Turlington that it apparently had changed somewhat by 1983. But the links between assessment policy, curriculum, and instruction would become major focal points of educational reform in years to come.

Instructional Validity and Discrimination Rejoined in 1999

The Texas case was *GI Forum v. Texas Education Agency*, representing its principal litigants. Many Hispanic and African American students failed the Texas Assessment of Academic Skills, or TAAS, which had been introduced in 1990. Unlike the earlier Texas Educational Assessment of Minimum Skills, it was intended to measure higher-order thinking, problem-solving skills, and knowledge. This change reflected a national movement away from MCT exams to standards-based assessments aimed at greater proficiency in various academic domains. But 67 percent of African American and 59 percent of Mexican American eleventh grade students failed to meet the cut score in 1991, compared to 31 percent of white students. They were offered remediation and multiple opportunities to retake the test, and passing rates improved. But significant racial and ethnic disparities remained, with minority students about twice as likely to initially fail as white students.[57] The fundamental issue, consequently, was the disparate impact of the TAAS, a striking parallel to the Florida case two decades earlier.

The Texas plaintiffs alleged a violation of Title VI of the 1965 Civil Rights Act, a different legal foundation from that in *Debra P. v. Turlington*. But another major difference concerned the question of test validity. TAAS was more carefully designed to assess skills and knowledge represented in the state-approved curriculum than the Florida exam, and its development was informed with substantial input from educators around the state. The state provided evidence on these points, including survey data from teachers and testimony from educators and others involved in developing the test. Consequently, the court expressed little concern about the test's curricular validity and deemed no additional study of the issue necessary.[58]

The question of instructional validity, however, remained unsettled, even if vestiges of segregated schooling was not an issue. The plaintiffs raised questions about how minority students had been taught and how resources varied across districts and schools. Although the court did not use the term "instructional validity," a somewhat parallel set of questions arose. The plaintiffs provided clear evidence of differences in the extent and quality of instruction that many minority students received, despite the defense contention that similar curricular standards existed statewide.[59]

Addressing this point directly, plaintiffs demonstrated that minority students were underrepresented in advanced placement courses and gifted and talented programs, and were disproportionately taught by uncertified teachers. But the court found that because of a "rigid, state-mandated correlation" between curricular standards and the assessment, "all Texas students have an equal opportunity to learn the items presented on the TAAS test." It further found that remediation for students who failed represented "more concentrated, targeted educational opportunities."[60] As in Florida, this court sidestepped the question of instructional validity by assuming that state and local educational authorities required teachers to deliver an appropriate curriculum, and that remediation and multiple testing opportunities obviated the need to consider remaining inequities.

Dropout rates became another feature of the *GI Forum* case that was not addressed in Florida. Walter Haney of Boston College testified that inordinate numbers of minority students left Texas high schools in their freshman year, ostensibly to avoid taking the TAAS. This would artificially raise test scores if most were likely to fail, which relatively low passage rates suggested was the case. It also potentially compromised the supposed effect of the testing regime, rendering these students unable to benefit from improved academic standards. A 2003 investigation by the *Washington Post* confirmed that minority students were prevented from taking tests by being held back in grade, with many dropping out. The court, however, did not find that Haney had drawn a clear link between the advent of the TAAS and statewide dropout patterns, consequently ruling his testimony irrelevant. This was helpful to the defense, but it did document a link between exit exams and accelerated dropout rates, an issue that received attention in other studies.[61]

Additional questions in the Texas case also made it depart somewhat from *Debra P. v. Turlington*. On disparate impact the court found that the plaintiffs had a compelling case under the Four Fifths Rule and the *Shoben* formula, legal parameters for identifying adverse impact. But it ultimately found that "an examination of cumulative pass scores in more recent years does not evince adverse impact" under these rules, despite continuing evidence of disparities. The court added that the effects of remediation made prima facie evidence of disparate impact considerably less persuasive.[62] Additionally, the question of cut scores proved less controversial than in Florida. This was due both to the consultative process used in setting them, which appeared less arbitrary, and the opportunity for students who failed to improve their performance.[63]

Altogether, the *GI Forum* case was less contentious than *Debra P.*, partly because the question of content validity was somewhat settled by industry procedures linking curricula more closely to assessment. The question of instructional validity, a term invoked in Florida, remained germane, but courts in both cases chose not to intervene in matters considered to be the province of educational administrators, seeing that teachers deliver the prescribed curriculum. The fact that students had recourse to remediation and multiple opportunities to pass the tests also proved to be critical. Perhaps most importantly, however, both courts accepted the proposition that states had a compelling interest in requiring such exams, in pursuit of higher standards and greater equity. The successful defense of these prerogatives was a major accomplishment and paved the way for wider adoption of such measures. At the same time, it also laid to rest many questions of racial and ethnic performance differences on such assessments, including the potential effects of bias and discrimination. While these continued to be important concerns in the public square and academic discourse, they ceased to be potent matters of legal contention.[64] And this helped to effect an important shift for civil rights organizations with respect to testing: instead of a barrier to equal opportunity, it gradually came to be seen as a lever to help enable equitable educational reform.

Discovering Stereotype Threat and Its Significance

As indicated earlier, there was considerable interest in psychological factors affecting minority test performance during the 1970s, and it was mentioned in the NAACP report at the time. But two decades passed before a breakthrough occurred in that regard, led by psychologist Claude Steele of Stanford University. He and his collaborators found that minority students tended to perform lower on tests they believed to represent a reflection of their academic or cognitive abilities. Steele argued that this represented an affirmation of stereotype, triggering anxiety that impeded successful performance. This was established in experimental research, and it was not limited to African Americans. A range of studies documented its impact on other minority groups, and women in certain circumstances. Its discovery was an important contribution to the field of social psychology, and to understanding achievement gaps.[65]

The psychological mechanism involved in this phenomenon is fear of stereotypes that affect members of relevant groups. A central feature of racialized social distinctions, of course, concerns mental abilities. And myths of Black inferiority were sustained by standardized assessments, starting with IQ tests. Steele and his collaborators found that African American students performed more poorly when informed that a test measured cognitive or academic ability than if it was said to be less evaluative. They hypothesized that stress led to performance monitoring, narrowing of attention, and efforts to suppress adverse responses, which impacted outcomes.[66] This line of research suggested that group differences could widen as a result. Similar effects were found for women in mathematics and other STEM (science, technology, engineering, and mathematics) fields, although not necessarily to the same extent.[67]

These finding held significant implications for understanding racial and gender differences in standardized assessment, especially those associated with high stakes, such as graduation requirements. Effects potentially included racial differences in high school exit exams and long-standing differences on other tests. Stereotype threat was also linked to overall academic performance in some circumstances.[68] Of course it did not explain all racial and gender differences in test outcomes, as a host of additional factors also impact them, including poverty, parental education, family structure, and institutional effects. Motivation can affect performance too: students who care little about outcomes are unlikely to do well. And stereotypes can only exert influence if students know about derogatory labels to begin with.[69]

In 2006 the American Psychological Association published a statement declaring that "stereotype threat widens [the] achievement gap" and "reminders of stereotyped inferiority hurt test scores." It highlighted the harmful role that stigma and prejudice can play in assessing students who have suffered them historically.[70] But because the preponderance of pertinent research was conducted under controlled conditions, the larger impact of these effects remains unclear. As some researchers have pointed out, stereotype effect may not account for most racial or gender differences in test performance. And it is unclear how its effects are manifest among younger people in a variety of circumstances and community settings. Rather, it appears that its effects may be widespread but rather variable in degree or strength.[71]

The Racial Achievement Gap and Its Causes

Dramatic racial and ethnic differences on high school exit exams in Florida and Texas suggested that such disparities were a pervasive and persistent problem. But passage rates for minority students improved in both states, and racial and ethnic differences also shrank, at least in absolute terms. More significantly, Black–white differences on the NAEP also diminished markedly between 1971 and the latter 1980s. Aggregate disparities for Black and white seventeen-year-olds fell by about 50 percent on both verbal and quantitative assessments. The principal source of change was rising African American scores; assessment outcomes for white students remained largely constant. For nearly two decades, African American performance on the "gold standard" of educational assessment improved dramatically. Yet questions about race and cognitive ability continued to be sources of controversy.[72]

Both academic and popular attention began to focus on the achievement gap as an important issue during the 1990s, although it certainly was recognized before that.[73] Publication of Richard Herrnstein and Charles Murray's book,

The Bell Curve: Intelligence and Class Structure in American Life in 1994 brought the question back into public view, drawing media attention and becoming a bestseller. Utilizing data largely from armed forces testing, it argued that IQ was a primary factor in determining social status and success in American life. Published without customary review procedures, it met with widespread academic criticism despite its apparent popularity.[74]

Among the academic responses to *The Bell Curve* was a collection of essays edited by Christopher Jencks and Meredith Phillips titled *The Black–White Test Score Gap*. In many respects its publication marked the beginning of sustained interest in racial test scores differences from both academic researchers and the public. Most contributors to the book were social scientists and not measurement experts, and its chapters largely focused on social and economic factors impacting test scores. It was a fitting research-based response to Herrnstein and Murray, and its major points continue to resonate today.[75] Altogether, there can be little doubt that *The Bell Curve* and the responses it provoked helped to put the racial achievement gap onto the national agenda.[76]

As suggested above, many factors in addition to race and ethnicity affected test scores. Students from poverty backgrounds typically have done poorly on standardized assessments. Those with college-educated parents usually had an advantage. Students residing in two-parent households normally did better than those with single parents, even when income and education were similar. And all three of these factors impacted many African American students, who were considerably more likely than white students to live in poverty neighborhoods, have less educated parents, and live in single-parent households. In short, a number of the factors that potentially undermine test performance were compounded for them. By the 1990s, as many as a third lived in circumstances where all of these factors had an impact. Black students in schools with large numbers of impoverished students usually fared poorly on standardized assessments, while those attending institutions in more affluent settings did considerably better. The former conditions have been described as concentrated disadvantage, a confluence of problems that no other group has experienced in recent history. And it has contributed substantially to perpetuating the racial achievement gap.[77]

In recent years African American children were three times more likely to live in poverty households than white children, and more than twice as likely to live in single-parent households. Many resided in high poverty neighborhoods, where schools often struggled to provide robust educational experiences. And as studies have pointed out, Black–white test score gaps are evident at all levels of family income, even the highest. Yet these data demand scrutiny. A range of additional factors affect the achievement gap, including stability of household income, capital assets, parental education, neighborhood and school quality, and depth of poverty. These conditions affect many minority groups, including American Indians, but their effect on African Americans is especially severe. Studies have shown that statistically controlling for them reduces the portion of gaps attributable to race considerably.[78] And of course it is possible that some portion of the gap results from the psychological effect of stereotype threat, although its overall magnitude is unknown.

A large body of research thus suggests that much of the racial achievement gap can be attributed to these so-called structural factors, the extremely difficult circumstances that large numbers of African Americans experience on a daily basis. For many, conditions of severe poverty have existed for generations, depriving families of resources that may enable children to succeed. Even middle-class Black families experience economic instability, possess fewer capital assets, have less parental education, and enjoy less disposable income than white families on average. They are also less likely to reside in well-heeled communities with high performing schools, which are often overwhelmingly white. Continuing racial segregation means that many such families send their children to city schools that often do not perform as well. As Edmund Gordon wrote in 2001, "income and wealth have replaced, or greatly reduced the significance of, the color line in our society," but segregation has continued to impact most African Americans.[79] These are circumstances that have dictated much of the racial achievement gap for decades.

Schools of the Department of Defense (DoDEA) offer an interesting alternative case. They served 112,000 students in 1998, equivalent to a small state or large urban district, with half eligible for free or reduced lunch and a 35 percent annual turnover rate due to military rotations. Forty percent of enrollment was minority students, but the composition of schools varied considerably, as some exceeded 80 percent minority and low income students due to housing based on military rank. Students with single parents, however, were below national levels (6.2 percent versus 27 percent), and budgets were "adequately but not lavishly financed" at about 22 percent higher than the national average. Teacher compensation was higher too. DoDEA schools were smaller than most public schools, and staff collaboration was emphasized. Parental involvement also was high and students reported that teachers were supportive and challenging. Students were not normally placed into "tracks" or levels of academic work. These features reportedly fostered shared values and expectations, reflecting "the value placed upon education and training that permeates the military community." Racial achievement gaps were considerably smaller than in public schools, by nearly 50 percent among eighth graders, showing what was possible when many social and institutional problems facing other schools were less pronounced.[80]

So-called cultural factors also may affect minority achievement, and these too may have been less evident on military bases. Considerable research and commentary have focused on such considerations.[81] The prevalence of rap music highlighting rejection of traditional values, and labeling school success as "acting white" have been construed as evidence of such influences.[82] But other cultural elements also are evident, such as antagonistic responses from white students and families to the very presence of Black students in suburban institutions. This is documented in studies examining course placements, punitive disciplinary practices, and special education assignments that collectively have compromised African American academic success.[83]

Given these general circumstances, along with pervasive poverty and discrimination, and police harassment and coercion, it is little wonder that some Black adolescents reject academic accomplishment and institutional accommodation. While this response does not characterize most Black youth, it also reflects working-class rejection of formal education, well documented among whites.[84] It likewise echoes youth culture from the past, which may explain its appeal to teens from a variety of backgrounds. In this respect Black resistance to schooling can be considered quite conventional, and certainly not a unique animus against social norms. Severe deprivation may contribute to its potency, but that too is hardly an exception historically. In the end, structural and socioeconomic factors appear to account for more of the racial achievement gap than the so-called cultural influences highlighted by some observers.[85]

The racialized achievement gap has been a topic of considerable commentary and debate. Among the more thoughtful responses was a report issued by the National Study Group for the Affirmative Development of Academic Ability, chaired by Edmund W. Gordon and published in 2004. It focused on "improving the learning opportunities and academic achievement of minority and low income students" through coordinated intervention in classrooms, schools, and communities. Its authors highlighted the need for trust as essential to developing "compassionate and independently critical thinking members of humane communities," where "intellectual competence reflects intellective character." Instead, the federal program labeled No Child Left Behind promulgated a policy regime premised on sanction for schools and educators that failed to remedy achievement gaps.[86] Its shortcomings are addressed in chapter 5.

Conclusion

Race and standardized assessment continued to be linked during the latter twentieth century, but the circumstances of their connection began to change. Testing became especially controversial as debates over racial disparities in test scores gained national attention. The NAACP made it a focal point, culminating in a historic conference posing a range of questions for the assessment industry. Even if many such issues were not subsequently addressed, it did contribute to efforts at reducing potential bias in tests and commitments to ensure fairness in outcomes. As a consequence, bias of the sort alleged at the time was likely reduced substantially. This, however, did not end controversies regarding race and testing.

Legal battles over MCT and graduation requirements did not result in decisions curtailing these policies. The period's principal cases opened the door to such exit exams, which spread most notably across the South. The racial impact was likely substantial, with somewhat higher dropout rates and a greater focus on test preparation instead of other subjects. As noted in the previous chapter, there is little evidence that these policies improved educational outcomes, as their proponents—and the courts—suggested would be the case.

The 1990s brought new developments, with discovery of psychological factors that potentially contributed to racial test disparities, renewed debate about race and IQ testing, and a resulting focus on achievement gaps and their causes. Echoes of the NAACP's Conference on Minority Testing were evident, demonstrating that much remained to be done in addressing these questions. With concerns about test bias being addressed somewhat, standardized assessment gradually came to be seen as a crucial element in achieving educational equity. In this respect, debates over testing during the closing years of the twentieth century made it possible to realize a dramatic turn in policy at the start of the twenty-first.

3

A Time of Transition

Testing Takes a Back Seat in the 1980s

The 1980s were a time of considerable ferment in American education. Ronald Reagan's presidential election signaled a conservative turn in national politics, and rejection of the equity-minded reform agenda of previous decades. Reagan had promised to abolish the newly formed Department of Education, arguing that schooling was the purview of the states. But it turned out to be an empty threat, as education—and testing—continued to be significant public concerns. Just how that would find expression, however, took a while to be revealed.[1]

If there was a single event that defined the decade, it was publication of *A Nation at Risk* in 1983, a federal report that declared a crisis in American education. Perhaps motivated by the education department's precarious status, it called attention to national problems of academic underperformance. Assessment was a key element of this, as test scores became a major source of evidence regarding it. Moreover, a steady decline in college entrance exam scores had aroused considerable public concern. And American students fared relatively poorly on international assessments comparing education systems.[2] Given these developments, it was little wonder that the report found a receptive audience.

The response to *A Nation at Risk* elevated education as a public issue, focusing attention on educational excellence. This was different from the emphasis on basic skills in the seventies. As noted earlier, the MCT movement expanded in the 1980s, but critics then argued that it did little to promote higher levels of accomplishment.[3]

New reform initiatives took shape, setting the stage for subsequent developments in assessment for years to come. It was a time of transition regarding both educational reform and testing policies. Public interest in education as a national issue increased dramatically, and politicians responded. Reagan devoted little attention to education, but his successor, George H. Bush, made it a theme in his campaign and administration. At the same time, a fresh generation of state governors became champions of school reform, making institutional performance a cornerstone of plans for economic development. This was a clear manifestation of the human capital agenda of educational change for growth. It was especially important in the South, while extending to other parts of the country, and it received enthusiastic support from corporate executives.[4] If *A Nation at Risk* put education reform on the national agenda, state and business leaders gave it shape. But assessment policy received less attention than it had in the 1970s.

These developments stirred educational researchers, and they too helped to move reform conversations forward. They gave voice to key proposals and offered feedback on policy. Many became advisors to political leaders, offering perspective and insight. It was out of this diverse mélange of voices that reform moved forward, laying the groundwork for a new conceptualization of assessment that eventually found expression toward the end of the decade.

A Conservative Turn

Ronald Reagan swept into the White House in 1980, marking a sharp break from the liberal orientation of prior years. Popular dissatisfaction with economic problems during the 1970s sealed his victory, along with the seeming ineptness of his predecessor, Jimmy Carter. Courting national teacher unions, Carter had created a cabinet-level Department of Education, which Reagan vowed to eliminate, in line with his neoliberal, smaller government principles.[5] These plans were thwarted, however, by congressional Democrats, and Reagan recruited Terrel Bell, commissioner of education under Richard Nixon, to head the department and close it down. But Bell had other plans: in 1981 he appointed a commission to study American schools. While this was partly intended to ensure the department's survival, it also helped to galvanize public interest in education reform.[6]

The commission's report, *A Nation at Risk*, was published at a time when the public was already quite concerned about American schools. This was partly due to a highly publicized decline in performance on the SAT, the most widely used college admission exam.[7] Between 1963 and 1980 scores dropped fifty-four points on the verbal section and thirty-seven points in mathematics. Only a third of test takers in 1980 performed as well as half did seventeen years earlier. Commentary at the time pointed out that more students took the exam, especially those who scored lower, but it also pilloried the schools. As the *New York Times* reported, the decline was widely "regarded as a prime symbol of educational deterioration." Critics charged that curricular changes led to less emphasis on academic skills, along with lower daily attendance and grade inflation in high schools. Student motivation reportedly had dropped too, reflected in declines on other assessments. Much of the public was unhappy about this, reflecting anxieties about social promotion and lagging standards that had motivated MCT requirements. According to the Gallup Poll, between 1975 and 1980 American adults giving schools a rating of A or B declined from 43 percent to little more than a third, a low point in recent history. If *A Nation at Risk* was critical of the schools, the country certainly was ready for its message.[8]

In light of this, it is little wonder that assessment data figured prominently in the report. *A Nation at Risk* was distributed widely across the country and hundreds of newspapers and other periodicals featured articles about it.[9] Written in an accessible manner, it was framed in dramatic terms. Its authors declared that "the educational foundations of our society are presently being eroded by a rising tide of mediocrity that threatens our very future as a Nation and a people," calling for a renewed pursuit of excellence. And test scores predominated in the narrative. Nine of thirteen "Indicators of the Risk" concerned declining or comparatively poor results on standardized assessments. These included "international comparisons of student achievement," followed by an observation that "23 million American adults are functionally illiterate." There also was a statement that average high school achievement "on most standardized tests" was "now lower than 26 years ago, when Sputnik was launched." Other such declarations adduced similar figures from different sources, including the SAT and tests of college graduates. Faltering graduation rates also were cited, along with complaints about inadequate skills from business and military leaders. But assessment data clearly played a leading role in arguments alleging a general decline in American education.[10]

Regarding schools, the report suggested curricular standards had waned in many states, with lower expectations for coursework in key subjects. It also asserted that homework expectations had worsened, with many states allowing secondary students to take frequent electives, including "less demanding personal service courses." Perhaps most telling, however, commission members declared "'minimum competency' examinations (now required in 37 states) fall short of what is needed, as the 'minimum' tends to become the 'maximum,' thus lowering educational standards for all." This struck directly at a major policy impetus of the 1970s and the heart of accountability measures in Florida and other states. Rather than raising academic standards, as reform leaders had suggested, MCT policies were depicted as undermining them. This idea also appeared in other discussions of MCT, despite its growing use as an instrument of accountability.[11]

Given its critique of lowered expectations, it followed sensibly that the commission's report would focus on raising curriculum standards. Consequently, it recommended greater attention to traditional subjects such as English, mathematics, science, and social studies, with computer science included for good measure. This was a thinly veiled rejection of the curricular flexibility and experimentation of prior decades. The report also identified grade inflation as a growing problem, suggesting standardized tests as a remedy. Longer school days and an extended academic calendar also were recommended. No longer satisfied with basic literacy and mathematical skills, the commission outlined fundamental curricular changes to provide a pathway to higher standards.[12]

Academic excellence was hardly an end in itself, of course, and commission members cited "demand for highly skilled workers in new fields" that were "accelerating rapidly" as rationales for pursuing it. Science educator Paul DeHart Hurd declared "we are raising a new generation of Americans that is scientifically and technologically illiterate." Reading scholar Paul Copperman suggested that "for the first time in the history of our country, the educational skills of one generation will not surpass, will not even approach, those of their parents."[13] Such statements were dramatic, if not entirely accurate, and featuring them in a report sanctioned by the Department of Education may have been intended to provoke alarm. It also highlighted a clear human capital rationale for change. Featuring this message, *A Nation at Risk* succeeded in gaining national attention. Its publication marked a turning point of sorts in educational history, and much of its evidence was based on standardized testing of one sort or another, further legitimizing this mode of assessment.[14]

The report was met with skepticism too, especially when its claims were subjected to critical scrutiny. But it took a while for telling critiques to register. In the meantime, the report succeeded somewhat in shifting attention from minimum competency to questions of excellence. It linked the loss of American academic, scientific, and technological leadership to national security and economic ascendency, suggesting that raising performance on standardized assessments was vital to the future. Not since Sputnik in the latter 1950s had such a challenge been issued. But it also was different this time. Instead of topping foreign powers in military technology, it called for surpassing them on test scores. Whether this was truly indicative of critical skills and knowledge, or economic and military performance, was another question.

Perhaps the most tangible problem cited in *A Nation at Risk* was declining national test scores. It was evident in a variety of assessments, but most notably in the SAT, which exhibited a fairly continual decline of 1 to 3 percent of a standard deviation annually. Other tests also showed drops, although not as dramatic. While the commission report suggested that such changes reflected a "rising tide of mediocracy," others noted that more minority and poor youth took such tests after 1963, groups with less access to relevant academic resources. It also appeared that some students took such tests less seriously, especially in the 1970s when college admissions became less competitive. While these developments did not account for all changes in scores, long-term declines apparently were not primarily caused by lower academic standards. In fact, test scores for some groups rose during these years. A comprehensive analysis by the Congressional Budget Office concluded that scores started improving ten years earlier, and both compositional and educational factors likely were involved.[15] Since *A Nation at Risk* focused on declines as evidence of problems in the schools, these findings posed a serious threat to one of its central arguments. But the general public paid little heed to such technicalities.

Critics also questioned the relevance of test scores to education and economic development. Dean Theodore Sizer of the Harvard Graduate School of Education, for example, wondered whether more required courses would make students better writers or creative thinkers. Henry Levin, an economist at Stanford University, challenged the idea that schools were a source of problems for American businesses. "The easiest way," he declared, "to take pressure off of themselves for producing a lousy product with too many middle managers, too high executive salaries and too little creativity is to say, 'How can we do it? We have a lousy workforce.'" Additionally, survey data suggested that rhetoric about growing demand for high-skilled jobs was not entirely accurate. The Economic Policy Institute, based in Washington, DC, estimated that improving occupational skills would raise wages less than half of 1 percent. But such points had little impact on public opinion. Since most of the commission's critics failed to gain much publicity, and were broadly contested by government officials, their objections failed to cast much doubt on the report.[16]

In the end, Bell's efforts to save his agency from political extinction largely succeeded. Reagan could hardly abolish the department or exclude it from cabinet status following the report's publication and its popular reception. Education had become a national issue, but it was scarcely clear how to address it. Despite some sporadic evidence of improved achievement, MCT accountability had not transformed American schools. Reagan exhibited little interest in reform, focusing instead on problems of discipline and order in schools. He stressed these issues in speeches to teacher organizations and other groups, urging Attorney General Edwin Meese to investigate school violence.[17] But even if that issue was possibly linked to academic performance, stricter discipline could hardly guarantee higher achievement. And the Reagan administration was not about to propose a federally sponsored school reform program. While *A Nation at Risk* clearly lent a conservative tone to educational reform, the focal point of change remained in the states, with business leaders also playing a role.[18]

Reform Politicians Take the Stage

It did not take long for policy makers to react to concerns voiced in *A Nation at Risk* and rising public interest in school reform. George H. W. Bush, vice president under Reagan, ran for the presidency in 1988 and declared education to be a national priority. For Republicans this was a dramatic pivot away from abolishing the education department as an objective.[19] But Americans were dissatisfied with schools, despite most supporting their local institutions, and political leaders began to respond accordingly. In 1986 the National Governors' Association (NGA) published a report about problems facing American education, titled *Time for Results*. The NGA had formed seven task forces to study these questions and propose recommendations. Among the most important issues were the quality of teaching, school leadership, parent involvement and choice, and poverty and family structure. While the governors agreed education needed reform, they also discovered that its problems were multifaceted.[20]

The NGA additionally concluded that "the nation—and the states and school districts—need better report cards about results, about what students know and can do," suggesting that accountability systems needed improvement. Accordingly, its report implicitly endorsed the emphasis on testing in *A Nation at Risk*, but it devoted surprisingly little additional attention to accountability. An NGA Task Force on Readiness offered a brief discussion of assessment, yet it was meant to help students and parents see areas for improvement, not to make them work harder or comply with curricular expectations. And the widespread MCT movement was ignored altogether. In this respect, *A Time for Results* was a noteworthy departure from most state policy frameworks.[21]

This did not mean testing had fallen off the national agenda, however. The Education Commission of the States (ECS) also issued a report in 1983 that voiced many of the concerns expressed in *A Nation at Risk*. Calling for school improvement through "firm and demanding requirements," it argued that "teaching and student achievement should be objectively evaluated," code words for using standardized tests. While not explicitly endorsing strict accountability, ECS suggested that evaluative assessment was indispensable. Just how to accomplish it was another question. Following *A Nation at Risk*, MCT approaches seemed to be falling out of favor, but public opinion polls clearly appeared to support test-based accountability.[22]

Subtle pressure from Washington also contributed to the impression that state-level assessments would remain important. Secretary Bell created a "wall chart" at the Department of Education, showing the standing of each state on standardized test scores, principally the SAT and ACT, and other data. And it continued with his successor, William Bennett. While hardly a comprehensive comparison, it did stimulate greater interest in state-level educational outcomes. ECS also began compiling comparative information on school outcomes. State policy makers often were exasperated by this sort of attention, but the level of interest—or notoriety—it provoked led some to ponder more methodical approaches to comparative assessment.[23]

One obvious candidate for such a role was the NAEP, and Secretary Bennett appointed a committee to study how to make state-level data available from it. This idea quickly proved controversial, however, as some state leaders objected to it. Consequently, such comparative data were not made accessible until the early 1990s.[24] In the meantime, the Southern Regional Education Board created a Commission for Educational Quality, which issued a report in 1988 calling for higher educational standards across the region, along with assessments to ensure local accountability. While this did not have an immediate effect, as MCT exit exams still predominated there, it was a harbinger of things to come. These developments underscored the appeal of greater consistency in test-based accountability.[25]

Just as the NGA released its report, results of the Second International Mathematics Study, conducted in 1982, indicated once again that American students did not fare well. While scoring near the international average in algebra and computational arithmetic, they were well below it in geometry and problem solving. Japan had the highest overall math scores, which generally reflected how its national curriculum covered the tested material. This impacted public opinion, as Japanese auto makers were then taking larger shares of U.S. and global car markets. The human capital connection between school performance and economic development could hardly seem clearer. If American companies were to succeed in the world economy, it appeared that the schools must improve.[26]

These concerns echoed across the corporate sector of American business. The Committee for Economic Development, representing major companies, issued a 1985 report linking national competitiveness to the quality of schools. Arguing that education had a "direct impact on employment, productivity and growth," it pointed to a number of problems. These included "lack of preparation for work" among high school graduates, and the deficient skills of many college students. Japanese schools, by contrast, were praised for keeping students in class longer and graduating them at higher rates.[27] If the United States was losing to international rivals, education was targeted as a critical question. This, of course, further fueled public anxiety and the concerns of political leaders.[28]

Also apprehensive about public education, the Carnegie Corporation of New York created the Carnegie Forum on Education and the Economy, and issued a critical report on teacher preparation. In 1987 it created a National

Board for Professional Teaching Standards, intended to improve educator training and performance. While receiving a cool reception from major teacher organizations, these developments did highlight the importance of highly effective instruction. In 1988 the Carnegie Forum moved from New York City to Rochester and became the National Center on Education and the Economy. Its subsequent record of research and advocacy continued to be influential, often with implications for assessment.[29]

At the same time, reports that American teens lacked basic knowledge of the country's history and functions of government added to worries about the schools. In 1987 Diane Ravitch and Chester Finn published a book about student performance on a test about history and civics. About half the sample of high school juniors performed poorly, correctly answering less than 60 percent of the questions. They were especially deficient in explaining historical events and functions of government. Results were similar on NAEP history and civics assessments in 1988. These developments also contributed to calls for educational reform, and to doubts about young people becoming informed citizens and voters.[30]

In 1989 President George H. W. Bush, who had vowed to become an "education president," addressed the Business Roundtable, which represented more than 200 corporations. Just five months after being inaugurated, he declared the nation's schools to be in "real trouble." International test data revealed that American students still did not perform very well, especially compared to their Asian peers. Bush proposed a new education policy advisory committee, representing "leaders of business and labor, educators from every level, state and local government officials and the media," intended "to bring [him] innovative ideas." For its part, the Roundtable devoted its meeting wholly to the topic, hearing from a number of educational leaders.[31] As far as national business leaders were concerned, American schools continued to be a problem, inhibiting prospects for economic competitiveness in the future.

A culmination of all this activity was a presidential "education summit" with the governors in September 1989. This too was a sign of the attention schools had gained, and it occurred shortly after the Business Roundtable meeting. National polling indicated broad support for higher standards, broader testing, and curricular reform.[32] Bush thus started his presidency with considerable political momentum for a rhetorical commitment to educational improvement. But his administration was slow in launching a practical reform program. Its initial proposals were neither original nor vigorously pursued as a legislative agenda, and were hampered by Democratic congressional majorities.[33] In the end it was the NGA that reached out to explore the possibility of a conference with the president regarding educational issues. Following a White House meeting, all parties agreed to convene an educational summit.[34] Even if Bush did not have a clear vision himself, he was willing to abide meetings devoted to the question.

Discussion leading to the summit, held at Charlottesville, Virginia, focused on national goals for reform. Within the Department of Education a number of assessment ideas percolated in connection with this, including "a system of statewide achievement tests to ensure that students who pass through the system attain the subject area mastery necessary to progress to meaningful employment or on to postsecondary education." Another suggested that "all students would be expected to pass achievement tests that measure basic and higher level skills in reading, math, history, and science." College-bound students would take additional exams for mastery of higher-level work. National report cards also were proposed, and "a system of school improvement plans that requires failing schools to alter their educational programs."[35] Prescient as they may have been, however, these sorts of proposals did not play well at the summit. While accountability remained an important concern, recommendations for more comprehensive assessment failed to gain traction at the time.

Certain governors at the summit bolstered their standing as educational leaders, particularly Bill Clinton of Arkansas and Lamar Alexander of Tennessee, and both would become important national reform figures. Despite disagreements over the federal role in education, summit organizers suggested that its outcomes should include goals that would "guarantee an internationally competitive standard" in each of seven areas. Following school readiness, the second item on that list was "the performance of students on international achievement tests, especially in math and science," acknowledging the importance of assessment. Other goals were broader in scope, including fewer dropouts and better performance for "at risk" students, improving literacy among adults, training a competitive workforce, creating safe and drug-free schools, finding more qualified teachers, and adding up-to-date technology. And the conference closing statement included a call for annual report cards on progress toward those objectives, which undoubtedly would have required systematic assessment.[36]

For his part, President Bush did affirm the seven goals in a joint communiqué with the governors. Before long, however, his own version of national goals looked somewhat different. Bush reduced the number to six, announcing them as focal points in his 1990 State of the Union address.[37] He called for improving the performance of American students on international assessments to first in the world by 2000, along with demonstrating competency in "challenging subject matter." Workforce training and increasing qualified teachers were not mentioned, and neither were the curriculum changes suggested in *A Nation at Risk*. Such measures could have entailed federal guidance and financial support, and hence generally were unacceptable to the president's largely Republican constituency.[38]

Bush also advocated a "voluntary national test," but his domestic assessment goals were framed in terms of competency and were linked to gateway decision points at grades four, eight, and twelve. In this respect the president's educational objectives seemed somewhat backward looking, at least regarding testing. Although never fully formulated, his thinking appeared to reflect the remedial accountability policies still evident in many state policies. Bush's reform initiative, titled America 2000, was torpedoed in Congress by conservatives in his own party (which he did little to rectify), and the national test was opposed by civil rights groups worried about its potential for harming minority students. But despite declaring "these goals are about excellence," his proposals hardly represented the reform program advocated in *A Nation at Risk*, including its critique of MCT.[39] Ideas from his own Department of Education even failed to find expression. Instead, Bush's education budgetary priorities focused on increasing school choice and supporting exemplary institutions to serve as models.[40] It would take a new administration, and different approaches to assessment, for federal policy to change in the years to come.

Shifting Reform Priorities in the States

As noted earlier, the 1980s witnessed widespread adoption of MCT programs, with more than a third of the states requiring such exams for high school diplomas. Despite the fanfare garnered by *A Nation at Risk*, little immediate effort was devoted to replacing these tests with assessments measuring higher levels of achievement. As a practical matter, relatively few states had the resources to develop more sophisticated assessments, relying instead upon local expertise or commercial vendors to develop MCT exams. Matching relevant curricular content with exams, of course, had been a problem in Florida during the 1970s. Just because a test was evaluated for construct validity, after all, did not mean that it was appropriately aligned with curricula and teaching. Eventually, of course, widespread use of these exams meant that curricula often shifted to better reflect content that tests appeared to require.[41] Eventually this created potential validity problems, as instructional practices responded to annual exams, undermining the likelihood of comprehensively and accurately measuring relevant knowledge and skill domains.

As suggested by the NGA's reform initiatives, the 1980s was also a time of change in the states. Once again, much of the action occurred in the South, with figures like Richard Riley in South Carolina, Bill Clinton, and Lamar Alexander emerging as education governors, but reform occurred elsewhere too. Following the examples of Florida and North Carolina, MCT and basic skills accountability predominated throughout the region, but improvement efforts focused on other features of education systems.[42] As a reform-minded "new" Democrat, Clinton took the lead in Arkansas, manifest in the Arkansas Quality Education Act in 1983. He persuaded the legislature to increase sales taxes for additional school funding, nearly a 24 percent increase over three years. Reforms included increased graduation requirements, longer school days and school years, class size reduction, and more math and science instruction. Districts were expected to submit improvement plans regarding a variety of issues, including evaluation. As for assessment, MCT prevailed in Arkansas, with a gateway exam at grade eight. Teachers also were tested, with possible dismissal for failure. Grants and merit scholarships were intended to promote excellence, but higher levels of achievement were not targeted in the assessment system.[43]

Alexander followed suit in Tennessee, engineering passage of a Comprehensive Education Reform Act in 1984. Gaining the support of teachers and both parties in the legislature was key. The reform plan was quite extensive, including changes in teacher professional standards and curricular focal points. After legislative wrangling, key points became more money for educators and a new professional career ladder, funds for math and science instruction and gifted and talented programs, a longer school year, and computerized scoring of MCT exams. It too was paid for with state sales taxes and helped make Alexander a national figure in educational reform. But with respect to assessment, the focus remained on basic skills.[44]

Riley also launched his initiative in 1984, likewise convincing legislators to approve sales taxes to support changes, including higher teacher salaries. The focal point was at the school level, however, with rewards and sanctions for educators, not students (although South Carolina did have an exit exam). The assessment system utilized the California Test of Basic Skills (CTBS), a commercially produced and nationally normed exam, and scores improved. Its success was partly due to a significant portion of the new resources being devoted to support for accountability. Much of this was earmarked for "remedial and compensatory education improvements," often focused directly on improved test scores. Observers praised these programs, but few wondered whether "remedial" instruction threatened the validity of the CTBS as a high stakes assessment.[45]

Clinton and the other educationally minded governors also made a mark on the national scene, contributing to the NGA goals initiative. Clinton, of course, would play a pivotal role as president in the 1990s, along with Riley as his secretary of education. But in 1987 he already was writing about national educational reform, noting progress in the states but arguing that change was necessary across the country. Echoing ideas then quite familiar, he declared that "if the United States does not move toward a high-wage, high-technology, innovative economy, each succeeding generation will have to accept a standard of living lower than the one before." It was a clear statement of the human capital rationale for change, dictated by the idea of a competitive global marketplace for superior cognitive skills. Education, particularly in mathematics and science, was thus seen as crucial to economic success. Clinton touted the NGA's *A Time for Results* as a blueprint for reform, repeating its principal points. He was joined in this by fellow reform governors Riley and Alexander, along with Thomas Kean of New Jersey, Richard Lam of Colorado, and Ted Schwinden of Montana, among others. But here too, assessment received little attention. Instead, these states devoted resources mainly to keeping pace with national trends, including teacher salaries and programs for the most talented students.[46]

By the mid-1980s MCT had become business as usual regarding assessment, but it was highlighted less frequently in policy deliberations than earlier. Standards of performance, represented by passing (cut) scores, were typically set by consulting panels of educators, disciplinary experts, and other individuals asked to judge the likelihood of students answering questions successfully. It was an approach suggested by William Angoff at ETS in 1971, but subsequently went through many permutations. While hardly perfect, as panelists often disagreed widely, it was better than the rather arbitrary approach initially used in Florida during the 1970s.[47]

Following *A Nation at Risk*, journalist Jonathan Friendly expressed a common concern, wondering if "minimums would become goals unless students, teachers and administrators are rewarded for going further than they have to." Consequently, states turned to curriculum changes and improving the quality of teaching. Forty of them increased course requirements for graduation by 1984, with most also changing curriculum standards. In 1985 the *New York Times* found some states and districts considering incentives for more regular attendance and greater engagement, "carrots instead of sticks," and inducements for new teachers. It suggested that a shift had occurred, from focusing on "the performance of students" to "the quality of the teaching force and the conditions in which teaching must function." As one observer remarked "It's easy to raise standards. It's a lot tougher to figure out how to help these kids who can't meet them to make the grade."[48] Demanding minimum competency was one thing, but getting all students to accomplish it was another.

Occasionally there was talk about tests going beyond basic skills. For instance, a mandate to improve standards led New Jersey Commissioner Saul Cooperman to recommend a more rigorous assessment for high school freshmen in 1983. But the political reality of high failure rates in urban districts gave state politicians pause. Governor Thomas Kean did eventually launch a new "proficiency" test requirement in 1986, featuring a writing component and higher order problems to solve. But in practical terms it remained simply a harder MCT that failed to track different achievement levels. It still meant trouble for many students, as it soon became mandatory for graduation. And predictably, schools began rapidly changing curricula to address it, using test materials to inform instruction and raising the specter of Campbell's Law. Extensive remedial education created additional validity questions but made the exam politically palatable. As in Florida, such measures helped assuage concerns about failure rates in impoverished districts, which became quite high. Cooperman defended the test with familiar arguments about making diplomas meaningful. But other educators acknowledged that enhanced testing alone would not improve the schools, or close the achievement gap between urban and suburban students. Kean left office in 1990 and new governor Jim Florio shifted the state's educational focus to greater equity in resources, offering a clear example of political change impacting education policy.[49]

Other states followed New Jersey's lead by focusing on improved test results. W. James Popham continued to be an enthusiastic proponent of MCT assessment and wrote about its use in improved learning. He advocated "measurement-driven instruction," directing lessons to topics and skills featured on the tests. As he put it, "the competencies that are covered by the test will become curricular magnets that draw instruction toward themselves." Reports from Texas, Detroit, South Carolina, and Maryland corroborated this, providing accounts of educators tailoring instructional time for improving test scores. They also emphasized the importance of remedial or compensatory education for struggling students. But the chief evidence of improvement was rising scores on the MCT exams, not audit tests of one sort or another. Little mention was made of innovative teaching, curricular advances, student engagement, or other means of documenting educational improvement. Instead, Popham endorsed the idea of focusing instruction rather narrowly on accountability tests, with little heed to Campbell's Law. Such was the state of thinking among many MCT advocates while it became the country's predominant mode of test-based accountability.[50]

Perhaps because it had become so commonplace, however, accountability testing ceased to be a major focal point of school improvement efforts. Education leaders at the state level largely turned away from assessment questions in the 1980s. Instead, they focused on enhancements that held the promise of boosting performance on the tests at hand. Having MCT assessments may have been necessary to persuade legislatures to appropriate additional funding, especially for teacher salaries, but they were scarcely a centerpiece of reform. There were efforts to experiment with alternative forms of assessment, but that generally was an issue for the next decade. By and large, calls for more sophisticated tests were ignored through much of the 1980s, or they were deliberated cautiously.[51] Symptomatic of this, New Jersey commissioner Cooperman declared upon retirement in 1988 that his greatest accomplishments were efforts to improve the quality of teaching. He also pointed to effective schools programming and an urban initiative, without dwelling on assessment.[52] Leaders in South Carolina, Tennessee, Arkansas, and other states likely would have agreed, as changes generally focused on better teaching, improved resources, and curricular enhancements. It was a reform agenda quite different from the preceding decade.[53]

Testing Controversies Redux

Standardized tests may have become commonplace in the 1980s, but that did not mean that they were any less contentious. Questions of bias, content and construct validity, and fair use continued to abound, even if not necessarily at the same level of attention as during the seventies. Arguments conducted by experts of one sort or another predominated, but they continued to address considerable public skepticism about testing. Major debates over fairness and bias had quieted somewhat, yet many Americans still felt besieged by assessment of various sorts and wondered about its necessity.[54]

Among the most critical appraisals of the topic appeared in a 1990 booklet titled *From Gatekeeper to Gateway: Transforming Testing in America*. It was produced by the National Commission on Testing and Public Policy (NCTPP), which began in 1987 with a grant from the Ford Foundation. It included representatives from leading academic and research institutions, civil rights groups, and others including Bill Clinton. Based at Boston College, George Madaus served as its executive director and the report reflected perspectives long associated with the faculty there. While not a government publication, it did provide an apt summary of concerns felt by many informed observers about large-scale assessment.[55]

The NCTPP report cited a range of problems, some featured in earlier debates and others of more recent vintage. It noted that accountability tests relied heavily upon multiple choice formats, which were often unreliable and perhaps unfair when employed without other criteria to consider. It revisited the issue of arbitrary cut scores, with accounts of talented individuals unreasonably excluded from opportunities when failing by a single point. The report also argued that such assessments were used far too often, amounting to millions of lost days of instruction and perhaps nearly a billion dollars in direct and indirect costs. With respect to curriculum and instruction, it suggested that "as teaching turns into test preparation, test results cease to reflect what examinees really know or can do." This, of course, was a challenge to concepts such as Popham's "measurement driven instruction," although the authors did not mention it. Echoing the 1975 NAACP conference, the report also called for greater oversight of the testing enterprise, noting that "the industry whose products regulate access to opportunities is itself unregulated and unaccountable."[56]

Additionally, the NCTPP focused on racial and ethnic bias in testing, concerns also expressed fifteen years earlier at the NAACP conference. It recommended that "the more test scores disproportionally deny opportunities to minorities, the greater the need to show that tests measure characteristics relevant to the opportunities being allocated." In short, it suggested that tests should not be used for selection beyond documenting the ability to succeed in a particular educational program or line of employment. The 1990 report also noted that test anxiety, test familiarity, attitudes toward testing, and cultural background could also impact performance on standardized assessments, anticipating insights revealed by the stereotype threat research.[57] Observations such as these, underscored with a number of revealing examples, made the commission's report an especially comprehensive critique, albeit one that received little public attention.

A somewhat similar report was issued by the U.S. Commission on Civil Rights (USCCR) several years later, titled *The Validity of Testing in Education and Employment*. Considerably longer, it touched upon many similar themes but focused on validity and fairness. It also noted that test anxiety and familiarity could affect performance, especially along racial, ethnic, and gender lines. It featured essays by a number of experts with different views but in the end there was a general acknowledgment that bias did continue to be evident in standardized testing and that authorities such as the USCCR could help to limit its impact. Beyond that, the USCCR report echoed other themes addressed by the NCTPP, such as inappropriate use of standardized tests and oversight of the testing industry.[58]

Experts testifying for the USCCR included James Loewen, a University of Vermont sociologist, Nancy Cole, an ETS vice president, Monty Neil from the National Center for Fair and Open Testing (or FairTest), Barry Goldstein, an NAACP Legal Defense Fund attorney, and Lloyd Bond, a University of North Carolina psychometrician, among others. This group agreed that measures by the assessment industry were somewhat effective in reducing bias, and that it probably was not the chief source of difference between Black and white test takers. But critics such as Loewen, Goldstein, and Neil were insistent on the need for greater attention to it, while those more involved in the testing field such as Cole or Bond, were considerably less so. The report certainly was not the final word on these questions, but it documented the extent to which debates from the 1970s continued to resonate.[59]

If a coherent vision for assessment was evident in these reports, it entailed a sharply reduced role for standardized testing. All recommended that such assessments should not be the single criterion for high-stakes decisions about educational success and failure. Factors such as school grades and personal accomplishments were recommended for consideration too. Alternative forms of assessments also were suggested, including writing samples, constructed response items, and portfolios of student work.[60] Additionally, these themes were highlighted by FairTest, founded in Massachusetts in 1985 to provide a critical perspective on the testing industry. While much of its attention was focused on gateway exams such at the SAT or ACT, FairTest also objected to graduation exams and the growing numbers of MCTs that students took overall.[61] Highly publicized testing conflicts from the 1970s and early 1980s may have become somewhat distant memories by 1990, but issues of fairness and validity continued to motivate the quest for alternative and presumably better assessments.

These sorts of academic debates did not get much public attention, but other testing issues did. Renewed controversy erupted in 1987 when John Jacob Cannell, a West Virginia physician, published a paper demonstrating that all fifty states claimed norm-referenced test results above national averages. This led to widespread clamor and different studies to determine just how it could occur. The seeming paradox was labeled the "Lake Wobegone Effect," after the mythical Minnesota town of Public Radio fame where all children were considered above average; and eventually it was linked to certain underlying assessment problems that had received relatively little attention.[62]

The uproar focused on the elementary grades, where norm-referenced tests such as ITBS and CTBS still were used by districts and results were often aggregated to state averages. Part of the problem was that test scores typically rose after national norms were reported, with many students eventually scoring higher than the latter, lending the impression that they were "above average" based on earlier standards. The underlying question, however, was whether scores rose because children were learning more or because teachers had become more familiar with the test and focused on preparing them for it.[63]

Following a flurry of derisive commentary, more thoughtful studies of the matter appeared. One was conducted by a team led by Linn and another by Lorrie Shepard, both sponsored by the Center for Research on Evaluation, Standards, and Student Testing at UCLA. Linn's team found that norms established at earlier points were indeed a major factor in the effect, but evidence also suggested that achievement may have increased in the interim, indicated in NAEP data. The Linn et al. study, however, could not rule out the possibility that instruction was being guided by tests, explicitly or implicitly preparing students to achieve higher scores. This was a considerably more serious problem than misaligned norming cycles.[64]

The Shepard study explored the question of test-aligned instruction in greater depth . She reported that commercial test producers typically did not change test forms much, if at all, for considerable lengths of time, and educators acknowledged that curricula and instruction often were guided by assessments. Outright cheating was reportedly rare, but Shepard discussed a number of approaches that allowed teachers to focus instruction on boosting scores. "The old complaint again norm-referenced tests," she wrote, "was that they were insensitive to instruction . . . [and] It would take an enormous amount of instruction . . . to move the class average by a single item. Our examples from the norms tables illustrate, however, that teaching to specific items is enormously more efficient. In this sense, norm referenced tests are quite sensitive or vulnerable to teaching to specific items."[65]

While Shepard's paper was hardly comprehensive, it did uncover evidence of a widespread disposition to link instructional content to tests that districts—and even entire states—used at the elementary level. This was associated with accountability pressures to increase scores, exacerbated by media coverage where assessment data were publicly reported. Some educators described school and district leaders losing jobs because of unsatisfactory results, a powerful incentive to bend rules in order to succeed. This may not have been difficult, since Shepard reported that "the same form of the test is administered year after year," often on a six- or seven-year cycle. This made it relatively easy to gear instruction to particular aspects of the exams. And once that occurred, she noted, high scores did not "guarantee that apparent gains generalize to other tests," or even new forms of an old test. In short, this sort of preparation was a serious threat to the validity of normed assessments such as ITBS or CTBS.[66]

The problem of accountability policy distorting test results also was highlighted by Daniel Koretz in a 1988 article published by the American Federation of Teachers. He pointed out that when responsibility for assessment results was assigned to educators, and they could be threatened by low scores, it created perverse inducements to cheat in various ways. Koretz argued that verifiable achievement gains *did not* account for improvements in norm-referenced tests, prima facie evidence of this sort of trouble. Instead, it appeared that Campbell's warnings about test-based accountability were being borne out. Koretz worried that the "above average" scores that states and districts reported were clearly the results of teaching to tests in one fashion or another.[67]

This rather high-profile imbroglio led many to call for more frequent norm setting, including Dr. Cannell and test producers, but Shepard was less sanguine about that response. "The solution should be fresh tests," she wrote, "not annual norms." Updating norms more frequently, she pointed out, could simply add greater pressure to game the tests. And what if norms themselves reflected such gaming? In that case, Shepard declared, "the standard of comparison based on user norms would be spurious and inflationary."[68] In other words, it could make problems of test validity in the Lake Wobegon Effect even worse. A far better answer was producing new assessments each year, but that would be very expensive for test developers, raising the cost of assessment considerably. This was a major challenge to the industry, even if rarely acknowledged at the time.

These were problems well known in the testing field, yet rarely aired in such a public fashion.[69] In the end, this episode created pressure for testing organizations to update norms and introduce new tests more often. But if accountability pressures could produce these problems in the 1980s, when consequences for failure still were relatively modest, it was an ill portent for what would eventually follow. Many of the issues raised then would return in even more troubling form somewhat later.

The Question of Standards

As noted earlier, *A Nation at Risk* posed the challenge of achieving academic excellence to American educators. It also issued an implicit challenge to the testing industry, arguing that MCT instruments were inadequate to either assessing or promoting progress toward that goal. Developing tests to perform these functions was difficult, however, as long as state and federal policy offered little guidance on criteria to measure "excellence" in various knowledge and skill domains. This, no doubt, along with politically sensitive questions that standardized tests often posed, helped to keep relatively modest MCT requirements in place during the eighties.

Setting cut scores was a long-standing question that became more important as testing organizations contemplated how to move beyond MCT-style assessments. As noted earlier, critics had long highlighted the somewhat arbitrary decision to declare a certain percentage of correct answers a criterion dividing line. This usually meant that many students who answered correctly just below a given threshold could have the same level of competence as those scoring slightly above it. Determining such dividing lines was a big challenge, but on tests intended to identify multiple levels of performance, the issue could be seriously compounded. If assessments were to take up the challenge of identifying students as "highly proficient" or "advanced," clear criteria for such categories would have to be identified in a manner deemed legitimate.[70]

The problem was demonstrated in 1990, when the National Assessment Governing Board (NAGB) convened panels to rate student performance on the NAEP as "advanced," "proficient," or "basic." NAGB recruited subject experts and educators to identify test items and responses that would qualify for such broad categories, expecting variation in such judgments but also that a consensus would eventually emerge. But this proved elusive in practice, and no such agreement materialized. With this, expectations that criteria developed through such an inductive process appeared to be tenuous at best.

A team of measurement and testing specialists found that the judgment of evaluators recruited by NAGB varied widely, throwing the trustworthiness of performance categories into question. In a subsequent report, the authors concluded that "our analyses indicate that the achievement levels are seriously flawed—seriously enough that they cannot credibly support the conclusions to be based upon them." They recommended that "the achievement levels developed so far not be used in any public reporting of . . . NAEP results." A subsequent study by the National Academy of Education reached similarly negative conclusions.[71] This was disappointing news for NAGB, but underscored the challenge of developing assessments that went beyond certifying competence in basic academic skills. It also raised serious policy questions in addressing the admonitions of *A Nation at Risk*. And if this was true at NAEP, with the human and fiscal resources at its disposal, it was doubly so in many states where relevant expertise and funding were far less abundant.

An answer to this dilemma was posed in a 1991 paper coauthored by Marshall Smith and Jennifer O'Day, respectively the dean and a doctoral student at Stanford University's School of Education. They called for systematic state structures to guide both instruction and assessment. Such a reform regime would feature clear and challenging standards for achievement, with guidance for schools and teachers on implementing them in local curricula and instructional practice. It was not quite the same as uniform curricula for various subject domains, but rather a matter of identifying ambitious goals for more advanced knowledge and skills. The Smith–O'Day essay addressed the widespread frustration felt after a decade of reforms in states and districts that failed to produce a national picture of progress. Localized school improvement relied upon the skill and enthusiasm of particular leaders and educators, but the uncoordinated result often was described as "policy fragmentation" that yielded little sustained state or national advancement.[72]

Critics noted that accountability systems featured tests emphasizing broad coverage of facts and the ability to find designated answers to multiple choice items. Reformers called for complex problem solving and higher-order thinking, assessed in a variety of ways. To make this work, however, teachers themselves needed the knowledge and skills required if schools were to deliver a more challenging curriculum. Smith and O'Day argued that a fragmented policy system contributed to poor quality curricular materials, and that coherent state-level policy guidance held great promise for changing it. A well-known example was California, which developed curricular frameworks and mandated statewide adoption of textbooks, permitting identification of standards to assess performance. Connecticut, Kentucky, and New York also were cited frequently as states moving toward such reforms and corresponding assessment systems. With respect to assessment, Smith and O'Day called for new tests tied to state content frameworks, administered relatively infrequently for accountability purposes. Using Advanced Placement exams as an example, they advocated assessment focused on higher-level goals such as depth of knowledge, complex thinking, solving difficult problems, and producing well-reasoned results.[73]

An influential model was provided in the *Curriculum and Evaluation Standards for School Mathematics* announced in 1989 by the National Council of Teachers of Mathematics (NCTM). The result of discussion between mathematicians, teachers, curriculum developers, and other stakeholders, these standards featured statements about mathematical concepts and operations that students should know at different points in their school careers. Emphasis was placed on abstract understanding and utility rather than memorization and procedural rules. This created some controversy among mathematics educators accustomed to traditional instructional approaches, but relatively clear stages of development ultimately were outlined. The standards were also criticized for being vague, slogan-like, and restrictive, but they did provide goals to consider and sequential pathways to improved mathematical instruction and student mastery. In these respects they were also useful for the assessment field. NCTM offered a relatively clear picture of different levels of knowledge and skill in an academic subject, and an account of their curricular sequence. And mathematics, of course, was a discipline considered foundational by policy makers and educators alike.[74]

The mathematics standards provided a start, but doing this across other fields was a tall order, especially given the decentralized governance and instructional decision making that characterized American education. The Smith–O'Day proposal would link higher-order teaching to more complex and demanding assessment, and in this respect it also was a challenge to the testing industry, even if not fully appreciated at the time. It did not take long, however, for its implications to become clear. Spurred by *A Nation at Risk* and widespread discussion of improved standards, other reform efforts were taking shape. The National Alliance for Restructuring Education focused on underperforming urban schools, an outgrowth of the National Center for Education and Economy. Altogether, the early 1990s witnessed a flurry of activity around state and national standards in various subject fields, along with proposed changes in assessment. But change in policy at these levels was difficult to accomplish, not to mention the challenge of aligning local curricula, instruction, and assessment practices.[75] It was one thing, after all, to articulate visionary reform measures, and quite another to achieve an even modest institutional transformation. That was a task for the following decade.

Conclusion

The 1980s started with a historic commitment to change in American education, represented in publication of *A Nation at Risk*. But it largely was a period of rhetorical commitments to excellence at the national level followed by piecemeal reform in the states, and relatively little change in assessment. MCT, often attached to graduation requirements, was widely used by the states, and calls to measure higher levels of achievement largely went unheeded. President George H. W. Bush helped to highlight reform as a national priority, and initiated debate over key issues, but in the end he did little to move things forward. The idea of national assessments was floated toward the end of his presidency but failed to gain traction in Congress. Despite a good deal of reform impetus in the states, and the emergence of reform governors, test-based accountability did not begin to change until the early 1990s.

Critiques of educational assessment continued to echo concerns from the 1970s or earlier, especially concerning equity issues and civil rights, but major court decisions discussed earlier opened the way for MCT to become the decade's principal framework for ensuring accountability. Controversy regarding the Lake Woebegone episode raised validity concerns about tests at the elementary level that had not been voiced quite so clearly. In a telling analysis of MCT testing, Mary Catherine Ellwein, Gene V. Glass, and Mary Lee Smith argued that its purposes were largely symbolic and political, and it resulted in relatively little effort to improve schools. It was not until the end of the decade that reform-minded scholars began linking curricular standards, instructional excellence, and assessment in a conceptually coherent and potentially productive fashion. At the same time, African American test scores improved dramatically, even as overall trends in academic achievement remained uncertain.[76] These matters would become focal points of change in decades to come, and they also contributed to changes in accountability practices that eventually would impact the nation's public schools in an unprecedented fashion.

4

New Standards and Tests

Accountability on the National Stage

In 1989 Kentucky Governor Wallace Wilkerson appointed a task force to draft an educational reform act that would prove widely influential. The impetus was a state supreme court decision declaring that schools were failing a constitutional duty to "expect a high level of achievement of all children." The resulting legislation, titled the Kentucky Education Reform Act, or KERA, was revolutionary in several respects. Among other things, it called for an assessment system with high standards and rewards for educators that met or exceeded them. It also specified consequences for failing to meet standards, and called for "continuous improvement" regardless of prior achievement. Altogether it was an ambitious program of accountability, with assessments including standardized test questions and "alternative" items such as essays, portfolios, and performance events. This was a clear break from MCT assessments that held students accountable, shifting responsibility to teachers and schools. And the new exams aimed for higher-order learning, moving beyond basic skills. In many regards KERA was a portent of the future, both for the accountability system it mandated and the controversy it engendered. But it would take time for these eventualities to be realized.[1]

At the national level, George H. W. Bush's flirtation with a national testing program, along with the NGA's reform goals, led to renewed interest in assessment. While Bush's plans failed to find legislative support, partly due to his intransigence on school choice, the standards movement began picking up steam. Following Bill Clinton's ascent to the White House in 1992, education remained a national issue and ranked among the top concerns in public opinion polls. In this context, hortatory politics dictated that assessment play a somewhat different role in reform.[2] The admonition to go beyond basic skills in *A Nation at Risk* finally found expression. It was a time of considerable experimentation and debate.

The systemic reform model that Marshall Smith and Jennifer O'Day articulated also turned out to be quite influential, linking assessment to curricular reform and standards for test development. Following the NCTM's example, national education and research groups embraced the task of devising such standards, sometimes prompting controversy. At the same time, international test results continued to suggest that American students did not perform very well, especially teenagers.[3] This too triggered political commentary, fueling public concern about the quality of education and more demands for accountability.

All this contributed to Clinton's decision to push for a national test, somewhat comparable to Bush's proposal and ultimately meeting a similar fate. Clinton was an energetic advocate of accountability, often with little regard for the problems it entailed. He frequently echoed corporate advocacy of assessment, and concern about American schools competing internationally.[4] These were elements of a human capital agenda that he had long advocated. Meanwhile, past controversies regarding assessment found new life, although critics of accountability still wielded little influence.[5]

While debate ensued in Washington, action occurred at the state level, this time in Kentucky, Vermont, California, Connecticut, North Carolina, and elsewhere. New accountability systems took form, and tests were designed to assess higher order thinking and problem-solving skills. So-called alternative and performance-based items became new features of such exams. This triggered a host of responses, many quite critical.[6] Researchers also identified problems in the new tests, questioning their long-term viability, but also finding attributes to commend.[7] It was a volatile time in that respect too, making assessment a focal point of reform in new ways.

Renewed attention was devoted to racial test score differences, leading to widespread discussion of a Black–white "achievement gap." This disparity was evident during the 1970s and 1980s, of course, but it gained renewed attention in the 1990s. Test bias in this context ceased to be a major worry, despite lingering concerns, and most observers acknowledged that disparate scores reflected tangible differences in academic skills. Consequently, questions turned to closing the gaps through greater resources, improved instruction, and culturally relevant curricula, among other measures. Even if it was hardly clear how testing could enhance minority achievement,[8] civil rights organizations began to focus on improving rather than challenging test results.[9] It was a development of historic proportions.

Making NAEP results available at the state level also contributed to apprehensions about the quality of education, creating a perception of winners and losers in different parts of the country. This produced pressure to improve school performance, contributing to support for new assessment systems addressing higher skill levels. Educational reform continued to be a hot political button, often in states where NAEP results did not compare well.[10] Altogether, the 1990s witnessed sustained public engagement with educational issues, at all levels of policy discourse.

A National Assessment Proposal

The 1990s began with a national testing plan. President H. W. Bush issued one as a component of his America 2000 reform initiative stemming from the 1989 summit. In response to proposals from a number of groups, including business leaders, Bush's new secretary of education, Lamar Alexander, outlined ideas in 1991 for a national assessment and higher curricular standards. Details about how such a test would be developed and administered remained unclear, but the administration declared it key to ensuring accountability and institutional change. Bush also called for greater school choice and vouchers to permit dissatisfied parents to send students to private schools.[11]

Bush's proposals got a chilly reception in Congress, where Democrats objected to its modest budget and robust choice component. But the idea of a national test was also controversial, on both sides of the aisle. Local control of schooling was a long-standing and sacrosanct tradition in American education, and critics worried that a national test would lead to a nation-wide curriculum, even if unintentionally. As a result, Secretary Alexander recommended creating a National Council on Educational Standards and Testing (NCEST), to develop proposals for national standards and assessments and to move reform goals forward. NCEST was created by Congress in 1991, and included leaders from both parties and technical experts, including Marshall Smith and Eva Baker. It was charged with developing a plan of action within a short time frame of about six months.[12]

NCEST proposals arrived on time in January 1992, in a lengthy report titled *Raising Standards for American Education*. It called for a "quality system of national standards" to be "set at world class levels."[13] Proposed standards would be developed with guidance from a National Education Standards and Assessment Council (NESAC), to be appointed by a National Educational Goals Panel (NEGP). While the question of standards proved somewhat contentious, the idea of a nationally coordinated assessment system prompted the strongest objections, especially from civil rights organizations. Much of the debate over standards hinged on resources for schools to meet higher expectations, such as NCTM standards, and ultimately was settled by recommending greater local flexibility in earmarking funds. But testing proposals proved more difficult.[14] As Eva Baker later reported, debates within the council's assessment task force hinged on the feasibility of assessing more demanding standards, going beyond traditional formats to address problem solving, textual interpretation, and creative abilities. NESAC ultimately called for a 'national assessment system" rather than a single test, with common elements for state comparisons, covering a range of subjects. With the first tests projected for deployment in two years, it was a challenging proposition, and Baker doubted that most measurement professionals in the states would find it feasible.[15]

The controversy over national testing was a telling sign of the opposition that standardized exams still could elicit. But the stakes were even higher for such a proposal. It was one thing, after all, to require testing in the states, where legislatures and education authorities wielded power, and another in Washington, where partisan debates often were acute and national interest groups exerted greater influence. For their part, civil rights organizations complained that nationwide assessments would result in disadvantageous test-score gaps for minority students. A coalition coordinated by FairTest asked members of Congress "not to authorize or appropriate funds for the development of a national test or examination system at this time." It included the NAACP, the National Parent Teacher Association (PTA), the Mexican American Legal Defense Fund, and groups representing school superintendents and principals. Their complaints reflected issues dating from the 1970s, including long-standing stereotypes about minority children that could be reinforced by such assessments.[16]

Other critics, including many Republicans, worried that proposed reforms could undermine local control of schools and districts. They suggested that national standards and assessments could open the door to common curricular frameworks, compromising communities' ability to determine what children should learn.[17] And additional concerns surfaced as well. In testimony to Congress, Daniel Koretz argued that "external tests coupled with serious consequences generally narrow the curriculum" and could contribute to "the inflation of test scores." He added that "innovative" or alternative forms of assessment "are not yet ready to be a linchpin of national policy." In short, high-stakes tests of this sort potentially came with many worrisome consequences. These comments represented a minority viewpoint but pointed to underlying technical problems with the testing NCEST recommended. In the opinion of critics, a national test could create more problems than it resolved.[18]

In the end, the Bush proposal for a national assessment program failed to inspire the type of positive response that could ensure its success. Hampered by his opposition to additional public school resources and an insistence on school choice as a centerpiece of reform, Bush failed to become the education president he pledged to be. Critiques of testing proposals from scholars and civil rights organizations did not help. But America 2000, NEGP, and the proposed assessment program represented important precedents for federal reform initiatives, despite opposition in Congress.[19] Bush was a one-term president, but his successor was Bill Clinton, a "new" Democrat and reform governor who again would make education a priority upon arriving in Washington.

Identifying and Assessing National Standards

The announcement of mathematics standards in 1989 marked the beginning of a sustained effort to develop similar guidelines for other subjects. A convenient definition of content standards was "broad descriptions of the knowledge and skills students should acquire in a particular subject area."[20] And reformers worried that without them schools lacked the curricular coherence that could improve academic performance. As NCEST declared in 1992, "In the absence of well-defined and demanding standards, education in the United States has gravitated toward de-facto national minimum expectations, with curricula focusing on low-level reading and arithmetic skills and on small amounts of factual material in other content areas."[21] Such comments suggested that educational reforms conducted at the state level had done little to improve the nation's academic performance.

Leading assessment scholars often disagreed with such bleak views, but they wielded little influence. Robert Linn declared that "despite the negative picture, there is considerable evidence regarding improvements in achievement that critics do not choose to acknowledge."[22] But NCEST echoed *A Nation at Risk* from nearly a decade earlier: "Most current assessment methods reinforce the emphasis on these low-level skills and processing bits of information rather than on problem solving and critical thinking."[23] This was a message that many testing scholars welcomed, albeit with reservations. If higher curricular standards were to succeed, an appropriately calibrated examination system also would have to be created.[24] The big questions concerned how to go about that, and the answers were rarely easy.

Establishing clear standards of assessment had long been difficult for the measurement field, extending back to Gene Glass's critique of MCT and earlier. Eventually, however, generally acceptable methods for making distinctions between different levels of performance emerged in practical terms. As indicated earlier, many involved expert panelists tasked with imagining or specifying student scores on separate test items. Initially, the most widely used approaches were variants of Angoff's method, asking panelists to estimate the likelihood of "minimally competent students" answering questions successfully.

Estimates were summed and averaged to establish expected performance standards.[25]

While variants of this approach were used to set cut scores on MCT exams, standards for higher levels of achievement were a different question. To identify levels of proficiency, panelists often were provided "maps" showing questions of varying difficulty, and asked to estimate how well students of divergent ability would answer them. The results informed the identification of proficiency standards at different levels of achievement, creating a new class of assessments for accountability. Panelists also were asked to identify students clearly above and below a standard of proficiency, and resulting groups were compared to ascertain distinctions between them. In the end, such methods were widely used to organize tests scores into tiers of proficiency, or achievement levels, that appeared to be clear and objective, but actually represented considerable variation in judgment. There was also evidence that political considerations occasionally could influence numbers reported at different achievement levels, typically at state education agencies.[26]

Such was the response to the challenge of defining higher degrees of achievement as mandated by the standards movement. Ideally, test questions could be linked to standards to reflect levels of knowledge and skill, and development of national and state curricular standards certainly facilitated creation of disciplinary maps for panels to consider. But human judgment is highly variable, even with training and structured collaboration. And this was a problem even for tests comprised principally of multiple choice questions. When so-called authentic or performance assessments became more commonplace, new approaches were needed to contend with the problems they posed. The array of methods used to address these issues pointed to the manifold difficulties that higher standards posed for the assessment field.[27]

Reform Governors Come to Washington

In many respects, the Clinton administration picked up where Bush and Lamar Alexander left off regarding educational reform. Clinton was an NGA leader on the issue and his new secretary of education was Richard Riley, South Carolina's reform governor and also an NGA activist. Shortly after taking his cabinet seat, Riley proved adept at turning a revised version of Bush's goals into a new initiative titled Goals 2000. This measure added teacher training and parent involvement to Bush's proposal and, more importantly, focused on systemic reform. The latter point was especially crucial, as it stipulated alignment of curricular standards and tests. This added momentum to calls for new assessments to replace the MCT systems that still predominated in most states.[28] But the federal role in ensuring such changes was hardly clear. Bush's reform plan had been soundly rebuffed, including his national assessment proposal, and it took Clinton a while to address the question.[29]

Unlike the Bush administration, Clinton and Riley were initially quite successful in Congress, passing Goals 2000 and a reauthorization of the Elementary and Secondary Education Act (ESEA) in two years. It was accomplished despite predictable partisan opposition from certain quarters. The final version of Goals 2000 identified voluntary objectives for states, building upon ideas promulgated by the NGA and Bush. But while symbolically important, its practical impact was limited. Despite providing funds to help schools elevate standards, it otherwise was largely emblematic, with few direct implications for assessment. The ESEA reauthorization, on the other hand, firmly linked federal Title 1 funds to enhanced state standards in reading and mathematics. Titled the Improving America's Schools Act, it was the first federal legislation to embrace systemic reform. Its general framework was articulated by the Commission on Chapter 1, a group representing civil rights and education organizations and educational researchers (including Marshall Smith and George Madaus, among others). The commission issued a 1992 report calling for assessments to hold schools accountable for higher standards. Under new ESEA rules, states were expected to promulgate enhanced standards, and implement assessment plans by the year 2000. This was a step toward nationwide assessment of curricular reform, highlighting the impact of the standards movement in just a few years.[30] Just how such an appraisal was supposed to take place, however, was a different question.

Given the vagaries of Washington politics, Clinton's early success in reform initiatives was short lived. A Republican wave in 1994's midterm elections elevated Georgia congressman Newt Gingrich to a leadership role and changed the political landscape, making additional policy initiatives difficult. In the next two years Republicans challenged Clinton's education programs, reducing funds for Goals 2000 and attempting to eliminate the education department.[31] But schools remained a bellwether national issue. In the spring of 1996, forty-one governors from both parties met in Palisades, New York, with forty-nine corporate leaders to discuss educational problems, highlighting the need for additional reforms. It was labeled "The National Education Summit" and many "education experts" also attended. Riley was an observer and Clinton made a speech on the need for a national assessment. Corporate leaders proved strong advocates of using tests to ensure that higher standards were being achieved. This stance reflected popular opinion, as polls showed considerable public interest in education issues, and testing in particular. Republican intransigence on these issues proved costly in the 1996 election cycle, undercutting Gingrich in Congress. Clinton won reelection and returned with renewed commitment to educational change, advocating a national test to make Americans more competitive on the global stage.[32]

By then circumstances had changed since Bush's 1991 national assessment proposal. The standards movement had forged ahead, with new curricular frameworks in science, history, and other subject fields. Some of these proved controversial, such as when the history standards received a sharp rebuke in the U.S. Senate.[33] But others proved quite useful in charting how assessments might be scaled to identify different levels of proficiency. These included National Science Education Standards developed by the National Research Council in 1996, which emphasized a constructivist approach to instruction in various scientific fields. Standards for English language arts were developed by the National Council for the Teaching of English and the International Reading Association, which featured an expansive definition of literacy and the skills it entailed. While these innovative curricular proposals also proved controversial, they did provide guidance to the assessment field regarding exams that moved beyond MCT.[34]

By the mid-1990s, consequently, the stage was set for additional steps in assessment policy, and Clinton was keen to move forward. Proponents of additional testing, however, would soon find that much of the public was not enamored of a national exam. Once again conflict over assessment played out in the halls of Congress.

National Testing Returns

The Bush vision for a national testing program may have fallen by the wayside, along with much of the rest of his education reform initiative, but the idea of an exam for the entire country did not die. And in the mid-nineties a new assessment crisis gave it added allure. In 1995 the Third International Math and Science Study (TIMSS) was conducted, then the largest cross-national assessment of its kind. It examined students at multiple grade levels and also collected data on curricula, instructional methods, and other contextual factors that potentially affected achievement. Once again, American students ranked below peers in other industrialized nations, particularly many in Asia. While fourth graders did relatively well, secondary students performed disappointingly. This revived calls for school reform and more rigorous assessment, putting education back in the spotlight somewhat dramatically.[35]

In the wake of these developments the Clinton administration, along with business leaders, expressed interest in national assessments to raise achievement standards. This was the context of Clinton's remarks at the 1996 Palisades meeting, where he also endorsed exit exams. Corporate leaders found the idea of nationwide standards and tests quite amenable. Some had expressed frustration with the country's decentralized education system. Paul O'Neill, CEO of Alcoa Aluminum, for instance, asked why different standards and tests existed, when "nine times nine should produce the same number in all the states." Many of his peers wondered it too, concluding that America's patchwork approach to reform was a major impediment to progress. In their minds education was back on the agenda and assessment became a focal point of change.[36]

Following Clinton's reelection, his administration launched a concerted push for a national test that could raise achievement across the country, making students more competitive on international assessments. While this idea had been a source of debate since *A Nation at Risk*, concrete proposals ran into determined opposition. Recognizing this, Clinton argued that funds could be earmarked for a "voluntary" national test from ESEA legislation passed in his first term, and that congressional approval was not—strictly speaking— necessary. His proposal, moreover, was more straightforward than the Bush assessment plan of coordinated state tests. Instead, proponents argued that it was rather modest in scope, limited to a reading exam in fourth grade and a mathematics test for eighth graders. The former was to be based on NAEP and the latter on TIMSS, and both would be norm referenced for national and international comparisons. Beyond that, they would be voluntary for states and districts interested in knowing where their students stood. It was an idea that drew considerable support, even from former Bush education officials Chester Finn and Diane Ravitch.[37]

Almost immediately, however, the proposed tests encountered a buzzsaw of congressional opposition, mostly from Republicans. Given that the general idea was similar to Bush's, it conceivably could have drawn bipartisan support. But it turned out to be quite contentious regardless. Some of the opposition was simply political, but a greater impediment was charges that such a test could undermine state and local prerogatives. Educators were ambivalent about it too, and civil rights organizations echoed the concerns they had registered in 1992. The force of this multifaceted opposition led Riley eventually to discontinue work on the proposal. Although the National Assessment Governing Board, which oversaw NAEP, ultimately was authorized to develop a pilot test, the idea of standardized exams for all American students proved far too contentious to gain traction. Education—and assessment—thus remained a largely state and local concern, despite the problems that many continued to see in schools across the country.[38]

Notwithstanding this setback, Clinton remained an eager proponent of testing. The following year districts in affluent suburbs north of Chicago persuaded authorities to administer the TIMSS exam in their schools, and they performed quite well. Their well-heeled students scored second in the world in science, and fifth in mathematics. Labeled the "first in the world" consortium, this endeavor drew the president's favor, and he showed up at a local ceremony to announce that American youth could indeed perform at a high level. Of course it also demonstrated that privileged students could test well on such instruments, so the general point was hardly clear. But this fact did little to temper the president's enthusiasm.[39]

In his 1999 State of the Union address, Clinton touted a testing program launched by the Chicago Public Schools (CPS), which used the ITBS as a gateway exam for eighth grade students to enter high school. The ITBS was norm referenced with little direct relationship to the CPS curriculum, and thousands of students who consequently failed to meet required scores were forced to take remedial summer classes or repeat a grade. Eye exams revealed that nearly a third needed glasses, raising further questions about the causes of poor performance. Clinton ignored these aspects of the CPS testing program, however, praising it for halting "social promotion." This was a politically calculated gesture, but hardly sound assessment policy. While the ITBS requirement did have a short-term effect of improved achievement in Chicago grade schools, it did not endure and the testing program eventually was dropped.[40]

The troubling Chicago experience pointed to yet another source of opposition to gateway exams and norm-referenced tests: the nation's principal civil rights organizations. They represented a key point of resistance to Clinton's plans, situated largely within the Democratic party. Such exams, they argued, reinforced long-standing stereotypes about minority students branded as inferior to whites. Maxine Waters, chair of the Congressional Black Caucus, declared that it "cannot support any testing that may further stigmatize our children and force them into lower educational tracks and special education classes." The caucus feared that national exams would simply highlight racial differences while doing little to redress them. Civil rights leaders argued that such "gaps" in test scores were largely due to poverty and inequitable schooling, and that national assessments could aggravate those problems. While they supported state assessments to improve schools, these groups had grave misgivings about national, norm-referenced tests. This represented a serious roadblock to Clinton's policy proscriptions from one of his party's core constituencies.[41]

The Clinton administration's experience with national exam proposals was instructive. The historic legacy of federalism proved to be a formidable obstacle to such ideas, regardless of their virtues. Opposition from civil rights groups contributed to its political liabilities. In the end, there was simply too much disagreement to make a national exam possible, and Clinton had other problems to contend with.[42] For test-based accountability to be launched on a national scale, another approach would be necessary. And that task would fall to Clinton's White House successor.

Focusing on the Racial "Achievement Gap"

The misgivings of civil rights groups about a national test, even one linked to subject matter standards and curricular frameworks, pointed to long-standing racial and ethnic differences in achievement. But during the 1970s and 1980s, aggregate NAEP results revealed a significant improvement in African

American achievement in both mathematics and reading. Critics of the national test had legitimate concerns about the status and self-image of racial and ethnic minority students, but substantial progress in their performance had been made already, suggesting further improvement was possible.[43]

During the 1990s, however, the racial and ethnic "test-score gaps" in NAEP data ceased this process of narrowing, again raising concerns about the schools serving minority youth. Apprehension about this led to greater scrutiny of relevant data, and research on factors that contributed to improved test results. As indicated in chapter 2, this led to publication of *The Black–White Test Score Gap*, which helped put the issue on the national agenda. Editors Christopher Jencks and Meredith Phillips, along with contributing authors such as Claude Steele and William Julius Wilson, argued that differences on standardized tests represented substantial skill and knowledge disparities that compromised the life prospects of minority students. While acknowledging social and economic inequality, they suggested that attention also be devoted to psychological and cultural factors, such as preparing children to deal with adversity.[44] While many of the book's ideas failed to gain traction in policy arenas, it did succeed in putting the so-called "achievement gap" on academic agendas, and eventually on the national political stage.

At about the same time, civil rights organizations began to sponsor more programs to boost the performance of minority and poor students on standardized assessments. The Urban League was a frontrunner in this regard, led by Hugh B. Price, who became its CEO and president in 1994. From the beginning, he later wrote, "I was determined to make the promotion of academic achievement the centerpiece of my tenure."[45] In local chapters around the country, the league organized test preparation classes and worked with inner-city youth to change attitudes about standardized exams. Much of this work was conducted following publication of Claude Steele's work on stereotype threat, which suggested that some of the gap could be due to psychological barriers. Other civil rights and community organizations organized similar programs, albeit on a somewhat smaller scale. Rather than rejecting tests as inherently biased, this stance asserted that minority students could substantially improve their achievement by approaching exams with greater confidence and resolve. Raising test performance also entailed working harder in school, and this too was a focal point for the Urban League and other organizations.[46] The goal was changing a mindset that too often rejected scholastic success as unobtainable or alien.

By the latter 1990s, therefore, the nation's civil rights community held somewhat contradictory views regarding testing. They continued to be skeptical about the validity and value of norm-based assessment, especially given its use in racist theories about the status of racial and ethnic minority groups. These concerns animated their opposition to national exams. But success in closing achievement gaps, along with Steele's work on psychological obstacles to minority test performance, gave rise to optimism that progress could be made. Research suggested that bias was no longer a major problem on most achievement exams, and that test results signaled critical differences in knowledge and skill. For leaders such as Price this was a clarion call for focusing on improved academic performance for students from poor and minority backgrounds.[47] It was a stance that would prove quite influential in a relatively short time.

Critical Perspectives on Testing

Familiar critiques of standardized testing continued to be voiced during the 1990s. The process of aligning curricula and exams revived questions about test integrity. Cheating remained a concern, as assessment instruments often were available to educators during examination periods. More significantly, an often unequivocal connection between assessments and curricula enabled educators to tailor instruction to material likely to be featured on tests. As suggested earlier by many observers, this was potentially a major source of inflation in scores, undermining their validity. There were other ways to boost results too, such as excluding students by classifying them as disabled or not promoting them to grades being tested (as in Texas). This could occur regardless of the exam, its degree of difficulty, or the ability of students. Campbell's Law, after all, continued to be operative as long as assessment regimes held obvious consequences for educators. And as accountability pressures increased, its likelihood became ever greater.[48]

In 1989 the National Research Council issued a report on problems associated with large-scale testing and its appropriate uses. Titled *High Stakes: Testing for Tracking, Promotion, and Graduation*, it was commissioned by Congress in the wake of national exam debates to "ensure that tests are used properly and fairly." Supervised by a special Committee on Appropriate Test Use, the project was codirected by Columbia University legal scholar Jay Heubert and Robert M. Hauser, a prominent University of Wisconsin sociologist. By and large, the study echoed points made earlier by the NCTPP, led by George Madaus, and the NAACP conference report in the 1970s. It offered a capsule history of standardized assessment, including federal court cases. It also discussed public opinion and political perspectives on assessment, the validity of test results, and the role of tests in high-stakes decisions about student placement, promotion, and graduation, among other issues. More than 300 pages long, it was both comprehensive and thoughtful.[49]

Acknowledging that standardized testing remained popular, despite failure rates on gateway exams, the report concluded that testing had little overall effect on achievement. In no uncertain terms, the authors argued that test scores alone should not dictate important student outcomes, especially promotion and graduation. The study highlighted the ambiguous rationale for cut scores and the highly disparate impact of such assessments on minority students and others from less advantaged backgrounds. As in earlier critiques, it also suggested that tests had a valuable role to play in schools, principally for understanding student strengths and weaknesses. Balanced and objective in tone, *High Stakes* represented a firm indictment of many assessment practices employed in the recent past. As a technical government document, however, it also proved unlikely to exert popular influence or yield a political impact. Like other such reports it failed to garner public attention, although it did generate considerable interest in academic circles.[50]

Despite admonitions from such critics, standardized exams were required for graduation or grade promotion in most states through the 1990s and remained a source of controversy. Many educators experienced anxiety about their students' success, especially in impoverished communities, and new curricular standards did not always help. "I just feel like there's too much pressure," a Boston teacher declared in 1999, "because no matter what, it's going to come back on us [when students fail]." Others expressed similar concerns. Assessments with higher standards usually meant greater challenges, often without additional resources. These circumstances, routinely reported in the press, contributed to educators' misgivings about test-based accountability, although it remained popular nationally. Nearly three out of four adults in one poll supported sanctions for "failing schools," measures opposed by more than three-quarters of teachers. A nationally representative survey in 2001 found that teachers in high accountability states were especially prone to tailoring instruction to standardized test specifications. Higher numbers also sought transfers out of tested grade levels, and a majority found test-based accountability to exert unwelcome pressures on teaching.[51] Responses like these ensured that assessment and accountability would remain a volatile political issue.

Clinton's national testing proposal drew critical commentary from certain assessment experts, many of whom had also raised concerns about MCT. Campbell's Law was invoked in this context as well, along with familiar worries about changing standards, arbitrary cut scores, and higher rates of failure for poor and minority students. As educational researcher Andrew Porter noted, "The enormous array of individual differences among students represents a serious challenge to the equity goal of hard content for all students." A push for higher scores also was labeled a threat to ingenuity and imagination, for students and teachers alike. The fact that corporate leaders and national political figures supported it did not help matters. Critics pointed out problems that such tests produced elsewhere, especially in Asia, arguing that American traditions of local control and innovative freedom were essential to educational vitality. But others, including most policy makers, believed that testing made progress possible, and rarely acknowledged potential problems.[52]

In 2000, the American Educational Research Association (AERA) issued a "Position Statement on High Stakes Testing," reflecting concerns voiced in the past. These included "protections against high stakes decisions based on a single test," "alignment between the test and the curriculum," ensuring "validity of passing scores and achievement levels" and "validation for each separate use," as well as "full disclosure of likely negative consequences of high stakes testing," among other issues. The statement also called for providing "adequate resources and opportunities to learn," "opportunities for meaningful remediation" for those failing such tests, and attention for those with disabilities and language differences. Linked to the 1999 Standards for Educational and Psychological Testing jointly sponsored by AERA, the American Psychological Association, and the National Council on Measurement in Education, the statement was "intended as a guide and a caution to policy makers, testing professionals, and test users involved in high-stakes testing programs." As a supplement to the 1999 edition of the *Standards for Educational and Psychological Testing*, it drew a variety of reactions, ranging from firm support, to partial or qualified endorsement, to calls for even more stringent guidelines. While hardly resolving debates, in that case, it did add the imprimatur of these major academic and professional organizations to a number of concerns that had been expressed for decades.[53]

In concert with the development of standards, there was also a concerted push for alternative forms of assessment, moving away from the multiple choice format commonplace in standardized examinations historically. This was a major concern of FairTest and other groups critical of conventional exam formats.[54] So-called constructed response questions often seemed to better reflect students' knowledge and skill, not just the ability to choose correct answers to questions. Critics suggested that tests that did not constrain student responses were more "authentic" indicators of learning and competence. But there was limited evidence that including such items on exams helped students who did poorly on conventional test questions. And some worried that too much emphasis was placed on these items as a solution to more general challenges posed by standardized tests. As George Madaus observed, "there is a danger that technological solutions, such as alternative educational assessment, will blind policymakers and the public to the reality that we Americans cannot test, examine, or assess our way out of our educational problems."[55]

Essay responses also were proposed as a genuine form of constructed response, calling for students to utilize a range of skills and knowledge in addressing a topic or problem. In a potentially revealing form of assessment, students developed portfolios of work to demonstrate achievement in various knowledge and skill domains. These products usually were evaluated by educators and other experts, a difficult and time-consuming process. Each of these approaches to assessment was considered by many to be advances over traditional standardized testing and appeared to promise higher standards of knowledge and skill, and perhaps better teaching.[56] The problem, however, was that such responses on many thousands of tests posed significant assessment challenges, including substantially higher costs and lower reliability. As Eva Baker observed in 1994, "Technical findings from the research community continue to indicate concerns for task generalizability, equity, instructional sensitivity, and practicality of performance assessments." There was also the persistent problem of identifying levels of proficiency, as coordinating the judgments of subject experts organized into panels was even more difficult with such tests. And the writing skills of most American students were not highly developed in any case. These were major issues facing educational measurement in the 1990s, and most of them defied easy resolution.[57]

Assessment Reform in the States

While certainly influencing events at the national level, the standards movement made its biggest impact on the states. Education was chiefly a state responsibility, and the experience of Florida and other states in aligning curricula with assessments highlighted the issue. The "system" in the Smith and O'Day formulation of reform, furthermore, was defined at the state level. And it did not take long for many states to jump on the systemic reform bandwagon. A flurry of activity got the ball rolling, articulating standards and linking them to new assessments. Kentucky, Vermont, California, and New Jersey were leaders, but others quickly followed. The transition was not necessarily easy, as matching assessments to new curricular standards proved more difficult than many imagined. But by the decade's end, most states had initiated reforms that generally could be characterized as systemic. A new day seemed to be dawning, and it quickly brought fresh challenges.[58]

While little progress was made in creating a national assessment program, there was considerable experimentation across the states with different types of tests. It was during the 1990s that the admonition to move beyond MCT finally found a variety of responses. As the Council of Chief State School Officers noted, "possibly the greatest changes in the nature of state student assessment programs have taken place in the 1990s, as more states have incorporated open-ended and performance exercises into their tests, moving away from reliance on only multiple-choice items."[59] Kentucky was a leader in this regard, spurred by its state court decision calling for increased school funding. Vermont and California attempted assessment reform too, with variable success. Connecticut, Maryland, and New Jersey also tried new test formats, influencing other states. Texas became a focal point of controversy. In some cases changing assessments were linked to a rekindled accountability impulse, albeit with considerable variation in standards. In others, new tests were simply improvements intended to better reflect what students had learned, although educators complained that overly broad standards were less helpful than more specific ones. Altogether, however, this represented a moment of substantial innovation in assessment, some of which ultimately would not be considered successful.[60]

As suggested earlier, Kentucky was a forerunner in this phase of reform. Changes began with Governor Wilkerson and a court ruling in 1989 finding its schools both inequitable and inadequate. After some legislative wrangling, this led to passage of KERA, widely touted as a sweeping shift in education policy. It mandated organizational and curricular changes, along with improvements in technology, professional development, and teacher salaries. But perhaps its most controversial feature was a groundbreaking assessment system. With advice from David Hornbeck, a consultant and former commissioner in Maryland, reform in Kentucky moved into the limelight.[61]

Responsibility for accountability within KERA fell to the Kentucky Instructional Results Information System, or KIRIS. This was another new feature of the education system and integral to its reform. KIRIS was mandated to develop assessments that measured higher levels of achievement, moving beyond basic skills and rote knowledge. KERA specified six learning goals for schools, including the use of basic skills to address problems, and students' application of academic "core concepts and principles . . . to situations they will encounter throughout their lives." Other goals concerned self-sufficiency, family responsibility, problem solving, and continued learning and growth. Altogether, the general orientation was progressive in spirit, focusing on life skills and capacity for future learning, but traditional school subjects were addressed too. From the standpoint of assessment, consequently, it presented a formidable challenge.[62]

KIRIS was intended to be a somewhat nontraditional assessment system. With exams given in grades four, eight, and twelve, it broke from the tradition of using multiple choice formats for all questions. Instead it featured constructed responses, writing prompts and portfolios of student work to gauge a wide range of skills and knowledge. It also employed matrix sampling, with different questions for many students, making it hard to game instructionally. Student scores fell into categories: novice, apprentice, proficient, and distinguished. Group performance tasks were included occasionally too. The goal was a more "authentic" appraisal of student abilities and knowledge, asking them to express responses in their own words. And it was supposed to foster writing and problem-solving abilities by incentivizing teachers to cultivate them.[63]

These assessments became a key element in the state's accountability scheme. Schools were evaluated largely on test and portfolio performance, with a goal of averaging at "proficient." They were supposed to set improvement goals on a two-year cycle, with monetary rewards for schools and educators exceeding them. Those that did not succeed were given assistance, although sanctions and loss of local control also became possible. As mentioned earlier, accountability focused on teachers and institutions rather than students, unlike most MCT programs. In this respect KIRIS was less punitive than earlier state assessment systems, at least regarding students. But it placed substantial pressure on educators, despite rewards for positive performance that could be substantial and benefit them individually. Notwithstanding such inducements, KIRIS did not prove popular among teachers.[64]

Despite its innovations, or perhaps because of them, KIRIS only lasted until 1998, when it was replaced by the Commonwealth Accountability Testing System (CATS), marking a return to more traditional assessment practices. KIRIS had proven expensive and difficult to justify psychometrically. Writing assignments and portfolios, along with group projects, proved challenging in terms of reliability, and were unpopular among parents accustomed to conventional testing. CATS retained some constructed response and extended writing items, and portfolios remained for twelfth graders, but it added a traditional MCT that could serve as a baseline reference for both educators and parents. Like other states, Kentucky experimented with alternative or authentic assessment, and eventually returned to more conventional approaches for several reasons. While it was often praised for sweeping reforms and groundbreaking assessments, the state's NAEP and ACT scores did not change dramatically and poorly performing schools typically failed to improve despite sanctions. While reform had reduced inequality in school funding, the resulting impact on equity in achievement was negligible. Irrespective of its promising start, Kentucky's experiment in reform failed to produce sustained progress.[65]

Yet another attempt to conduct alternative or authentic assessments occurred in Vermont. It had no comprehensive accountability program until 1988 when, in the words of an evaluation team, it embarked on "the development of an innovative statewide performance assessment program."[66] The timing was noteworthy, as it preceded both the standards movement and formation of NCEST. It thus can be considered a uniquely localized approach assessment in a rather small state. Regarding accountability, test results were principally intended for local use in assessing the schools. This reflected an especially strong ethos of local autonomy, somewhat unique among states then considering assessment reform.[67]

The Vermont approach consisted of a "uniform test" and student portfolios, evaluated by teachers at statewide meetings. The uniform portion was standardized, but not only with multiple choice items. In writing it featured a single prompt, scored with rubrics also used for portfolios. The math exam had more multiple choice questions, but also included constructed response items. Portfolios highlighted both math and writing, with rubrics developed by teams of teachers. These collections of work featured items judged by students and their teachers to represent their best efforts. Only a sample of these documents, however, was assessed by the state, given the time and expense that it entailed. And an even smaller sample of portfolios was assessed by second raters. Results were reported to students' districts for program evaluation and review, but not for sanctions or rewards. Districts also conducted their own assessments of these materials for review purposes, including feedback on instructional practice.[68]

Vermont's assessment system was described as democratic, as local educators often helped students prepare portfolios and assessed them. Then again, having teachers evaluate these materials resulted in widely ranging scores for similar items, despite detailed rubrics for both mathematics and writing. Reliability measures were quite low, with score correlations for writing only in the .5 to .6 range in a comprehensive evaluation. Mathematics correlations were similar to start but improved to the .7 to .8 range. Second raters did not reportedly improve matters. This inconsistency raised significant questions about the validity and viability of the overall accountability system. By the mid-1990s it became a cautionary tale about the challenges of alternative assessment of accountability, despite its many innovative and praiseworthy qualities.[69]

A third example of state-level reform took place in California. In 1993 the state adopted a new testing program, the California Learning Assessment System (CLAS), designed to supplant the California Assessment Program. CLAS was considered an improvement at the time, designed to align more closely to changing curricular frameworks. It also featured more alternative items, including open-ended writing prompts and mathematical problem solving. Like KIRIS, CLAS was intended to respond to critics arguing that multiple choice frameworks provided limited information about student skills. CLAS was initially supported by Governor Pete Wilson, legislative leaders, and the state's education department, which oversaw its development.[70]

It did not take long, however, for problems to surface. Parent and neighborhood groups complained about topics that students were asked to write about, objecting to seemingly value-laden statements that made them uncomfortable. As in Vermont, the expense of grading these exams led the state to evaluate just a sample of them, limiting feedback to districts and schools. This did not satisfy Wilson and other political leaders, who hoped to use the test to evaluate individual students and teachers. It led to acrimonious debate between a variety of stakeholders, making the exam's political future uncertain. After just a year, Wilson vetoed reauthorization of CLAS, ending California's experiment with assessment reform as seen in Kentucky and Vermont.[71]

The California experience offered yet another cautionary tale. Even if actual complaints about CLAS were rather few, critics wielded considerable political influence in making their complaints heard. It did not help that some previously high-performing districts did not do well on the exams. In addition, a technical review panel chaired by Stanford University's Lee Cronbach concluded that CLAS exhibited reliability and validity problems, even when reporting aggregate results. This, of course, was a familiar complaint about performance-based assessment, but the exam's rapid development and rollout had forestalled the possibility of addressing such issues adequately. These circumstances only amplified public concerns.[72]

Authentic or performance-based assessment may have seemed a wonderful idea until it encountered these types of critical responses. Part of this, of course, might have been avoided if the test developers had consulted potential critics to start but, in large and culturally diverse states such as California, assessment of textual interpretation could provoke negative responses regardless of such efforts. Test developers also went beyond curricular guidelines in some domains, believing that assessment could instigate curricular change. This did not sit well with educators, or parents wondering why test scores often were lower than expected.[73]

California was a rather extreme example of assessment reform politics, but it highlighted many problems that so-called authentic assessment encountered. Eventually the state adopted a nationally normed assessment, at least for a while, but it too encountered problems.[74] Similar controversies occurred in other states, though not on the same scale. Performance tasks proved inherently difficult to assess with high rater agreement, signaling persistent reliability and validity troubles. Time and cost constraints led to few such items being included in most assessments, and reliability remained an issue. Students and teachers complained about these questions as unfamiliar or difficult, and parents worried about worse than expected results. Some families wanted scores compared to national norms, which was very difficult with these exams. While many educators welcomed these changes as supporting higher standards, others were troubled by scoring inconsistencies and student objections. Additionally, state education leaders and politicians worried about higher costs. California's decision to score just a sample of CLAS assessments gave leaders elsewhere pause in considering similar reforms.[75] Altogether, the decade's experiments with "authentic" assessment were hardly a resounding success, although its supporters remained hopeful. In the end, performance assessment would remain a vital but unresolved question for the foreseeable future.[76]

Despite these troublesome developments, the measurement field moved resolutely beyond MCT during the 1990s. It became commonplace to identify levels of proficiency in state accountability tests, even if standards varied a good deal. The availability of state NAEP data invited comparisons among state assessment programs. In some respects, national organizations spurred these changes, such as the NEGP, which published data on state education systems.[77] And more detailed data in various assessments could sometimes prove contentious, especially in cases of widely reported successes or shortcomings.[78]

Texas was perhaps the best-known example of such controversy, as Governor George W. Bush made its record of alleged success a national issue during his 2000 presidential campaign, and the *GI Forum* case drew attention to it as well. The TAAS was intended to measure "higher order thinking skills and problem solving ability," like other proficiency tests appearing then. In its first four years, scores increased dramatically for both fourth and eighth grade students, registering substantial treatment effect sizes. If legitimate, these gains surely would have been "miraculous," but NAEP scores did not correspond with such improvements. This, of course, cast considerable doubt on advancements that the state assessments appeared to document. The same was true of reported improvements in achievement gaps. A team of investigating RAND corporation researchers concluded that "the stark differences between TAAS and NAEP (and other non-TAAS tests) raise very serious questions about the generalizability of the TAAS scores."[79]

In particular, these and other researchers pointed to evidence of Campbell's Law impacting TAAS scores and holding certain students back from grades subject to testing. In other words, their findings suggested that the Texas miracle was more likely a mirage, reflecting widespread teaching to tests and excluding students judged a threat to TAAS results. An analysis of the program's economic impact showed higher attainment and earnings for many graduates, but "large negative impacts on attainment and earnings for the lowest-scoring students." Altogether, Texas appeared to offer yet another cautionary tale, highlighting the pitfalls of attaching political significance to test results without acknowledging dangers of score inflation induced by educator responses to accountability.[80]

Changing examination systems thus raised new questions and failed to resolve long-standing ones. Texas demonstrated problems that had haunted the measurement field for decades, extending back to Lindquist's well-known admonition. But new forms of assessment raised additional questions. The idea of authentic or performance-based assessment became especially prominent, even if such exams often represented a limited range of items. In 1996 the National Society for the Study of Education devoted a yearbook to the issue. Reflecting the views of many educators and researchers, its contributors hailed the prospect of more nuanced, practical, and customized assessments. They argued that these evaluations permitted consideration of sophisticated student work, supported innovative and thoughtful teaching, and accommodated curricular advancement. They also suggested it could be more equitable. But some acknowledged that these assessments posed serious reliability and validity questions, especially regarding school-based instruction.[81] Robert Linn and Eva Baker proposed that exams featuring complex and multifaceted tasks "may be general intelligence tests in disguise," and that more specifically focused test items may not represent higher-level skills and knowledge, especially if there were small numbers of them.[82] In the end they argued that long-term research was necessary to demonstrate the validity of these approaches to assessment, "but until that future arrives, we must continue to operate on faith."[83] This was hardly a ringing endorsement of such assessment reform, but it accurately expressed the state of the measurement field at the time. While large-scale testing had matured in many respects, significant questions remained, and it stood poised for new challenges that lay just around the proverbial political corner.[84]

Conclusion: The Tangled Politics of Testing

There can be little doubt that the nineties witnessed standardized accountability testing becoming a national issue. It started with George H. W. Bush's proposal for a voluntary national testing program, taken up six years later by the Clinton administration. The latter was the far more serious attempt, rousing determined opposition in Congress before receiving the barest of approvals for development. Bill Clinton was an enthusiastic practitioner of hortatory politics with regard to testing, framing it as a cure for social promotion and other problems in education. In the end, of course, a national test never materialized, as Clinton's second term became consumed with other issues. But debates at the time clearly showed that large-scale assessment was an inescapably political issue, destined to be embroiled continuously in controversy.

Goals 2000 was a significant symbolic achievement, crowning years of debate over national standards for American schools. But it was just a voluntary mandate. More important were provisions in the 1994 ESEA reauthorization linking improved state standards to Title 1 funds. Because of political wrangling, however, and inertia in the states, little was accomplished by the year 2000 deadline for these changes. By then a new authorization of ESEA was underway and political winds in Washington had shifted significantly. The reauthorization failed and there was little follow-up to the 1994 requirements. It was left to the next administration to address these questions.[85]

The national standards movement also was contentious, although considerably less so than testing proposals. Finding consensus within disciplinary fields was often difficult, but standards in mathematics and science set the pace for other fields. Reading standards remained controversial, although the relevant groups found grounds for moving forward. The history standards, on the other hand, proved very controversial and their proponents struggled to find a consensus. Other fields developed standards at their own pace, but it was mathematics, language arts (English), and science that predominated in assessments across the country. This simplified matters somewhat. Yet even the best developed curricular standards and tests needed to be carefully aligned, and many states struggled to do this successfully. And relatively little consideration was given to changing instructional practices.[86]

Politics figured in the attention devoted to "achievement gaps" as well, with civil rights groups eventually embracing achievement tests to highlight the need for additional instructional and curricular resources for minority and poor youth. Closing the gaps would become a focal point for this sector of the national polity, a development with profound implications for assessment. Calls for more "authentic" testing were also quite political, and as Kentucky, Vermont, and (especially) California demonstrated, opposition to new assessments could be formidable. But the overall effect of "performance-based assessment" was rather modest. As Edward Haertel and Robert Linn observed, "Because of their cost in development, administration time, scoring time, and other resources, relatively few performance tasks can be included in an assessment." Making changes to long-established assessment regimes was not easy, as alterations of any significant scope usually entailed new problems. Fundamental psychometric concerns were hardly the least of these.[87]

But there could be little doubt that testing had moved ahead since the heydays of MCT. New assessments were more sophisticated, offered various question formats, and sought to identify different levels of achievements. Informed by standards representing relatively firm curricular expectations, their foundation as criterion-based exams was somewhat sounder than in the seventies. Important questions remained, such as how to best set cut scores, along with the familiar problem of Campbell's Law, not to mention disparities in instructional practice. There was also the unsettling matter of "failing" schools that accountability regimes invariably identified.[88] Despite the many changes in standardized tests, it still was unclear whether they measured skills and knowledge as effectively as most people imagined. While this was an issue with little public resonance, it remained an Achilles' heel for the field as a whole.

5

A Millennium Dawns

The Origins and Impact of NCLB

The advent of a new millennium brought a dramatic shift in federal educational policy. George W. Bush narrowly won the 2000 presidential election, leading to change in many policy domains, but particularly in education and assessment. The return of Republican control to the federal executive branch meant an end to dreams of a national test to make American students more competitive on international exams. Instead, a new policy framework returned responsibility to the states, but with a clear and compelling federal mandate.

Bush had attended the 1996 NGA Palisades conference and clearly agreed with many of the ideas conveyed there. A son of former president George H. W. Bush, he became an educational reform governor in Texas and a champion of accountability. This made him broadly comparable to "new" Democrats such as Clinton and Riley, and he campaigned on this record, bringing it to Washington. Seeking a broad base of support after winning the presidency, Bush reached out to members of Congress, governors from both parties, and business leaders for support. He clearly recognized that education remained an important political issue, which continued to resonate with the public at large. And he was determined to address it.[1]

As suggested earlier, corporate leaders articulated a human capital agenda that called for a globally competitive labor force. They also wanted greater accountability for both schools and students, with more demanding tests to make it work. This had been true since *A Nation at Risk*, if not earlier. What had changed, however, was that many civil rights organizations also came to favor school accountability and rigorous assessment. They were interested in closing achievement gaps, which required tests to identify needs and to gauge improvements. It was a rare historical moment when the interests of these quite distinct political interest groups aligned with respect to educational reform and assessment.[2]

The result was new federal legislation for renewing ESEA, given the evocative title of No Child Left Behind. The bill's name, popularly shortened to NCLB, reflected an interest in maximizing prospects for all American youth, a goal that spoke to both the business human capital agenda and the civil rights concern about achievement gaps. The measure duly received bipartisan support in Congress, reflecting its supporters' links to both major parties. Signed by President Bush in early 2002, it marked a new era in American education, and the assessment field in particular.[3]

Despite its auspicious origins, NCLB soon became controversial. Federally mandated accountability provisions, which relied upon state assessment systems, often proved difficult to abide. And before long, much of the public grew frustrated with these testing requirements. While states and school districts had been slow to address assessment expectations in the 1994 ESEA authorization, NCLB left considerably less discretion. Consequently, assessment soon become the object of much attention. A 2007 survey found that 57 percent of the adult public favored NCLB's reauthorization, but just 42 percent of public school employees agreed. More than 30,000 educators and concerned citizens signed an online petition for its repeal. Initially hailed as a policy milestone, NCLB eventually became a point of heated debate.[4]

Among the most telling critiques of NCLB were reports highlighting variability in testing programs from one state to another, readily evident soon after it went into effect. As accountability's skeptics had long noted, setting cut scores could be a somewhat political process, with limited foundation in psychometrics or policy studies, even if work on these issues continued. States with weaker education systems often set lower proficiency scores than those with stronger ones, as high failure rates could produce political problems. Test performance in math and reading, consequently, did not always correspond to NAEP results. Beyond that, many long-standing critiques of test-based accountability proved highly relevant to NCLB's assessment regime. Widespread evidence of educators tailoring instruction to tests soon emerged, along with narrowing of curricula and even outright cheating. Achievement gaps remained persistently evident, and American performance on international assessments did not improve substantially.[5]

Since NCLB was associated with the Bush administration, many critics were surprised when President Barack Obama preserved many of its requirements following his election in 2008. In fact, his administration—with leadership from Secretary of Education Arne Duncan—added new wrinkles to its accountability program. Announcing a "Race to the Top" initiative in 2012, Duncan and Obama asked states to compete for federal funds to boost achievement. Much of the impetus for this came from civil rights organizations, which continued to see assessment as indispensable to closing achievement gaps. By and large, the Obama administration appeared quite willing to embrace test-driven accountability to promote educational reform, along with supporting charter schools to spur innovation. These market-oriented (or neoliberal) policy choices dated from the Clinton years, if not earlier, and Obama doubled down on them.[6]

Ultimately there were signs of change, most clearly evident in the Every Student Succeeds Act of 2015. This legislation provided greater leeway to the states regarding accountability and assessment and dropped strict school improvement requirements. But proficiency tests were still required and achievement gaps remained a focal point. Test-based accountability continued to be a cornerstone of American educational policy, albeit in a somewhat milder form. It thus remains an open question about how or when this particular approach to educational improvement eventually may be supplanted.[7]

A New Bush Administration and Educational Reform

George W. Bush was no stranger to education reform when running for president. In fact, his record in Texas became a key factor in the campaign. The state's accountability system was established under his predecessor, Democrat Ann Richards, and featured the TAAS. As governor, Bush embraced this annual testing regime, including the exit exams that were challenged in the *Gi Forum* case. Raising education spending with bipartisan support, his administration pushed higher teacher salaries, sensible class sizes, and reading skills. And it proved rather successful. As noted earlier, it was labeled the "Texas miracle," led by rising elementary school test scores. Although TAAS and other aspects of accountability received considerable criticism, Texas fourth graders performed highly on NAEP in 1996, and African Americans compared favorably to peers nationally. At the same time, achievement gaps remained evident, dropout rates increased, and NAEP did not show similar gains in other grade levels. Nonetheless, national commentary often highlighted positive aspects of this record. Given public interest in education, it was broadly seen as an advantage in his presidential bid.[8]

Regarding policy choices, Bush advocated investment in early education, persuading the legislature to fund additional instruction for third grade reading. He justified this by citing research showing that skill gains were considerably harder in later grades. Bush also rejected criticism of testing as racially biased, asserting "I strongly say it is racist not to test, because by not testing we don't know and by not knowing we are just moving children through the system." Unlike many other Republican leaders, he did not dwell on divisive points like school vouchers or private education. Altogether he proved a firm advocate of test-based accountability, focusing on public schools. "Texas has a very good accountability system that began to develop thanks to others who preceded me," he declared, adding that "I have worked hard to strengthen it, to continue to raise the bar."[9] This background suited him well for educational policy deliberations in Washington.

Despite advocating state-level accountability, Bush also touted local control of curriculum, instruction, and everyday policy decisions. In keeping with Republican Party principles, he felt that local educators could best determine how to meet standards set by the state. He was generally amenable to ideas voiced at the Palisades conference regarding standards and assessments, if not a national test. It was unclear whether he was supportive of his father's proposed national assessment plan, with states coordinating tests for uniformity. Having witnessed the opposition that national testing proposals provoked, and the fate of Goals 2000, he was understandably reluctant to proffer similar proposals. His approach to educational reform left considerable discretion to state authorities but included a robust federal role too.[10]

Bush also was quick to reach out to congressional Democrats after the election, despite the rather contentious way his victory had been decided (in the Supreme Court). He borrowed substantially from Democratic proposals for authorizing ESEA, which had failed during the waning days of Clinton's administration. He remained an advocate of school accountability and continued to see testing as critical to making it work. While he made reference to vouchers as alternatives to "failing" public schools, practically a requirement for national Republican candidates, it was not a centerpiece of his policy proposals. George W., as he was called, was willing to consider greater federal aid to schools in conjunction with accountability measures. This opened the door to moderate Democrats and bipartisan agreement on national educational policy.[11]

Gaining congressional renewal of ESEA was hardly smooth, however, given traditionally conservative and liberal positions regarding education. But Bush set the tone for a new policy orientation in an opening position that mirrored a centrist Democratic proposal offered by Senator Joseph Lieberman. It addressed Republican advocacy of block grants to replace targeted program funding streams, such as Title 1, which Democrats resolutely supported. Lieberman, and Bush, proposed fewer targeted funding streams and stronger accountability provisions to insure effectiveness. This allowed Republicans to claim progress on reducing support for some federal school programs, while permitting Democrats to focus on important ones, especially Title 1. And both groups favored greater accountability, chiefly at the state level. The proposal to create NCLB did not end debates over federal involvement in education, but it did create a pathway that allowed both sides to claim a degree of success. And Bush was adamant about pushing things forward.[12]

The Making of NCLB

Like the acrimonious record of past policy debates, conflicts over the legislation that ultimately gave rise to NCLB turned out to be quite rancorous. With the question of programming generally settled, however, disputes focused on testing and funding, topics also featuring sharp partisan divisions. Legislators from both parties, but mainly Democrats, worried that accountability provisions that included annual testing and performance improvement would burden schools and saddle states with added costs. Critics argued that many schools soon could be labeled as failing. A provision that NAEP be employed to ascertain the quality of state assessments led Republicans to object that it paved the way to a national test, which they still vehemently opposed. Disagreements about funding levels and disabled students led Senator Jim Jeffords of Vermont to switch parties, giving Senate control to the Democrats. This put Senator Ted Kennedy of Massachusetts in a position of leadership, which also turned out to be crucial.[13]

Traditional education interest groups, such as the National Education Association and organizations representing administrators and state legislators, were strongly opposed to accountability and testing provisions in the legislation. Kennedy had long-standing ties to these groups and helped to hold them at bay while finding congressional points of agreement. Organizations that supported previous proposals for higher standards and accountability, such as the NGA and the Business Roundtable, were generally encouraging. And, as suggested earlier, civil rights groups also were supportive, a significant shift in their stance toward testing, even if their misgivings about funding remained. This appeared especially important to Kennedy and other liberal legislators. Much of the discussion about Title 1 focused on achievement gaps, and the prospect of addressing them through subgroup testing and school-level accountability appealed to liberals. The result was a momentous alignment of interests.[14]

It is also possible that the September 11 attacks on the World Trade Center, the Pentagon, and other targets helped push NCLB through Congress during a time of national unity and bipartisan determination to move ahead. This was acknowledged by various observers, including some predicting that state-level standards and tests would result in a hodgepodge of programs with little comprehensive power to improve schools.[15] Describing the NCLB legislation as "a disaster in the making," Thomas Toch of the Brookings Institution minced few words: "the Bush plan lets the states choose their own tests and set achievement standards, a strategy that practically guarantees mismatched tests, low standards, and scant hope for real accountability. Most of the flaws in the Bush testing plan stem from the simple fact that Congress and the White House want the benefits of national tests without actually having to mandate them."[16]

And that was just the beginning. Additions to its standards and accountability principles eventually made NCLB considerably more complicated than previous ESEA iterations. Choice components were added, allowing students from low-performing schools to attend other state-approved institutions. Students at low-performing schools also could get supplementary services. These provisions allowed private entities to receive public funds, including religious schools and service providers, a Republican priority. The bill also required public school teachers to be "highly qualified" in terms of certification and relevant subject-matter knowledge, although states were permitted wide latitude in setting such standards. A new elementary reading program, "Reading First," was authorized, requiring that curricula and instruction be "research based." This initiative, along with another for preschool children, was consistent with Bush's long-standing interest in early reading instruction. Altogether, the bill was intended to substantially bolster academic achievement, as measured by standardized assessments.[17]

Altogether, the passage of NCLB was a momentous legislative accomplishment, and at its heart was a federally mandated accountability system requiring states to test public school students regularly, including racial and ethnic subgroups, and hold institutions responsible for their success or failure. But it also was familiar in many respects, mirroring many state accountability policies from the prior decade. The goal was a steady record of improvement, with all students reaching proficiency by 2014, defined by each state, using NAEP to appraise standards. The opposition included Republicans resisting any expanded federal education role and liberal Democrats concerned about inadequate funding and excessive testing. Many educators also opposed the law, and the National Education Association unsuccessfully challenged it in court. While a solid majority of legislators from both parties supported NCLB, issues raised by its critics would remain points of controversy. In the end it represented a grand compromise that ultimately proved problematic to many Americans, even if they failed to agree on alternatives.[18]

Implementing NCLB

The Bush administration moved quickly to roll out NCLB requirements for states, which were considerably greater than the expectations in 1994's ESEA reauthorization. State authorities were supposed to have standards and related exams in place by 2005, and schools failing to register suitable improvements thereafter were subject to sanctions. Districts were expected to report progress toward meeting "highly qualified" status for teachers, although relevant state requirements varied considerably. These stipulations were especially onerous for districts serving mainly poor and minority students, even if many Black educators initially supported the law. And schools in more affluent settings sometimes also struggled to meet these expectations. This was especially true in mathematics and science, where well trained and experienced teachers often were in short supply. Given the typically adverse response of institutional systems to demands for change, the Bush administration's Department of Education soon began receiving challenges from states. The number of appeals was small but significant, with Connecticut filing a legal complaint describing the law as an unfunded mandate. Some school districts individually resisted participating too. These developments were a portent of problems to come.[19]

At the heart of NCLB was a provision for "Adequate Yearly Progress," or AYP, calculated to "ensure that not later than 12 years after the 2001–2002 school year, all students . . . will meet or exceed the state's standards." Progress was supposed to be assessed in reading and mathematics, and later science, and was meant to include graduation rates too. And it was expected to include at least 95 percent of students in designated subgroups, including racial and ethnic minorities, special education students, and low income students. While it was left to the states to develop appropriate subject standards and "statistically valid and reliable" assessments for a half dozen grade levels, AYP expectations were set by the U.S. Department of Education. The requirement of ongoing advancement toward universal proficiency was widely decried as unrealistic, especially without additional resources. Since there was little guidance regarding standards, or requirements to meet a given level of achievement, AYP obligations became an inducement to lower expectations so that gains could be more easily realized. State graduation rates also were subject to differing definitions, often showing high rates of success along with data revealing problems. But even locally controlled standards could pose a challenge to many institutions, which were encountered from the outset. And increased testing requirements led to rising demand for psychometric expertise as assessment providers scrambled to meet new expectations. Given all this, accountability provisions at the center of NCLB soon became a source of considerable controversy.[20]

The task of creating and aligning standards and assessments put enormous pressure on state accountability programs, resulting in a retreat from the so-called authentic assessments, and a return to multiple choice and constructed response ("open ended") items. In 2009 the federal Government Accountability Office found that nearly four out of five states used multiple choice items for all or most test items.[21] Two years later a RAND study examined more than 5,000 test items and found that multiple choice questions remained the principal format. Altogether, these items comprised 78 percent of mathematics questions, 86 percent in reading, and 85 percent in writing. Using a four-level analytical framework for assessing the skill and knowledge level of questions, and panels of experts to rate items, RAND authors concluded that high levels of skill and knowledge were rarely assessed. For instance, nearly 60 percent of mathematics items were rated at level 1 (recall of a fact, concept, or procedure) and nearly all others at level 2 (using information, concepts, and procedures in two or more steps). Level 3 (use reasoning, a plan, or sequence of steps, with complexity and more than one answer) appeared rarely and level 4 (investigation, processing multiple conditions, and performing nonroutine manipulation) not at all. In reading, the study rated 80 percent of the multiple choice questions at or below the first two levels, along with the majority of constructed response items. It was only in writing that 10 percent of the questions were rated at level 4, and some states did not assess it at all.[22] Consequently, it appeared that state NCLB assessments largely failed to focus on higher order forms of knowledge and ability that enhanced standards were supposed to represent, and to boost American performance on international assessments. It was also possible that such tests made it easier for teachers to tailor instruction accordingly, focusing on skills and knowledge likely to appear on the exams.

To be fair, the RAND study did document considerable variation in items utilized in state tests. All or most items were multiple choice for mathematics in California, Texas, Ohio, New York, New Jersey, Missouri, Maryland, and Massachusetts. But in Kentucky, Connecticut, and Colorado most math questions were open ended, suggesting the possibility of more demanding skill expectations. In others, such as four New England states and Washington, there was a balance of items. Differences were evident in reading too, although only Colorado, Connecticut, and Missouri featured mostly open-ended questions. On writing exams only Ohio, Texas, and the New England states mainly used multiple choice items. As a rule, states with more open-ended (or constructed response) items were likely to have higher skill requirements, with mathematics often featuring relatively few such questions. Larger states such as California, Texas, Ohio, and New York utilized tests dominated by multiple choice questions, suggesting that cost and convenience continued to be important factors influencing standardized assessments. Experimentation in performance-based assessment slowed significantly, although interest concerning it remained in a few states.[23] The RAND study failed to consider the related question of cut scores, and how they were defined across states.[24]

NCLB did not dictate a singular national testing program, but it did create a national system of testing requirements with more draconian consequences than imagined during debates of the 1990s. Its style of accountability was similar to reforms in Kentucky, Texas, and other states that held institutions responsible for educational outcomes. While many states continued to require graduation or promotion exams, NCLB shifted the focus to AYP and achieving near universal proficiency. With unremitting pressure to show improvement on tests, it became even more difficult for educators to resist tailoring instruction to the task of improving scores. Nationally, about a quarter of all schools failed to meet AYP expectations in the first round of NCLB follow-up assessments, and the numbers were considerably higher in certain states. A report found that schools needing improvement were "most likely to be high poverty, high minority, large urban schools to which Title I has historically directed substantial resources." In these respects NCLB underscored long-standing points of inequality in education.[25]

Demanding that all schools improve the percentage of students judged proficient eventually put pressure on most institutions, and the numbers failing to meet AYP increased. Federal requirements for improved test scores proved a substantial shock to the nation's education system, leading the Bush administration to offer some flexibility in accountability requirements. As a South Carolina school superintendent declared, expecting "everyone to be proficient or advanced is . . . pushing it too far," and the state estimated that over two-thirds of its schools would struggle with AYP targets. For many institutions NCLB proved challenging from the very start, and the pressure increased with time.[26]

Dilemmas of High-Stakes Accountability

Since repeated failure to "make" AYP could result in dire consequences for educators and institutions, the NCLB accountability regime created a powerful incentive to game the system. This took a variety of forms, including restricting topics covered in state assessments, limiting curricula and instruction to tested topics, focusing on students judged likely to improve, and excluding students believed unlikely to pass the tests. None of these practices honored the intention of NCLB, reflecting a strategy for raising test scores without improving the quality of education or expanding the range of skills and knowledge that students could exhibit.[27]

The basic idea of standards-based reform, of course, was that curriculum and instruction should be carefully aligned with assessments, so that tests could determine whether students were achieving greater proficiency in prescribed material. Substantial effort, consequently, was devoted to determining whether such alignment was evident, and how it could be enhanced. Despite this, there was considerable inconsistency in how teachers adapted instruction to standards and assessments, and how schools and districts ensured such alignment. A study of five urban districts, for instance, found generally weak topical alignment of mathematics and science instruction with assessments, although alignment with standards was stronger. Of course, it was possible that linking instruction closely to assessment could threaten the validity of tests as measures of wider standards. A study of several states noted a related problem:

"standards that are too broad or numerous to guide decisions about what to teach might lead to negative consequences, such as excessive reliance on the test rather than the standards to decide what to teach."[28] And as pressure to meet AYP goals became greater, "alignment" could become narrowly focused indeed.[29]

At perhaps its most basic level, of course, the linkage between instruction and assessment could lead to "teaching to the test." Since past assessments were typically available to schools, and often guidelines for current tests too, many teachers could focus instruction on topics emphasized on exams, boosting scores at the expense of other aspects of the curriculum. As sociologists Jennifer Jennings and Jonathan Bearak found, "students performed better on items testing frequently assessed standards in both ELA (English Language Arts) and math—standards that composed a larger fraction of the state test in prior years—suggesting that state test results may have overstated students' mastery of the state standards."[30] School leaders sometimes made this an unambiguous expectation, incentivizing teachers to prioritize test scores over other instructional goals. Outright cheating also occurred in some instances, including changing answer sheets to produce higher scores. Teaching to tests reportedly was commonplace in many schools serving poor and minority student bodies, where scores were lower to start. The result often was "drill and kill" instruction, focused on specific math and reading skills to the exclusion of other topics and subjects. But perhaps more broadly, testing had greater impact on topical content than pedagogical practice. A pronounced narrowing of the elementary curriculum became a well-documented feature of the NCLB era, hardly an outcome that its proponents had advocated.[31]

As suggested earlier, teaching to the test was facilitated by assessments that focused on a narrow range of skills without much change annually. But having fewer and less specific standards also could encourage it by providing little practical support for instruction, making exams a much better source of guidance. States with limited school resources, or with conservative legislatures, may have been more likely to cut corners this way. A goal may have been higher scores at a lower cost, but it also made teaching to tests considerably easier if educators could anticipate what to expect on exams.[32] This practice also contributed to narrowing the curriculum within tested subjects, along with less attention to untested ones. A national study in 2006 suggested that overall curricular narrowing became quite widespread: "Seventy one percent of school districts reported that they have reduced instructional time in at least one other subject to make more time for reading and mathematics. In some districts, struggling students receive double periods of reading or math or both . . . sometimes missing certain subjects altogether."[33]

Beyond this, researchers found that some educators focused attention on students judged improvable enough to achieve proficiency, giving less consideration to those less likely to succeed. The most advanced students, those deemed likely to do well, also got less attention in many classrooms. Such "triage" was especially evident in less affluent institutions, where accountability posed the biggest challenges. And the instruction that such children often received was focused resolutely on tested material. Inflation of mandated test scores resulted from this, typically evident in misalignment with NAEP results at the state level.[34]

There also was evidence of students being excluded. States set criteria for assessment eligibility, and students who moved frequently could be barred by enrollment deadlines for testing. Additionally, institutions with small numbers of minority students were not required to report subgroup scores, even if substantial achievement gaps existed. Incomplete tests could be discarded too. Altogether, these conditions contributed to underreporting for many thousands of student assessments each year, much of which helped to raise score averages. In 2004 more than 70,000 tests were discounted in Illinois, mostly because of "late enrollment." Another 56,000 minority students were not recognized due to subgroup size requirements. The result was substantial underrepresentation of poor and minority students, who were most affected by these rules. As a general proposition, these were significant gaps in NCLB's accountability regime, which also likely contributed to score inflation.[35]

Perhaps the most glaring problem with NCLB, however, was evidence of outright cheating, typically orchestrated by teachers and administrators. Following the law's passage, an "epidemic" of fraudulent efforts to improve test results became evident. Highly publicized cases in Atlanta, Philadelphia, Dallas, and other cities demonstrated that conspiracies to change answer sheets, provide questions in advance, and other forms of cheating were organized on a large scale. In Atlanta some 200 educators reportedly changed student answers on tests, and eleven were sentenced to prison terms for coordinating it. In Philadelphia eight educators pleaded guilty to similar charges. A review of tests in Washington, District of Columbia, found "high rates of erasures from wrong to right answers at 103 of 168 schools." And these were just the best known cases: observers estimated that evidence of cheating elsewhere likely went undetected. But the most highly publicized instances involved urban schools under pressure to improve scores in the face of draconian accountability measures. As W. James Popham remarked in 2006, educators did this to avoid "a sanction-laden improvement track capable of 'improving' [them] into nonexistence." Given the potential consequences, these cases represented rather extreme instances of Campbell's Law at play. While such actions cannot be excused, they were shaped by an accountability regime that posed immense challenges while providing relatively meager resources to address long-standing problems. Unfortunately, this reaction only further compromised public confidence in educators and the credibility of urban institutions, suggesting to many that even stricter accountability was warranted.[36]

Beyond questions of cheating and exclusion of students, however, there was little evidence that NCLB was succeeding. Symptomatic of variability in state standards, there was mixed confirmation of correspondence between results on state assessments and NAEP. Researchers found that improvements in state scores were not matched by comparable gains on NAEP in many cases, including alleged reform leaders such as Texas, North Carolina, and Connecticut. On the other hand, states with higher or clearer standards appeared to perform better on NAEP, at least in the early stages of NCLB. Massachusetts and New York were sometimes cited in this regard. There also were important differences in fidelity for various student subgroups, with African Americans often doing worse than others. This may have been due to local decisions to focus more on overall institutional performance than subgroup minority student, and long-standing discriminatory attitudes regarding African Americans. Altogether, it was not clear whether this mismatch between state assessments and NAEP was the result of weaker state standards, narrowing of test material, or teaching to the test, although all of these circumstances likely were contributing factors. Frustrated with these inconsistencies, in 2008 Secretary of Education Margaret Spellings created a dashboard featuring data on state performance with a number of indicators, like Secretary Bell's "Wall Chart" more than two decades earlier.[37] In the end, however, it was hardly clear that the accountability requirements that NCLB had mandated exerted many positive effects on student achievement.

These sorts of responses suggested that Campbell's Law was widely at play following implementation of NCLB. The principle that inspired the legislation held that test scores were primarily—if not exclusively—a reflection of educators' efforts and abilities, and that student background characteristics were secondary or perhaps even trivial considerations. Long-standing observations about the difficulty of teaching impoverished students were dismissed as excuse making that potentially harmed children. But such objections ignored decades of sociological research that documented the substantial impact of family background factors on academic achievement. This line of inquiry had found that such effects were clearly evident on standardized tests of all sorts.[38]

To the extent this was true in schools serving poor communities, AYP represented a particularly severe burden, one that invited significant narrowing of instruction—if not outright cheating. And even then, success in meeting AYP expectations often proved very challenging. By the end of the decade, reports suggested that slightly over half of the nation's schools were in danger of failing. While early achievement gains often were made possible by focusing on tested topics and teaching students how to take standardized assessments, further progress required deeper knowledge and increased skill levels. There also was evidence that pressure to produce higher scores contributed to discipline problems, especially for children from poverty backgrounds. Such circumstances created enormous difficulties for many local authorities, some of whom lobbied Washington for relief from accountability. These issues did not help NCLB's popularity, which dipped dramatically within just a few years.[39]

Given the many challenges that NCLB posed, it was little wonder that it quickly fell out of favor among educators, along with many educational researchers and other observers. Teachers also objected to pressures to restrict their instruction to subjects and topics covered on tests. In a survey of California educators, more than 90 percent reported that teaching to tests, to one degree or another, was the biggest change NCLB had wrought. School systems across the country invested in additional exams to target instruction to students in need of extra assistance, typically those just shy of proficiency. States were also allowed to develop alternative tests for students with disabilities in 2008, complicating things further. The result was more time dedicated to testing, but also greater accountability triage, wherein the poorest performing and least prepared students at times were the last to get assistance.[40] This, of course, was a practical response to the logic of accountability with limited resources. But it also represented a gross perversion of the law's title, No Child Left Behind.

In the push to meet AYP requirements, pragmatic decision making could mean that some children were literally left behind, simply because they represented the biggest challenges. In other cases students were excluded from testing, especially those labeled as disabled in one way or another. This created an incentive to classify low-performing students as needing special education, and researchers soon found that disabilities subgroups became a leading reason for institutions failing to make AYP. These were responses that NCLB's authors apparently had not considered, even though they were predictable in light of Campbell's Law and other critiques of accountability regimes. Research also found that schools encountering AYP problems often were staffed by less experienced teachers, suggesting that more seasoned educators either avoided or left them when possible. This too was contrary to the hopes of NCLB's sponsors, who had argued that accountability provisions, including teacher qualifications, would create better learning opportunities for vulnerable students.[41]

Other critics pointed to the sheer amount of time devoted to testing, noting that it meant shorter periods of instruction and heightened anxiety levels for students and teachers alike. Even though these tests typically had little practical relevance to students' futures, many felt pressure to perform. For those wanting to please their teachers, this easily could contribute to apprehension.[42] And failure to perform adequately could be disheartening. This was an additional incentive to tailor instruction to ensure student success, and evidence indicated that certain state assessment scores eventually became seriously inflated when compared to benchmarks such as NAEP. In 2007, economist Brian Jacob found "considerable evidence of test score inflation in several different states, including those with quite different state testing systems."[43] Other scholars concurred, with some suggesting that such assessments could be exhibiting the classic signs of exaggerated results evident in earlier accountability systems.[44]

This, of course, raised questions about the validity of many state and local tests, and the federally imposed accountability regime that elevated their importance. Noting assessment variability across states, and fluctuating degrees of improvement on both NAEP and state tests, assessment experts wondered about the feasibility of NCLB goals from the beginning. "One could agree that schools should improve and that holding schools accountable will contribute to improvement," wrote Robert Linn, Eva Baker, and Damian Betebenner in 2001, "but still conclude that the goal of having 100% of students reaching the proficient level or higher, as proficient is currently defined by NAEP or by many state tests, is so high that it is completely out of reach." And this raised concerns about the ultimate effect of the reform strategy. "Setting a goal that is unobtainable," they continued, "no matter how hard teachers try, can do more to demoralize than to motivate greater effort."[45] These turned out to be unusually prescient observations. In the end, it was a work of legislation that promised far more than it could deliver, and it set many of the nation's public school educators on a course for sustained frustration and disappointment.[46]

The Impact of NCLB

To the extent that NCLB had a positive effect on achievement, results were most clearly evident in the elementary grades. Overall it appeared that accountability requirements were associated with improved math performance in the fourth and eighth grades by 2010, but had somewhat less bearing on reading. Positive results were also evident in international assessments, as American fourth graders also improved in mathematics on the Trends in International Math and Science Study exam (TIMSS). Those reaching "advanced" and "high" benchmarks increased from 46 percent in 1995 to 60 percent in 2011, with bigger increases coming after 2003. There was somewhat less improvement among eighth grade students, however, begging the question of whether the NCLB had as much impact with older students or more advanced topics. Sanctions for schools also appeared to have positive initial effects, at least in certain settings.[47] These were results calculated at the state and national levels, however, with considerable variation from one district or school to another. As indicated earlier, schools serving largely impoverished students often struggled to meet AYP and were more likely to focus instruction specifically on tested subjects.[48]

As suggested by the low correlation of NAEP and NCLB assessments, the overall effect of NCLB was considerably less dramatic than hoped for, despite these positive effects in elementary grades. Average fourth and eighth grade mathematics scores on NAEP grew until 2009, but leveled off thereafter (both also had improved during the 1990s). Scores for high school students did not change meaningfully, nullifying gains in the earlier grades. In years to follow, NAEP scores for all students changed little, indicating that NCLB accountability, such as it was after Duncan–Obama revisions, had negligible longer-term effects.[49] Insofar as NAEP served as an unbiased indicator of change, it offered little sustained support for the theory that AYP-driven test-based accountability was an effective reform strategy.

Similarly, changes in racial or ethnic achievement gaps evident in NAEP also occurred in the early years of NCLB and stabilized thereafter. A thirty-one-point Black–white difference in fourth grade math in 2000 had been reduced to twenty-six points by 2005, but remained about there for fifteen years thereafter. Hispanic fourth grade students made greater progress, reducing the gap with white (non-Hispanic) students to eighteen points by 2019. The results for eighth graders were largely similar, with African Americans reducing the gap with whites from forty points to thirty-two by 2007, but little thereafter. Hispanic eighth graders closed their gap with white eighth graders from thirty-one points to twenty-six during that time, and dropping a bit afterwards. Similar patterns were evident in reading, except there was little change in eighth grade Black–white differences. There was even less progress for twelfth graders, again pointing to the fleeting effects of elementary school improvement. A 2019 Black–white difference of thirty-one points in secondary mathematics was virtually the same as in 2005, and the Hispanic–White gap had closed just a couple of points to twenty-one. In reading, it appeared that gaps among twelfth graders had actually widened somewhat by 2019, as overall achievement dropped nationally.[50]

In general, consequently, NCLB appeared to deliver little overall progress on achievement gaps, except perhaps for Hispanic students, although it is hardly clear that accountability contributed to their gains. The theory that tracking the performance of racial and ethnic minority groups would help in closing achievement gaps also does not appear to have borne fruit. As critics of NCLB suggested, simply testing students was unlikely to improve their educational experiences without other changes, especially regarding instructional strategies and resources for lower-performing institutions. In the nation's biggest cities, with large numbers of minority and impoverished students, only about 20 percent of eighth graders met or exceeded state proficiency standards in 2013, despite slight improvements on tests and narrowing achievement gaps.[51] Clearly, testing and accountability alone were insufficient to overcome the challenges faced by students in these settings.

The results of international assessments told a similar story. In 2011 American fourth graders ranked eleventh in mathematics on an updated version of TIMSS, and eighth graders ranked ninth (among fewer countries). Both cohorts showed little movement in rankings since 2003, despite improved scores overall.

In 2015, after the point when they were supposed to be at or near the top of TIMSS standings, American fourth grade students came in at fourteenth, and eighth graders were eleventh. Once again, scores improved slightly, but the standing of American students did not. If one of the goals of the NCLB accountability regime was to raise the position of the nation's students on international assessments, it could hardly be judged a success.[52]

The 2011 TIMSS report revealed other problems that illustrated the limitations of NCLB. Looking at teachers of American eighth grade students taking the math test, a far larger proportion of students than the international average had teachers without a college major in mathematics, 56 percent compared to 24 percent. Nearly a third had teachers who lacked even a focus on mathematics education. Research had demonstrated that advanced teacher mathematics training was associated with higher achievement. It was little wonder, therefore, that just 37 percent of American eighth graders scored above the advanced or high benchmarks, placing them at twelfth among the forty-two countries. This was above the median, but a far cry from the aspirations voiced by corporate and political leaders more than two decades earlier. It also revealed that NCLB requirements that teachers be highly qualified had relatively little impact. The performance of students in this grade cohort had changed little since 1999.[53]

Part of the problem also was compositional: not only were American eighth graders taught by teachers with relatively weak mathematics preparation, but they attended schools with larger numbers of impoverished students. TIMSS reported that over half (55 percent) of these students attended schools where more than a quarter came from "economically disadvantaged homes," with math scores lower than the international mean. The international average was 36 percent. Just 22 percent of American students attended institutions where more than a quarter came from "economically affluent homes," with average scores well above the mean, compared to nearly a third of their international peers. The fact that so many American students came from schools where teacher credentials were weak, and parental ability to support high achievement likely was constrained, undoubtedly affected performance on this and other international assessments.[54] As suggested earlier, this was a conundrum NCLB was ill suited to remedy.

Students from the United States performed even more poorly in the PISA exams in 2012, administered to fifteen-year-olds, scoring thirty-sixth in mathematics out of sixty-five nations participating that year. The PISA assessment was positively correlated with TIMSS, but focused on applications of skills, many related to life circumstances. Test takers identified as "top performers" were judged able to "develop and work with models for complex situations, and work strategically using broad, well-developed thinking and reasoning skills." Fewer than 9 percent of American youth scored at that level, while more than a quarter were in the "low achievers" category. This put the United States below the international mean, along with other countries boasting relatively few high achievers. U.S. scores in reading and science were slightly better, but also fell below the international average. There had been little change since 2009 on PISA and, in 2015, the U.S. math performance actually fell.[55] This too was hardly a ringing endorsement of NCLB.

Critics of PISA argued that it was not a test tied to a particular curriculum, whereas TIMSS attempted to examine curricular standards and practices. But they overlapped considerably, and both offered a measure of external validity for national testing systems.[56] Not only did NCLB's brand of accountability fail to produce substantial improvements on NAEP, it also did little to improve U.S. performance on international assessments, one of the publicly stated motivations for undertaking accountability reform. The reasons for this were likely manifold, and certainly included incentives to "game" or circumvent NCLB accountability, but these test results also suggested that the principles behind the law were seriously flawed. If the ultimate goal of test-based accountability was to make American education a world leader, it clearly failed.[57]

NCLB and the Obama Administration

With the election of Barack Obama as president in 2008, with Democratic control of Congress, led many observers to expect substantial changes to NCLB. Teachers were a core party constituency and, along with many other critics of the law, they were generally opposed to its form of test-based accountability. But educators did not exercise much influence in the presidential race, as schools did not become a critical issue. Obama advocated higher standards and accountability but argued that Bush had failed to adequately fund NCLB. His principal Democratic opponent, Hillary Clinton, vowed to end NCLB, but it made little difference in primaries where she lost decisively. A centrist stance set the tone for Obama's approach to educational policy, despite the widespread opposition that NCLB had generated.[58]

True to his word, and perhaps his bipartisanship, Obama became a largely steadfast supporter of the test-based accountability. His choice for secretary of education, former Chicago Schools CEO Arne Duncan, initially proposed no major changes to NCLB, focusing instead on early childhood programs, charter schools, and teacher training. He clearly supported reporting scores for student subgroups, long favored by civil rights groups. As Duncan declared in 2011, "NCLB's goals were the right ones—holding all students to the same challenging standards; closing achievement gaps; and providing transparency and accountability for the proficiency and graduation rates of all students." While he also acknowledged that some states had lowered their standards, many teachers tailored instruction to tests, and subjects like history and the arts suffered neglect, he suggested that greater flexibility could make accountability workable. For their part, Republican senators generally supported his confirmation, including former education secretary Lamar Alexander, additional evidence of the overall policy continuity that Duncan and Obama represented.[59]

Race to the Top, Duncan and Obama's major education initiative, was funded with stimulus money intended to boost the economy during the Great Recession of 2009 and did not require congressional approval. Originating as such, it was a clear reflection of their thinking about educational reform. Structured as a competition among states for federal funds, it aimed to advance changes in education systems, with points assigned to goals deemed important by the Obama–Duncan team. First among these was improved educator effectiveness, with training and support programs to sustain progress. Then came state reform agendas, standards and assessments, support for charter schools, improved funding and data systems, and a focus on STEM subjects. Proposals from the states were expected to be comprehensive and supported by local districts and political leaders, although many teachers were not happy with this approach to reform. The Duncan-led U.S. Department of Education administered the competition and chose winners. The theory was that successful states would provide influential models of reform, leading eventually to nationwide change. In this regard the reform strategy aimed to create a marketplace of policy ideas, very much in line with Obama's neoliberal proclivities.[60]

A key aspect of the original NCLB legislation was a waiver provision for states or other localities facing difficulty in meeting the law's requirements. While a limited number were approved under the Bush administration, many more were permitted after Obama and Duncan took control. As time passed, more states encountered difficulties with NCLB's AYP targets and remediation procedures. The Obama administration announced a new waiver program in 2011, and states were expected to apply for such dispensation, subject to approval by the Department of Education. And it did not take long for many to do so.[61]

Not surprisingly, given the Obama–Duncan priorities, waivers came with expectations that states link teacher evaluation to student achievement and adopt so-called college and career readiness curricular standards, which soon became known as the Common Core. States could also apply for a waiver to delay the 2014 deadline for achieving 100 percent proficiency, which most measurement scholars believed unattainable. The number of waivers increased dramatically, far surpassing those awarded under Bush. The basic purpose of the program was greater flexibility and encouraging innovation in response to NCLB. It helped some states develop better accountability systems, but in others it did not appear to improve matters much at all. As one study concluded, many states "missed opportunities to design more effective school accountability systems that might minimize negative unintended consequences of these policies."

Yet waivers did permit Obama's administration to pursue its own reform priorities without attempting an ESEA reauthorization. In these respects, the waiver program was linked to Race to the Top in spirit, if not formally.[62]

With Race to the Top, Obama and Duncan preserved the NCLB accountability system but added new wrinkles with waivers and focusing on teachers. The expectation that states should evaluate teachers potentially moved accountability to the classroom level. It also opened the door to using test results for judging teacher effectiveness, creating even greater pressure to hew instruction closer to topics on state assessments. More egregious forms of cheating also may have been encouraged. While draft guidelines for the competition had emphasized charter schools and teacher evaluation, greater flexibility on those points was granted following public commentary. But Race to the Top and new waivers were strictly executive-branch gambits, while the original legislative requirements of NCLB remained in place.[63]

The issue of teacher performance also gave rise to renewed interest in value-added modeling, as methodologists contemplated using student test scores to evaluate instruction. The trick was measuring students' achievement growth, net of prior knowledge and skills. It was complicated by findings that children learned at different rates, regardless of instruction, and that most teachers taught relatively small classes, especially at the elementary level, making trustworthy estimates difficult to realize. There was also the problem of accounting for nonschool influences, especially for affluent students. While methodologists debated approaches to such difficulties, evaluation of teacher performance remained a controversial and generally unsettled question. Experts believed that this information could be useful, but many argued that it should be combined with additional evidence in making personnel decisions.[64]

As indicated earlier, calls for improved curricular guidelines contributed to yet another reform initiative of the Obama–Duncan era, the so-called Common Core Standards. The basic idea stemmed from NGA meetings going back to Charlottesville, advocating a single set of robust standards for all American schools. In 2009 the governors' association convened leaders from relevant disciplinary and educator groups, and the assessment field, to begin drafting such guidelines, focusing on making them clear, consistent, and sufficiently vigorous. The effort was also supported by the Council of Chief States School Officers, the principal organization of state-level education leaders. National standards were also a long-standing goal of business and corporate leaders, who wondered why educational expectations varied so widely across the country. These different constituencies represented a powerful coalition seeking a dramatic departure from traditional American deference to local priorities regarding education, and curricular matters in particular.[65]

Both Obama and Duncan were outspoken supporters of the Common Core Standards, and states were encouraged in Race to the Top to consider adopting them as evidence of reform. The Department of Education also provided funding for developing standards and assessments for English-language learners, a major group in some states. Alternative assessments were developed for special education students. All this made the Common Core appealing, and by 2010 more than forty states joined the initiative. Race to the Top also proved very attractive, with forty-four states eventually applying for funds. Each of these developments was evidence that the Obama–Duncan program of reform, built upon NCLB without fundamentally changing it, was moving toward its goals. It appeared that the country was verging on a rather momentous educational change.[66]

As Common Core Standards were being approved by states, testing consortia were formed to allow sharing assessments aligned with them. The largest was the Smarter Balanced Assessment Consortium, which developed adaptive online exams for a number of states. It also developed a digital library of assessment tools and test items for member states. At its peak, some thirty states belonged to Smarter Balanced, although the number dropped to twenty by the decade's end (and thirteen in 2023). A similar but smaller consortium, the Partnership for Assessment of Readiness for College and Careers, or PARCC, received Race to the Top funding to develop assessments for college and career readiness standards. Both consortia played leading roles in creating computerized test formats, permitting more individualized assessments and greater item variety. At the outset some twenty-four states joined PARCC, along with the District of Columbia, although a number also belonged to Smarter Balanced. By 2014, however, just fourteen states and the District of Columbia remained in PARCC, reflecting a concern about its costs, technical glitches, and political apprehension about Common Core Standards. Some parents also complained that its tests were too difficult. Many Americans continued to worry about federal influence in education and the possibility of a national curriculum and related assessments, long-standing points of political controversy.[67]

Given NCLB's unpopularity, it did not take long for Race to the Top and the Common Core to encounter a storm of controversy. Critics saw Race to the Top as evidence of the Obama administration's fealty to test-based accountability and AYP provisions in NCLB, made worse by compelling states to compete for dollars by enhancing such policies. Local politicians labeled the Common Core a case of federal overreach, bringing ideas and standards from Washington to supersede local prerogatives. Urban school leaders complained that their students already took too many tests. Evaluating teachers and administrators proved especially divisive, as educator unions denounced quantitative assessments as technically flawed and potentially discriminatory. Measurement scholars also debated the merits of "growth models" purporting to document teacher abilities and effort with limited numbers of students. Despite the Obama administration's liberal waiver policy, Race to the Top seemed to represent the very worst aspects of NCLB, made even more egregious by focusing sanctions on allegedly poor-performing educators.[68]

Following early enthusiasm about common curricular standards to bring schools closer to offering rigorous coursework, local control advocates mounted a campaign to denounce shared standards as federal intrusion. These criticisms received wide publicity as states moved to adopt the Common Core. In 2015 a Gallup poll showed a slight majority of Americans opposed the new standards, but there was considerable variation in responses. Opposition appeared to be greatest where reforms were tied to teacher evaluation, and among more affluent parents. In New York nearly one in five students in 2015 opted out of taking new achievement tests, perhaps fearing their difficulty, although teacher unions may have encouraged it also. Test opposition surfaced elsewhere too, as New Jersey and Colorado became hot spots for opt-out advocates. In California, on the other hand, there was considerably less opposition and few students choosing to opt out, despite its history of protest against exams. Minority parents expressed less opposition to the Common Core than white parents, perhaps because they thought that it would help improve the schools. And nearly 40 percent of poll respondents declared that standards were too low in schools, even if they opposed the Common Core. By and large, much popular resistance appeared to partly represent traditional distrust of federal involvement, similar to sentiments that derailed national testing proposals in the 1990s, but more liberally minded parents often opposed tests in local schools too.[69]

In December 2015 the Obama administration's reauthorization of ESEA was finally signed into law. Named the Every Student Succeeds Act, it reflected a modification of NCLB that addressed some critics' concerns, while preserving its key accountability provisions. Consistent with the policy of more liberally extending waivers, the law offered greater flexibility in implementing accountability measures. AYP was no longer required, although testing remained a mandated necessity. This may have been partly a response to changing public opinion, as polls in 2015 also showed considerable ambivalence about accountability testing, and substantial opposition to using scores to evaluate teachers. Under ESSA, states had flexibility to propose provisions that suited their needs. Greater emphasis was placed on graduation rates, especially for poor and minority students, and less importance was assigned to evaluating teachers than in Race to the Top. The achievement gap also remained a concern, as civil rights groups, represented by the Leadership Conference on Civil and Human Rights, continued to insist on assessment of group differences within schools and districts. And deeper learning was a stated expectation too.[70]

Business groups were steadfast in supporting test-based accountability, as were many Republicans, but opponents of federal involvement on both sides of the aisle favored greater flexibility in meeting mandated requirements. A coalition of organizations proposed a "Testing Bill of Rights," with "fewer and fairer assessments" and making them "more useful and less burdensome for parents." Members included the Urban League, the National PTA, and the liberal Center for American Progress, among other organizations. While recognizing the problem of "over testing," they declared assessment critical to school improvement, and ESSA a step forward. Acknowledging testing's opponents, the Center for American Progress's Catherine Brown cautioned that "when students and parents opt-out, they miss an opportunity to identify persistent learning gaps that can stand in the way of college or career readiness." Speaking in favor of responsible testing, Delaware governor Jack Markell insisted that "we all should be able to agree that high quality assessments play an essential role in making our continued progress and improvement possible." Supporters of this initiative thus asserted that test-based accountability should be preserved. In the end ESSA was a grand compromise, but it affirmed the Obama–Duncan approach to accountability, offering a less draconian assessment regime than NCLB, but preserving a commitment to testing requirements nevertheless.[71]

Obama's administration backed away from the strict assessment obligations that George W. Bush advocated, but argued that some form of test-based accountability was necessary to improve American schools. While Duncan and Obama may have recognized many drawbacks of standardized assessment, and perhaps its growing unpopularity, they still accepted the logic of external accountability. They continued to focus on academic outcomes as a driver of school improvement, and test-based achievement in particular. And they accepted the neoliberal logic of using exam scores to exert pressure on schools in a marketplace of educational options. It was an approach to reform dating in one form or another to the latter 1960s, even if testing had evolved a good deal. Whether it was viable strategy to make American students competitive internationally was another question. Like their predecessors, Obama and Duncan did not appear to seriously consider alternative approaches, although ESSA opened the door to greater use of performance assessments. In any case, test-based accountability continued to be largely unchallenged, even if it had lost some of its bite.[72]

An Apex or Turning Point?

In many respects, NCLB was a logical apogee in the search for an accountability system that would transform American education and make it the world leader that many Americans wanted. Leaving no child behind represented powerful political rhetoric, and universal proficiency was unassailable as an aspiration. But as a policy that employed assessment to spur institutions—and educators—to action, it was hobbled by the fact that test scores were largely dictated by out-of-school factors. Pronouncements that taking such realities into account was simply "making excuses" may have played well in public opinion, but ignored decades of research. To the extent that measurement professionals went along with this, not to mention other educational researchers, their responses bordered on professional malpractice. The fact that prominent scholars continually pointed this out made it all the more egregious. In the end, educators across the country, but especially in the most economically deprived communities, were expected to metaphorically defy gravity in raising test scores without suitable resources. It is little wonder that they usually did not succeed, and that some resorted to cheating as a consequence.[73]

It was very difficult to judge NCLB as a success, and yet assessment-based accountability continued to predominate as a policy regime throughout Obama's time in office. It was understandable that George W. Bush would advocate strict test-based accountability. Like many Republicans, he saw it as a way of compelling recalcitrant or ineffectual educators to behave more responsibly, and he believed that Texas offered a successful model to emulate. Liberals like Ted Kennedy went along, seeing subgroup reporting features of NCLB as addressing the achievement gap and hoping that funding inequities eventually could be addressed. But the stance of the Obama administration is harder to explain. Like their predecessors, Obama and Duncan were unwilling to allow educators responsibility for running their organizations without oversight from federal and state authorities. This may have been partly a political decision, as much of the public appeared to agree in 2009, and educators were unlikely to abandon the Democratic Party. But as Race to the Top demonstrated, Obama and Duncan were firm believers in the supposed virtues of test-based accountability, and a market-oriented approach to finding solutions to educational problems. Civil rights organization also continued to support this approach to reform (along with African Americans in polls), as did the business community, so maintaining the basic framework that Bush and Kennedy launched was politically straightforward, and very much in line with Obama's centrist policy orientation. But whether the NCLB and ESSA accountability regimes were a success was another question altogether, and the available evidence suggests they were not.[74]

In certain respects NCLB's test-based accountability was the worst possible amalgam of policy options. While dictating national testing requirements, it did not establish a national test. It also imposed a schedule of constant improvement yet provided few additional resources to accomplish it. The result was a variety of state accountability systems, with inconsistent standards of rigor in proficiency expectations, although there eventually was evidence of assessments converging somewhat with NAEP.[75] With educators bearing the burden of dire consequences for failure, it became a classic formula for Campbell's Law to exert undue influence. Abundant evidence of such problems came to light, much of which had been anticipated for decades and was well known within the testing industry. Yet the voices of dissent were relatively few. Policy makers could hold out hope that problems identified by

Robert Linn, Daniel Koretz, or Lorrie Shepard, among others, could be corrected, much as questions of bias generally had been settled.[76] But that did not occur and test-based accountability continued to predominate through the Obama years. Things did change somewhat in 2017 with the advent of a new Republican administration preoccupied with school choice but testing still remained critically important for many schools and the central features of ESSA remained operative. Finding an alternative to test-based accountability thus remains a compelling question for educational reform in the twenty-first century.

Conclusion

A Troubled History and
Prospects for Change

An era of test-based accountability has shaped American education for a half century and does not appear likely to end anytime soon. The technology of standardized assessment has remained at its center, despite the many problems it posed, most of which also have endured for quite some time. History reveals that it is impossible to understand this dilemma without considering the politics that have animated it. As noted in the introduction, Lorraine McDonnell suggested that hortatory politics have played an outsized role in accountability, although aspirational politics also could be an accurate label. It seemed that for most Americans accountability was about improving public schools, and they generally accepted the proposition that testing was an efficient and effective means of doing it. These concerns often were rooted in human capital theories that held academic skills to be critical for the future. Anxiety about American economic competitiveness and future prosperity helped to fuel public interest in such questions. Despite the debates it prompted, these circumstances have made accountability an enduring theme in contemporary educational reform.[1]

Simplicity routinely defeats complexity in public debates, and critics of high-stakes testing repeatedly failed to convince policy makers, much less the public, that problems they documented were vitally important. Education became a point of widespread public concern during this era, and political leaders responded accordingly. Their answer was greater accountability, and testing became a relatively inexpensive mechanism to ensure it. This may have been influenced by a new focus on outcomes in the evaluation of public policy and institutions, and exams became widely used for such purposes in education. And the rising cost of schooling, especially at the state level, undoubtedly was a major factor as well. For much of the public, the suggestion that standardized tests were objective measures of learning and ability, and hence reliable tools of accountability, seemed like common sense. This was borne out in opinion polls, despite something of a decline in support for testing after 2010. The teaching profession had lost favor in the wake of unionization, strikes, and allegations of social promotion, along with perceptions of rising school discipline problems. Test-based accountability was supposed to get educators and students focused on the right priorities and restore an emphasis on academic skills worthy of greater financial support. U.S. students' performance on international assessments only intensified fears that schools were failing in their educational responsibilities, especially given the nation's alleged standing as a world leader.[2]

There can be little doubt that such concerns animated policy makers' interest in accountability, at both state and national levels. For some this was simply political opportunism, as attacking schools or advocating accountability became a way to curry favor with many voters. But for most it was a question of how best to prepare children for the future, which almost certainly would require greater reliance on specialized forms of knowledge and reasoning. This was a driver of hortatory politics, extending to the federal level in the 1990s and beyond. And at every step, standardized testing of one sort or another was called into service, both to ensure that schools were doing their job and to provide the public with information to evaluate institutions. Though less emphasized by policy makers, accountability for school choice also was important in a country with more than 13,000 districts and a relatively mobile population.[3] At the same time that assessments were supposed to improve education, consequently, they also provided a convenient map for anyone searching for apparently better schools. This was yet another source of political support for test-based accountability, particularly when high-scoring institutions could help to boost property values. In this respect testing was well suited to the market-based (or neoliberal) logic of public policy reform that became so influential at the time.[4]

Challenges for the Assessment Industry

If the public failed to heed critiques of standardized assessments, the testing business did take some seriously. It faced a potential crisis during the latter 1960s and 1970s, as charges of systematic bias were leveled against assessments of all sorts. Distressed about IQ controversies, some organizations called for boycotting standardized tests, or curtailing their use. As noted in chapter 2, the NAACP and other civil rights groups made test bias a focal point of discussions regarding equality of opportunity. In response, testing organizations worked on methods of detecting potential unfairness in tests, and reducing or eliminating it. And in the end they appeared to have generally succeeded.[5] Racial disparities in test results continued to be evident, however, and the discovery of stereotype threat in high-stakes assessment helped to explain why. In the 1990s a new consensus emerged, holding that the "racial achievement gap" was largely a product of social and educational inequality and could be addressed by schools and other institutions, even if racial segregation, educational inequality, and extreme poverty remained formidable problems.[6]

Beginning in the 1970s, so-called criterion-based exams became a focal point of assessment for accountability, posing new questions of test validity. Racial disparities in test outcomes continued to be a point of contention, particularly as African American students faltered on exit exams at relatively high rates. Content validity became a central point in federal trials challenging this, although the courts ultimately declined to hold states culpable for racial test score gaps.[7] The related questions of how to establish proficiency standards on such tests and aligning them to curricula eventually gave rise to the standards movement and the next generation of statewide assessment regimes in the 1990s. But as tests were asked to go beyond minimum competency measures regarding accountability, content validity remained an important matter of contention.[8]

A third challenge to the assessment field was complaints that the most commonplace test item, the multiple choice question, was a poor indicator of meaningful knowledge and skills. This gave rise to the "authentic assessment" movement, and the appearance of FairTest in the mid-1980s. Many critics became dedicated to reform of traditional forms of assessment, if not their outright elimination. The result was experimentation with new assessment approaches, and alternative forms of evidence to document student learning. But these tests turned out to be considerably more expensive than conventional ones, and acceptable levels of reliability in scoring them proved difficult to reach and sustain.[9] The public was not always receptive to alternative assessment either, partly because conventional testing had become so familiar. Many parents wanted to know how well their children compared to others, and had little patience with assessment results that proved difficult to interpret.[10]

There was also the controversy over apparent score inflation that gained widespread attention in the 1980s, when most states reported results supposedly above national averages. It turned out that nationwide benchmarks were calculated at multiyear intervals, giving state scores time to catch up or even exceed them. But the more basic question was just how scores could improve so quickly, while often dropping when new forms of a test were introduced. As a number of scholars pointed out, this was evidence of even more insidious test score inflation: "teaching to the test" when educators became familiar with exams. This, of course, could threaten the integrity of both testing and the educational process.[11]

With NCLB and its intensified accountability provisions, this problem appears to have grown even worse. In light of these developments, Campbell's Law concerning the effect of accountability provisions on testing has come clearly into view. It became especially problematic when schools were in danger of censure or loss of local control because of relatively low test scores. And cases of outright cheating also have been documented, with educators providing students with correct responses or changing answer sheets to boost school-level scores. These should have been sobering developments for policy makers who had advocated accountability, but most viewed them as aberrations to be addressed by assessment professionals. In these respects it is reasonable to conclude that test-based accountability compromised the process of education for millions of students.[12]

In short, the assessment field has faced some daunting issues over the past half century, most linked directly to accountability as a policy regime. Persistent questions about the validity and value of tests have gradually undermined public confidence in educational reform since the passage of NCLB. As indicated in chapter 5, there is little evidence of overall improvement in the performance of American students in the past two decades. While NAEP scores did increase initially in elementary grades, with similar improvements on TIMSS these gains did not persist through high school. Critics suggest that initial improvement may have resulted from educators focusing on tested subjects, but absent more fundamental instructional changes and additional resources to struggling schools, longer-term enhancement of test performance was highly unlikely. In any case, the widely proclaimed goal of making all American students proficient in tested subjects by 2014 was unrealistic to start with. As Robert Linn, William Coffman, and others observed, there was far too much variability in the conditions under which children learned in the United States to make such dramatic improvements feasible without other changes. But the logic of hortatory politics made such goals an aspirational obligation, despite the limitations of testing for documenting it and underlying problems with accountability as a policy regime for making it happen.[13]

The Politics of Aspiration

Accountability was premised on hortatory politics from the beginning, aiming to end social promotion, making teachers and students work harder, and clarifying goals for everyone. And it flowed from both sides of the political spectrum. Calls to increase accountability rarely entailed greater resources for schools, although accountability measures often followed state legislation that increased educational funding. In those instances it was intended to ensure that dollars were well spent, presuming that educators were unlikely to do so on their own. But federal policy pronouncements such as Goals 2000 and policy regimes such as NCLB and ESSA were a different matter. Their purposes were almost purely hortatory, as if declaring goals and utilizing standardized testing alone was enough to produce remarkable changes. In fact, declaring that simply demanding higher expectations for schools was sufficient to produce change became a familiar refrain, especially following *A Nation at Risk*. And even if the advocates of these goals claimed that they too would be held accountable for the policies they endorsed, such reckoning rarely occurred.[14]

Historical contingencies contributed to these events, along with long-standing patterns of inequality in American education. As suggested in chapter 1, it probably was no accident that accountability was embraced so enthusiastically in the South. The region struggled with economic development, and education was widely seen as crucial to attracting investment. Some leaders, and much of the public, apparently felt that the quality of education had declined with desegregation, which had swept the region by the seventies. They saw MCT-based accountability as a mechanism to ensure that high school students possessed skills and knowledge generally expected of graduates. Ralph Turlington was an enthusiastic proponent of such requirements, despite the problems they posed for students, especially African American youth. The *Debra P v. Turlington* case effectively closed the controversy about whether this was discriminatory in legal terms. It contributed to the adoption of this form of accountability throughout the country, setting the stage for subsequent developments.[15]

Given these circumstances, it was hardly a surprise that southern governors took charge in promoting higher standards and accountability as a national agenda in the 1980s, Indeed, it is possible to assert that test-based accountability sprang largely from southern roots. Bill Clinton, Lamar Alexander, and Richard Riley were among the leaders at national meetings leading to the first Bush administration's America 2000 reform proposals, including a proposed national testing program. While Bush did not succeed in getting his reform package through Congress, President Clinton had considerably more success after 1992. Goals 2000 and a reauthorization of ESEA were approved quite expeditiously, but a proposed national test ran aground with bipartisan opposition during his second term. In the meantime, the standards movement swept into focus, starting with Kentucky, Maryland, Connecticut, and other early adopters. Even though federal legislation required states to report on reforms, the results were uneven and incomplete. By the end of his presidency Clinton was immersed in scandal and controversy, but the stage was set for another southern governor to launch a decidedly different reform plan, one that expanded upon state accountability programs while taking expectations to an altogether new level.[16]

In many respects the passage of NCLB marked a pinnacle in the saga of test-based accountability. Inspired by George W. Bush's Texas experience and informed by other accountability programs, its political fate hinged on a historic alliance of corporate leaders and civil rights organizations, along with key Washington figures committed to its success. Its underlying logic held that higher expectations were the principal driver of educational improvement, and that continually advancing achievement requirements could pull proficiency ever higher. It clearly reflected the concerns of corporate leaders, who worried about the academic skills and knowledge of American students. Test-based accountability was well aligned with their human capital agenda. For civil rights organizations, NCLB also required schools to address the achievement gaps that had long remained evident in annual testing. This addressed growing concerns about how well schools were serving minority students. This alignment of interests was crucial to NCLB's legislative success, but also to test-based accountability as a policy framework. Failure to conform to the new expectations it represented often posed dire consequences for educators. And public airing of test results was intended to produce competitive pressure for reform, reflecting the market orientation of neoliberal policy thinking at the time. It ultimately created tremendous stress for many institutions, resulting in widespread narrowing of curricula and instruction, along with the appearance of cheating in various forms.[17]

These requirements, along with others regarding teacher qualifications and research-based approaches to instruction, marked a new level of federal involvement in education. States that resisted this mandate risked losing federal Title 1 funds, as much as 20 percent or more of local school budgets. While NCLB initially proved popular among educators and the public, its appeal faded quickly as demands for improvement mounted. This led the Obama administration to employ widespread use of waivers to allow greater flexibility in meeting federal requirements, and to support new initiatives such as value-added teacher evaluations and the Common Core. Eventually ESSA's passage did away with mandated improvements in test scores but kept annual assessment requirements and reporting of achievement gaps. States were afforded greater flexibility regarding school staffing and proficiency expectations. But the principle of improvement through accountability remained intact, with public airing of test results to inform school-choice market dynamics. Despite its many problems, the age of test-based accountability rolled onward in a somewhat kindlier, more accommodating guise.[18]

A Devolving Mandate?

In the years since ESSA, political change in Washington has shifted federal education policy somewhat. Shortly after taking office, President Donald Trump declared a focus on "restoring local control" to education and reducing federal influence.[19] As a result, certain Obama initiatives were dropped, such as rules regarding transgender students and programs addressing racially disproportionate disciplinary practices. But Trump's education secretary, Betsy DeVos, was limited by law regarding changes she could make, and her department did enforce ESSA rules. Beyond that, DeVos displayed little interest in test-based accountability, instead promoting school choice and support for private, religious institutions. Her proposals for tax credits to supplement private school tuition failed in Congress, and additional moves to support such institutions were limited to just a few states.[20] She also advocated reduced federal funding for charter schools, a focal point of the Obama administration.[21] But DeVos and Trump ultimately did little to undercut the ESSA commitment to test-based accountability, though perhaps more from ineptness than explicit policy choices.

Despite the Trump administration's failure to change policy mandates, it is hardly apparent today that the historic coalition that stood by NCLB remains committed to this way of conducting educational reform. The failure to overcome achievement gaps has produced concern among civil rights activists, and the corporate leaders who championed tests for accountability have largely exited the scene. In recent years a debate has emerged as more African Americans have denounced standardized testing, noting its historic links to eugenics and racist propositions about intelligence and achievement.[22] In the wake of controversies during the Trump presidency, corporate leaders reportedly have chosen to focus on social justice and equity issues rather than standards-based reform and testing.[23] A limited but highly vocal antitesting movement has appeared in different parts of the country, principally among suburban families.[24] While each of these developments has been rather limited in scope, together they may reflect a modest shift away from test-based accountability as a reform strategy. If so, it could signal a change of historic proportions.

The big question is what would take its place, especially if so many problems that accountability was supposed to address have continued to remain salient. The achievement levels of many American students continue to be disappointing, both on NAEP and on international assessments. And racial achievement gaps are still far too substantial to sustain the country's long-standing principles of equal opportunity into the future. Some criticisms directed at testing resurrect outdated critiques of test bias, assertions about norm-referenced assessments, or suggestions that not all children learn the same way.[25] These points have been addressed at length within the assessment field and reflect a misunderstanding of how contemporary achievement tests differ from past intelligence tests, and norm-referenced exams such as the SAT or ACT. While it is true that today's subject-based standardized assessments still rely upon tiered scales of item difficulty and response rates, among other factors that produce a range of scores, it also remains hypothetically possible for all students to perform equally well. And even if proficiency levels—cut scores—are set rather arbitrarily, students can generally improve performance with adequate preparation. In the end, achievement tests report differences in knowledge and skill, not only a ranking of students, and therein lies their lasting value.[26] Just what to do with such information, of course, remains a vital question.

Some critiques of test-based accountability resonate nostalgically, recalling a time when schools supposedly were democratic and each child learned at his or her own pace. But where such institutions existed, they tended to be located in relatively stable or middle-class communities and sorted students in ways that reinforced racial and social class divisions. Those who argue that standardized tests fail to reward students whose interests lie in the arts, sports, or other performance realms, also are treading on unsteady grounds. There is a long tradition suggesting that racial minorities and women, and perhaps other students, may be less able academically, but possess talents in music, other forms of artistic expression, or athletic ability. There is little solid research, however, to support the proposition that children learn in fundamentally different ways, even if they bring different experiences, goals, and dispositions into classrooms. Propositions regarding differing group abilities and interests also have a pernicious history. One only need to consult Thomas Jefferson's *Notes on Virginia*, first published in 1780, to find a famous slaveowner making such assertions about African American abilities in music and their physical prowess. Remarkably, it is possible to find somewhat similar claims today, suggesting that poor and minority students should not be held to conventional academic standards.[27] This is hardly an argument in favor of equality in achievement and the pathways to improved social status that often go with it.

More telling critiques of test-based accountability point to distortions that it can produce in classrooms, changing curricula and teaching to correspond more closely to material on tests. This undermines the integrity of assessments by artificially inflating scores and undercuts instruction by narrowing it significantly. It is the problem that Lindquist identified more than seventy years ago, and Campbell reiterated twenty-five years later. Daniel Koretz and other observers of the field have documented it more recently. In certain respects it now appears to be systemic, potentially making a mockery of the principles underlying test-based accountability: that standardized tests provide an objective, accurate, and fair accounting of what students have learned. As long as new test forms are introduced only every three, four, or more years, providing teachers time to adjust instruction to tested material, this will remain a significant problem. The result is a telltale sawtooth pattern of scores rising as exam forms remain in place and falling when new ones are introduced. It is quite pervasive and is perhaps the most revealing sign of just how widespread the problem has become. Outright cheating still comes to light occasionally too, despite the lower accountability pressures of ESSA. In these respects the educational process continues to be compromised for many students.[28]

And perhaps the most revealing critique concerns the tendency of achievement tests to align with socioeconomic differences in student family backgrounds, regardless of where they attend school. This is one of the great ironies of the accountability movement: tests intended to convey how well schools performed turned out to largely reflect long-standing differences in these socioeconomic factors. Such variation, of course, was mainly due to circumstances beyond the control of educators or even students themselves. Institutions with lower scores typically were located in settings wracked by poverty and a lack of institutional resources. Those that benefited from high test scores generally were located in communities with quite different profiles: higher levels of affluence, college-educated adults, and additional sociocultural assets. Given the power of these factors in dictating test results, it remains an open question just how well different institutions have contributed to improved achievement. It is possible, after all, that even the highest scoring institutions have added relatively little to their students' success, especially if large numbers were raised by highly educated, affluent parents who "cultivated" them for greater attainment.[29]

Finally, there are the other benefits of schooling, so-called noncognitive skills that economists have highlighted in recent years. As mentioned in the introduction, this line of research suggests that skills measured by standardized assessments may be less important than other attributes that are at least partially imparted in schools, such as punctuality, working with others, following directions, and behaving responsibly in institutional settings. Additional research has suggested that these behaviors also contribute to longer-term accomplishment. But the national obsession with test scores, dating at least to *A Nation at Risk*, has obscured the roles that such traits play in most forms of employment and other spheres of life. These qualities are especially significant as elements of civil discourse and democratic deliberation and decision making, fundamental features of the nation's political life. A test-driven preoccupation with reading and mathematics helped reduce instruction in social studies, history, and government in many schools. In this regard, the human capital agenda of improving a narrow range of knowledge domains and related skills has pushed aside other dimensions of public education, some of which have been central to its role historically.[30]

Notwithstanding the efforts of DeVos and the Trump administration, ESSA and its accountability program are still the law, and state testing programs remain firmly in place, even if the extreme pressures represented by NCLB have been relaxed somewhat. The school choice movement has largely been limited to larger cities, as suburbanites have soundly rejected vouchers, charter schools, and other facets of choice in favor of their well-regarded public schools. As noted earlier, accountability has featured an implicit choice dimension, as test scores were partly intended to inform the public about schooling options. But families exercising choice by moving to affluent districts had little interest in alternatives; in fact, many worried that choice options could jeopardize the status of their local public schools—along with property values linked to higher test scores. Given the fact that most American school children attend suburban schools today, this was a vast bulwark against the policies that DeVoss represented, and a source of opposition to changing accountability systems that make their local institutions look good. If most suburbanites had their say, some form of test-based accountability likely would remain in place, notwithstanding occasional complaints about excessive testing.

To summarize, in that case, while test-based accountability has grown somewhat less draconian in the challenges it poses, its basic principles remain firmly in place. NCLB ultimately may have become less popular, but enough political support appears to remain for some form of test-based accountability to persist into the foreseeable future. If that indeed turns out to be true, the next logical step for reformers may be finding ways to make it work better.[31]

Prospects for Change?

Even with all of the problems described herein, it is probably difficult for most Americans to conceive of public education without some sort of accountability. Standardized testing has been ubiquitous in schools historically, making it likewise difficult to imagine them without it. Consequently, future reformers must necessarily deal with many of the issues discussed above. Failing to do so will permit problems associated with accountability to persist. But there does seem to be some promising ideas to consider.

As suggested earlier, some of the most troubling problems with accountability testing stem from its cross-sectional orientation. Testing typically occurs once a year, usually in the spring. This makes it difficult to assess academic growth over time, partly because students often develop unevenly during summer months. Many students also change schools, especially in urban settings, further complicating such assessments.[32] But if schools were required to test twice a year, near the beginning and end, it would be possible to document advancement rather than achievement at a single point in time. This likely would be far more revealing of a school's educational success or shortcomings than a single test that is highly correlated with parental background. It basically requires each student to be compared to an earlier assessment of her or himself, potentially making background factors less important in determining scores. While schools in affluent areas may well have more resources to effect positive change, including parental support, urban institutions also can impact students profoundly, even if growth does not often raise scores to suburban levels (of course, additional resources can help boost their overall achievement). The key metric is value added, calculated at the building level, reflecting the collective effort of educators at a particular school.[33]

The term "value added," of course, became controversial during the Obama years when it often was applied to individual teachers. It was widely deemed problematic because of the small numbers of students typically available for such calculations, and the range of additional factors that inevitably impacted teacher performance and student outcomes. Some states have extended this to reporting "growth" for individual students, despite statistical problems associated with these sorts of estimates.[34] But the basic idea of measuring student growth is far more practical at the school level, where the numbers of students typically are greater, and the results can be attributed to the collective effort of educators working together as a group. While students changing schools would remain a problem, there are data management and statistical strategies for addressing such issues. And perhaps the greatest benefit to measuring growth would be to encourage educators to collaborate as teams, especially when a host of problems make academic success difficult to sustain. Research suggests that such collective efforts can foster improved instruction, which often is the key to sustained improvement in achievement.[35]

Testing twice instead of once per year is not likely to solve the problem of teaching to the test, however, and even may make it worse. As Robert Linn pointed out, "high-stakes accountability requires new high-quality assessments each year that are equated to those of previous years." He added that "getting by on the cheap will likely lead to both distorted results (e.g., inflated, nongeneralizable gains) and distortions in education (e.g., the narrow teaching to the test)." And this would be true even if focused on growth rather than annual snapshots. But there would be advantages too. It is also possible that such assessments could include more performance and constructed response items, especially if advances in machine scoring—powered by so-called artificial intelligence—can help improve reliability. And perhaps most importantly, matrix sampling of test items (or even test forms) can be utilized to make it more difficult to tailor instruction to particular questions and to narrow the curriculum. Linn also pointed out that multiple indicators can improve test validity.[36]

Developing assessments under these conditions could incentivize teachers to work together on covering the entire curriculum through the academic year, while focusing attention on student weaknesses identified on the initial exam. This will be more costly but could pay dividends both in the validity of results and motivation for educators to cover as much prescribed material as possible. If it can be accomplished, a somewhat different sort of accountability could emerge, focused on achievement growth, improved instruction, and collaborative problem solving. In the words of the late Richard Elmore, it could promote *internal* accountability, with educators working collectively to hold one another responsible for building-wide achievement gains. It could also contribute to so-called improvement science, recently advocated by Anthony Bryk and others in connection with the Carnegie Endowment for the Advancement of Teaching.[37]

An assessment system focused on student growth and not simply academic (and by extension social) status could represent a big improvement in accountability. It would help level the playing field, providing urban schools the opportunity to compete more effectively with their suburban counterparts. And growth targets could be made more reasonable in light of resource constraints and other factors affecting institutions. In the end, of course, many parents likely will be prone to selecting schools based on overall scores rather than growth, although the latter may prove appealing to those interested in raising the performance of their children. Should that occur, it may help shift the logic of accountability away from the hierarchy of presumed winners and losers that prevails today. The result could be a more nuanced and variegated school system, offering a range of opportunities for the public to consider. And students may embrace the variety as well. Excellence, after all, can be defined in different ways, and it can be experienced in a variety of settings. This could prove a potent new source of motivation for students who currently believe that their schools are simply inferior. And there are additional assessment ideas that have been suggested lately that might also prove fruitful, focusing again on institutions rather than students or teachers.[38]

Finally, the high-stakes accountability framework of NCLB should never be revisited. Strictly punitive consequences for relatively poor performance have *not* produced dramatic turnaround stories in most cases. Instead, policy should aim to help educators cooperatively focus on improving student achievement, setting reasonable targets for advancement, and utilizing approaches that make a difference. Cross-building collaboration also might be helpful, or the assignment of key administrators and teacher leaders to facilitate positive change. Larger districts may consider designating full-time school improvement specialists, working with institutions to focus on instructional enhancement and achievement growth. But greater teamwork *within schools* is especially important, and making it happen cannot be left to outside experts. One result of this could be the sort of collegial accountability that Elmore advocated, between teachers and administrators, along with less egregious forms of external accountability (such as basic reporting to the public) than in the past. This may be even more important in the wake of disruptions occasioned by the COVID-19 pandemic.[39] Establishing a pervasive culture of professionalized accountability would be an important step in the advancement of teaching as a profession, and perhaps an end to the type of draconian, politically motivated accountability that has prevailed in the past half century. That too would be a development of significant historic proportions.

Appendix

Oral History Sources

As mentioned in the acknowledgments, I benefited from insights and information offered by some three dozen individuals, representing a variety of backgrounds and perspectives. They included assessment scholars, historians, policy scholars, policy makers, activists, political advisors, and assessment administrators. All had lived through much of the period covered in the book, and had much to say about it. Many were eyewitnesses to key events. Altogether they provided a wealth of testimony to consider.

The study's interview protocol focused on the recent history of accountability testing and developments in the assessment industry. It was approved by the University of Kansas Human Research Protection Program, and participants who agreed to be included in the study signed a standard publisher's waiver for permission to use the interview. These sessions were conducted in person before the coronavirus pandemic prevented travel, and by phone thereafter. They ranged from an hour to nearly two in length. They were recorded digitally and transcribed through an online service.

Each participant was provided with a copy of the transcript for review and making corrections, which could be somewhat difficult when the recording quality was inconsistent. Not everyone agreed to allow use of their remarks, and their reasons varied. Some thought the transcription too poor; others retrospectively found their responses inadequate or incomplete, and at least one found the waiver too broad with respect to future use of interviews.

Most did agree to participate in the study, however, and many took pains to correct transcriptions or clarify their remarks. A number are cited in the book's notes, although none are quoted. But regardless of permissions and waivers, all of the interviews were very valuable, especially for providing information about events, people, ideas, and controversies to be investigated further with standard historical sources. As noted in the acknowledgments, some participants provided documents, reports, and publications that proved very helpful.

Validity checks were performed by comparing oral history interviews across participants, and with other, more conventional historical sources of evidence. While just a subset of interviews is cited in the book, all of them provided valuable information about a wide range of topics addressed in the book.

Names of participants were not anonymized, and those cited are identified by name and date of the interview. Since all provided useful testimony, however, I offer a full list of participants herein, regardless of their appearance in the book. Identifying them here, of course, does not imply that anyone agrees with everything in the text, nor should they be held culpable for my conclusions. The order is alphabetical by last name: Eva Baker, Henry Braun, Robert Brennan, Steven Brint, Michael Cohen, Larry Cuban, Dale Dennis, John Easton, Steve Ferrara, Michael Feuer, Edmund Gordon, Gwen Grant, Thomas Guskey, Edward Haertel, Walt Haney, Andrew Ho, Jack Jennings, Carl Kaestle, Neal Kingston, Daniel Koretz, Bob Lee, Ina Mullis, Joseph Pedulla, Diane Piche, W. James Popham, Hugh Price, John Poggio, Melissa Roderick, Mike Russell, Bob Schaeffer, Lorrie Shepard, Bob Schwarz, Marshall (Mike) Smith, Marth Thurlow, Jon Twing, and Maris Vinovskis.

The oral history dimension of the study was a key component of the research process, providing important insights, historical information, and suggestions about where to locate additional sources of evidence. I am extremely grateful to all of the participants for taking the time to contribute to the study. Without their contributions, it would have been considerably less complete and satisfactory.

Acknowledgments

Scholarship is a collective enterprise and I received a great deal of assistance in undertaking this study. It was generously supported by a small research grant from the Spencer foundation, which allowed for travel to archives and libraries, transcription of interviews, book purchases, and support for two very helpful research assistants, Ryan Belew and Jennifer Hurst.

I also spoke with many testing experts, policy analysts, policy makers, historians, and historical actors who also were very helpful (see the appendix regarding oral history interviews with most such individuals). A number of them shared documents or other materials of various sorts, including Edward Haertel, Ethan Hutt, Neal Kingston, Daniel Koretz, John Poggio, Lorie Shepard, and Maris Vinovskis. This assistance proved very useful indeed, and I am most grateful for their thoughtfulness and generosity.

Librarians at the Library of Congress, the Florida State Archives, Special Collections and Archives at the University of Iowa Library, the Gutman Library at the Harvard Graduate School of Education, Boston College's O'Neil Library, and the Anschutz Library at the University of Kansas were helpful in my utilizing collections relevant to this study. The advent of the COVID-19 pandemic in early 2020 made travel to additional research sites impossible.

Colleagues provided valuable feedback at various stages of the project. Ben Justice responded very positively to the initial proposal for the book, offering helpful advice, and subsequent readings as well. Neal Kingston read the entire manuscript, providing extensive commentary that was very valuable, and Joseph Pedulla also read portions of the book and offered positive feedback. Professor Rory Bahadur of Washburn University also read the manuscript and offered very helpful reactions. A revised version of chapter 1 was published in *Teachers College Record*, and its reviewers' commentary proved useful for the book as a whole. Anonymous readers for Rutgers University Press also provided valuable critical feedback, which informed the final revisions leading to the book's publication.

Senior editor Margaret (Peggy) Solic at Rutgers University Press adeptly steered the book through the various stages of review and preparation for publication. Editorial director Kimberly Guinta also was very helpful during the early stages of its consideration, and Sherry Gerstein was the very capable production editor. Copyediting was adeptly performed by Sally Quinn. I prepared the index myself.

Finally, my spouse Aida Alaka, along with friends and colleagues in Lawrence, have been very supportive throughout the process of conducting the research for this project, and writing the book. Their encouragement, patience, and forbearance has made the task altogether more manageable and gratifying.

As mentioned above, a revised version of chapter 1 was published as "The Origins of American Test-Based Educational Accountability and Controversies about Its Impact, 1970–1983," in *Teachers College Record* 124, no. 1 (January 2022), with Ryan and Jennifer, who assisted with revising and editing it, as coauthors.

Notes

Introduction

1   For an overview, see Lorrie A. Shepard, "A Brief History of Accountability Testing, 1965–2007," in *The Future of Test-Based Accountability*, ed. Katherine E. Ryan and Lorrie A. Shepard (New York: Routledge, 2008), 25–46; and Daniel P. Resnick, "Educational Policy and the Applied Historian: Testing, Competency and Standards," *Journal of Social History* 14, no. 4 (Summer 1981): 539–559. On *A Nation at Risk*, see James W. Guthrie and Matthew G. Springer, "'A Nation at Risk' Revisited: Did 'Wrong' Reasoning Result in 'Right' Results? At What Cost?" *Peabody Journal of Education* 79, no. 1 (2004): 7–35. On complaints about testing, see Michael Gonchar, "Do You Spend Too Much Time Preparing for Standardized Tests?" *New York Times*, April 12, 2013, https://archive.nytimes.com/learning.blogs.nytimes.com/2013/04/12/do-you-spend-too-much-time-preparing-for-standardized-tests/?searchResultPosition=5.

2   An introduction to relevant research on the global history of accountability may be found in Sherman Dorn and Christian Ydesen, "Towards a Comparative and International History of School Testing and Accountability," *Education Policy Analysis Archives* 22, no. 115 (2014): 1–11; and Brendan A. Rapple, "Payment by Results: An Example of Assessment in Elementary Education from Nineteenth Century Britain," *Education Policy Analysis Archives* 2, no. 1 (1994): 1–21.

3   On accountability and testing earlier in U.S. history, see William J. Reese, *Testing Wars in the Public Schools: A Forgotten History* (Cambridge, MA: Harvard University Press, 2013), chs. 6 and 7; and Jal Mehta, *The Allure of Order: High Hopes, Dashed Expectations, and the Troubled Quest to Remake American Schooling* (New York: Oxford University Press, 2013), ch. 3.

4   On early accountability measures see Raymond E. Callahan, *Education and the Cult of Efficiency: A Study of the Forces That Have Shaped the Administration of the Public Schools* (Chicago: University of Chicago Press, 1962), chs. 4–8; David Tyack and Elizabeth Hansot, *Managers of Virtue: Public School Leadership in America, 1820–1980* (New York: Basic Books, 1982), chs. 9–12. On more recent developments, see Kathryn A. McDermott, *High-Stakes Reform: The Politics of Educational Accountability* (Washington, DC: Georgetown University Press, 2011),

chs. 1–4; Sherman Dorn, "The Political Legacy of School Accountability Systems," *Educational Policy Analysis Archives* 6, no. 1 (January 1998): 1–31; Karen Seashore Lewis, Karen Febey, and Roger Schroeder, "State-Mandated Accountability in High Schools: Teachers' Interpretations of a New Era," *Educational Evaluation and Policy Analysis* 27, no. 2 (2005): 177–204; Richard M. Ingersoll and Gregory J. Collins, "Accountability and Control in American Schools," *Journal of Curriculum Studies* 49, no. 1 (2017): 75–95; and Diana D'Amico Pawlewicz, *Blaming Teachers: Professionalization Policies and the Failure of Reform in American History* (New Brunswick, NJ: Rutgers University Press, 2020), ch. 5.

5 Lorraine M. McDonnell, *Politics, Persuasion and Educational Testing* (Cambridge, MA: Harvard University Press, 2004), chs. 1 and 2. Also see Lorraine M. McDonnell, "Accountability as Seen through a Political Lens," in *Making Sense of Test-Based Accountability in Education*, ed. Laura S. Hamilton, Brian M. Stecher, and Stephen P. Klein (Santa Monica, CA: RAND, 2002), 101–120. For a somewhat different perspective, see Jal Mehta, "How Paradigms Create Politics: The Transformation of American Educational Policy, 1980–2001," *American Educational Research Journal* 50, no. 2 (April 2013): 285–324.

6 On geospatial inequality in education related to test score differences, see Christy Lleras, "Race, Racial Concentration, and the Dynamics of Educational Inequality across Urban and Suburban Schools," *American Educational Research Journal* 45, no. 4 (December 2008): 886–912; and Vincent J. Roscigno, Donald Tomaskovic-Devey, and Martha Crowley, "Education and the Inequalities of Place," *Social Forces* 84, no. 4 (June 2006): 2121–2145. On the historical roots of these issues, see Jack Dougherty, "Shopping for Schools: How Public Education and Private Housing Shaped Suburban Connecticut," *Journal of Urban History* 38, no. 2 (March 2012): 205–224.

7 McDonnell, *Politics, Persuasion*, chs. 2, 3, and 6. Also see Elizabeth DeBray-Pelot and Patrick McGuinn, "The New Politics of Education: Analyzing the Federal Education Policy Landscape in the Post-NCLB Era," *Education Policy* 23, no. 1 (January 2009): 15–42. On human capital, see Gary S. Becker, preface to *Human Capital: A Theoretical and Empirical Analysis, with Special Reference to Education*, 3rd ed. (Chicago: University of Chicago Press, 1994).

8 Shepard, "Brief History," 25; Daniel P. Resnick, "Minimum Competency Testing Historically Considered," *Review of Research in Education* 8 (1980): 10–14.

9 For comparison of polling data, see James N. Johnstone, "A Note on the Use of a Composite Education System Indicator: An Application to the Annual Gallup Poll on 'Attitudes to Education,'" *Educational Evaluation and Policy Analysis* 3, no. 1 (January–February 1981): 23–26. On student conflict in this era concerning a range of issues, see John Herbers, "High School Unrest Rises, Alarming U.S. Educators," *New York Times*, March 9, 1969, 1; and John L. Rury and Shirley A. Hill, *The African American Struggle for Secondary Schooling: Closing the Graduation Gap* (New York: Teachers College Press, 2012), chs. 4 and 5. Regarding other changes during the 1960s, see Kevin Boyle, *The Shattering: America in the 1960s* (New York: W. W. Norton, 2021). On social promotion as an issue, see Southwest Educational Development Laboratory, *The Literature on Social Promotion versus Retention* (Washington, DC: National Institute of Education, 1981).

10 On the state of public perceptions regarding the country's status, see Bruce J. Schulman, preface to *The Seventies: The Great Shift in American Culture, Society, and Politics* (New York: Free Press, 2001). Regarding the growth of political

interest in education, especially at the federal levels, after 1980, see Paul Manna, *School's In: Federalism and the National Education Agenda* (Washington, DC: Georgetown University Press, 2007), pt. II. On the significance of test scores, see Shepard, "Brief History," 29; Carl Kaestle, *Testing Policy in the United States: A Historical Perspective* (Gordon Commission on the Future of Assessment in Education, 2018), http://www.ets.org/Media/Research/pdf/kaestle; Susan M. Brookhart, "The Public Understanding of Assessment in Educational Reform in the United States," *Oxford Review of Education* 39, no. 1 (February 2013): 52–71.

11 On this trend, see Gary Gerstle, introduction to *The Rise and Fall of the Neoliberal Order: America and the World in the Free Market Era* (New York: Oxford University Press, 2022); Lily Geismer, *Left Behind: The Democrats' Failed Attempt to Solve Inequality* (New York: Public Affairs, 2022), ch. 8. Also see Kim Phillips-Fein, "The History of Neo-Liberalism," in *Shaped by the State: Toward a New Political History of the Twentieth Century*, ed. Brent Cebul, Lily Geismer, and Mason B. Williams (Chicago: University of Chicago Press, 2019). On NCLB, see Jesse Rhodes, *An Education in Politics: The Origin and Evolution of No Child Left Behind* (Ithaca, NY: Cornell University Press, 2012), chs. 5 and 6

12 Gerstle, *Rise and Fall*, pt. II.

13 For a broad discussion of these issues, and historical context, see Daniel Koretz, *Measuring Up: What Educational Testing Really Tells Us* (Cambridge, MA: Harvard University Press, 2008), chs. 4 and 10.

14 Reese, *Testing Wars*, chs. 3–7; U.S. Congress, Office of Technology Assessment, *Testing in American Schools: Asking the Right Questions* (Washington, DC: U.S. Government Printing Office, 1992), pp. 105–110.

15 Reese, *Testing Wars*, ch. 6; Stephan Jay Gould, *The Mismeasure of Man*, rev. ed. (New York: W. W. Norton, 1996), chs. 3, 4, and 5.

16 Gould, *Mismeasure of Man*, ch. 5; Gerardo Giordano, *How Testing Came to Dominate American Schools: The History of Educational Assessment* (New York: Peter Lang, 2005), ch. 3.

17 Gould, *Mismeasure of Man*, ch. 5; Clarence J. Karier, "Testing for Order and Control in the Corporate Liberal State," *Educational Theory* 22, no. 2 (April 1972): 154–180; Giordano, *How Testing*, chs. 2 and 4. Also see the essays in Michael Sokal, ed., *Psychological Testing and American Society, 1890–1930* (New Brunswick, NJ: Rutgers University Press, 1987). On the more general role of testing in American culture, see Joseph F. Kett, *Merit: The History of a Founding Ideal from the American Revolution to the Twenty-First Century* (Ithaca, NY: Cornell University Press, 2013), ch. 5.

18 Frederick J. Kelly, "The Kansas Silent Reading Tests," *Journal of Educational Psychology* 7, no. 2 (February 1916): 63–80; Giordano, *How Testing*, ch. 2. On earlier achievement tests, see Kaestle, *Testing Policy*, 16; and for reading tests after 1920, Arlene L. Barry, "The Evolution of Reading Tests and Other Forms of Educational Assessment," *Clearing House* 71, no. 4 (March–April 1998): 231–235.

19 Nicholas Lemann, *The Big Test: The Secret History of the American Meritocracy* (New York: Farrar, Straus and Giroux, 2000), ch. 1; Kaestle, *Testing Policy*, 19–20; Claude M. Fuess, *The College Board: Its First Fifty Years* (New York: Columbia University Press, 1950), 100–119.

20 Derrick Darby and John L. Rury, *The Color of Mind: Why the Origins of the Achievement Gap Matter for Justice* (Chicago: University of Chicago Press, 2018), ch. 4.

21 Fred J. Galloway, "Inferential Sturdiness and the 1917 Army Alpha: A New Look at the Robustness of Educational Quality Indices as Determinants of Interstate Black–White Score Differentials," *Journal of Negro Education* 63, no. 2 (Spring 1994): 251–266.

22 Karl Alexander and Stephen L. Morgan, "The Coleman Report at Fifty: Its Legacy and Implications for Future Research on Equality of Opportunity," *RSF: The Russell Sage Foundation Journal of the Social Sciences* 2, no. 5 (September 2016): 1–16. Also see Elizabeth Evitts Dickinson, "Coleman Report Set the Standard for the Study of Public Education," *Johns Hopkins Magazine* (Winter 2016), https://hub.jhu.edu/magazine/2016/winter/coleman-report-public-education/.

23 Lemann, *Big Test*, chs. 3–8. Regarding technical qualities of contemporary aptitude tests, see Robert J. Sternberg, Elena L. Grigorenko, and Donald A. Bundy, "The Predictive Value of IQ," *Merrill-Palmer Quarterly* 47, no. 1 (January 2001): 1–41. For discussion of various tests historically used in schools and elsewhere, see F. Allen Hanson, *Testing Testing: The Social Consequences of the Examined Life* (Berkeley: University of California Press, 1993), pt. II.

24 Julia Peterson, *The Iowa Testing Programs: The First Fifty Years* (Iowa City: University of Iowa Press, 1983), pt. I.

25 Regarding the rise of "testing culture" in American schools at this time, see Ethan Hutt and Jack Schneider, "A History of Achievement Testing in the United States Or: Explaining the Persistence of Inadequacy," *Teachers College Record* 120 (November 2018): 1–34. On the development of the ACT, see Peterson, *Iowa Testing Programs*, ch. 9.

26 Everett F. Lindquist, "Preliminary Considerations in Objective Test Construction," in *Educational measurement*, 2nd ed. (Washington, DC: American Council on Education, 1951), 152–153.

27 Donald T. Campbell, "Assessing the Impact of Planned Social Change," in *Social Research and Public Policies*, ed. Gene M. Lyons (Hanover, NH: University Press of New England, 1975), 35.

28 Koretz, *Measuring Up*, ch. 10; also see Daniel Koretz, *The Testing Charade: Pretending to Make Schools Better* (Chicago: University of Chicago Press, 2017), chs. 4 and 5; and Edward Haertel, "Getting the Help We Need," *Journal of Educational Measurement* 50, no. 1 (Spring 2013): 84–90.

29 Koretz, *Testing Charade*, ch. 4; Kimberly West-Faulcon, "The Real Cheating Scandal of Standardized Tests," *Pacific Standard*, June 14, 2017, https://psmag.com/education/the-real-cheating-scandal-of-standardized-tests-35282. Also see Richard Rothstein, "Holding Accountability to Account: How Scholarship and Experience in Other Fields Inform Exploration of Performance Incentives in Education" (Working Paper 2008-04, National Center on Performance Incentives, Vanderbilt University, February 2008), https://files.epi.org/2014/holding-accountability-to-account.pdf.

30 Koretz, *Testing Charade*, chs. 2 and 5; Alia Wong, "Why Would a Teacher Cheat? Educators Often Choose to Inflate Students' Scores on Standardized Tests, and the Motivations—and Effects—Indicate That a Little Deception Isn't Always a Bad Thing," *Atlantic*, April 27, 2016, https://www.theatlantic.com/education/archive/2016/04/why-teachers-cheat/480039/.

31 On the need for qualitative measures, see Daniel L. Duke, "What Is the Nature of Educational Excellence, and Should We Try to Measure It?" *Phi Delta Kappan* 66,

no. 10 (June 1985): 671–674; and Kathleen Porter-Magee, "Trust but Verify: The Real Lessons of Campbell's Law," Thomas B. Fordham Institute, February 26, 2013, https://fordhaminstitute.org/ohio/commentary/trust-verify-real-lessons -campbells-law.

32 For an early discussion of the use and potential problems of these tests, see James W. Popham, introduction to *Criterion-Referenced Measurement: An Introduction* (Englewood Cliffs, NJ: Educational Technology Publications, 1971); and Anthony J. Nitko, "Distinguishing the Many Varieties of Criterion-Referenced Tests," *Review of Educational Research* 50, no. 3 (Autumn 1980): 461–485. For a more critical perspective, see George F. Madaus, "The Distortion of Teaching and Testing: High-Stakes Testing and Instruction," *Peabody Journal of Education* 65, no. 3 (Spring 1988): 29–46; and Peter W. Airasian and George F. Madaus, "Linking Testing and Instruction: Policy Issues," *Journal of Educational Measurement* 20, no. 2 (Summer 1983): 103–118; also see Robert L. Linn, "Two Weak Spots in the Practice of Criterion-Referenced Measurement," *Educational Measurement: Issues and Practice* 1, no. 1 (Spring 1982): 12–13, and his later discussion of these problems in "Assessments and Accountability," *Educational Researcher* 29, no. 2 (March 2000): 4–16. For a more recent and somewhat different discussion of problems, see W. James Popham, "Criterion-Referenced Measurement: Half a Century Wasted? Four Areas of Confusion Have Kept Criterion Referenced Measurement from Fulfilling Its Potential," *Educational Leadership* 71, no. 6 (March 2014): 62–68.

33 For a recent summary of this perspective, see Douglas Downey, *How Schools Really Matter: Why Our Assumption about Schools and Inequality Is Mostly Wrong* (Chicago: University of Chicago Press, 2020), Part I. Also see Heather C. Hill, "The Coleman Report, 50 Years On," *Annals of the American Academy of Political and Social Science* 674 (November 2017): 9–26; John R. Logan, Elisabeta Minca, and Sinem Adar, "The Geography of Inequality: Why Separate Means Unequal in American Public Schools," *Sociology of Education* 85, no. 3 (July 2012): 287–301; Gary Orfield, "Tenth Annual Brown Lecture in Education Research: A New Civil Rights Agenda for American Education," *Educational Researcher* 43, no. 6 (August–September 2014): 273–292; Annette Lareau, *Unequal Childhoods: Class, Race, and Family Life*, 2nd ed. (Berkeley, CA: University of California Press, 2011), chs. 1 and 2. Also see Selcuk R. Sirin, "Socioeconomic Status and Academic Achievement: A Meta-Analytic Review of Research," *Review of Educational Research* 75, no. 3 (Fall 2005): 417–453.

34 Dennis S. Davis and Angeli Willson, "Practices and Commitments of Test-Centric Literacy Instruction: Lessons from a Testing Transition," *Reading Research Quarterly* 50, no. 3 (July–August–September 2015): 357–379; Howard Machtinger, "What Do We Know about High Poverty Schools? Summary of the High Poverty Schools Conference at UNC-Chapel Hill," *High School Journal* 90, no. 3 (February–March 2007): 1–8; Erin Rooney, "'I'm Just Going Through the Motions': High-Stakes Accountability and Teachers' Access to Intrinsic Rewards," *American Journal of Education* 121, no. 4 (August 2015): 475–500; Grace Enriquez, "'But They Won't Let You Read!': A Case Study of an Urban Middle School Male's Response to School Reading," *Journal of Education* 193, no. 1 (2013): 35–46. On problems associated with narrowly framed instruction, see Kennon M. Sheldon and Bruce J. Biddle, "Standards, Accountability, and School Reform: Perils and Pitfalls," *Teachers College Record* 100, no. 1 (Fall 1998): 164–180.

35   James J. Heckman and Paul A. LaFontaine, "Bias-Corrected Estimates of GED Returns," *Journal of Labor Economics* 24, no. 3 (July 2006): 661–700; James Heckman and Tim Kautz, "Achievement Tests and the Role of Character in American Life," in *The Myth of Achievement Tests: The GED and the Role of Character in American Life*, ed. James J. Heckman, John Eric Humphries, and Tim Kautz (Chicago: University of Chicago Press, 2014), 3–56. For a related commentary on the validity of test score data, see Daniel M. Koretz, "Limitations in the Use of Achievement Tests as Measures of Educators' Productivity," *Journal of Human Resources* 37, no. 4 (Autumn 2002): 752–777.

36   James J. Heckman, "Schools, Skills, and Synapses," *Economic Inquiry* 6, no. 3 (July 2008): 289–324.

37   James J. Heckman and Tim Kautz, "Hard Evidence on Soft Skills," *Labor Economics* 19, no. 4 (August 2012): 451–464. On this point, also see Jack Schneider, *Beyond Test Scores: A Better Way to Measure School Quality* (Cambridge, MA: Harvard University Press, 2017), ch. 3.

38   Quoted in Heckman and Kautz, "Achievement Tests," 13–14.

39   James J. Heckman, John Eric Humphries, Paul A. LaFontaine, and Pedro L. Rodriguez, "The GED Testing Program Induces Students to Drop Out," in Heckman et al., *Myth of Achievement Tests*, 293–317. Also see John H. Tyler, "Economic Benefits of the GED: Lessons from Recent Research," *Review of Educational Research* 73, no. 3 (September 2003): 369–403; and Steven W. Hemelt and Dave E. Marcotte, "High School Exit Exams and Dropout in an Era of Increased Accountability," *Journal of Policy Analysis and Management* 32, no. 2 (Spring 2013): 323–349. For a somewhat different perspective on high school exit exams, see Sean F. Reardon, Nicole Arshan, Allison Atteberry, and Michal Kurlaender, "Effects of Failing a High School Exit Exam on Course Taking, Achievement, Persistence, and Graduation," *Educational Evaluation and Policy Analysis* 32, no. 4 (December 2010): 498–520.

40   Daniel Koretz, interview by author, February 7, 2020; Lorrain McDonnel, interview by author, September 8, 2020. Both of these scholars argued that policy makers were aware of problems with standardized testing, but believed political risks of eschewing accountability were too great or hoped that such problems could be eventually resolved.

41   On the origins of accountability, see Shepard, "Brief History," 25–27; and Lorraine M. McDonnell, "Stability and Change in Title I Testing Policy," *RSF: The Russell Sage Foundation Journal of the Social Sciences* 1, no. 3 (December 2015): 170–186. On the development of accountability policies in the South, see Scott Baker, Anthony Myers, and Brittany Vasquez, "Desegregation, Accountability, and Equality: North Carolina and the Nation, 1971–2002," *Education Policy Analysis Archives* 22, no. 117 (2014), http://dx.doi.org/10.14507/epaa.v22.1671.

42   References regarding these developments can be found in chapter 1, but key points are addressed in the following: W. James Popham and T. R. Husek, "Implications of Criterion-Referenced Measurement," *Journal of Educational Measurement* 6, no. 1 (Spring 1969): 1–9; John Robert Warren and Rachael B. Kulick, "Modeling States' Enactment of High School Exit Examination Policies," *Social Forces* 86, no. 1 (September 2007): 215–229; and R. Scott Baker, "Desegregation, Minimum Competency Testing, and the Origins of Accountability: North Carolina and the Nation," *History of Education Quarterly* 55 (February 2015): 33–57.

43 References regarding these issues can be found in chapter 2, but key points about the trials discussed therein are addressed in the following publications: Benjamin Michael Superfine, *The Courts and Standards-Based Educational Reform* (New York: Oxford University Press, 2008), 71–82; W. James Popham and Elaine Lindheim, "Implications of a Landmark Ruling on Florida's Minimum Competency Test," *Phi Delta Kappan* 63, no. 1 (September 1981): 18–20; and Diana Pullin, "Minimum Competency Testing and the Demand for Accountability," *Phi Delta Kappan* 63, no. 1 (September 1981): 20–22; Jennifer Jellison Holme, Meredith P. Richards, Jo Beth Jimerson, and Rebecca W. Cohen, "Assessing the Effects of High School Exit Examinations," *Review of Educational Research* 80, no. 4 (December 2010): 476–526.

44 These events are discussed in chapter 3 and references for them can be found there. Key sources include Maris A. Vinovskis, *From A Nation at Risk to No Child Left Behind: National Education Goals and the Creation of Federal Education Policy* (New York: Teachers College Press, 2009), chs. 1, 2, and 3; Laura Hersh Salganik, "Why Testing Reforms Are so Popular and How They Are Changing Education," *Phi Delta Kappan* 66, no. 9 (May 1985): 607–610; Richard J. Coley and Margaret E. Goertz, *Educational Standards in the 50 States: 1990* (Princeton, NJ: Policy Information Center, Educational Testing Service, 1990), 3–26; National Commission on Testing and Public Policy, *From Gatekeeper to Gateway: Transforming Testing in America* (Chestnut Hill, MA: NCTPP, 1990); and McDonnell, *Politics, Persuasion*, chs. 3 and 4. On authentic assessment, see Larry Cuban, "Whatever Happened to Authentic Assessment?" Wordpress, September 28, 2020, https://larrycuban.wordpress.com/2020/09/28/whatever-happened-to-authentic-assessment/. Also see Robert L. Linn and Joan L. Herman, *A Policymaker's Guide to Standards-Led Assessment* (Denver, CO: Education Commission of the States, 1997), 1–6.

45 Chapter 4 deals with these events and, once again, Vinovskis, *From A Nation at Risk* is an indispensable source regarding national politics. Also see Rhodes, *An Education in Politics*, chs. 3, 4, and 5; Patrick J. McGinn, *No Child Left Behind and the Transformation of Federal Education Policy, 1965–2005* (Lawrence: University Press of Kansas, 2006), chs. 2 and 4–7; and Elizabeth H. DeBray, *Politics, Ideology & Education: Federal Policy during the Clinton and Bush Administrations* (New York: Teachers College Press, 2006), pts. 1 and 2. Useful insights are also offered by Jack Jennings, *Why National Standards and Tests? Politics and the Quest for Better Schools* (Thousand Oaks, CA: Sage, 1998), and his more recent book, *Presidents, Congress, and the Public Schools: The Politics of Educational Reform* (Cambridge, MA: Harvard Education Press, 2015).

46 Regarding NCLB, the principal topic of chapter 5, Rhodes (*Education in Politics*, chs. 5 and 6), Vinovskis (*From A Nation at Risk*, chs. 6, 7, and 8), and DeBray (*Politics, Ideology & Education*, pt. III) provide somewhat different perspectives, along with Christopher Cross, *Political Education: National Policy Comes of Age* (New York: Teachers College Press, 2010), chs. 7 and 8; and W. Lee Anderson, "The No Child Left Behind Act and the Legacy of Federal Aid to Education," *Education Policy Analysis Archives* 13, no. 24 (2005), http://epaa.asu.edu/epaa/v13n24/. On antecedents, see David J. Hoff, "Made to Measure," *Education Week*, June 16, 1999, https://www.edweek.org/teaching-learning/made-to-measure/1999/06; and for a noteworthy response at the time, Robert L. Linn, "Accountability: Responsibility and Reasonable Expectations," *Educational Researcher* 32, no. 7

(October 2003): 3–13. On racial achievement gaps, see James D. Anderson. "The Historical Context for Understanding the Test Score Gap," *National Journal of Urban Education and Practice* 1, no. 1 (2007): 1–20.

47 These issues also are discussed in chapter 5. See, for instance, Thomas Dee and Brian Jacob, "The Impact of No Child Left Behind on Student Achievement" (Working Paper 15531, National Bureau of Economic Research, November 2009), https://www.nber.org/system/files/working_papers/w15531/w15531.pdf; and Morgan S. Polikoff, Andrew J. McEachin, Stephan L. Wrabel, and Mathew Duque, "The Waive of the Future? School Accountability in the Waiver Era," *Educational Researcher* 43, no. 1 (February 2014): 45–54. On Obama's generally neoliberal orientation, see Gerstle, *Rise and Fall*, ch. 6.

48 Alyson Klein, "The Every Student Succeeds Act: An ESSA Overview," *Education Week*, March 31, 2016, https://www.edweek.org/policy-politics/the-every-student -succeeds-act-an-essa-overview/2016/03; Council of Chief State School Officers, *Accountability Identification Is Only the Beginning: Monitoring and Evaluating Accountability Results and Implementation* (Washington, DC: CCSSO, 2018), 2–8; Jeffrey R. Henig, David M. Houston, and Melissa Arnold Lyon, "Lessons Learned or Politics Reaffirmed?" in *The Every Student Succeeds Act (ESSA): What It Means for Schools, Systems, and States*, ed. Frederick M. Hess and Max Eden (Cambridge, MA: Harvard Education Press, 2017), 29–42.

49 David J. Hoff, "Not All Agree on Meaning of NCLB Proficiency," *Education Week*, April 17, 2007, https://www.edweek.org/policy-politics/not-all-agree-on -meaning-of-nclb-proficiency/2007/04; Daniel Koretz, "How Do American Students Measure Up? Making Sense of International Comparisons," *Future of Children* 19, no. 1 (Spring 2009): 37–51; Jeremy Kilpatrick, "TIMSS 2007 Mathematics: Where Are We?" *MAA FOCUS* (February–March 2009), https:// www.maa.org/sites/default/files/pdf/pubs/febmar09pg4-7.pdf; and Ludger Woessmann, "The Importance of School Systems: Evidence from International Differences in Student Achievement," *Journal of Economic Perspectives* 30, no. 3 (Summer 2016): 3–31; Andreas Schleicher, "Seeing the United States Education System through the Prism of International Comparisons," *Middle School Journal* 40, no. 5 (May 2009): 11–17.

50 Jill Koyama, "Global Scare Tactics and the Call for US Schools to Be Held Accountable," *American Journal of Education* 120, no. 1 (November 2013): 77–99; John B. Holbein and Helen F. Ladd, "Accountability Pressure and Non-Achievement Student Behaviors" (Working Paper 122, National Center for Analysis of Longitudinal Data in Education Research, Duke University, February 2015), https://caldercenter.org/sites/default/files/WP%20122.pdf; Lisa Guisbond, Monty Neill, and Bob Schaeffer, "NCLB's Lost Decade for Educational Progress: What Can We Learn from This Policy Failure?" *Counterpoints* 451 (2013): 7–26; Jennifer Jennings and Heeju Sohn, "Measure for Measure: How Proficiency-Based Accountability Systems Affect Inequality in Academic Achievement," *Sociology of Education* 87, no. 2 (April 2014): 125–141.

51 On the decline in confidence for American institutions, see Robert Putnam, *The Upswing: How America Came Together a Century Ago and How We Can Do It Again* (New York: Simon & Schuster, 2020), chs. 4 and 5. Regarding public opinion and NCLB accountability, see Frederick M. Hess, "Accountability without Angst? Public Opinion and No Child Left Behind," *Harvard*

Educational Review 76, no. 4 (Winter 2006): 587–610. On educators' attitudes, see Stephen Brint and Sue Teele, "Professionalism under Siege: Teacher Views of NCLB," in *No Child Left Behind and the Reduction of the Achievement Gap: Sociological Perspectives on Federal Educational Policy*, ed. Alan R. Sadovnik, Jennifer A. O'Day, George W. Bohrnstedt, and Kathryn M. Borman (New York: Routledge, 2008), 131–152.

Chapter 1 The Origins of Test-Based Accountability

1 Ralph D. Turlington, "How Can We Prove What We Are Doing Better?" in *Accounting for Accountability* (Denver, CO: Cooperative Accountability Project, 1975), 11–12.

2 Lesley Browder, "Stewards, Reviewers and the Future: An Overview," in Turlington, *Accounting for Accountability*, 8.

3 A longtime leader in the Florida legislature, Turlington saw education as crucial to the state's future. For a capsule biography, see "Ralph Turlington," People Pill, accessed May 16, 2020, https://peoplepill.com/people/ralph-turlington/.

4 The quote is from Lorraine M. McDonnell, "Stability and Change in Title I Testing Policy," *RSF: The Russell Sage Foundation Journal of the Social Sciences* 1, no. 3 (December 2015): 171–172. On the influence of Coleman's study and NAEP, see Christopher Cross, *Political Education: Setting the Course for State and Federal Policy*, 2nd ed. (New York: Teachers College Press, 2014), 34. Also see Jack Jennings, *Presidents, Congress, and the Public Schools: The Politics of Education Reform* (Cambridge, MA: Harvard Education Press, 2015), ch. 2.

5 Elizabeth Pop Berman, *Thinking Like an Economist: How Efficiency Replaced Equality in U.S. Public Policy* (Princeton, NJ: Princeton University Press, 2022), ch. 5. For a more sweeping account of economistic reasoning in this era, see Daniel T. Rogers, *Age of Fracture* (Cambridge, MA: Belknap Press of Harvard University, 2011), ch. 2.

6 These were influential developments that highlighted the potential for testing to inform educational policy. On their advent in the 1960s, see Cross, *Political Education*, 38.

7 Stanley M. Elam, ed., *Gallup Polls of Attitudes toward Education, 1969–1984: A Topical Summary* (Bloomington, IN: Phi Delta Kappa, 1984), 69. When asked about supporting greater resources for schools, a higher proportion of respondents responded positively in 1969 and 1971 than in later years, although a plurality was always opposed. A majority in those years also supported the idea of more state support for the schools (p. 28). A majority in 1970 felt that discipline was a major problem in the schools, but a plurality believed that this was more a responsibility of parents than educators (p. 50). A solid majority supported national testing to compare achievement across districts, an idea often linked to accountability. On the latter point, see George Gallup, "The Third Annual Survey of the Public's Attitudes toward the Public Schools, 1971," *Phi Delta Kappan* 53, no. 1 (September 1971): 33. On parents, see Scarvia B. Anderson, "Public Expectations," in *Proceedings of the Conferences on Educational Accountability*, ed. Educational Testing Service (Princeton, NJ: Educational Testing Service, 1971), 101. On subsequent developments, see Paul Peterson, "Ticket to Nowhere," *Education Next* 21, no. 2 (Spring 2021), https://www.educationnext.org/tickettonowhere/. For a contemporaneous take on SAT scores, see David G. Savage, "The Long

Decline in SAT Scores," *Educational Leadership* 35, no. 4 (January 1978): 290–293.

8   For early expressions of this, see Conrad Briner, "Administrators and Account-ability," *Theory into Practice* 8, no. 4 (October 1969): 203–206; Luvern L. Cunningham, "Our Accountability Problems," *Theory into Practice* 8, no. 4 (October 1969): 285–292; and W. James Popham, "Focus on Outcomes: A Guiding Theme of ES '70 Schools," *Phi Delta Kappan* 51, no. 4 (December 1969): 208–210.

9   David K. Cohen, "Social Accounting in Education: Reflections on Supply and Demand," in *Proceedings of the 1970 Invitational Conference on Testing Problems* (Princeton, NJ: Educational Testing Service, 1970), 129–148. For a telling critique of Cohen's discussion, see James J. Gallagher's comments in the same collection (pp. 170–173). Regarding additional advocacy of vouchers as a remedy for institutional nonresponsiveness at the time by one of Cohen's Harvard colleagues, see Christopher Jencks, "Giving Parents Money for Schooling: Education Vouchers," *Phi Delta Kappan* 52, no. 1 (September 1970): 49–52.

10 Anderson, "Public Expectations," 32; Myron Lieberman, "An Overview of Accountability," *Phi Delta Kappan* 52, no. 4 (December 1970): 194–195.

11 Leon Lessinger, "Engineering Accountability for Results in Public Education," *Phi Delta Kappan* 52, no. 4 (December 1970): 217–225; Felix M. Lopez, "Account-ability in Education," *Phi Delta Kappan* 52, no. 4 (December 1970): 231–235.

12 Stephen M. Barro, "An Approach to Developing Accountability Measures for the Public Schools," *Phi Delta Kappan* 52, no. 4 (December 1970): 196–205; Rich-ard M. Durstine, "An Accountability Information System," *Phi Delta Kappan* 52, no. 4 (December 1970): 236–239.

13 Robert E. Campbell, "Accountability and Stone Soup," *Phi Delta Kappan* 53, no. 3 (November 1971): 177.

14 Educational Testing Service, *Proceedings*; Anderson, "Public Expectations," 101–102. For a related set of concerns, see Vito Perone and Warren Strandberg, "A Perspective on Accountability," *Teachers College Record* 73, no. 3 (February 1972): 347–355, which called for using a "Personal Record of Educational Experiences" to document student learning.

15 John E. Morris, "Accountability: Watchword for the 70's," *Clearing House* 45, no. 6 (February 1971): 323–328; K. Fred Daniel, "Moving toward Educational Accountability: Florida's Program," *Educational Technology* 11, no. 1 (Janu-ary 1971): 41–42. Also see George R. la Noue and Marvin R. Pilo, "Teacher Unions and Educational Accountability," *Proceedings of the Academy of Political Science* 30, no. 2 (December 1970): 146–158; and Medill Bair, "Developing Accountability in Urban Schools: A Call for State Leadership," *Educational Technology* 11, no. 1 (January 1971): 38–40. For a slightly later perspective, see Gene I. Maeroff, "Schools Now Are Taking Account of Accountability," *New York Times*, October 10, 1976, 182.

16 Arthur R. Jensen, "How Much Can We Boost IQ and Scholastic Achievement?" *Harvard Educational Review* 39, no. 1 (Spring 1969): 1–123. Also see Leon Kamin, introduction to *The Science and Politics of IQ* (Mahwah, NJ: Lawrence Erlbaum Associates, 1974).

17 Lee Edson, "Jensenism, n. The Theory That I.Q. Is Largely Determined by the Genes: Jensenism, n. An I.Q. Theory Learning Ability, Says Jensen, Comes in Two Distinct Forms," *New York Times*, August 31, 1969; Sandra Scarr-Salapatek "Race,

Social Class, and IQ," *Science* 174, no. 4016 (December 24, 1971): 1285–1295; N. L. Gage, "Replies to Shockley, Page, and Jensen: The Causes of Race Differences in I.Q.," *Phi Delta Kappan* 53, no. 7 (March 1972): 422–427; Thomas Sowell, "Arthur Jensen and His Critics: The Great IQ Controversy," *Change* 5, no. 4 (May 1973): 33–37; Mallory Wober, "Race and Intelligence," *Transition* no. 40 (December 1971): 16–26; Kenneth Kaye, "I. Q.: A Conceptual Deterrent to Revolution in Education," *Elementary School Journal* 74, no. 1 (October 1973): 9–23; Paul Gomberg, "IQ and Race: A Discussion of Some Confusions," *Ethics* 85, no. 3 (April 1975): 258–266.

18 Edward B. Fiske, "Controversy Over Testing Flares Again," *New York Times*, May 1, 1977, ED1; "Blacks Win IQ Test Ruling," *Los Angeles Sentinel*, December 5, 1974, A4; Greg Mims, "Board's IQ Tests Challenged by NAACP Group," *Pittsburgh Courier*, August 31, 1974, 1; "Educators Aim to Reform 'Racial Tests,'" *Chicago Defender* (Big Weekend Edition), March 31, 1973, 14. Statements in opposition to testing are reported in the *Journal of Black Psychology* 4, nos. 1 & 2 (August 1977): 26–31. For a response to this, see William E. Coffman, "Moratorium? What Kind?" (Presidential address to NCME, Iowa Testing Program Occasional Papers, No. 1, March 1973).

19 See, for instance, Richard D. Lyons, "Scientists Shun Confrontation on Causes of Differences in I.Q.," *New York Times*, May 3, 1970, 58; Robert Cassidy, "'Academic racism': University Professors under Attack," *Chicago Tribune*, March 26, 1974, 14; Philip Hager, "Shockley and Innis Debate in S.F.," *Los Angeles Times*, August 24, 1974, 17; James Turman Barron, "Free Speech at Princeton," *Washington Post*, September 7, 1974, A19; and Robert L. Williams, William Dotson, Patricia Don, and Willie S. Williams, "The War against Testing: A Current Status Report," *Journal of Negro Education* 49, no. 3 (Summer 1980): 263–273. For a somewhat more practical perspective from a big city district leader, see Manfred Byrd Jr., "Testing under Fire: Chicago's Problems" (Paper presented at Conference of the Educational Records Bureau, "Testing in Turmoil: Problems and Issues in Educational Measurement," New York, October 1970), ERIC, ED047013, TM000388.

20 For a brief overview of this distinction, see Linda A. Bond, *Norm- and Criterion-Referenced Testing* (ERIC Development Team, ERIC/AE Digest, ED410316 1996-12-00, December 1996), https://files.eric.ed.gov/fulltext/ED410316.pdf.

21 W. James Popham and T. R. Husek, "Implications of Criterion-Referenced Measurement," *Journal of Educational Measurement* 6, no. 1 (Spring 1969): 1–9. Popham later specifically contrasted IQ and criterion-referenced tests in 1980, W. James Popham, "Criterion-Referenced Tests for Black Americans," *Journal of Negro Education* 49, no. 3 (Summer 1980): 297–305. Also see W. James Popham, "Normative Data for Criterion-Referenced Tests?" *Phi Delta Kappan* 57, no. 9 (May 1976): 593–594; and Samuel A. Livingston, "Criterion-Referenced Applications of Classical Test Theory," *Journal of Educational Measurement* 9, no. 1 (Spring 1972): 13–26.

22 Popham and Husek, "Implications," 4. Also see Popham's book published later, *Criterion-Referenced Measurement* (Englewood Cliffs, NJ: Prentice Hall, 1978).

23 Popham and Husek, "Implications," 9. On concerns about such tests expressed at an early point in their development, see Ronald K. Hambleton and Melvin R. Novick, "Toward an Integration of Theory and Method for Criterion-Referenced Tests," *National Council on Measurement in Education* 10, no. 3 (Autumn 1973):

163–165. Hambleton and Novick expressed misgivings about the problems with setting a standard too high or too low, resulting in Type I or Type II errors that could be costly in terms of slowing student progress and wasting teacher resources or failing to identify students needing additional support, which would also end up costing educational resources and could create problems for the student.

24 See Cohen, "Social Accounting in Education" and Popham, "Focus on Outcomes." Also see W. James Popham, "Objectives-Based Management Strategies for Large Educational Systems," *Journal of Educational Research* 66, no. 1 (September 1972): 4–9. On MCT, see John T. Guthrie, "Research Views: Minimum Competency Testing: A Brief History," *Reading Teacher* 34, no. 7 (April 1981): 874–876; and W. James Popham and Stuart C. Rankin, "Minimum Competency Tests Spur Instructional Improvement," *Phi Delta Kappan* 62, no. 9 (May 1981): 637–639.

25 Gene V. Glass, "Standards and Criteria," *Journal of Educational Measurement* 15, no. 4 (Winter 1978): 237–261. His point about the logic of criterion-based tests being essentially normative in orientation was also made in a National Academy of Education report that year, *Improving Educational Achievement: Report of the National Academy of Education Committee on Testing and Basic Skills to the Assistant Secretary for Education* (Washington, DC: National Academy of Education, 1978), 3. Although not addressed in these exchanges, perhaps the nation's best known tests of basic skills at the time, the Iowa Test of Basic Skills, was normatively structured, comparing individual test takers to a nationally representative sample of students taking the exam each year. The Iowa Testing Service resisted pressure to adopt a different approach in the 1970s, arguing that it was not scientifically responsible. On this point, see Julia Peterson, *The Iowa Testing Program: The First Fifty Years* (Iowa City: University of Iowa Press, 1983), 211. Also see Robert L. Linn in the same issue as the Glass article, "Demands, Cautions, and Suggestions for Setting Standards," *Journal of Educational Measurement* 15, no. 4 (Winter 1978): 301–308.

26 W. James Popham, "As Always, Provocative," *Journal of Educational Measurement* 15, no. 4 (Winter 1978): 297–300. Suggesting that public opinion effectively identified competence, of course, was hardly a telling response to the charge that minimum standard setting did not have a scientific or educationally sound foundation. For other responses to Glass see John Fremer, "In Response to Gene Glass," *Phi Delta Kappan* 59, no. 9 (May 1978): 605–606, 625; and Michael Scriven, "How to Anchor Standards," *Journal of Educational Measurement* 15, no. 4 (Winter 1978): 273–275.

27 Lorraine McDonnell, interview by author, September 29, 2020. This point was also made by Gene V. Glass and Mary Lee Smith in "The Technology and Politics of Standards," *Educational Technology* 18, no. 5 (May 1978): 12–18.

28 Everett F. Linquist, "Preliminary Considerations in Objective Test Construction," in *Educational Measurement*, 2nd ed. (Washington, DC: American Council on Education, 1951), 152–153; Donald T. Campbell, "Assessing the Impact of Planned Social Change," in *Social Research and Public Policies*, ed. Gene M. Lyons (Hanover, NH: University Press of New England, 1975), 35.

29 This general point was made about high stakes testing more generally in Daniel Koretz, *The Testing Charade: Pretending to Make Schools Better* (Chicago: University of Chicago Press, 2017), ch. 4.

30 Gene V. Glass, "Minimum Competence and Incompetence in Florida," *Phi Delta Kappan* 59, no. 9 (May 1978): 602–605; Walt Haney and George Madaus, "Making Sense of the Competency Testing Movement" (National Consortium on Testing, Staff Circular No. 2, Huron Institute, Cambridge, MA, 1978). On the question of validity and high stakes, also see Joan C. Baratz, "Policy Implications of Minimum Competency Testing," in *Minimum Competency Achievement Testing: Motives, Models, Measures and Consequences*, ed. Richard M. Jaeger and Carol K. Tittle (Berkeley, CA: McCutchan, 1978), 84–85. Baratz quoted Donald Campbell on the question of validity, or "corruption" of tests saddled with policy implications, and other contributors to the Jaeger and Tittle volume raised similar concerns.

31 On this issue, see Lorrie Shepard, "Norm-Referenced vs. Criterion-Referenced Tests," *Educational Horizons* 58, no. 1 (Fall 1979): 26–32; and Ronald K. Hambleton, Hariharan Swaminathan, James Algina, and Douglas Bill Coulson, "Criterion-Referenced Testing and Measurement: A Review of Technical Issues and Developments," *Review of Educational Research* 48, no. 1 (Winter 1978): 1–47. Also see William H. Schmidt, "Content Biases in Achievement Tests," *Journal of Educational Measurement* 20, no. 2 (Summer 1983): 165–178; and William A. Mehrens and Robert Ebel, "Some Comments on Criterion-Referenced and Norm-Referenced Achievement Tests," *NCME Measurement in Education* 10, no. 1 (Winter 1979): 1–7.

32 W. James Popham, "The Case for Minimum Competency Testing," *Phi Delta Kappa International* 63, no. 2 (October 1981): 90.

33 On the difficulty of establishing such cut scores, see Stephen L. Koffler, "A Comparison of Approaches for Setting Proficiency Standards," *Journal of Educational Measurement* 17, no. 3 (Autumn 1980): 167–178, which argued that different approaches to the question did not produce consistent results, although other studies reported more consistent results when the same groups of judges were used. On the latter point, see Craig N. Mills, "A Comparison of Three Methods of Establishing Cut-Off Scores on Criterion-Referenced Tests," *Journal of Educational Measurement* 20, no. 3 (Autumn 1983): 283–292. Calculating reliability measures also presented problems; see Ronald A. Berk, "A Consumers' Guide to Criterion-Referenced Test Reliability," *Journal of Educational Measurement* 17, no. 4 (Winter 1980): 323–349.

34 The Arizona legislature passed an accountability measure in 1975, but it called for the state's Board of Education to work with local districts in developing specific tests, and the same was true of New Mexico. See Arizona State Department of Education, *Suggested Guidelines for the Development and Implementation of a Continuous Uniform Evaluation System* (Phoenix: Arizona State Department of Education, 1977), ERIC, ED147348, https://files.eric/docview/63823280 /B2EB6BD168644849PQ/4?accountid=14556. Also see Gary D. Estees, Lloyd W. Colvin, and Colleen Goodwin, "A Criterion-Referenced Basic Skills Assessment Program in a Large City School System" (Paper presented at the annual meeting of the American Educational Research Association, San Francisco, April 1976), https://files.eric.ed.gov/fulltext/ED124587.pdf.

35 Turlington was just the second elected commissioner of education in Florida's history, and served for twelve years, making him the state's longest constitutional office-holding elected official in history. For a biographical sketch, see "Ralph

Turlington," Wikipedia, accessed March 15, 2020, https://en.wikipedia.org/wiki /Ralph_Turlington.

36 A useful if sympathetic overview of the Florida accountability program's development can be found in Thomas H. Fisher, "The Florida Competency Testing Program," in Jaeger and Tittle, *Minimum Competency Achievement Testing*, 217–238; also see James C. Impara, "A System of Educational Assessment in the State of Florida" (Paper presented at the annual meeting of the American Educational Research Association, Chicago, April 1972), ERIC, ED063335. On Askew and the push for funding reform in Florida, see Sherman Dorn and Deanna L. Michael, "Education Finance Reform in Florida," and Deanna L. Michael and Sherman Dorn, "Accountability as a Means of Improvement: A Continuity of Themes," in *Education Reform in Florida: Diversity and Equity in Public Policy*, ed. Kathryn M. Borman and Sherman Dorn (Albany: State University of New York Press, 2007), 53–116. SSAT stood for Student Statewide Assessment Test.

37 Thomas H. Fisher, "Florida's Approach to Competency Testing," *Phi Delta Kappan* 59, no. 9 (May 1978): 599.

38 For discussion of the validity study, see Fisher, "Florida Competency Testing Program," 226.

39 On the test chronology, see Florida Department of Education, "A Chronology of Events: 1968–1978," Assessments and Publications Archive, www.fldoe.org /accountability/assessments/k-12-student-assessment/archive/history-fl-statewide -assessment/hsap6878.stml. Also see Princess Palmer, Sande Milton, and Linda Fears, "Florida's Minimum Competency Program: A Survey of Teachers' Opinions," *High School Journal* 66, no. 2 (December 1982–January 1983): 104–105. Quotes are from Glass, "Minimum Competence," 602–604; Fisher, "Florida Competency Testing Program," 225–226. The technical term for the secondary level was SSAT II. For a telling account of the Florida standard setting approach, see National Research Council, *Ability Testing: Uses, Consequences, and Controversies* (Washington, DC: National Academies Press, 1982), 166–168. The quote from the *Miami Herald* can be found on p. 168.

40 Michael Silver, "Half of Black Students Expected to Fail Test," *Sentinel Star*, November 7, 1977.

41 United Press International, "Turlington Sees 'Test Year' as Crucial One for Schools," *Fort Lauderdale News*, September 6, 1977. Turlington also suggested that the basic skills test would improve Florida students' performance on the SAT and other national tests where declines had been registered. On this point, see Associated Press, "Turlington: State Follows Pattern Slide," *Fort Lauderdale News*, August 25, 1977.

42 Michael Silver, "Educators Strive to Make Literacy Test Accepted," *Sentinel Star*, November 13, 1977.

43 United Press International, "Turlington Sees 'Test Year'"; Jeff Golden, "Reporters Find the State's Literacy Tests Aren't That Easy," *Miami Herald*, November 9, 1977; Glass, "Minimum Competence," 603. On compensatory education, see Turlington's September 8, 1978, memorandum regarding funds for remedial education in forty-five counties, Florida State Archives, Department of Public Instruction, Subject Files, S1466, Box 8, Ralph D. Turlington, Statements.

44 Passage rates on the SSAT for a number of years, beginning in 1977, were reported in "State Achievement in Florida: A Comparative Analysis of Minimum

Performance Standards by School District-Region: 1977–1981–1982" (State of Florida Department of Education, 1983). Also, see Ralph D. Turlington to District Superintendents, memorandum, March 11, 1983; and Douglas W. Crawford to District Superintendents, memorandum, update on March 1984 Statewide Assessment, Table: "Percent Passing of Students Taking the Test for the First Time, State Student Assessment Test, Part II, 1977 through 1983" (no page number). Each of these documents can be found in Florida State Archives, Department of Public Instruction, Subject Files, S1466, Box 9 (unorganized). On generally positive media responses in Florida, see Fisher, "Florida Minimum Competency Program," 231–232. On the national press reaction, see "Math a Big Problem for Florida Schools: Failure Rate of 40 to 50 Percent is Reported in Proficiency Tests Given throughout the State," *New York Times*, December 7, 1977; and "Good Pupils Fail Florida Test," *Washington Post*, December 19, 1977. Also see "Florida Flunks," *Time*, December 12, 1977.

45 "Good Pupils Fail Florida Test."

46 Ron Brandt, "Conflicting Views on Competency Testing in Florida," *Educational Leadership* 36, no. 2 (November 1978): 99–106, 102.

47 "Good Pupils Fail Florida Test." On support for the test, see Jane Singer, "State Educators Defend Functional Literacy Tests," *Clearwater Sun*, November 8, 1977. State education officials remained steadfast in the face of charges that the test had been "sprung" on high school students, was culturally biased, and the cut score was arbitrary. "This [test] will lead to greater confidence and support in the public school system," Turlington declared. "We in America have had a lessening of expectations. We can do more in terms of helping children by raising expectations. We can get better results." On Turlington's response to critics, noting improvement in scores, see Ralph D. Turlington, "Good News from Florida: Our Minimum Competency Program Is Working," *Phi Delta Kappan* 60, no. 9 (May 1979): 649–651; and a second article he wrote, "Florida's Testing Program: A Firm Foundation for Improvement," *Phi Delta Kappan* 63, no. 3 (November 1981): 204.

48 Palmer et al., "Florida's Minimum Competency Program," 104–105.

49 Because of legal challenges to the accountability program, the test did not directly affect graduation for Florida students until 1983–1984. On this point see Florida Department of Education, "Monday Report," vol. XV, no. 22 (March 16, 1981): 1.

50 On state graduation rates, see Florida Department of Education, "Historical Summary of Florida's Graduation Rate," updated 2017, http://www.fldoe.org/core/fileparse.php/7584/urlt/GradRateHistorical17.pdf. The rates for years 1976 to 1986 were calculated by dividing the number of graduates each year by the number of first-time freshmen statewide four years earlier. Graduation rates calculated in this manner improved after 1986, when a new test was adopted, and dropped again in 1999 when a cohort method of calculating graduation rates was adopted. On Black and white graduation rates in 1979 and 1980, see Florida Department of Education, "Monday Report," 1.

51 John Y. Sessums, "The Impact of the Florida State Student Assessment Test on Students in Hillsborough County, Florida: Equity vs. Standards of Minimum Competency" (unpublished PhD diss., University of Florida, 1981).

52 Palmer et al., "Florida's Minimum Competency Program," 107. Further discussion of the shortcomings of the testing program, including the problems of poorly prepared students, can be found in Ron Brandt, "Conflicting Views on

Competency Testing in Florida," *Educational Leadership* 36, no. 2 (November 1978): 99–106.

53 These points are summarized in Koretz, *Testing Charade*, ch. 4. Also see Kennon M. Sheldon and Bruce J. Biddle, "Standards, Accountability, and School Reform: Perils and Pitfalls," *Teachers College Record* 100, no. 1 (Fall 1998): 164–180.

54 Political scientists have suggested that racial integration became associated with a threat to educational quality for whites, and exclusionary measures (testing in this case) could be interpreted as correcting. On this point, see Heather McCambly and Quinn Mulroy, "The Rise of (E)quality Politics: The Political Development of Higher Education Policy, 1969–1999" (EdWorkingPaper 22-571, Annenberg Institute at Brown University, May 2022), https://doi.org/10.26300/3zh7-0c82. Also see J. Eric Oliver, *The Paradoxes of Integration: Race, Neighborhood, and Civic Life in Multiethnic America* (Chicago: University of Chicago Press, 2010), ch. 6.

55 On the ITBS and CAT, see Peterson, *Iowa Testing Program*; and Joseph Harris, *What Every Parent Needs to Know about Standardized Tests* (New York: McGraw Hill, 2001), ch. 7. For a picture of state approaches at the time of Florida's first MCT exam, see Chris Pipho, "Minimal Competency Testing: A Look at State Standards," *Educational Leadership*. 34, no. 7 (April 1977): 516–520. On the New York Regents exams, see "History of the Regents Examinations, 1865 to 1987," NYSED, Office of Assessment Policy, Development and Administration, November 24, 1987, https://web.archive.org/web/20120719060813/http://www.p12.nysed.gov/apda/hsgen/archive/rehistory.htm.

56 Califano as quoted in John Fremer, "What Is the National, State, and Local Context for MCT Program Development?" *Researcher* 17 (December 1, 1978): 3. He was especially clear that the federal government could not directly support MCT assessment development. Califano, however, asked the National Academy of Education to convene a panel to study the question, which recommended against the use of MCT exams. See Gene I. Maeroff, "Panel Opposes Testing Students to Gauge Minimum Competency," *New York Times*, March 3, 1978, A11.

57 Brief accounts of each state can be found in Chris Pipho, *State Activity: Minimum Competency Testing* (Denver, CO: Department of Research and Information, Education Commission of the States, February 1, 1980), 1, 2, and 11. On national developments, see Gene I. Maeroff, "Basic Skills Tests Pushed for High School Diploma," *New York Times*, March 14, 1976, 1. Also see Gene I. Maeroff, "Coast Schools Split on Proficiency Tests," *New York Times*, October 2, 1977, 21; and "California's Proficiency Test," *Christian Science Monitor*, October 20, 1980.

58 For an overview of events in North Carolina, see Scott Baker, "Desegregation, Minimum Competency Testing, and the Origins of Accountability: North Carolina and the Nation," *History of Education Quarterly* 55 (February 2015): 33–57; and Scott Baker, Anthony Myers, and Brittany Vasquez, "Desegregation, Accountability, and Equality: North Carolina and the Nation, 1971–2002," *Education Policy Analysis Archives* 22, no. 117 (2014), http://dx.doi.org/10.14507/epaa.v22.1671.

59 On North Carolina, see James J. Gallagher and Ann Ramsbotham, "The Competency Program in North Carolina," *High School Journal* 61, no. 7 (April 1978): 302–312; James J. Gallagher, "Setting Educational Standards for Minimum Competency Testing," in *Minimum Competency Achievement Testing: Motives, Models, Measures and Consequences,* ed. Richard M. Jaeger and Carol K.

Tittle (Berkeley, CA: McCutchen Publishing, 1978), 239–256; Robert C. Serow, James J. Davies, and Barbara M. Parramore, "Performance Gains in a Competency Test Program," *Educational Evaluation and Policy Analysis* 4, no. 4 (Winter 1982): 535–542; Robert C. Serow and James J. Davies, "Resources and Outcomes of Minimum Competency Testing as Measures of Equality of Educational Opportunity," *American Educational Research Journal* 19, no. 4 (Winter 1982): 529–539; and Baker, "Desegregation," 33–57. On Virginia, see James C. Impara, "Virginia's Approach to Minimum Competency Testing," in Jaeger and Tittle, *Minimum Competency Achievement Testing*, 284–308; and A. Graham Down, "Implications of Minimum-Competency Testing for Minority Students" (Paper presented at the annual meeting of the National Council of Measurement in Education, San Francisco, CA, April 11, 1979), ERIC, ED178616, TB01001B. On Maryland, see David Hornbeck, "Maryland's 'Project Basic,'" *Educational Leadership* (November 1977): 98–101; and Office of Project Basic, "Project Basic Instructional Guide, Writing Supplement" (Maryland State Department of Education, Baltimore, MD, January 1984). My interview with Steve Ferrara on April 3, 2020, also was helpful regarding Maryland's testing programs during this period.

60 For an account of state and local MCT programs, see William P. Gorth and Marcy R. Perkins, *A Study of Minimum Competency Programs: Final Comprehensive Report* (Amherst, MA: National Evaluation Systems, 1979), ERIC, ED185123, TM800350. But not all programs were equivalent: in New York, for instance, educators reportedly believed that the tests were too easy, see New York State Education Department, Division of Educational Testing, *A Report to the Board of Regents on the Basic Competency Testing Program* (Albany, NY: NYSED, May 1978). New York also reported a low failure rate on the Regents Competency Exam, Gene I. Maeroff, "Few Are Finding Proficiency Test Bar to Diploma," *New York Times*, August 15, 1983, B1. On controversy in New York and New Jersey see Norman Goldman, "The State and 'Basic Kills' in School," *New York Times*, March 2, 1980, NJ26; and Gene I. Maeroff, "Competency Exams Test Schools as Well as Pupils," *New York Times*, July 2, 1980, E6.

61 See, for example, the discussion in Marshall D. Herron, "Graduation Requirements in the State of Oregon: A Case Study," in Jeager and Tittle, *Minimum Competency Achievement Testing*, 258–283.

62 On tendencies in the South, see Baker et al., "Desegregation."

63 John Robert Warren and Rachael B. Kulick, "Modeling States' Enactment of High School Exit Examination Policies," *Social Forces* 86, no. 1 (September 2007): 215–229. For a comprehensive review of research on this question, which arrives at conclusions similar to Warren and Kulick, see Jennifer Jellison Holme, Meredith P. Richards, Jo Beth Jimerson, and Rebecca W. Cohen, "Assessing the Effects of High School Exit Examinations," *Review of Educational Research* 80, no. 4 (December 2010): 476–526.

64 See the discussion of these themes in Baker, "Desegregation," 33–57. On white racial attitudes affecting southern politics, see Rory McVeigh, David Cunningham, and Justin Farrell, "Political Polarization as a Social Movement Outcome: 1960s Klan Activism and Its Enduring Impact on Political Realignment in Southern Counties, 1960 to 2000," *American Sociological Review* 79, no. 6 (December 2014): 1144–1171; and Doug McAdam and Karina Kloos, *Deeply Divided: Racial Politics and Social Movements in Post-War America* (New York: Oxford University Press, 2014), chs. 3–6. Also see James W. Button, *Blacks and*

Social Change: Impact of the Civil Rights Movement in Southern Communities (Princeton, NJ: Princeton University Press, 1989), chs. 1 and 2. On racial conflict in schools, see John L. Rury and Shirley A. Hill, *The African American Struggle for Secondary Schooling, 1940–1980: Closing the Graduation Gap* (New York: Teachers College Press, 2012), ch. 5.

Southern states frequently worked together in regional coordination efforts. Much of this was conducted through the Southern Regional Education Board, which issued a 1981 report declaring that "the region's immediate challenge is to implement minimum standards across the board" and pursue improvements thereafter. The quote is from Lynn Cornett, *Measuring Educational Progress in the South: Student Achievement* (Atlanta, GA: Southern Regional Education Board, 1984), 1, ERIC, ED246, HE017437.

65　These are also themes in Baker's writing. Of the dozen southern states that had established testing requirements of one sort of another by 1980, two-thirds of them were initiated in legislation, which often contained rather specific language about the objectives and even the content of testing instruments. These circumstances speak to the political orientation of accountability programs in these settings. This was true of the region's four high school graduation testing programs: Florida, North Carolina, Virginia, and Maryland. Outside the South most testing programs were initiated by state boards of education, many of which were also politically motivated but with much closer connections to their professional education communities. It is also worth noting that the initial wave of statewide test-based accountability regimes in the South took root in states with greater urban populations and somewhat higher levels of wealth. Other states in the immediate vicinity, such as Georgia, Alabama, and South Carolina, were more rural and may have faced budgetary constraints, along with somewhat lower commitments to educational reform, and hence may have been reluctant to undertake statewide assessments that could entail significantly higher educational costs. It is noteworthy that bills introduced in their legislatures in the mid-1970s intended to initiate Florida-like reform measures were not successful. All of these trends are quite clear in the detailed legislative record compiled by the Education Commission of the States in 1979, reprinted in *Minimum Competency Testing: A Manual for Legal Services Programs* (Cambridge, MA: Center for Law and Education, 1979). For a review of legal questions concerning MCT, see Merle Steven McClung, "Are Competency Testing Programs Fair? Legal?" *Phi Delta Kappan* 59, no. 6 (February 1978): 397–400.

66　Warren and Kulick, "Modeling States' Enactment," 226–227; Thomas S. Dee and Brian A. Jacob, "Do High School Exit Exams Influence Educational Attainment or Labor Market Performance?" in *Standards-Based Reform and the Poverty Gap: Lessons for No Child Left Behind*, ed. Adam Gamoran (Washington, DC: Brookings University Press, 2007), 154–197; Steven W. Hemelt and Dave E. Marcotte, "High School Exit Exams and Dropout in an Era of Increased Accountability," *Journal of Policy Analysis and Management* 32, no. 2 (Spring 2013): 323–349; and James S. Catterall, "Standards and School Dropouts: A National Study of Tests Required for High School Graduation," *American Journal of Education* 98, no. 1 (November 1989): 1–34. Also see discussion of the larger literature in Holme et al., "Assessing the Effects." On the racial impact of MCT policies in Georgia, see "A Third May Fail Exam for Graduation," *Atlanta Daily World*, April 10, 1981, 1.

67 A brief but useful summary can be found in Charmine J. Girrbach and Richard N. Claus, *Competency Testing: A Review of the Literature* (Lansing: Michigan Department of Evaluation Services, 1982), https://files.eric.ed.gov/fulltext /ED214974.pdf. For a more complete account, see Merle Steven McClung, "Competency Testing Programs: Legal and Educational Issues," *Fordham Law Review* 47, no. 5 (1979): 652–711. For more philosophical and ethical considerations, see Jerrold R. Coombs, "Can Minimum Competency Testing Be Justified?" *High School Journal* 62, no. 4 (January 1979): 175–180; and Allan E. Dittmer, "A Pound of Flesh and More: The Price of Minimum Competencies," *English Journal* 69, no. 9 (December 1980): 34–37.

68 Paul Thurston and Ernest R. House, "The NIE Adversary Hearing on Minimum Competency Testing," *Phi Delta Kappan* 63, no. 2 (October 1981): 87–89. The quote is from Barbara Jordan's introductory remarks, recorded at the "Minimum Competency Testing Clarification Hearing" (National Institute of Education, Washington, DC, July 8–10, 1981), 6, https://files.eric.ed.gov/fulltext/ED215001 .pdf. NIE had planned an evaluation of MCT programs, but arranged the debate instead, as pointed out in David A. Gamson and Laura E. Pirkle-Howd, "Competencies, Inequities, and Contradictions: The Rise of Minimum Competency Testing Movement, 1970s–1980s," a paper presented at the annual meeting of the American Educatioonal Research Association, April 15, 2023.

69 "Minimum Competency Testing Clarification Hearing," 2–10. On Barbara Jordan's role and her view of the utility of the hearing, see "Interview with Barbara Jordan," *Educational Evaluation and Policy Analysis* 3, no. 6 (November–December 1981): 79–82.

70 "Minimum Competency Testing Clarification Hearing," 322.

71 "Minimum Competency Testing Clarification Hearing," 19–21.

72 "Minimum Competency Testing Clarification Hearing," 602.

73 "Minimum Competency Testing Clarification Hearing," 346.

74 "Minimum Competency Testing Clarification Hearing," 604

75 "Minimum Competency Testing Clarification Hearing," 635.

76 George F. Madaus, "NIE Clarification Hearing: The Negative Team's Case," *Phi Delta Kappan* 63, no. 2 (October 1981): 92–94.

77 Madaus, "NIE Clarification Hearing," 93. For a similar argument on declining skills and test scores, also see Gordon Cawelti, "National Competency Testing: A Bogus Solution," *Phi Delta Kappan* 59, no. 9 (May 1978): 619–621.

78 "Minimum Competency Testing Clarification Hearing," 490–491.

79 "Minimum Competency Testing Clarification Hearing," 465

80 See, for instance, "Minimum Competency Testing Clarification Hearing," 501–503.

81 "Minimum Competency Testing Clarification Hearing," 481.

82 "Minimum Competency Testing Clarification Hearing," 494.

83 "Minimum Competency Testing Clarification Hearing," 543.

84 Warren and Kulick, "Modeling States' Enactment," 228.

85 "Minimum Competency Testing Clarification Hearing," 491.

86 "Minimum Competency Testing Clarification Hearing," 843. A survey of viewers who watched the MCT debate found that most favored such testing in the end; reported in Gamson and Pirkle-Howd, "Competencies, Inequities, and Contradictions."

87 See, for instance, Jal Mehta, *The Allure of Order: High Hopes, Dashed Expectations, and the Troubled Quest to Remake American Schooling* (New York: Oxford
University Press, 2013), ch. 1.

88 Susan M. Brookhart, "The Public Understanding of Assessment in Educational
Reform in the United States," *Oxford Review of Education* 39, no. 1 (Febru-
ary 2013): 52–71; Frank Newport, "Americans Strongly Behind Mandatory School
Testing: Public Also Perceives Education as Top Priority," *Oxford Review of
Education* 39, no. 1 (February 2013): 52–71. Also see Alec M. Gallup and Stan-
ley M. Elam, "The 18th Annual Gallup Poll of the Public's Attitudes toward the
Public Schools," *Phi Delta Kappan* 68, no. 1 (September 1986): 43–59.

89 A useful summary of the critique of MCT is Robert L. Linn, George F. Madaus,
and Joseph J. Pedulla, "Minimum Competency Testing: Cautions on the State of
the Art," *American Journal of Education* 91, no. 1 (November 1982): 1–35. Another
helpful summary of these points can be found in Robert L. Ebel, "The Paradox of
Educational Testing," *NCME Measurement in Education* 7, no. 4 (Fall 1976): 1–7.

90 John Robert Warren and Eric Grodsky, "Exit Exams Harm Students Who Fail
Them: And Don't Benefit Students Who Pass Them," *Phi Delta Kappan* 90, no. 9
(May 2009): 645–649, 646. For a somewhat different view, which does not dispute
research on academic outcomes, see Mathew F. Larsen, "High-School Exit Exams
Are Tough on Crime: Fewer Arrests Where Diplomas Require a Test," *Education
Next* 20, no. 3 (Summer 2020), https://www.educationnext.org/high-school-exit
-exams-tough-on-crime-fewer-arrests-diplomas-require-test/.

91 National Research Council, *Ability Testing*, 166.

92 W. James Popham, *The Truth about Testing: An Educators Call to Action* (Alexandria, VA: ASCD, 2010), ch. 1. Also see Koretz, *Testing Charade*, ch. 1; Lorrie A.
Shepard, "A Brief History of Accountability Testing, 1965–2007," in *The Future
of Test-Based Educational Accountability*, ed. Katherine E. Ryan and Lorrie A.
Shepard (New York: Routledge, 2008), 25–46; and Lorraine M. McDonnell, "The
Politics of Educational Accountability: Can the Clock Be Turned Back?" in Ryan
and Shepard, *Future of Test-Based Educational Accountability*, 47–67. It is also
possible that policy makers recognized the limits of testing but decided that an
imperfect reform was better than none at all, and they may have believed that
psychometric problems could eventually be resolved. Lorraine McDonnell
suggested this in my interview with her on September 8, 2020.

93 On the evolution and impact of accountability at the national level, see Jack
Jennings, *Presidents, Congress and the Public Schools: The Politics of Educational
Reform* (Cambridge, MA: Harvard Education Press, 2015), Part II.

Chapter 2   Standardized Testing and Race

1 Edmund W. Gordon and Molidawn D. Terrell, "The Changed Social Context of
Testing," *American Psychologist* 36, no. 10 (October 1981): 1167–1171, 1170.
Dr. Terrell completed the doctoral program in psychology at Yale in 1989,
https://psychology.yale.edu/graduate/history/psychology-dept-phd-graduates.

2 Reports at the time held that African American dissatisfaction with the schools
was growing especially in the North: see A. Graham Down, *Implications of
Minimum-Competency Testing for Minority Students* (Princeton, NJ: ERIC
Clearinghouse on Tests, Measurement, and Evaluation, 1979), 3–4. These issues
are dealt with at length in subsequent chapters. For a brief overview see Jesse H.

Rhodes, introduction to *An Education in Politics: The Origin and Evolution of No Child Left Behind* (Ithaca, NY: Cornell University Press, 2012).

3   A useful contemporaneous overview of these issues is Ashley Montagu, ed., introduction to *Race and IQ* (New York: Oxford University Press, 1975).

4   On this question, see Cecil Reynolds, "Bias in Mental Testing," in *Perspectives on Bias in Mental Testing* (New York: Springer, 1984), 1–39. Also see, for example, Ross Gelbspan, "Standardized Testing Falling Victim to Suits, Charges of Discrimination," *Boston Globe*, October 22, 1985, 100.

5   On this phenomenon, see Michael Inzlicht and Toni Schmader, eds., introduction to *Stereotype Threat: Theory, Process, and Application* (New York: Oxford University Press, 2012).

6   On the contemporaneous controversy that the book produced, see Steven Fraser, ed., *The Bell Curve Wars: Race, Intelligence and the Future of America* (New York: Basic Books, 1995). For policy implications discussed at the time, see Claude S. Fischer, Michael Hout, Martín Sánchez Jankowski, Samuel R. Lucas, Ann Swidler, and Kim Voss, *Inequality by Design: Cracking the Bell Curve Myth* (Princeton, NJ: Princeton University Press, 1996), chs. 6 and 7.

7   Test Prep Project, NAACP Papers, Library of Congress, Part VII, Box VII, 80. A capsule history of developments prior to the project was provided, with the quote regarding the 1974 convention on p. 3.

8   NAACP Invitational Conference on Minority Testing, 1975, NAACP Papers, Library of Congress, Part VIII, Box VIII, 349, passim. As noted in chapter 1, the Association of Black Psychologists also called for a moratorium, as did the National Education Association with respect to accountability programs in 1971. Also see materials on the conference in the Edmund W. Gordon Archives, 1933–2010, University of Texas, Benson Latin American Collection, Texas Archival Resources, Box 51, Folder 1 "NAACP Conference on Minority Testing." For coverage of the meeting, see "NAACP Holds Meet on Testing," *Chicago Defender*, October 6, 1975, 8; and Peter Keepnews, "NAACP Urges Moratorium on 'Biased' Tests," *New York Post*, May 17, 1976.

9   "NAACP-Minority Testing, 1975–76," Conference Final Report, NAACP Papers, Library of Congress, Part VIII, Box VIII, "Conveners Introduction," 1.

10 "NAACP-Minority Testing, 1975–76," 1 and 2.

11 See, for instance, Evan Jenkins, "Heredity Backer Scored in Debate on Intelligence," *New York Times*, June 1, 1973, 38; Robert Reinhold, "Shockley Debates Montagu as Innis Angrily Pulls Out: Tests Called Biased," *New York Times*, December 5, 1973, 38.

12 NAACP Invitational Conference on Minority Testing, 1975, 349, Task force memberships and listed on pp. 8 through 13 (unnumbered), followed by their draft reports.

13 NAACP Invitational Conference on Minority Testing, 1975, prologue and charge.

14 "NAACP-Minority Testing, 1975–76"; Buel Gallagher, "Introduction," Conference Final Report, May 17, 1976, i. Dr. Gallagher was then president emeritus of the City College of New York, and vice chairman, emeritus, of the NAACP Board. The question of cultural bias underlay many grievances listed in conference resolutions, particularly those concerning school-aged children. But it was difficult to make the same charge about tests used for graduate and professional school admission, or for teachers. These were college graduates and presumably possessed the skills and knowledge that other graduates taking the tests had

acquired. But this did not mean that the potential for discrimination did not exist. Too often, the NAACP report suggested, such exams were employed in an exclusionary manner, rather than simply determining whether applicants possessed the skills and knowledge for success in a program of education or a profession. If such assessments had predictive validity, after all, applicants who scored high enough to succeed should not have been excluded simply because their scores were lower than others. The same principle applied to the SAT, ACT, and other assessments used to compare applicants to colleges and universities. In this context, the report also recommended that such examinations be focused on predicting the probability of success, and not principally as a means of exclusion. The use of assessments in this fashion was likely to result in discrimination against African American and other minority candidates (and often women too), largely because of historical inequities in education, income, wealth, and other factors. Conferees demanded that the testing industry take steps to mitigate the unfairly exclusionary quality of many such gateway assessments.

15 NAACP Invitational Conference on Minority Testing, 1975, conference notes, 3.
16 NAACP Invitational Conference on Minority Testing, 1975, conference notes, 3.
17 NAACP Invitational Conference on Minority Testing, 1975, conference notes, 9.
18 NAACP Invitational Conference on Minority Testing, 1975, conference notes, 10.
19 NAACP Invitational Conference on Minority Testing, 1975, conference notes, 7.
20 NAACP Invitational Conference on Minority Testing, 1975, Conference Final Report, 26–27 and 30.
21 See, for instance, Patricia McCormick, "NAACP, Others Challenging Standardized Tests: They Can Unfairly Wipe Out Job, School Opportunities," *Baltimore Afro-American* (1893–1988), September 13, 1980, 6.
22 On the salience and persistence of these issues, see Nancy S. Cole, "History and Development of DIF," in *Differential Item Functioning*, ed. Paul W. Holland and Howard Wainer (Hillside, NJ: Lawrence Erlbaum Associates, 1993), 25–29.
23 On this point, see Russell T. Warne, Yoon Myeongsun, and Chris J. Price, "Exploring the Various Interpretations of 'Test Bias,'" *Cultural Diversity and Ethnic Minority Psychology* 20, no. 4 (October 2014): 570–582; as the authors note on p. 571, "According to the standards set by the American Educational Research Association (AERA), the American Psychological Association (APA), and the National Council on Measurement in Education (NCME), test bias . . . is said to arise when deficiencies in a test itself or the manner in which it is used result in different meanings for scores earned by members of different identifiable subgroups," in American Educational Research Association, American Psychological Association, & National Council on Measurement in Education, *Standards for Educational and Psychological Testing* (Washington, DC: American Educational Research Association, 1999, p. 74). Also see Kurt F. Gessinger, "The History of Bias in Assessment in Educational and Psychological Testing," in *Fairness in Educational and Psychological Testing: Examining Theoretical, Research, Practice and Policy Implications of the 2014 Standards*, ed. Jessica L. Johnson and Kurt F. Geisinger (Washington, DC: American Educational Research Association, 2022), 13–31. On test prep programs, see "NAACP Test Preparation Program Shows Success," *Baltimore Afro-American*, July 28, 1984, 7. For historical perspective on these questions, see Nancy S. Cole and Michael J. Zieky, "The New Faces of Fairness," *Journal of Educational Measurement* 38, no. 4 (Winter 2001): 369–382.

24 For a contemporaneous discussion of this, see Jane R. Mercer, "Test 'Validity,' 'Bias,' and 'Fairness': An Analysis from the Perspective of the Sociology of Knowledge," *Interchange* 9, no. 1 (1978): 1–16.

25 Robert Reinhold, "Standardized Tests Defended by Panel: Study Reports No Built-In Bias but Warns of Overreliance," *New York Times*, February 3, 1982, A1; Muriel Cohen, "Study Says There Is No Systematic Antiminority Bias in Standardized Tests," *Boston Globe*, February 3, 1982, 1. On related questions, also see Robert L. Linn, "Selection Bias: Multiple Meanings," *Journal of Educational Measurement* 21, no. 1 (Spring 1984): 33–47.

26 Arthur Jensen, *Bias in Mental Testing* (New York: Free Press, 1980). This 786-page book provided a wealth of data to support the claim that bias of the sort popularly linked to racial differences in test scores probably played a small role in such variation. But as Lorrie Shepard pointed out, "bias in the tests cannot explain away the observed difference between blacks and whites. But the evidence reviewed here does not support the conclusion that there is absolutely no bias nor the dismissing of the bias issue as a worthy scientific question." See her article, "The Case for Bias in Tests of Achievement and Scholastic Aptitude," in *Arthur Jensen: Consensus and Controversy*, ed. Sohan Modgil and Celia Modgil (New York: Falmer Press, 1987), 189. Edmund W. Gordon and Tresmaine J. Rubain, "Bias and Alternatives in Psychological Testing," *Journal of Negro Education* 49, no. 3 (Summer 1980): 350–360, 352. The article explored various arguments regarding these questions in considerable depth, including attempts to create "Culture free tests," and addressed criterion-based tests as well. In the end it repeated Gordon's point cited earlier that "The purposive bias in mental testing which has favored quantification and sorting has almost precluded attention to the diagnostic and prescriptive functions of testing" (p. 353).

27 Gordon and Rubain, "Bias and Alternatives," 358. For a statement regarding the need for greater flexibility both in instructional approaches and assessment, see Edmund W. Gordon, "Toward an Equitable System of Educational Assessment," *Journal of Negro Education* 64, no. 3 (Summer 1995): 360–372.

28 William Angoff, "A Technique for the Investigation of Cultural Differences" (Paper presented at American Psychological Association Meeting, Honolulu, Hawaii, September 1972). Specifically, Angoff noted that "although the technique is not intended as a measure of item or test bias, it is useful in diagnosing cultural differences and comparing different types of groups" (from the abstract).

29 For an overview of this process, see William H. Angoff, "Perspectives on Differential Item Functioning Methodology," in Holland and Wainer, *Differential Item Functioning*, 3–23.

30 See, for instance, Ronald L. Flaugher, "Patterns of Test Performance by High School Students of Four Ethnic Identities," *ETS Research Bulletin 71-25* (June 1971); Donald M. Medley and Thomas J. Quirk, "Race and Subject Matter Influences on Performance on General Education Items of the National Teacher Examination," *ETS Research Bulletin 72-43* (1972); Ronald L. Flaugher, "Minority versus Majority Group Performance on an Aptitude Test Battery," *Project Access Research Report #3* (Princeton, NJ: Educational Testing Service, 1972); Joel T. Campbell and Leon H. Belcher, "Word Associations of Students at Predominantly White and Predominantly Black Institutions," *ETS Research Bulletin 75-29* (1975); Jonathan R. Warren, "Prediction of College Achievement among Mexican American Students in California," *ETS Research Bulletin 76-12* (1976).

For a critique of methods at that time, see Nancy S. Petersen and Melvin R. Novick, "An Evaluation of Some Models for Culture-Fair Selection," *Journal of Educational Measurement* 13, no. 1 (Spring 1976): 3–29.

31 These events are described in the ETS publication, *Building Equity since 1947: 1996 Annual Report* (Princeton, NJ: Educational Testing Service, 1996).

32 ETS, *Building Equity*.

33 The latter point refers to the Golden Rule Settlement, resulting from a lawsuit in Illinois regarding an insurance licensing exam that allegedly discriminated against Black students. On this point, see Robert L. Linn and Fritz Drasgow, "Implications of the Golden Rule Settlement for Test Construction," *Educational Measurement: Issues and Practice* 6, no. 2 (Summer 1987): 13–17.

34 Lorrie Shepard, Gregory Camilli, and Marilyn Averill, "Comparison of Procedures for Detecting Test-Item Bias with Both Internal and External Ability Criteria," *Journal of Educational Statistics* 6, no. 4 (Winter 1981): 317–375, 369. For further developments in this era, see Lorrie A. Shepard, Gregory Camilli, and David M. Williams, "Validity of Approximation Techniques for Detecting Item Bias," *Journal of Educational Measurement* 22, no. 2 (Summer 1985): 77–105; and Gregory Camilli and Lorrie A. Shepard, *Methods for Identifying Biased Test Items* (Thousand Oaks, CA: Sage, 1994). The Camilli and Shepard publications deal primarily with statistical procedures for calculating DIF measures, although there is discussion of "Judgmental Methods and Sensitivity Review" as well.

35 ETS, *Building Equity*. Also see Paul W. Holland and Dan Robinson, "Interview: Paul W. Holland," *Journal of Educational and Behavioral Statistics* 30, no. 3 (Autumn 2005): 348. Holland noted that he advocated for the "Mantel–Haenszel common odds-ratio measure, which was widely used in biometrics," but thought of his contribution to DIF "as being an advocate for responsible methods and for using the best that were available at the time rather than 'solving' the problem forever."

36 Paul W. Holland and Dorothy T. Thayer, "Differential Item Functioning and the Mantel–Haenszel Procedure," *ETS Research Report Series* (December 1986), doi .org/10.1002/j.2330-8516.1986.tb00186.x. Also see John R. Donoghue, Paul W. Holland, and Dorothy Thayer, "A Monte Carlo Study of Factors That Affect the Mantel–Haenszel and Standardized Measures of Differential Item Functioning," in Holland and Wainer, *Differential Item Functioning*, 137.

37 On developments in a major private test producer, CBT/McGraw Hill, see Donald Ross Green, "Racial and Ethnic Bias in Achievement Tests and What to Do About It" (unpublished report, 1973), https://eric.ed.gov/?id=ED084285. Also see the later report by the same author, "Procedures Used for Reducing Bias at CBT/McGraw Hill, 1966–1980" (unpublished report available in NAACP Papers, Library of Congress, Part V, Box V, 2070, "Testing and Tracking Report and Recommendations").

38 On variability in review panel judgment, see Barbara S. Plake, "A Comparison of a Statistical and Subjective Procedure to Ascertain Item Validity: One Step in the Test Validation Process," *Educational and Psychological Measurement* 40, no. 2 (1980): 397–404; and Jonathan Sandoval and Mary W. Mille, "Accuracy of Judgments of WISC-R Item Difficulty for Minority Groups," *Journal of Consulting and Clinical Psychology* 48, no. 2 (April 1980): 249–253. Research on these questions is summarized in Camilli and Shepard, *Methods for Identifying*, 135–138.

39 Lorrie. A. Shepard, "Definitions of Bias" (Paper presented at the John Hopkins University National Symposium on Educational Research, Washington, DC, November 7, 1980), 15–16, as cited in Stafford Hood and Laurence J. Parker, "Minority Bias Review Panels and Teacher Testing for Initial Certification: A Comparison of Two States' Efforts," *Journal of Negro Education* 58, no. 4 (Autumn 1989): 511–519.

40 W. James Popham, interview by author, April 6, 2020; John Poggio, interview by author, May 4, 2020. For an example of research about responses to "cultural content" on standardized exams, see Cynthia B. Schmeiser and Richard L. Ferguson, "Performance of Black and White Students on Test Materials Containing Content Based on Black and White Cultures," *Journal of Educational Measurement* 15, no. 3 (Autumn 1978): 193–200. Also see James J. Diamond, James Ayrer, Roger Fishman, and Paul Green, "Are Inner City Children Test-Wise?" *Journal of Educational Measurement* 14, no. 1 (Spring 1977): 39–45.

41 Patrícia Martinková, Adéla Drabinová, Yuan-Ling Liaw, Elizabeth A. Sanders, Jenny L. McFarland, and Rebecca M. Price, "Checking Equity: Why Differential Item Functioning Analysis Should Be a Routine Part of Developing Conceptual Assessments," *Life Sciences Education* 16, no. 2 (Summer 2017), https://www.ncbi.nlm.nih.gov/pmc/articles/PMC5459266/. Also see Rebecca Zwick, *A Review of ETS Differential Item Functioning Assessment Procedures: Flagging Rules, Minimum Sample Size Requirements, and Criterion Refinement* (ETS Research Report, 2012), doi.org/10.1002/j.2333-8504.2012.tb02290.x; and Rebecca Zwick and Kadriye Ercikan, "Analysis of Differential Item Functioning in the NAEP History Assessment," *Journal of Educational Measurement* 26, no. 1 (Spring 1989): 55–66. On recent debates over the power and limitations of DIF in college admission testing, see Maria V. Santelice and Mark Wilson, "Unfair Treatment? The Case of Freedle, the SAT, and the Standardization Approach to Differential Item Functioning," *Harvard Educational Review* 80, no. 1 (Spring 2010): 106–133.

42 The national office of the NAACP was asked to join the case but declined due to concerns that Justice Marshall would have to recuse himself if it went to the Supreme Court. On this point, see Nathaniel R. Jones to Earl T. Shinhoster Esq., Regional Director of Bay Area Legal Services, Inc., Tampa, Florida, January 17, 1979, NAACP General Counsel, NAACP Papers, Library of Congress, Part V, Box 394, "Debra P. v. Turlington."

43 For a detailed account of both cases in this discussion, see Benjamin Michael Superfine, *The Courts and Standards-Based Educational Reform* (New York: Oxford University Press, 2008), 71–82. My account relies heavily on the case summary provided in Debra P. v. Turlington, 564 F.Supp. 177 (1983), 11 Ed. Law Rep. 893, 13 Fed. R. Evid. Serv. 1041, written by George C. Carr, federal district judge.

44 This account relies on the case summary, GI Forum v. Texas Education Agency, Civil Action No. SA-97-CA-1278-EP (W.D. Tex., 2000), Edward C. Prado, district judge presiding.

45 On North Carolina, see Scott Baker, "Desegregation, Minimum Competency Testing, and the Origins of Accountability: North Carolina and the Nation," *History of Education Quarterly* 55, no. 1 (February 2015): 49. On the Georgia case see Thomas J. Flygare, "De Jure: Graduation Competency Testing Fails in Georgia," *Phi Delta Kappan* 63, no. 2 (October 1981): 134–135; and Anderson v.

Banks, 540 F.Supp. 761 (S.D. Ga. 1982). For discussion of these cases and their differences, see Martha M. McCarthy, "Minimum Competency Testing for Students: Educational and Legal Issues," *Educational Horizons* 61, no. 3 (Spring 1983): 103–110.

46 "Exit Exam to Be Revamped in La.," *Philadelphia Tribune*, November 1, 1994, 20F. Also, Rankins v. State Board of Elementary and Secondary Education, 637 So. 2d 548 (La. Ct. App. 1994), https://www.leagle.com/decision /19941185637s02d5481883.

47 Sandlin v. Johnson, 643 F.2d 1027 (4th Cir. 1981), decided March 11, 1981; Bester v. Tuscaloosa City Bd. of Educ, 722 F.2d 1514 (11th Cir. 1984), decided January 16, 1984; Erik v. ex rel. Catherine V. Causby, 977 F.Supp. 384 (E.D.N.C. 1997), decided August 28, 1997.

48 On these points and others, see Steven Schreiber, "High School Exit Tests and the Constitution: *Debra P. v. Turlington*," *Ohio State Law Journal* 41, no. 4 (1980): 1113–1142.

49 Superfine, *Courts*, 71–76.

50 The quote is from *Debra P.*, 564 F.Supp. 177, 12. Carr dismissed charges of bias in test questions, arguing that because items had been vetted professionally they could not account for the racial disparities in scores.

51 *Debra P.*, 564 F.Supp. 177, 4. Turlington's cover letter and instructions to district personnel regarding the IOX study can be found in Florida State Archives, Department of Public Instruction, Subject Files, S1466, Box (unorganized), and is dated September 14, 1982.

52 *Debra P.*, 564 F.Supp. 177, 5.

53 *Debra P.*, 564 F.Supp. 177, 5 and 6. In a rather lengthy review of the Florida case in a chapter on competency testing, Richard Jaeger largely agreed with Linn and Calfee, challenging the idea of curricular validity as a criterion for judging the validity of an instrument such as the Florida MCT. See Richard Jaeger, "Certification of Student Competence," in *Educational Measurement*, ed. Robert L. Linn, 3rd ed. (New York: Macmillan, 1989), 502–509.

54 *Debra P.*, 564 F.Supp. 177, 11. Plaintiff's attorneys argued that ongoing racial discrimination affected the extent and quality of instruction that African American students received, but the court ruled that such testimony was not conclusive, nor within the jurisdiction of the court to address. Also see Associated Press, "Court Rules Florida Can Deny Diplomas: To Those Failing High School Literacy Test," *Boston Globe*, May 5, 1983, 1. Diana Pullin later wrote that "the courts in Florida ultimately deferred in 1984 to the testimony of an expert in curriculum and instruction rather than relying on testing experts," suggesting that James Popham was somewhat less qualified to serve as an expert in the case than Linn or Calfee. See Diana C. Pullin, "Do Standards Promote Fairness and Legitimacy in the Changing Marketplace for Testing?" in Jonson and Geisinger, *Fairness*, 67.

55 The district court opinion in *Debra P. v. Turlington* was challenged and upheld upon appeal. See Debra P. by Irene P. v. Turlington, 730 F.2d 1405 (11th Cir. 1984), decided April 27, 1984, R. Lanier Anderson III, circuit judge.

56 See the discussion of the case by Popham and Diana Pullin: W. James Popham and Elaine Lindheim, "Implications of a Landmark Ruling on Florida's Minimum Competency Test," *Phi Delta Kappan* 63, no. 1 (September 1981): 18–20; and Diana Pullin, "Minimum Competency Testing and the Demand for

Accountability," *Phi Delta Kappan* 63, no. 1 (September 1981): 20–22. Both emphasize the significance of content validity for such tests, especially Popham and Lindheim.

57 GI Forum v. Texas Education Agency, Civil Action No. SA-97-CA-1278-EP, 1 and 2.

58 On this point see Cynthia A. Ward, "*GI Forum v. Texas Education Agency*: Implications for State Assessment Programs," *Applied Measurement in Education* 13, no. 4 (2000): 419–426; and William D. Schafer, "*GI Forum v. Texas Education Agency*: Observations for States," *Applied Measurement in Education* 13, no. 4 (2000): 411–418.

59 Regarding these and other measurement issues in the case, see S. E. Phillips, "GI Forum v. Texas Education Agency: Psychometric Evidence," *Applied Measurement in Education* 13, no. 4 (2000): 343–385.

60 *GI Forum*, Civil Action No. SA-97-CA-1278-EP, 6 and 7.

61 For an elaboration of his findings, see Walt Haney, "The Myth of the Texas Miracle in Education," *Education Policy Analysis Archives* 8, no. 1 (2000), https://epaa.asu.edu/ojs/article/view/432/828. Haney's discussion dealt with a variety of issues, including the validity of the TAAS exam, the conditions under which it was administered, and dropout rates in Texas high schools following introduction of the TAAS assessment. For the 2003 investigation, see Michael Dobbs, "Education 'Miracle' Has a Math Problem: Bush Critics Cite Disputed Houston Data," *Washington Post*, November 8, 2003, A1. For a critical account of Haney's account of dropout rates, see Laurence A. Toenjes and A. Gary Dworkin, "Are Increasing Test Scores in Texas Really a Myth, or Is Haney's Myth a Myth?" *Education Policy Analysis Archives* 10, no. 17 (2002), https://epaa.asu.edu/ojs/article/viewFile/296/422.

62 *GI Forum* Civil Action No. SA-97-CA-1278-EP, 11 and 12.

63 *GI Forum* Civil Action No. SA-97-CA-1278-EP, 13.

64 Superfine, *Courts*, 82–86. For discussion of a somewhat parallel case in California, see Arturo J. Gonzalez and Johanna Hartwig, "Diploma Denial Meets Remedy Denial in California: Tackling the Issue of Remedies in Exit Exam Litigation after the Vacated *Valenzuela v. O'Connell* Preliminary Injunction," *Santa Clara Law Review* 47, no. 4 (2007): 711–753. On the positive reputation Texas acquired for testing, see Robert Digitale, "Testing Ground: Local Schools May Have Lessons to Learn from Texas," *Press Democrat; Santa Rosa, Calif.* April 25, 1999, A1.

65 For an introduction to the concept, see Claude M. Steele, *Whistling Vivaldi: How Stereotypes Affect Us and What We Can Do* (New York: W. W. Norton, 2010), chs. 1, 2, 5, 6, and 7. Also see Inzlicht and Schmader, *Stereotype Threat*, introduction and pt. 1; and Ryan P. Brown and Eric Anthony Day, "The Difference Isn't Black and White: Stereotype Threat and the Race Gap on Raven's Advanced Progressive Matrices," *Journal of Applied Psychology* 91, no. 4 (2006): 979–985; and Paul R. Sackett, Chaitra M. Hardison, and Michael J. Cullen, "On Interpreting Stereotype Threat as Accounting for African American–White Differences on Cognitive Tests," *American Psychologist* 59, no. 1 (January 2004): 7–13.

66 Claude M. Steele, "A Threat in the Air: How Stereotypes Shape Intellectual Identity and Performance," *American Psychologist* 52, no. 6 (June 1997): 613–629.

67 Charlotte R. Pennington, Derek Heim, Andrew R. Levy, and Derek T. Larkin, "Twenty Years of Stereotype Threat Research: A Review of Psychological Mediators," *PLoS ONE* 11, no. 1 (2016), doi:10.1371/journal.pone.0146487;

Steven J. Spencer, Christine Logel, and Paul G. Davies, "Stereotype Threat," *Annual Review of Psychology* 67 (2015): 415–437. On gender effects, see Colleen M. Ganley, Leigh A. Mingle, Allison M. Ryan, Katherine Ryan, Marina Vasilyeva, and Michelle Perry, "An Examination of Stereotype Threat Effects on Girls' Mathematics Performance," *Developmental Psychology* 49, no. 10 (2013): 1886–1897; and Gilbert Stoet and David Geary, "Can Stereotype Threat Explain the Gender Gap in Mathematics Performance and Achievement?" *Review of General Psychology* 16, no. 1 (2012): 93–102, which suggests these effects are hardly universal.

68 Markus Appel and Nicole Kronberger, "Stereotypes and the Achievement Gap: Stereotype Threat Prior to Test Taking," *Educational Psychology Review* 24, no. 44 (December 2012): 609–635.

69 On potential impact see Geoffrey D. Borman and Jaymes Pyne, "What If Coleman Had Known about Stereotype Threat? How Social-Psychological Theory Can Help Mitigate Educational Inequality," *RSF: The Russell Sage Foundation Journal of the Social Sciences* 2, no. 5 (September 2016): 164–185. Despite the sizable literature on this concept it continues to be somewhat controversial. See, for instance, Michael Inzlicht, Sonia K. Kang, and Alexa M. Tullett, "Lingering Effects: Stereotype Threat Hurts More Than You Think," *Social Issues and Policy Review* 5, no. 1 (December 2011): 227–256; J. Aronson and M. Inzlicht, "The Ups and Downs of Attributional Ambiguity: Stereotype Vulnerability and the Academic Self-Knowledge of African-American Students," *Psychological Science* 15 (2004): 829–836. Oren R. Shewach, Paul R. Sackett, and Sander Quint, "Stereotype Threat Effects in Settings with Features Likely versus Unlikely in Operational Test Settings: A Meta-Analysis," *Journal of Applied Psychology* 104, no. 12 (2019): 1514–1534.

70 "Stereotype Threat Widens Achievement Gap: Reminders of Stereotyped Inferiority Hurt Test Scores. What the Research Shows," American Psychological Association, July 15, 2006, https://hcpss.instructure.com/courses/29219/files /22811856/download?verifier=jjRVcA1DHCrjubKwEvGIUYS5xlHz9UoCWsdL EWi6&wrap=1.

71 Regarding this, see Shewach et al., "Stereotype Threat." Also see Maya A. Beasley and Mary J. Fischer, "Why They Leave: The Impact of Stereotype Threat on the Attrition of Women and Minorities from Science, Math and Engineering Majors," *Social Psychology of Education* 15 (2012): 427–448. On addressing its effects, see Catherine Good, Joshua Aronson, and Michael Inzlicht, "Improving Adolescents' Standardized Test Performance: An Intervention to Reduce the Effects of Stereotype Threat," *Applied Developmental Psychology* 24 (2003): 645–662.

72 On trends in the racial achievement gap nationally, see Paul E. Barton and Richard J. Cooley, *The Black–White Achievement Gap: When Progress Stopped* (Princeton, NJ: Policy Information Center, Educational Testing Service, 2010), 3–8. On developments in the states, see Nancy Kober, Victor Chudowsky, and Naomi Chudowsky, "Slow and Uneven Progress in Narrowing Achievement Gaps on State Tests," in *Narrowing the Achievement Gap: Perspectives and Strategies for Challenging Times*, ed. Thomas B. Timor (Cambridge, MA: Harvard Education Press, 2012), 11–33. Also see Derrick Darby and John Rury, *The Color of Mind: Why the Origins of the Achievement Gap Matter for Justice* (Chicago: University of Chicago Press, 2018), ch. 1. On the question of racial score differences on tests of

cognitive ability, see Janet E. Helms, "Why Is There No Study of Cultural Equivalence in Standardized Cognitive Ability Testing?" *American Psychologist* 47, no. 9 (Summer 1992): 1083–1101.

73 See, for instance, Ronald Sullivan, "State's Pupil Tests Show a Black-Urban Lag," *New York Times*, May 25, 1974, 63; Mary Jordan, "Fear of Racist Label Kept Scores Quiet, Official Says: Alexandria Test Gap Known for Years," *Washington Post*, August 21, 1985, C1; and Tom Vesey, "Community Help Asked for Youths: NAACP Cites Concern Over Black Students," *Washington Post*, December 17, 1987, M1. These incidents apparently both led to discussion of how to close the gaps, a portent of things to come. Also see Robert Hanley, "New Jersey Schools: Rich, Poor, Unequal," *New York Times*, March 5, 1990, B1.

74 Richard J. Herrnstein and Charles Murray, *The Bell Curve: Intelligence and Class Structure in American Life* (New York: Free Press, 1994); for critical responses see Fischer et al., *Inequality by Design*; Arthur S. Goldberger and Charles F. Manski, "Review Article: The Bell Curve by Herrnstein and Murray," *Journal of Economic Literature* 36, no. 2 (June 1995): 762–776; James J. Heckman, "Lessons from the Bell Curve," *Journal of Political Economy* 103, no. 5 (1995): 1091–1120; and John L. Rury, "IQ Redux," *History of Education Quarterly* 35, no. 4 (December 1995): 423–438. Regarding the book's popular reception, on Amazon's website in 2020, 90 percent of 723 readers rated the book with four (11 percent) or five (79 percent) stars. This, of course, contrasted dramatically with its academic reception, even if it undoubtedly reflected the responses of many people predisposed to favor the book, as suggested by a decision to purchase it to begin with.

75 Christopher Jencks and Meredith Phillips, *The Black-White Test Score Gap* (Washington, DC: Brookings Institution Press, 1998). Contributors dealt with issues such as bias in testing (without mentioning DIF), possible genetic influences, family background factors, the historic narrowing of the gap, and the impact of schools on it in various ways, among other issues. In many respects they anticipated—or influenced—subsequent inquiry, and ways to think positively about how persistent gaps might be addressed.

76 In a search for "achievement gap" or "test score gap" in the *New York Times* ProQuest database, only 14 out of 427 articles containing these terms appeared before 1994. Similarly, on JSTOR less than 8 percent of 4,874 articles containing them appeared earlier than 1996. Both figures suggest that it was after the mid-1990s that these questions assumed their contemporary significance.

At about the same time, a conference sponsored by the Ford Foundation in Washington, DC, called attention to bias in testing, along with other issues, calling for creation of "an independent commission to make sure that national student tests are free of sexual, racial and cultural bias," without specifically mentioning the achievement gap; see William Celis, "Educators Seek Panel to Keep Tests Bias-Free," *New York Times*, March 14, 1993, 32.

77 A comprehensive overview of these factors, with pertinent references, can be found in Paul E. Barton and Richard J. Coley, *Parsing the Achievement Gap II* (Princeton, NJ: Policy Information Center, Educational Testing Service, 2009), 18–30. Also see Richard L. Kohr, James R. Masters, J. Robert Coldiron, Ross S. Blust, and Eugene W. Skiffington, "The Relationship of Race, Class, and Gender with Mathematics Achievement for Fifth-Eighth, and Eleventh-Grade Students in Pennsylvania Schools," *Peabody Journal of Education* 66, no. 2 (Winter, 1989): 147–171. On declining academic performance of inner-city schools, see Jay

Mathews, "Tests at Minority Schools Show a Ten Year Decline: Report Kindles Debate on Standards," *Washington Post*, November 4, 1987, A14.

78 These points are summarized in Barton and Cooley, *Black–White Achievement Gap*, 18–34. Also see Patrick Sharkey, *Neighborhoods and the Black–White Mobility Gap* (Pew Memorial Trusts, July 2009, pt. I), and Ezekiel J. Dixon-Roman, Howard T. Everson, and John J. McArdle, "Race, Poverty and SAT Scores: Modeling the Influences of Family Income on Black and White High School Students' SAT Performance," *Teachers College Record* 115 (April 2013), https://eric.ed.gov/?id=EJ1018120. Also see "Why Family Income Differences Don't Explain the Racial Gap in SAT Scores," *Journal of Blacks in Higher Education*, no. 62 (Winter 2008/2009): 10–12. On American Indians, see Dean Chavers and Patricia Locke, *The Effects of Testing on Native Americans* (Boston: National Commission on Testing and Public Policy, 1989), ERIC, ED336445, UD028174. See Mark Berends and Daniel Koretz, *Reporting Minority Students' Test Scores: How Well Can the NAEP Account for Differences in Social Context?* (Washington, DC: National Center for Education Statistics, 1996), for discussion of the need for contextual data to address factors affecting minority student test performance.

79 Dixon-Roman et al., "Race, Poverty and SAT Scores"; Jesse Rothstein and Nathan Wozny, "Permanent Income and the Black–White Test Score Gap," *Journal of Human Resources* 53, no. 4 (October 2018): 891–917. Also see "Why Family Income Differences," 10–12; and "The Black–White Scoring Gap on SAT II Achievement Tests: Some of the News Is Cheering," *Journal of Blacks in Higher Education*, no. 38 (Winter 2002–2003): 61–63. The Gordon quote is from his brief newsletter article, "Affirmative Development of Academic Abilities," *Inquiry and Praxis*, no. 2 (September 2001): 4.

80 Claire Smrekar, James Guthrie, Debra F. Owens, and Pearl G. Sims, *March toward Excellence: School Success and Minority Student Achievement in Department of Defense Schools* (Washington, DC: National Education Goals Panel, National Institute on Early Childhood Development and Education, 2001), 20 passim.

81 See, for instance, Edmund W. Gordon and Constance Yowell, *Educational Reforms for Students at Risk: Cultural Dissonance as a Risk Factor in the Development of Students* (Washington, DC: Office of Educational Research and Improvement, 1992), ERIC, ED366696, UD029720.

82 Signithia Fordham and John Ogbu, "Black Students' School Success: Coping with the 'Burden of "Acting White,"'" *Urban Review* 18 (1986): 176–206; Eric McNamara Horvat and Kristine Lewis, "Reassessing the 'Burden of Acting White': The Importance of Peer Groups in Managing Academic Success," *Sociology of Education* 76, no. 4 (2003): 265–280, http://www.jstor.org/stable/1519866; Karolyn Tyson, William Darity Jr., and Domini R. Castellino, "It's Not 'A Black Thing': Understanding the Burden of Acting White and Other Dilemmas of High Achievement," *American Sociological Review* 70, no. 4 (2005): 582–605, https://doi.org/10.1177/000312240507000403.

83 Amanda Lewis and John B. Diamond, *Despite the Best Intentions: How Racial Inequality Thrives in Good Schools* (New York: Oxford University Press, 2015), ch. 1; Karolyn Tyson, *Integration Interrupted: Tracking, Black Students and Acting White after Brown* (New York: Oxford University Press, 2011); Maika Watanabe, "Tracking in the Era of High Stakes State Accountability Reform: Case Studies of Classroom Instruction in North Carolina," *Teachers College Record* 110, no. 3

(2008): 489–534; Roslyn Arlin Mickelson and Bobbie J. Everett, "Neotracking in North Carolina: How High School Courses of Study Reproduce Race and Class-Based Stratification," *Teachers College Record* 110, no. 3 (2008): 535–570. On discipline see Russell J. Skiba, Robert S. Michael, Abra Carroll Nardo, and Reece L. Peterson, "The Color of Discipline: Sources of Racial and Gender Disproportionality in School Punishment," *Urban Review* 34, no. 4 (December 2002): 317–342, https://doi.org/10.1023/A:1021320817372. On special education, see Russell J. Skiba, Lori Poloni-Staudinger, Sarah Gallini, Ada B. Simmons, and Renae Feggins-Azziz, "Disparate Access: The Disproportionality of African American Students with Disabilities across Educational Environments," *Exceptional Children* 72, no. 4 (2006): 411–24, https://doi.org/10.1177/001440290607200402; and Alfredo J. Artiles, Beth Harry, Daniel J. Reschly, and Philip C. Chinn, "Over-Identification of Students of Color in Special Education: A Critical Overview," *Multicultural Perspectives* 4, no. 1 (2002): 3–10, https://doi.org/10.1207/S15327892MCP0401_2. Much of this research is summarized in Darby and Rury, *Color of Mind*, chs. 7 and 8.

84   On the numbers of Black students who encounter "acting white" commentary, see Ronald F. Ferguson, *Toward Excellence with Equity: An Emerging Vision for Closing the Achievement Gap* (Cambridge, MA: Harvard Education Press, 2007), ch. 2. On working-class white youth, see Jay MacLeod, *Ain't No Makin' It: Aspirations and Attainment in a Low-Income Neighborhood* (Boulder, CO: Westview Press, 2009), pt. 1.

85   On the balance of cultural and structural factors that influence behavior in deprived African American communities, see William Julius Wilson, *More Than Just Race: Being Black and Poor in the Inner City* (New York: W. W. Norton, 2009), chs. 1 and 5. On the persistence of racial achievement gaps across different levels of socioeconomic status and parental education, see Wayne J. Camara and Amy Elizabeth Schmidt, *Group Differences and Standardized Testing and Social Stratification* (New York: College Entrance Examination Board, 1999). On p. 3, the authors report that high socioeconomic status Black and Hispanic twelfth grade students scored at levels equivalent to middle socioeconomic status white peers on NELS 88 Reading and Math Assessments. Observed racial gaps within socioeconomic status groups were generally equivalent at each level.

86   National Study Group for the Affirmative Development of Academic Ability, executive summary in *All Students Reaching the Top: Strategies for Closing Academic Achievement Gaps* (Naperville, IL: Learning Point Associates, 2004), https://eric.ed.gov/?id=ED483170. On the ineffectiveness of NCLB in this regard, see Douglas N. Harris and Carolyn D. Herrington, "Accountability, Standards, and the Growing Achievement Gap: Lessons from the Past Half-Century," *American Journal of Education* 112, no. 2 (February 2006): 209–238.

Chapter 3   A Time of Transition

1   Christopher T. Cross, *Political Education: National Policy Comes of Age*, updated ed. (New York: Teachers College Press, 2010), 71.

2   Maris A. Vinovskis, *From A Nation at Risk to No Child Left Behind: National Education Goals and the Creation of Education Policy* (New York: Teachers College Press, 2009), 14–17.

3   For an overview, see Chandra Muller, "The Minimum Competency Exam Requirement, Teachers' and Students' Expectations and Academic Performance," *Social Psychology of Education* 2, no. 2 (June 1997): 200–201. Also see John H. Bishop, Ferran Mane, Michael Bishop, and Joan Moriarty, "The Role of End-of-Course Exams and Minimum Competency Exams in Standards-Based Reforms" (CAHRS Working Paper #00-09, Cornell University, School of Industrial and Labor Relations, Center for Advanced Human Resource Studies, Ithaca, NY, 2000), http://digitalcommons.ilr.cornell.edu/cahrswp/88.

4   Vinovskis, *From A Nation at Risk*, ch. 1. On the growing public interest in education and changing priorities in this era, see Christina Wolbrecht and Michael T. Hartney, "'Ideas about Interests': Explaining the Changing Partisan Politics of Education," *Perspectives on Politics* 12, no. 3 (September 2014): 603–630; also see Frederick M. Hess and Patrick J. McGuinn, "Seeking the Mantle of 'Opportunity' Presidential Politics and the Educational Metaphor, 1964–2000," *Educational Policy* 16, no. 1 (January–March 2002): 72–95. On the emphasis on growth among young governors at the time, see Lily Geismer, *Left Behind: The Democrats' Failed Attempt to Solve Inequality* (New York: Public Affairs, 2022), ch. 1.

5   On the rise of Reagan and his governing philosophy, see Gary Gerstle, *The Rise and Fall of the Neoliberal Order: America and the World in the Free Market Era* (New York: Oxford University Press, 2022), ch. 4.

6   For an overview of the process leading up to the report, see James W. Guthrie and Matthew G. Springer, "'A Nation at Risk' Revisited: Did 'Wrong' Reasoning Result in 'Right' Results? At What Cost?" *Peabody Journal of Education* 79, no. 1 (2004): 10–14. On problems with the Carter presidency, see Bruce J. Schulman, *The Seventies: The Great Shift in American Culture, Society, and Politics* (New York: Free Press, 2001), ch. 5.

7   David G. Savage, "The Long Decline in SAT Scores," *Educational Leadership* 35, no. 4 (January 1978): 290–293.

8   For a contemporaneous overview of the test score decline, including the SAT and other assessments, see Willard Wirtz, *On Further Examination: Report of the Advisory Panel on the Scholastic Aptitude Test Score Decline* (New York: College Entrance Examination Board, 1977); and James M. McGeever, *The Decline of Standardized Test Scores in the United States from 1965 to the Present* (Charleston, WV: Appalachia Educational Laboratory, 1983), ERIC, ED252565, TM850036. The quote can be found in Gene I. Maeroff, "Issue and Debate: The Concern Over Scores on the Scholastic Aptitude Test," *New York Times*, May 11, 1978, B16. Also see "15-Year Decline in Test Scores May Be Ending," *Washington Post*, January 23, 1982, A10; and Shane J. Lopez, "Americans' Views of Public Schools Still Far Worse Than Parents'," *Gallup News*, August 25, 2010, https://news.gallup.com /poll/142658/americans-views-public-schools-far-worse-parents.aspx. Jal Mehta has noted a general decline in public confidence in a range of professionalized institutions during this era: see his book, *The Allure of Order: High Hopes, Dashed Expectations and the Troubled Quest to Remake American Schooling* (New York: Oxford University Press, 2013), 119–120.

9   Maris A. Vinovskis, *The Road to Charlottesville: The 1989 Education Summit* (Alexandria, VA: National Education Goals Panel, 1999), 10–11. Also see "Bell Names Commission to Study Ways to Raise Schools' Standards: 'Challenging the Outer Limits,'" *New York Times*, August 27, 1981, A28.

10 National Commission on Excellence in Education, *A Nation at Risk: The Imperative for Educational Reform* (Washington, DC: National Commission on Excellence in Education, 1983), Findings (hereafter *A Nation at Risk*), https://eric .ed.gov/?id=ED226006.

11 *A Nation at Risk*; Muller, "Minimum Competency," 200–205. Also see Gerald W. Bracey, "On the Compelling Need to Go beyond Minimum Competency," *Phi Delta Kappan* 64, no. 10 (June 1983): 717–721; Roger Farr and Jill Edwards Olshavsky, "Is Minimum Competency Testing the Appropriate Solution to the SAT Decline?" *Phi Delta Kappan* 61, no. 8 (April 1980): 528–530.

12 *A Nation at Risk*, Recommendations.

13 *A Nation at Risk*, Introduction. On the pivotal nature of the report, see Cross, *Political Education*, 76–80; Vinovskis, *From A Nation at Risk*, 14–17; and Guthrie and Springer, "A Nation at Risk," 10–14, who report that millions of copies were distributed and hundreds of newspaper and magazine stories were published about the report.

14 For a contemporaneous perspective from a national figure who worried that an opportunity for change may be lost, see Harold Howe II, "Education Moves to Center Stage: An Overview of Recent Studies," *Phi Delta Kappan* 65, no. 3 (November 1983): 167–172.

15 Lawrence Steadman and Marshall Smith made this point shortly after the report's publication: see their article, "Recent Reform Proposals for American Education," *Contemporary Education Review* 2, no. 2 (October–December 1983): 85–104. Also see Julie A. Miller, "Report Questioning 'Crisis' in Education Triggers an Uproar," *Education Week* 11, no. 6 (October 9, 1991): 1; and Daniel Koretz, *Educational Achievement: Explanations and Implications of Recent Trends* (Washington, DC: Congressional Budget Office, 1987), pts. IV and V.

16 Fred M. Hechinger, "Experts Split on Issue of Quality of Schools," *New York Times*, September 17, 1985, C12; Jonathan Weisman, "Skills and Schools: Is Education Reform Just a Business Excuse?" *Washington Post*, March 29, 1992, C1; Miller, "Report Questioning," 32. Also see George F. Madaus, "Test Scores as Administrative Mechanisms in Educational Policy," *Phi Delta Kappan* 66, no. 9 (May 1985): 611–617.

17 Robert Pear, "Reagan Expected to Present Plan to Fight Crime in Public Schools," *New York Times*, January 1, 1984, 1; Steven R. Weisman, "Reagan Asks Drive on Unruly Pupils: Court Briefs Planned in Effort to Widen Teachers' Rights," *New York Times*, January 8, 1984, 1; Bernard Weinraub, "Reagan Orders Meese to Examine Ways to Curb Violence in Schools," *New York Times* (1923–current file), March 1, 1985, B9. The Congressional Research Service did prepare a compendium of readings published in response to the report in 1985, for use in high school and college debates on the issue. See Congressional Research Service, *Should More Rigorous Academic Standards Be Established for All Public Elementary and/or Secondary Schools in the United States? Intercollegiate Debate Topic, 1985–1986, Pursuant to Public Law 88-246, House of Representatives, 99th Congress, First Session* (Washington, DC: Library of Congress, Document No. 99-95, 1986).

18 On the shifting politics of education during this time, see Wolbrecht and Hartney, "Ideas about Interests."

19 Vinovskis, *From A Nation at Risk*, 20–22. Many polls at the time reported that while Americans were dissatisfied in general with the performance of schools, they were satisfied with their local institutions. On this point and others concerning

critiques of the critical tone of the time, see David C. Berliner and Bruce J. Biddle, *The Manufactured Crisis: Myths, Fraud, and the Attack on America's Public Schools* (New York: Basic Books, 1995), 112.

20 Lamar Alexander, "Chairman's Summary," in *Time for Results: The Governors' 1991 Report on Education* (Washington, DC: National Governor's Association, 1986), 1–8.

21 The quote is from the report of the Task Force on Readiness, *Time for Results*, 109.

22 Task Force on Education for Economic Growth, abstract in *Action for Excellence: A Comprehensive Plan to Improve Our Nation's Schools* (Denver, CO: Education Commission of the States, 1983), https://eric.ed.gov/?id=ED235588. On popular support for the schools, see Peter W. Airasian, "Symbolic Validation: The Case of State-Mandated, High-Stakes Testing," *Educational Evaluation and Policy Analysis* 10, no. 4 (Winter 1988): 301–313.

23 Leigh Burstein, *Educational Quality Indicators in the United States: Latest Developments* (CSE Report No. 265, Center for the Study of Evaluation, UCLA, 1986); Cross, *Political Education*, 80–81; and Leslie Maitland Werner, "State-by-State Comparisons Urged for U.S. Testing of Student Achievement," *New York Times*, March 22, 1987, 25. On the political appeal of comparable test data see Laura Hersh Salganik, "Why Testing Reforms Are So Popular and How They Are Changing Education," *Phi Delta Kappan* 66, no. 9 (May 1985): 607–610. Also see Terrel H. Bell, "Reflections One Decade after 'A Nation at Risk,'" *Phi Delta Kappan* 74, no. 8 (April 1993): 592; Lawrence Feinberg, "Private Schools Push District to SAT Gains: City Up 23 Points, Public Schools Down 3 Public School Scores Drop as D.C. SAT Rank Climbs," *Washington Post*, February 21, 1986, B1; Irvin Molotsky, "31 States Gain in Tests," *New York Times*, December 19, 1984, B6.

24 Vinovskis, *Road to Charlottesville*, 14 and 15. In the end, enabling legislation explicitly stated that NAEP data were not to be used for ranking state education systems, partly a legacy of Bell's unpopular wall chart. For a critical appraisal of state-level NAEP reports, see Daniel M. Koretz, "State Comparisons Using NAEP: Large Costs, Disappointing Benefits," *Educational Researcher* 20, no. 3 (April 1991): 19–21, as well as Robert L. Linn, "State-by-State Comparisons of Achievement: Suggestions for Enhancing Validity," *Educational Researcher* 17, no. 3 (April 1988): 6–9. The National Center for Educational Statistics published an even more ambitious comparison, featuring various aspects of individual states and a number of nations. Titled *Education in Nations and States,* it added another dimension to these potentially unflattering comparisons. See Richer P. Phelps, Thomas M. Smith, and Nabeel Alsalam, *Education in Nations and States: Indicators Comparing U.S. States with Other Industrialized Countries in 1991* (Washington, DC: NCES, 1996). Marshall Smith, interview by author, April 9, 2020.

25 Burstein, *Educational Quality Indicators.*

26 Ian D. Livingstone, *Second International Mathematics Study: Perceptions of the Intended and Implemented Mathematics* (Washington, DC: Center for Statistics (OERI/ED), 1986), 26–27, https://files.eric.ed.gov/fulltext/ED274525.pdf; Patricia J. Horvath, "A Look at the Second International Mathematics Study Results in the U.S.A. and Japan," *Mathematics Teacher* 80, no. 5 (May 1987): 359–368. Also see Edward B. Fiske, "American Students Score Average or Below in International Math Exams," *New York Times*, September 23, 1984, 30; and

Edward B. Fiske, "U.S. Pupils Lag in Math Ability, 3 Studies Find," *New York Times*, January 11, 1987, A1. For a discussion of contextual policy considerations impacting these assessments, see M. David Miller and Robert L. Linn, "Cross-National Achievement with Differential Retention Rates," *Journal for Research in Mathematics Education* 20, no. 1 (January 1989): 28–40.

27 Vinovskis, *Road to Charlottesville*, 6. Also see Jesse H. Rhodes, *An Education in Politics: The Origins and Evolution of No Child Left Behind* (Ithaca, NY: Cornell University Press, 2012), 48–49. The Committee for Economic Development issued a second report two years later, titled *Children in Need*, which dealt with equity questions in the schools.

28 Michael Timpane, "Business Has Rediscovered the Public Schools," *Phi Delta Kappan* 65, no. 6 (February 1984): 389–392.

29 "Excerpts from the Carnegie Report on Teaching," *New York Times*, May 16, 1986, A17. On the development of the National Center on Education and the Economy, see "About Us, accessed March 7, 2020, https://ncee.org/about-us//.

30 Diane Ravitch and Chester Finn, *What Do Our 17 Year Olds Know? A Report on the First National Assessment of History and Literature* (New York: Harper & Row, 1987), chs. 2–5; Kenneth J. Cooper, "Test Suggests Students Lack Grasp of Civics: Preparation for Citizenship Questioned," *Washington Post*, April 3, 1990, A5; and Michael Norman, "Lessons: Are Students Stupid? High School Seniors Try to Change an Image," *New York Times*, March 9, 1988, B8.

31 Edward B. Fiske, "Concerns Raised on School Quality," *New York Times*, June 6, 1989, 19. The Roundtable also released a report on the educational activities of its member corporations titled *Business Means Business about Education* and would continue to be actively engaged in influencing educational policy into the 1990s and beyond. "U.S. Students Place Low on Math and Science Tests," *New York Times*, February 1, 1989, B6.

32 Susan Chira, "Support Grows for National Educational Standards," *New York Times*, December 26, 1989, 1A.

33 Vinovskis, *From A Nation at Risk*, 39–42.

34 Vinovskis, *Road to Charlottesville*, 26–29.

35 Vinovskis, *Road to Charlottesville*, 31 and 32. Vinovskis also notes that other recommended goals included greater numbers of students reaching proficiency on NAEP and improved performance on international achievement tests.

36 David Hoffman and David S. Broder, "Summit Sets 7 Main Goals for Education," *Washington Post*, September 29, 1889, https://www.washingtonpost.com/archive /politics/1989/09/29/summit-sets-7-main-goals-for-education/a0c8a8a4-d58a -4036-9b4a-e5cebeebab40/. Also see Bernard Weintraub, "Bush and Governors Set Education Goals," *New York Times*, September 29, 1989, A1. On proposals for national report cards, see the "National Education Report Card Act of 1990." Hearing on S.2034 to Authorize the Creation of a National Education Report Card to be Published Annually to Measure Educational Achievement of Both Students and Schools and to Establish a National Council on Educational Goals, before the Subcommittee on Education, Arts and Humanities, Committee on Labor and Human Resources. Senate, One Hundred First Congress, Second Session (July 23 and September 10, 1990)" (Senate-Hrg-101-1017, Washington, DC, 1990); Bob Schwartz, interview by author, April 16, 2020.

37 Vinovskis, *Road to Charlottesville*, 40; "Transcript of Bush's State of the Union Message to the Nation," *New York Times*, February 1, 1990, D22.

38 John F. Jennings, *Why National Standards and Tests? Politics and the Quest for Better Schools* (Thousand Oaks, CA: Sage, 1998), ch. 2. For a sense of responses at the time, see David Shribman and Hillary Stout, "Politics & Policy 'Education President's' Ambitious Agenda Faces Formidable Obstacles Nationwide," *Wall Street Journal*, April 19, 1991, A16.

39 Thomas Ferraro, "Bush Announces Six 'National Education Goals,'" *UPI*, February 1, 1990, https://www.upi.com/Archives/1990/02/01/Bush-announces-six-national-education-goals/2945633848400/. The Bush priorities pointedly excluded policy recommendations with significant budgetary implications, such as improving the quality of the teaching force or providing more workforce training. He maintained that greater school choice could facilitate achievement of his other goals. For discussion of what a national test could have entailed, see National Endowment for the Humanities, introduction to *National Tests: What Other Countries Expect Their Students to Know* (Washington, DC: Government Printing Office, 1991), https://www.google.com/books/edition/National_Tests/l1 -dAAAAMAAJ?hl=en&gbpv=1

40 "America 2000: An Education Strategy," https://eric.ed.gov/?id=ED327009. Also see Vinovskis, *From A Nation at Risk*, 44–53. Bush pointedly argued that school choice was the best pathway to excellence, by then a Republican Party position that obviated the call for additional funding. His education legislation suffered from opposition on both the Right and Left, however, and preoccupied by a war in the Middle East and other matters, his administration did relatively little to bring the America 2000 act into existence. On the Bush proposal to develop exemplary "new American schools," see Mark Berends, "In the Wake of 'A Nation at Risk': New American Schools' Private Sector School Reform Initiative," *Peabody Journal of Education* 79, no. 1 (2004): 130–163. The president's stance regarding the problems of American education was further undermined in the fall of 1991 by publication of the so-called Sandia Report, which argued that several key points had been exaggerated, and that the schools had performed considerably better than suggested; see Miller, "Report Questioning 'Crisis,'" 1. On opposition to the national test proposal, see Kenneth J. Cooper, "Exams Opposed Over Potential Harm to Minorities: School Groups Urge Congress to Hold Off Administration Plan for Voluntary National Tests," *Washington Post*, June 12, 1991, A21.

41 A useful summary of this period can be found in U.S. Congress, Office of Technology Assessment, *Testing in American Schools: Asking the Right Questions*, OTA-SET-519 (Washington, DC: U.S. Government Printing Office, February 1992), ch. 2. Also see Richard J. Coley and Margaret E. Goertz, *Educational Standards in the 50 States: 1990* (Princeton, NJ: Policy Information Center, Educational Testing Service, 1990), 3–26, https://onlinelibrary.wiley.com/doi/pdf /10.1002/j.2333-8504.1990.tb01347.x. For developments in higher education, see Carol M. Boyer, Peter T. Ewell, Joni E. Finney, and James R. Mingle, *Assessment and Outcomes Measurement—A View from the States: Highlights of a New ECS Survey and Individual State Profiles* (Denver, CO: Education Commission of the States, 1987). On the development and use of these tests, see George F. Madaus, Peter W. Airasian, Ronald K. Hambleton, Robert W. Consalvo, and Lisanio R. Orlandi, "Development and Application of Criteria for Screening Commercial, Standardized Tests," *Educational Evaluation and Policy Analysis* 4, no. 3 (Autumn 1982): 401–415. Regarding the impact on teaching, see George F. Madaus, "The Distortion of Teaching and Testing: High-Stakes Testing and Instruction,"

Peabody Journal of Education 65, no. 3 (Spring 1988): 29–46. On underappreciated costs of large-scale testing, see James S. Catterall, "Estimating the Costs and Benefits of Large-Scale Assessments: Lessons from Recent Research," *Journal of Education Finance* 16, no. 1 (Summer 1990): 1–20.

42 Reginald Stuart, "South Pressing for Wide Changes to Upgrade Education Standards," *New York Times*, March 20, 1983, 26; William E. Schmidt, "Southern States Moving to Improve Schools," *New York Times*, January 11, 1984, A1; Keith R. Richburg, "Education Reform Effort Sweeps Southern States: Literacy Championed as Economic Boon," *Washington Post*, September 4, 1985, A3; Jean Latz Griffin, "Educators Draw Up Plans for 2d Wave of School Reform," *Chicago Tribune*, April 27, 1986, D1; Chris Pipho, "Kappan Special Report: States Move Reform Closer to Reality," *Phi Delta Kappan* 68, no. 4 (December 1986): K1–K8. In the mid-1980s the Southern Regional Education Board issued a series of reports regarding testing programs in its fifteen member states, encouraging, documenting, and critiquing such accountability measures; see Lynn Cornett, *Measuring Educational Progress in the South: Student Achievement* (Atlanta, GA: Southern Regional Education Board, 1984); Lynn Cornett, *Student Achievement: Test Results in the SREB States, 1985* (Atlanta, GA: Southern Regional Education Board, 1985); and Stephanie A. Korcheck, *Measuring Student Learning: Statewide Student Assessment Programs in the SREB States* (Atlanta, GA: Southern Regional Education Board, 1988). A 1992 report called for somewhat more sophisticated assessment practices, highlighting reforms in Kentucky; see Gale F. Gaines and Lynn M. Cornett, *School Accountability Reports: Lessons Learned in SREB States* (Atlanta, GA: Southern Regional Education Board, 1992), 5–12.

43 Allen Odden and Van Dougherty, *Education Finance in the States: 1984* (Denver, CO: Education Finance Center, Education Commission of the States, June 1984), 13 and 14. Also see "Arkansas Moves to Revamp Its Schools," *Washington Post*, November 13, 1983, A11. On Clinton's "new" Democratic perspective, see Geismer, *Left Behind*, ch. 8.

44 C. M. Achilles, W. H. Payne, and Z. Lansford, "Strong State-Level Leadership for Education Reform: Tennessee's Example," *Peabody Journal of Education* 63, no. 4 (Summer 1986): 23–44. On the rising importance of the South in this era, see Schulman, *Seventies*, ch. 4.

45 John Herbers, "Education Watch: A Governor Who Won Reforms in the Schools," *New York Times*, October 5, 1986, A.22; and L. Roger Kirk, "The South Carolina Educational Improvement Act of 1984," *Journal of Education Finance* 11, no. 1 (Summer 1985): 132–145. Also see Joe Davidson, "South Carolina Scores High Marks as States Act to Improve Their Educational Standards," *Wall Street Journal*, June 10, 1985, 1. Also see Chris Pipho, "Education Reform Comes in Big Packages," *Phi Delta Kappan* 66, no. 1 (September 1984): 5–6, which also discusses Texas; and Gary Putka, "South Carolina's Broad School Reform Includes Incentives or Punishment Based on Performance," *Wall Street Journal*, July 12, 1988, 1. For a somewhat critical perspective, see Rick Ginsberg and Barnett Berry, "Experiencing School Reform: The View from South Carolina," *Phi Delta Kappan* 71, no. 7 (March 1990): 549–552. According to W. James Popham, South Carolina eventually did shift to a more sophisticated assessment system, going into the 1990s; see James Popham and Michael W. Kirst, "Interview on Assessment Issues with James Popham," *Educational Researcher* 20, no. 2 (March 1991): 25.

46   Robert Reinhold, "School Reform: 4 Years of Tumult, Mixed Results," *New York Times*, August 10, 1987, A1; Bill Clinton, "The Next Educational Reform," *Issues in Science and Technology* 3, no. 4 (Summer 1987): 14–19. For discussion of financing for reform efforts across the country, see K. Forbis Jordan and Mary P. McKeown, "State Funding for Education Reform: False Hopes and Unfulfilled Expectations," *Journal of Education Finance* 14, no. 1 (Summer 1988): 18–29. On similar developments in yet another southern state, with a focus on merit pay for teachers, see Achilles et al., "Strong State-Level Leadership," 23–44.

47   Willam H. Anghoff, *Scales, Norms, and Equivalent Scores* (Princeton, NJ: Educational Testing Service, 1984). Also see Ronald A. Berk, "A Consumer's Guide to Setting Performance Standards on Criterion-Referenced Tests," *Review of Educational Research* 56, no. 1 (1986): 137–172; and Richard M. Jaeger, "Certification of Student Competence," in *Educational Measurement*, ed. Robert L. Linn, 3rd ed. (New York: Macmillan, 1989), 485–514. Jaeger noted the rather wide divergence in recommended standards (or cut scores) depending on which variant of panel study was employed in assessing test results, pointing to the continuing difficulty that the measurement field experienced in arriving at a consistent approach to addressing this question (pp. 497–500).

48   Jonathan Friendly, "States Shift toward Incentives for Achievement," *New York Times*, December 24, 1985, https://www2.lib.ku.edu/login?url=https://www-proquest-com.www2.lib.ku.edu/docview/111119394?accountid=14556; Edward B. Fiske, "Effort to Improve U.S. Schools Entering a New Phase," *New York Times*, April 27, 1986, https://www2.lib.ku.edu/login?url=https://www-proquest-com.www2.lib.ku.edu/docview/110942217?accountid=14556; Edward B. Fiske, "Amid Obstacles, Educators Aiming to Improve Schools," *New York Times*, September 9, 1984, https://www2.lib.ku.edu/login?url=https://www-proquest-com.www2.lib.ku.edu/docview/122557212?accountid=14556; Edward B. Fiske. "Redesigning the American Teacher: Growing National Anxiety about the Quality of American Schools—Coupled with the Prospect of a Teacher Shortage—Has Turned the Quality of Teacher Training into a Major Political and Educational Issue," *New York Times*, April 12, 1987, https://www2.lib.ku.edu/login?url=https://www-proquest-com.www2.lib.ku.edu/docview/110794115?accountid=14556. Regarding MCT in Kentucky and Massachusetts, somewhat later adopters, see *Kentucky Essential Skills Testing: Report of the Special Subcommittee on Kentucky Essential Skills Testing. Research Memorandum No. 435* (Frankfort: Kentucky State Legislative Research Commission, 1988); and Muriel Cohen, "Bay State Enters Era of Uniform School Tests," *Boston Globe*, March 23, 1986, 33. For a somewhat different approach in California, see Mark Fetler, "Accountability in California Public Schools," *Educational Evaluation and Policy Analysis* 8, no. 1 (Spring 1986): 31–44; on troubles encountered there, see Pamela Moorland, "'Danger Symptom': Goals Unmet at Many Schools," *Los Angeles Times*, June 20, 1986, A9. At the same time, local leaders in districts wondered if growing state-level mandates signaled a loss of local control in education; on this point, see Beverly Anderson and Chris Pipho, "State-Mandated Testing and the Fate of Local Control," *Phi Delta Kappan* 66, no. 3 (November 1984): 209–212; and Susan H. Fuhrman, "Education Policy: A New Context for Governance," *Publius* 17, no. 3 (Summer 1987): 131–143.

49   For an overview of the New Jersey testing system and the changes that the new exam represented in 1988, see Stephen L. Koffler, "Assessing the Impact of a State's Decision to Move from Minimum Competency Testing toward Higher Level

Testing for Graduation," *Educational Evaluation and Policy Analysis* 9, no. 4 (Winter 1987): 325–336. Koffler, who worked for ETS and was involved in creating the new test, suggested that the skills demanded by it made test preparation inconsequential but, when the test became mandatory for graduation, scores increased dramatically in just a year, strongly suggesting that instruction had shifted to focusing on tested skills and knowledge. On the New Jersey account-ability program prior to this change, see Edward A. Morante, Shari Faskow, and Irene Nomejko Menditto, "The New Jersey Basic Skills Assessment Program," *Journal of Developmental & Remedial Education* 7, no. 2 (Winter 1984): 2–4, 32. Also see Priscilla Van Tassel, "11th-Grade Skills Test Quietly Advances," *New York Times*, September 25, 1988, NJ 1; and "Suburban Pupils Write Best in a Jersey Exam," *New York Times*, November 6, 1983, 53. Although they were labeled as "proficiency exams," the state assessments in New Jersey largely functioned as somewhat more challenging MCTs with a writing component, which was the case in certain other states at the time, such as Connecticut. For additional discussion of the politics of urban–suburban differences in scores, see Robert Hanley, "New Jersey Schools: Rich, Poor, Unequal," *New York Times*, March 5, 1990, B1; and "4,000 Jersey Students Fail High School Test," *New York Times*, August 4, 1988, B5. On the changes in 1990, see Peter Kerr, "Florio Shifts Policy from School Testing to More Aid to Poor," *New York Times*, May 14, 1990, A1.

50   These points were made in a rather lengthy article that appeared in the middle of the decade, with reports from each of these places: W. James Popham, Keith L. Cruse, Stuart C. Rankin, Paul D. Sandifer, and Paul L. Williams, "Measurement-Driven Instruction: It's on the Road," *Phi Delta Kappan* 66, no. 9 (May 1985): 628–634. Authors of these reports, and Popham in particular, appear to have been tone deaf to the rather obviously problematic implications of a term such as "measurement-driven instruction," which can be readily likened to "teaching to the test." In an interview published six years later, Popham acknowledged that "the very [test] clarity that abetted instructional design decisions . . . may have been harmful to a number of students." He added that early competency tests provided "a clear understanding of what was to be taught," leading "many teachers to become preoccupied with a 'skill and drill' approach to teaching." He failed, however, to identify this behavior as teaching to the test, which it likely was; see Popham and Kirst, "Interview on Assessment Issues," 24. For discussion of a more comprehensive approach to assessment, see Michael Cohen, "Designing State Assessment Systems," *Phi Delta Kappan*, no. 8 (April 1988): 583–588, which unfortunately wielded little influence at the time. For criticism of testing, see Amy Goldstein, "Finding a New Gauge of Knowledge: Some States Are Designing Alternatives to Standardized Testing," *Washington Post*, May 20, 1990, a20. For a more general critique of standardized testing at this time, see Grant Wiggins, "A True Test: Toward More Authentic and Equitable Assessment," *Phi Delta Kappan* 70, no. 9 (May 1989): 703–713.

51   The 1990 ETS report noted that the majority of states still relied upon MCT at that time, with just eleven "using or developing instruments that will assess higher level skills or advanced achievement at the high school level." See Coley and Goertz, *Educational Standards*, 3. For a discussion of contemporaneous issues facing MCT programs, see Douglas R. Glasnapp and John P. Poggio, "Mandated Competency Testing Programs: Evaluating State and Local Initiatives," *Theory into Practice* 30, no. 1 (Winter 1991): 61–68; and in the same issue, John J. Bowers,

"Evaluating Testing Programs at the State and Local Levels," *Theory into Practice* 30, no. 1 (Winter 1991): 52–60; along with Richard M. Jaeger, "Legislative Perspectives on Statewide Testing: Goals, Hopes, and Desires," *Phi Delta Kappan*, no. 3 (November 1991): 239–242. On the development of alternative assessments, see Muriel Cohen, "Test Questions: A Subject for the '90s," *Boston Globe*, December 2, 1990, A33; Diego Ribadeneira, "Vermont Pioneers Portfolios," *Boston Globe*, December 2, 1990, A33.

52   Friendly, "States Shift"; Veronica T. Priscilla, "Cooperman Tenure Marked by Unusual Rate of Success: High Marks for Cooperman," *New York Times*, January 18, 1987, https://www2.lib.ku.edu/login?url=https://www-proquest-com .www2.lib.ku.edu/docview/110836197?accountid=14556. For details on the New Jersey Basic Skills Testing Program at this time, see Morante et al., "New Jersey Basic Skills," 2–4, 32.

53   A useful summary of these trends across a number of states can be found in Odden and Dougherty, *Education Finance*. Enhanced instructional resources included greater time in the classroom, as a popular change was a longer school year and extending the school day as well. Also see Chris Pipho, "Stateline: Education Reform: It Looks like a Keeper," *Phi Delta Kappan* 67, no. 10 (June 1986): 701–702; and his later article, "Stateline: A Decade of Education Reform," *Phi Delta Kappan* 74, no. 4 (December 1992): 278–279. For a nuanced and critical perspective stressing the need to consider local conditions, see Thomas B. Timar and David L. Kirp, "Education Reform in the 1980s: Lessons from the States," *Phi Delta Kappan* 70, no. 7 (March 1989): 504–511. For a summary of accountability systems in ten states toward the end of the decade, with a focus on comparing schools, see Office of Educational Research and Improvement, *Measuring Up: Questions and Answers about State Roles in Educational Accountability* (Washington, DC: Programs for the Improvement of Practice, 1988), 4–7.

54   See, for instance, Edward B. Fiske, "America's Test Mania," *New York Times*, April 10, 1988, 765; and Frances R. Hobbie, "The Quizzes of a Lifetime," *New York Times*, April 10, 1988, 769.

55   National Commission on Testing and Public Policy, *From Gatekeeper to Gateway: Transforming Testing in America* (Chestnut Hill, MA: NCTPP, 1990), xiii. Also see Susan Chira, "Study Finds Standardized Tests May Hurt Education Efforts," *New York Times*, October 16, 1992, A19; Malcomb Gladwell, "NSF Faults Science and Math Testing," *Washington Post*, October 16, 1992, A1; and Laurel Shaper Walters, "Study Finds Standardized Exams Constrain Teaching and Learning," *Christian Science Monitor*, October 26, 1992, 11. On test prep earlier in the decade, see Courtland Milloy, "Test Scores Too Good to Be True," *Washington Post*, June 29, 1983, DC1.

56   National Commission on Testing and Public Policy, *Gatekeeper to Gateway*, ix–xii. On the loss of instructional time in one state, see James Robinson and Michael Wronkovich, "Proficiency Testing in Ohio," *American Secondary Education* 20, no. 2 (1991): 10–15.

57   National Commission on Testing and Public Policy, *Gatekeeper to Gateway*, xi and 7. Also see Walter Haney and George Madaus, "Searching for Alternatives to Standardized Tests: Whys, Whats, and Whithers," *Phi Delta Kappan* 70, no. 9 (May 1989): 683–687; and Milbrey W. McLaughlin, "Test-Based Accountability as a Reform Strategy," *Phi Delta Kappan* 73, no. 3 (November 1991): 248–251.

58 U.S. Commission on Civil Rights, executive summary in *The Validity of Testing in Education and Employment* (Washington, DC: Government Printing Office, 1993), 1–7.

59 U.S. Commission on Civil Rights, *Validity of Testing*, 4–5 and 166–168.

60 U.S. Commission on Civil Rights, *Validity of Testing*, particularly the commentaries by Neill, Lowen, Goldstein, and Bolick. In the NCTPP report, see pp. ix–xii. On p. 87 Lowen suggested the interesting idea of simply inserting a constant for all or part of the difference in group scores in determining individual test scores, which could have the effect of controlling for differences that were attributable to group characteristics. In the case of race, for instance, this sort of adjustment would make variation within the Black population of test takers an important determinant of their scores, rather than Black–white differences, an approach the NAACP conference report had suggested more than a decade earlier.

61 Monty Neill, "Standardized Testing: Harmful to Civil Rights," in U.S. Commission on Civil Rights, *Validity of Testing*, 118–141. For discussion of this organization's perspective at the time, see Noe Medina and Monty Neil, *Fallout from the Testing Explosion: How 100 Million Standardized Exams Undermine Equity and Excellence in America's Public Schools* (Cambridge, MA: National Center for Fair and Open Testing, 1988); and *Standardized Tests and Our Children: A Guide to Testing Reform by FairTest Staff* (Cambridge, MA: FairTest, 1991).

62 Edward B. Fiske, "Standardized Test Scores: Voodoo Statistics?" *New York Times*, February 17, 1988, B9.

63 Associated Press, "Study Challenges Standardized Test Results: A Tailoring of Curriculums to Fit Tests Is Indicated," *New York Times*, November 28, 1987, 7; Phyllis Coons, "Educators, Publishers React to Criticism of Standard Tests," *Boston Globe*, March 20, 1988, 102. Also see John Jacob Cannell, *Nationally Normed Elementary Achievement Testing in America's Public Schools: How All Fifty States Are Above the National Average* (Daniels, WV: Friends for Education, 1987).

64 Robert L. Linn, M. Elizabeth Graue, and Nancy M. Sanders, *Comparing State and District Test Results to National Norms: Interpretations of Scoring "Above the National Average"* (CSE Technical Report 308, UCLA Center for Research on Evaluation, Standards and Student Teaching, January 1990); Muriel Cohen, "Standard Tests under Fire," *Boston Globe*, November 20, 1988, 1.

65 Lorrie A. Shepard, *"Inflated Test Score Gains": Is It Old Norms or Teaching to the Test?* (CSE Technical Report 307, UCLA Center for Research on Evaluation, Standards and Student Teaching, 1990), 8 and 10. On similar problems, including outright cheating, see Lee A. Daniels, "Schools Accused of Cheating on California Tests," *New York Times*, September 14, 1988, B8; Elaine Woo, "40 Grade Schools Cheated on Skill Tests, State Finds," *Los Angeles Times*, September 1, 1988, 12; Gary Putka, "Cheaters in Schools May Not Be Students, but Their Teachers," *Wall Street Journal*, November 2, 1989, A1; Steve Sanders, "Padded Scores Found in City School Tests," *Chicago Tribune*, July 21, 1984, 1; Muriel Cohen, "Basic Tests of Pupils Are Called Misleading," *Boston Globe*, March 17, 1988, 4; and Muriel Cohen, "Emphasis on Testing Challenged," *Boston Globe*, June 22, 1988, 1.

66 Shepard, *"Inflated Test Score Gains,"* 6; and Elaine Woo, "'Teaching to the Test': Dim Ethical Area for Educators," *Los Angeles Times*, September 19, 1988, B1. Also

see Robert Linn, *Test Misuse: Why Is It So Prevalent?* (Congress of the U.S., Washington, DC, Office of Technology Assessment, 1991).

67 Daniel Koretz, "Arriving in Lake Woebegon: Are Standardized Tests Exaggerating Achievement and Distorting Instruction?" *American Educator: The Professional Journal of the American Federation of Teachers* 12, no. 2 (Summer 1988): 8–15, 46. Also see Coons, "Educators, Publishers," 102. Daniel Koretz, interview by author, February 27, 2020.

68 Shepard, *"Inflated Test Score Gains,"* 11. Also see Leigh Burstein, *Looking Behind the "Average": How States Are Reporting Test Results* (CSE Technical Report 312, UCLA Center for Research on Evaluation, Standards and Student Testing, February 1990).

69 See, for instance, National Commission on Testing and Public Policy, *Gatekeeper to Gateway,* x.

70 Some of the problems in this regard were acknowledged in W. James Popham, "Preparing Policymakers for Standard Setting on High-Stakes Tests," *Educational Evaluation and Policy Analysis* 9, no. 1 (Spring 1987): 77–82. Also see Popham and Kirst, "Interview on Assessment Issues," 24–27.

71 Robert L. Linn, Daniel M. Koretz, Eva Baker, and Leigh Burstein, *The Validity and Credibility for the 1990 National Assessment of Educational Progress in Mathematics* (CSE Technical Report 330, UCLA Center for Research on Evaluation, Standards and Student Testing, June 1991). On the need for NAEP to test higher level skills and potential problems, see *The Nation's Report Card: Improving the Assessment of Student Achievement. Report of the Study Group, Lamar Alexander, Governor of Tennessee, Chairman, with a Review of the Report by a Committee of the National Academy of Education* (Cambridge, MA: National Academy of Education, 1987), 46–61. For the subsequent evaluation of NAEP standards that was also quite critical, see Lorrie Shepard, *Setting Performance Standards for Student Achievement: A Report of the National Academy of Education Panel on the Evaluation of NAEP Trial Assessment: An Evaluation of the 1992 Achievement Levels* (Stanford, CA: National Academy of Education, 1993), 148–149.

72 Marshall S. Smith and Jennifer O'Day, "Systemic School Reform," in *The Politics of Curriculum and Testing: The 1990 Yearbook of the Politics of Education Association,* ed. Susan Fuhrman and Betty Malen (New York: Falmer, 1991), 233–267.

73 "Putting the Pieces Together: Systemic School Reform" (CPRE Policy Briefs, Consortium for Policy Research in Education, New Brunswick, NJ, 1991); Marshall Smith, interview by author, April 9, 2020.

74 E. Joe Crosswhite, John A. Dossey, and Shirley M. Frye, "NCTM Standards for School Mathematics: Visions for Implementation," *Journal for Research in Mathematics Education* 20, no. 5 (1989): 513–522; Harold L. Schoen, "Beginning to Implement the Standards in Grades 7–12," *Mathematics Teacher* 82, no. 6 (September 1989): 427–430; Serkan Hekimoglu and Margaret Sloan, "A Compendium of Views on the NCTM Standards," *Mathematics Educator* 15, no. 1 (2005): 35–43.

75 The National Alliance for Restructuring Education was launched by the newly established National Center on Education and the Economy, which also promoted standards-based reform of the sort recommended by Smith and O'Day, if not quite as fully articulated or well implemented. On this point, see About Us, https://ncee.org/about-us/; Joshua L. Glazer, "External Efforts at District-Level

Reform: The Case of the National Alliance for Restructuring Education," *Journal of Educational Change* 10 (2009): 295–314. On the social and political context of the standards movement, see Maris A. Vinovskis, "An Analysis of the Concept and Uses of Systemic Educational Reform," *American Educational Research Journal* 33, no. 1 (Spring 1996): 53–85. Marshall Smith, interview by author, April 9, 2020.

76   Mary Catherine Ellwein, Gene V. Glass, and Mary Lee Smith, "Standards of Competence: Propositions on the Nature of Testing Reforms," *Educational Researcher* 17, no. 8 (November 1988): 4–9; also see Robert L. Linn and Stephen B. Dunbar, "The Nation's Report Card Goes Home: Good News and Bad about Trends in Achievement," *Phi Delta Kappan* 72, no. 2 (October 1990): 127–133.

Chapter 4   New Standards and Tests

1   Jane Clark Lindle, "'Hasn't Anyone Else Done This Right?' A Field Note on the Political Realities and Perceptions in Modifying Kentucky's High Stakes Accountability System" (Paper presented at the Annual Meeting of the American Educational Research Association, April 1999), 7, ERIC, ED464953. For a somewhat longer term perspective, see Prichard Committee for Academic Excellence, *Gaining Ground: Hard Work and High Expectations for Kentucky Schools* (Lexington: Partnership for Kentucky School Reform, 1999), 4–10.

2   For a detailed account of these developments, see Jesse H. Rhodes, *An Education in Politics: The Origin and Evolution of No Child Left Behind* (Ithaca, NY: Cornell University Press, 2012), chs. 3 and 4. On the importance of education in public opinion, see Christina Wolbrecht and Michael T. Hartney, "'Ideas about Interests': Explaining the Changing Partisan Politics of Education," *Perspectives on Politics* 12, no. 3 (September 2014): 603–630. On hortatory politics in the 1990s, see Lorraine M. McDonnell, *Politics, Persuasion and Educational Testing* (Cambridge, MA: Harvard University Press, 2004), chs. 1 and 2.

3   John F. Jennings, *Why National Standards and Tests? Politics and the Quest for Better Schools* (Thousand Oaks, CA: Sage, 1998), chs. 1 and 2.

4   Christopher T. Cross, *Political Education: National Policy Comes of Age* (New York: Teachers College Press, 2010), ch. 6.

5   On this point see Robert L. Linn, *Assessments and Accountability* (CSE Technical Report 490, UCLA National Center for Research on Evaluation, Standards, and Student Testing, 1998). Also see George F. Madaus, Michael K. Russell, and Jennifer Higgins, *The Paradoxes of High Stakes Testing: How They Affect Students, Their Parents, Teachers, Principals, Schools, and Society* (Charlotte, NC: Information Age, 2009), chs. 1 and 2.

6   McDonnell, *Politics, Persuasion*, chs. 1–3. Also see her article, "Assessment Policy as Persuasion and Regulation," *American Journal of Education* 102, no. 4 (August 1994): 394–420.

7   See, for instance, Harold F. O'Neil Jr. and Jamal Abedi, *Reliability and Validity of a State Metacognitive Inventory: Potential for Alternative Assessment* (CSE Technical Report 469, UCLA National Center for Research on Evaluation, Standards, and Student Testing, 1996); and Lyle F. Bachman, "Alternative Interpretations of Alternative Assessments: Some Validity Issues in Educational Performance Assessments," *Educational Measurement Issues and Practice* 21, no. 3 (September 2002): 5–18.

8   Christopher Jencks and Meredith Phillips, eds., introduction to *The Black–White Test Score Gap* (Washington, DC: Brookings Institution, 1998); Daniel M. Koretz, Robert L. Linn, Stephen B. Dunbar, and Lorrie A. Shepard, "The Effects of High-Stakes Testing on Achievement: Preliminary Findings about Generalization across Tests" (Paper presented at the Annual Meetings of the American Educational Research Association, Chicago, IL, April 3–7, 1991, and the National Council on Measurement in Education, Chicago, IL, April 4–6, 1991), ERIC, ED340730.

9   For example, see Hugh B. Price, *Achievement Matters: Getting Your Child the Best Education Possible* (New York: Kensington, 2002), chs. 4 and 5.

10   Maris Vinovskis, *From A Nation at Risk to No Child Left Behind: National Education Goals and the Creation of Federal Education Policy* (New York: Teachers College Press, 2009), 17–19. Also see Jack Jennings, *Presidents, Congress, and the Public Schools: The Politics of Education Reform* (Cambridge, MA: Harvard Education Press, 2015), ch. 5.

11   Jennings, *Why National Standards*, 17–20.

12   Jennings, *Why National Standards*, 20–25; Eva L. Baker, "Researchers and Assessment Policy Development: A Cautionary Tale," *American Journal of Education* 102, no. 4 (August 1994): 450–477.

13   National Council on Education Standards and Testing, *Raising Standards for American Education: A Report to Congress, the Secretary of Education, the National Education Goals Panel, and the American People* (Washington, DC: U.S. Government Printing Office, 1992), 24.

14   Jennings, *Why National Standards*, 20–25; Vinovskis, *From A Nation at Risk*, 51–55.

15   Baker, "Researchers and Assessment"; Vinovskis, *From A Nation at Risk*, 52–54. On assessment questions related to this issue, see Robert L. Linn, "Evaluating the Technical Quality of Proposed National Examination Systems," *American Journal of Education* 102, no. 4 (August 1994): 565–580.

16   Kenneth J. Cooper, "Exams Opposed Over Potential Harm to Minorities: School Groups Urge Congress to Hold Off Administration Plan for Voluntary National Tests," *Washington Post*, June 12, 1991, A21; "Groups Say No to National Test," *Washington Post*, June 20, 1991, DC5; "NAACP Legal Defense and Educational Fund," *Washington Informer*, October 29, 1997, 12.

17   Vinovskis, *From A Nation at Risk*, 42–51; Robert Rothman, "Group Urges 'Hitting the Brakes' on National Test," *Education Week*, January 29, 1992, https://www.edweek.org/ew/articles/1992/01/29/19brakes.h11.html.

18   Koretz's testimony was coauthored with George Madaus, Edward Haertel, and Albert Beaton, and published by the RAND Corporation: *National Educational Standards and Testing: A Response to the Recommendations of the National Council on Educational Standards and Testing* (Santa Monica, CA: Institute on Education and Training, RAND, 1992), 3–6. Also see Linda Darling-Hammond, "National Standards and Assessments: Will They Improve Education?" *American Journal of Education* 102, no. 4 (August 1994): 478–510.

19   Kenneth J. Cooper, "National Test for High School Seniors Gains Backing," *Washington Post*, January 31, 1991, A4. Also see Chester E. Finn, "Fear of Standards Threatens Education Reform," *Wall Street Journal*, March 23, 1992, A10.

20   Quoted in Lorrie Shepard, Jane Hannaway, and Eva Baker, *Standards, Assessments, and Accountability Education Policy White Paper* (Washington, DC: National Academy of Education, 2009), 3.

21 National Council on Education Standards and Testing, *Raising Standards*, i. Also see "'A Nation at Risk' + 10 Years = A Nation Still at Risk," *Christian Science Monitor*, April 26, 1993, 1; and Hilary Stout, "Bipartisan Panel on Education Urges National Standards, Voluntary Exams," *Wall Street Journal*, January 27, 1992, B4A. Also see National Research Council, *Investigating the Influence of Standards: A Framework for Research in Mathematics, Science, and Technology Education* (Washington, DC: National Academy Press, 2002), ch. 2. Symptomatic of these sentiments were headlines such as this: "Most 12th Graders Know Little American History, Survey Says," *New York Times*, November 2, 1995, A22.

22 Robert L. Linn, *Educational Assessment: Expanded Expectations and Challenges* (CSE Technical Report 351, UCLA National Center for Research on Evaluation, Standards, and Student Testing, January 1993), 3.

23 National Council on Education Standards and Testing, *Raising Standards*, i.

24 National Research Council, *Investigating the Influence*, ch. 6. Also see Milbrey W. McLaughlin and Lorrie Shepard, *Improving Education through Standards-Based Reform: A Report by the National Academy of Education Panel on Standards-Based Educational Reform* (Stanford, CA: National Academy of Education, 1995), pts. I and II. On efforts to update accountability systems in the South, see Gale F. Gaines and Lynn M. Cornett, *School Accountability Reports: Lessons Learned in SREB States* (Southern Regional Education Board, Atlanta, GA, 1992), ERIC, ED357471.

25 For discussion of the Angoff method, see William H. Angoff, *Scales, Norms, and Equivalent Scores* (Princeton, NJ: Educational Testing Service, 1984). Also see Ronald K. Hambleton and Mary Pitoniak, "Setting Performance Standards," in *Educational Measurement*, ed. Robert L. Brennen, 4th ed. (Westport, CT: Praeger, 2006), 433–470.

26 Gregory J. Cizek and Michael B. Bunch, *Standard Setting: A Guide to Establishing and Evaluating Performance Standards on Tests* (Thousand Oaks, CA: Sage, 2007), s. II: "Standards Setting Methods." Also see Hambleton and Pitoniak, "Setting Performance Standards," 464, where they note that "the role of the standard setting panel is to provide information in the form of recommended performance standards to the decision making body. That group may then choose to make adjustments to the performance standards before implementing them." Among the considerations influencing such adjustments, the authors include "organizational or societal needs" and "acceptable passing or failure rates." This is where the politics of test-based accountability could come into play. John Poggio, interview by author, November 1, 2019.

27 On the problem of variability in judgment seemingly endemic to most human endeavors, see Daniel Kahneman, Olivier Sibony, and Cass R. Sunstein, *Noise: A Flaw in Human Judgment* (New York: Little, Brown, 2021), pts. I and II. On the proliferation of approaches to standard setting by the latter 1990s, it is telling to note the differences in chapters dealing with these questions in the third and fourth editions of *Educational Measurement*, a reference work sponsored by the National Council on Measurement in Education and the American Council on Education, edited by Robert L. Linn (1989) and Robert L. Brennan (2007) respectively. While the relevant chapter in the former, by Richard Jaeger, was titled "Certification of Student Competence," the corresponding chapter in the latter by Hambleton and Pitoniak was titled "Setting Performance Standards" and featured a more extensive discussion of methods for setting standards of proficiency.

28 William Celis, "Administration Offers Plan for Better Schools," *New York Times*,
    April 22, 1993, A20; Helen Dewar, "Education Bill Caps Busy Week: Democrats
    in Congress Give Clinton a Victory after GOP Filibuster," *Washington Post*,
    March 27, 1994, A1; William Celis, "New Education Legislation Defines Federal
    Role in Nation's Classrooms," *New York Times*, March 30, 1994, B10. Also see
    Cross, *Political Education*, 108–113; Vinovskis, *From A Nation at Risk*, ch. 3; and
    Elizabeth H. DeBray, *Politics, Ideology and Education: Federal Policy during the
    Clinton and Bush Administrations* (New York: Teachers College Press, 2006),
    ch. 3.
29 James B. Steadman, *Goals 2000: Educate America Act Overview and Analysis*
    (Washington, DC: Congressional Research Service, 1993). On concerns about the
    effects of federal standards see David Cohen, "What Standards for National
    Standards?" *Phi Delta Kappan* 76, no. 10 (June 1995): 751–757.
30 Jesse H. Rhodes, *An Education in Politics: The Origins and Evolution of No Child
    Left Behind* (Ithaca, NY: Cornell University Press, 2012), ch. 4; Jennings, *Why
    National Standards*, chs. 4–6; Commission on Chapter 1, *Making Schools Work
    for Children in Poverty: A New Framework* (Washington, DC: Council of Chief
    State School Officers, 1992), pt. 1; Marshall Smith, interview by author, April 9,
    2020.
31 Dan Morgan, "Hill Leaders, Clinton Agree on $16.4 Billion in Cuts," *Washington
    Post*, June 30, 1995, A9; Jerry Gray, "104th Congress Falls Short of Revolution:
    G.O.P. Legislators Win Frugality Fight through Goals," *New York Times*,
    September 30, 1996, A14; Vinovskis, *From A Nation at Risk*, 86–100. On
    opposition to the goals, see Rochelle Sharp, "Federal Education Law Becomes Hot
    Target of Wary Conservatives," *Wall Street Journal*, August 30, 1995, A1; and
    Sabrina W. M. Lutz, "Whose Standards? Conservative Citizen Groups and
    Standards-Based Reform," *Educational Horizons* 75, no. 3 (Spring 1997): 133–142.
32 Peter Applebombe, "Education Summit Calls for Tough Standards to Be Set by
    States and Local School Districts," *New York Times*, March 27, 1996, 31; Rene
    Sanchez, "Governors Vow to Set Higher Academic Goals without Federal
    Involvement," *Washington Post*, March 28, 1996, A13; Cross, *Political Education*,
    115–116 and 117–120. Also see *A Review of the 1996 National Education Summit*
    (Washington, DC: Achieve, 1996), https://www.scribd.com/document/29608185
    /A-Review-of-the-1996-National-Education-Summit. Information regarding
    public opinion can be found on p. 19. On progress recorded subsequently, see
    National Education Goals Panel, *The National Education Goals Report: Building a
    Nation of Learners* (Washington, DC: U.S. Government Printing Office, 1998),
    10–17. On public opinion on testing and related issues, see Richard P. Phelps, "The
    Demand for Standardized Student Testing," *Educational Measurement: Issues and
    Practice* 17, no. 4 (Fall 1998): 5–23.
33 Associated Press, "Multicultural History Standards Rejected by Senate in 99–1
    Vote," *Los Angeles Times*, January 19, 1995; National Center for History in the
    Schools, *National Standards for History: Basic Edition* (Los Angeles: Center for
    History in the Schools, University of California, Los Angeles, 1996). Also see
    Ronald W. Evans, *The Social Studies Wars: What Should We Teach the Children?*
    (New York: Teachers College Press, 2004), 166–168.
34 Daniel M. Koretz and Laura S. Hamilton, "Testing for Accountability in K-12,"
    in Brennan, *Educational Measurement*, 4th ed., 156–157; National Council of
    Teachers of English, *Standards for the English Language Arts* (Urbana, IL: NCTE,

1996), pts. 1 and 3. On science standards see Okhee Lee, *Current Conceptions of Science Achievement and Implications for Assessment and Equity in Large Education Systems* (Madison, WI: National Institute for Science Education, 1998), 19–42. On the politics of curricular reform at the national level, see Michael W. Kirst, "The Politics of Nationalizing Curricular Content," *American Journal of Education* 102, no. 4 (August 1994): 383–393.

35 Richard Lee Colvin, "Global Study Finds U.S. Students Weak in Math," *Los Angeles Times*, November 21, 1996, VYA1; Peter Applebome, "A Prophecy Both False and Successful," *New York Times*, June 11, 1997, B9; National Center for Educational Statistics, *Highlights from TIMSS* (Washington, DC: Office of Educational Research and Improvement, U.S. Department of Education, 1996), 1. Also see Diana Jean Schemo, "Worldwide Survey Finds U.S. Students Are Not Keeping Up: U.S. Students Fail to Keep Up in Global Science and Math Tests," *New York Times*, December 6, 2000, A1. On evidence that younger students did better than older ones, see James Bennet, "Fourth Graders Successful, Study Shows," *New York Times*, June 11, 1997, B9. On the value of such comparative data, see Robert L. Linn and Eva L. Baker, "What Do International Assessments Imply for World-Class Standards?" *Educational Evaluation and Policy Analysis* 17, no. 4 (Winter 1995): 405–418.

36 Cross, *Political Education*, 115–116. For Clinton's remarks, see "Remarks to the National Governors' Association Education Summit in Palisades, New York," Administration of William J. Clinton, March 27, 1996, http://www.govinfo.gov/content/pkg/PPP-1996-book1/pdf/PPP-1996-book1-doc-pg511.pdf.

37 Chester E. Finn and Diane Ravitch, "A Yardstick for American Students," *Washington Post*, February 25, 1997, A17; Rene Sanchez, "Education Initiatives Off to a Slow Start: Clinton's Plan Faces Growing Opposition from Congress, State Officials," *Washington Post*, July 11, 1997, A18. Also see Susan H. Fuhrman, "Clinton's Education Policy and Intergovernmental Relations in the 1990s," *Publius* 24, no. 3 (Summer 1994): 83–97. Regarding the performance of U.S. students on TIMSS see Richard Lee Colvin, "U.S. Students Weak in Math in Global Tests," *Los Angeles Times*, November 21, 1996, OCA1; and Tom Schultz and Richard Colvin, "U.S. Students Fare Poorly in Comparison," *Los Angeles Times*, February 25, 1998, A1A.

38 Peter Applebome, "Proposal for School Testing Is Facing Wide Opposition," *New York Times*, August 3, 1997, 23; Rene Sanchez, "'House Republicans Fail to See the Need for Clinton's National Test Plan," *Washington Post*, August 19, 1997, A11; Gail Russell Chaddock, "Brouhaha on National School Testing Congress Will Try to Halt Development of US Voluntary Tests," *Christian Science Monitor*, September 3, 1997, 1–2. Also see John F. Harris, "Clinton Defends National Testing Plan: As Face-Off Looms, Opposition Grows on Both Ends of the Political Spectrum," *Washington Post*, September 4, 1997, A4; "Education Secretary Suspends the Drafting of National Tests," *New York Times*, September 28, 1997, 33; Robert Greene, "Conservatives and Liberals Band against Testing Plan," *Philadelphia Tribune*, September 30, 1997, 8A; Joan Beck, "Debating National Testing Program an Empty Gesture," *Chicago Tribune*, October 2, 1997, NW17; Jacques Steinberg, "Unlike Public, Teachers Oppose National Tests," *New York Times*, November 12, 1997, B7; Cross, *Political Education*, 117–120. For a frank assessment from educational researchers, see Anthony Carnevale and Ernest Kimmel, *A National Test: Balancing Policy and Technical Issues* (Princeton, NJ:

Educational Testing Service, 1997), ERIC, ED425488. Regarding congressional reaction on one side of the aisle, see Congressional Record Daily Edition—House, "Why Not Have National Tests for Math and Science?" 143 Cong. Rec. H8430 (October 6, 1997) (testimony of John B. Shadegg and Mark Edward Souder). On the ultimate fate of the Clinton testing proposal, see Tribune News Services, "Panel Urges Delay in National School Testing," *Chicago Tribune*, January 23, 1998, 20; Anjetta McQueen, "Panel Urges Funds for School Testing," *Philadelphia Tribune*, December 12, 2000, 8C; and Michael Guerra, "National Assessment Governing Board and Voluntary National Tests: A Tale of Tribulations without Trials" (Paper commissioned for the Twentieth Anniversary of the National Assessment Governing Board 1988–2008, March 2009), https://files.eric.ed.gov/fulltext/ED509400.pdf. For an example of technical objections to the national test proposal, see Hearing on "Overview of Testing/Standards and Assessments in the States," Committee on Education and the Workforce, House of Representatives, 105th Congress, Washington, DC, February 23, 1998, Testimony of Daniel M. Koretz, https://congressional-proquestcom. www2.lib.ku.edu/congressional/docview/t39.d40.b05710580055 000c?accountid=14556; and Hearing on "Overview of Testing/Standards and Assessments in the States," Committee on Education and the Workforce, House of Representatives, 105th Congress, Washington, DC, February 23, 1998, Testimony of Eva L. Baker, https://congressional-proquestcom. www2.lib.ku.edu/congressional/docview/t39.d40.b05710580055 000c?accountid=14556.

39 John F. Harris, "Clinton Urges Tougher Education Standards," *Washington Post*, January 23, 1997, A12; Romesh Ratnesar, "Why the President's Testing Plan Fails the Test," *Washington Post*, February 16, 1997, C4; Jo Thomas, "Questions of Excellence in Consortium Ranking: What Made an Illinois Group Do So Well?" *New York Times*, April 22, 1998, B11.

40 Pam Belluck, "In Chicago, the Story Behind the Rising Test Scores: An End to 'Social Promotion' Is but One Part of a Major Overhaul," *New York Times*, January 21, 1999, A20; Kenneth J. Cooper, "Pupils Sweat Out the 'Big Test'; End of Social Promotions Forces Chicagoans into Summer School," *Washington Post*, August 1, 1999, A03; Tracy Dell Angela, "12 Years In, School Reforms Mixed," *Chicago Tribune*, February 5, 2007, A1. Also see Melissa Roderick, Brian A. Jacob, and Anthony S. Bryk, "The Impact of High-Stakes Testing in Chicago on Student Achievement in Promotional Gate Grades," *Educational Evaluation and Policy Analysis* 24, no. 4 (Winter 2002): 333–357, which showed short-term gains in achievement; and Elaine Allensworth, *Ending Social Promotion: Dropout Rates in Chicago after Implementation of the Eighth Grade Promotion Gate* (Chicago: Consortium on Chicago School Research, 2004), 27–30. While students subject to retention as a result of this policy did not drop out at higher rates, overall system rates did not decline despite improvements in achievement.

41 Peter Applebome, "National Test Plan Runs into Minefield," *New York Times*, September 10, 1997, A21; for the Waters quote, see "Blacks, Latinos, Conservatives, Band against Testing Proposal," *Los Angeles Sentinel*, October 1, 1997, A8. John Easton, interview by author, April 13, 2020.

42 Lizette Alvarez, "Deal on National Test Faces Opposition from All Sides," *New York Times*, October 31, 1997, A25.

43 Kenneth J. Cooper, "Assessing Black Students in the '80s," *Washington Post*, April 8, 1990, 1; Michael A. Fletcher, "Students Gaining in Math Testing: Blacks,

{Hispanics Still Lag Behind Whites, Asians," *Washington Post*, August 3, 2001, A10; Derrick Darby and John L. Rury, *The Color of Mind: Why the Origins of the Achievement Gap Matter for Justice* (Chicago: University of Chicago Press, 2018), ch. 1.}

44 Jencks and Phillips, introduction to *Black–White*. Also see College Board, *Reaching the Top: A Report of the National Task Force on Minority High Achievement* (New York: College Board, 1999), 1–4.

45 Hugh B. Price, introduction to *Mobilizing the Community to Help Students Succeed* (Reston, VA: ASCD, 2008).

46 Larry Aubry, "Urban Perspective: Report Card on Education," *Los Angeles Sentinel*, August 22, 1991, A6; Hugh B. Price, "The Real Million Youth March: To Be Equal," *New Pittsburgh Courier*, October 3, 1998, 4; Marian Wright Edelman, "Harlem's Children's Zone: Child Watch," *New Pittsburgh Courier*, August 19, 2000, 4; Larry Aubry, "A Framework to Benefit African American Students," *Los Angeles Sentinel*, November 1, 2001, A7; Mashaun D. Simon, "Legislators Release Study to Improve Education," *Atlanta Daily World*, November 29, 2001, 1.

47 Hugh Price, interview by author, August 24, 2020. It was telling that the *Standards for Educational and Psychological Testing*, sponsored by the American Educational Research Association, the American Psychological Association, and the National Council on Measurement in Education, included no standards for "fairness" in 1985 but featured twelve such standards in 1999. On this change and others, see Wayne J. Camara and Suzanne Lane, "A Historical Perspective and Current Views on the Standards for Educational and Psychological Testing," *Educational Measurement: Issues and Practice* 25, no. 3 (Fall 2006): 36–41. For discussion of assessment for English-language learners, see National Research Council, *Testing English-Language Learners in U.S. Schools: Report and Workshop Summary* (Washington, DC: National Academies Press, 2000), ch. 1; Gwen Grant, interview by author, April 23, 2020; Hugh Price, interview by author, May 25, 2020.

48 These concerns are summarized in Robert L. Linn, "Assessments and Account-ability," *Educational Researcher* 29, no. 2 (March 2000): 4–16. Also see Daniel Koretz, "Alignment, High Stakes, and the Inflation of Test Scores," *Yearbook of the National Society for the Study of Education* 104, no. 2 (June 2005): 99–118; and Daniel Koretz, Robert L. Linn, Stephen B. Dunbar, and Lorrie A. Shepard, *The Effects of High-Stakes Testing on Achievement: Preliminary Findings about Generalization across Tests* (Los Angeles, CA: UCLA Center for Research on Evaluation, Standards, and Student Testing, 1991), ERIC, ED340730. Broadly similar points are made in George Hillocks, *The Testing Trap: How State Writing Assessments Control Learning* (New York: Teachers College Press, 2002), chs. 1 and 12. On the exclusion of students from testing and test prep, see David N. Figlio and Lawrence S. Getzler, "Accountability, Ability and Disability: Gaming the System" (Working Paper 9307, National Bureau of Economic Research, 2002); Walt Haney, "The Myth of the Texas Miracle," *Education Policy Analysis Archives* 8, no. 41 (August 2000); and Laurence A. Toenjes and A. Gary Dworkin, "Are Increasing Test Scores in Texas Really a Myth" *Education Policy Analysis Archives* 10, no. 17 (2002), https://epaa.asu.edu/index.php/epaa/article/view/296/. For additional perspective see Michael Bobbs, "Education 'Miracle' Has a Math Problem: Bush Critics Cite Disputed Houston Data," *Washington Post*, November 8, 2003; Karen Brandon, "Critics Call into Question Success of Texas

Schools," *Chicago Tribune*, March 5, 2001, C6; John Mintz, "An Education 'Miracle,' or Mirage?" *Washington Post*, April 21, 2000, A1; and Diana Jean Schemo and Ford Fessenden, "Gains in Houston Schools: How Real Are They?" *New York Times*, December 3, 2003, A1. For a somewhat different take on Texas, see David Grissmer and Ann Flanagan, *Exploring Rapid Achievement Gains in North Carolina and Texas: Lessons from the States* (Washington, DC: National Education Goals Panel, 1998), 24–33, ERIC ED425204, which is rather speculative and fails to consider issues raised in other sources cited herein.

49 National Research Council, *High Stakes: Testing for Tracking, Promotion, and Graduation* (Washington, DC: National Academies Press, 1999), 1 "Executive Summary," https://doi.org/10.17226/6336.

50 National Research Council, *High Stakes*, especially chs. 5 and 6, which deal with tracking, promotion, and retention. Chapters 11 and 12 feature recommendations on appropriate uses of tests. Tellingly, the study's publication did not receive attention in such major national papers as the *New York Times*, *Washington Post*, *Wall Street Journal*, or *Los Angeles Times*. To date, however, it has received more than 1,600 citations on Google Scholar.

51 The quote and poll numbers can be found in Mark Clayton, "Do High-Stakes Tests Change a School? Yes," *Christian Science Monitor*, April 6, 1999, 15. Also see Diego Ribadeneira, "Data: 40% of Hub Seniors Can't Read at 8th Grade Level," *Boston Globe*, December 16, 1989, 1; and Jeff Zorn, "Diplomas Dubiously Denied: A Taxonomy and Commentary," *English Journal* 91, no. 1 (September 2001): 73–78. For an overview of assessment features of state education systems in 1999, see Council of Chief State School Officers, *Key State Education Policies on K-12 Education, 2000: Time and Attendance, Graduation Requirements, Content Standards, Teacher Licensure, School Leader Licensure, Student Assessment. Results from the 2000 CCSSO Policies and Practices Survey, State Departments of Education* (Washington, DC: Council of Chief State School Officers, 2000), 48–54. For the survey of teachers, see Joseph J. Pedulla, Lisa M. Abrams, George F. Madaus, Michael K. Russell, Miguel A Ramos, and Jing Miao, *Perceived Effects of State-Mandated Testing Programs on Teaching and Learning: Findings from a National Survey of Teachers* (Chestnut Hill, MA: National Board on Educational Testing and Public Policy, 2003), 1–10. A report from North Carolina noted similar issues: M. Gail Jones, Brett D. Jones, Belinda Hardin, Lisa Chapman, Tracie Yarbrough, and Marcia Davis, "The Impact of High-Stakes Testing on Teachers and Students in North Carolina," *Phi Delta Kappan* 81, no. 3 (November 1999): 199–203. Sometimes scoring errors led to students failing, see Richard Lee Colvin and Martha Groves, "Schools Learn Perils of Using a Single Test," *Los Angeles Times*, September 25, 1999, A1; and Richard Jones and Dale Mezzacappa, "Testing Slighted Students' Abilities/The Revelation Renewed Criticism of the Process of Rewards and Sanctions Based on Test Results," *Philadelphia Inquirer*, January 13, 1998, B01.

52 A helpful overview of these issues is provided in Andrew C. Porter, "National Standards and School Improvement in the 1990s: Issues and Promise," *American Journal of Education* 102, no. 4 (August 1994): 421–449, 432. Also see Gregory J. Cizek, "Pockets of Resistance in the Assessment Revolution," *Educational Measurement: Issues and Practice* 19, no. 2 (Summer 2000): 20–27; and his related article, "More Unintended Consequences of High Stakes Testing," *Educational Measurement: Issues and Practice* 20, no. 4 (Winter 2001): 20–27; as well as Koretz

and Hamilton, "Testing for Accountability," 531–560. For a broad critique of test-based accountability utilizing self-determination theory, see Kennon M. Sheldon and Bruce J. Biddle, "Standards, Accountability, and School Reform: Perils and Pitfalls," *Teachers College Record* 100, no. 1 (Fall 1998): 164–180.

53 American Educational Research Association, "Position Statement on High-Stakes Testing," AERA, July 2000, https://www.aera.net/About-AERA/AERA-Rules -Policies/Association-Policies/Position-Statement-on-High-Stakes-Testing. For a range of reactions to the position statement, see Robert M. Hauser, Wayne Martin, Monty Neill, Audrey L. Qualls, and Andrew Porter, "Initial Responses to AERA's Position Statement concerning High-Stakes Testing," *Educational Researcher* 29, no. 8 (November 2000): 27–29.

54 See, for instance, D. Monty Neill and Noe J. Medina, "Standardized Testing: Harmful to Educational Health," *Phi Delta Kappan* 70, no. 9 (May 1989): 688–697; Grant Wiggins, "A True Test: Toward More Authentic and Equitable Assessment," *Phi Delta Kappan* 70, no. 9 (May 1989): 703–713; and Doug Archbald and Fred Newmann, *Beyond Standardized Testing: Assessing Authentic Academic Achievement in the Secondary School* (Reston, VA: National Association of Secondary School Principals, 1988). For an introduction to FairTest at this time, see Pamela H. Zappardino, "FairTest: Charting a Course for Testing Reform," *Clearing House* 68, no. 4 (March–April 1995): 248–252. On support for portfolios and other "exhibits" of student work, see Muriel Cohen, "Standardized Tests Challenged Again," *Boston Globe*, January 28, 1990, B91.

55 Ruth Mitchell, *Testing for Learning: How New Approaches to Evaluation Can Improve American Schools* (New York: Free Press, 1992); and Linda Darling-Hammond, Linda Ancess, and Beverly Falk, *Authentic Assessment in Action: Studies of Schools and Students at Work* (New York: Teachers College Press, 1995). On the impact of constructed response questions, see Peter Kennedy and William B. Walstead, "Combining Multiple Choice and Constructed Response Test Scores: An Economist's View," *Applied Measurement in Education* 10, no. 4 (1997): 359–375. Also see George F. Madaus and Laura M. O'Dwyer, "A Short History of Performance Assessment: Lessons Learned," *Phi Delta Kappan* 80, no. 9 (May 1999): 688–695; and George Madaus, "A Technological and Historical Consideration of Equity Issues Associated with Proposals to Change the Nation's Testing Policy," *Harvard Educational Review* 64, no. 1 (Spring 1994): 78.

56 See, for instance, James Hiebert, Thomas P. Carpenter, Elizabeth Fennema, Karen Fuson, Piet Human, Hanlie Murray, Alwyn Olivier, and Diana Wearne, "Problem Solving as a Basis for Reform in Curriculum and Instruction: The Case of Mathematics," *Educational Researcher* 25, no. 4 (May 1996): 12–21; and Robert C. Calfee and Pam Perfumo, *Student Portfolios and Teacher Logs: Blueprint for a Revolution in Assessment* (Berkeley: University of California, National Center for the Study of Writing, 1993). For an assessment of possibilities and problems at the end of the decade, see the essays in Gary W. Phillips, ed., *Technical Issues in Large-Scale Performance Assessment* (Washington, DC: National Center for Education Statistics, 1999), esp. chs. 1–4.

57 Robert L. Linn, Eva L. Baker, and Steven B. Dunbar, "Complex, Performance-Based Assessment: Expectations and Validation Criteria," *Educational Researcher* 20, no. 8 (November 1991): 15–21; Lauren B. Resnick and Daniel P. Resnick, *Issues in Designing and Validating Portfolio Assessments. Project 2.3: Complex Performance Assessments: Expanding the Scope and Approaches to Assessment* (Los Angeles, CA:

UCLA Center for Research on Evaluation, Standards, and Student Testing, 1993); Robert L. Linn, "Performance Assessment: Policy Promises and Technical Measurement Standards," *Educational Researcher* 23, no. 9 (December 1994): 4–14; Catherine Taylor, "Assessment for Measurement or Standards: The Peril and Promise of Large-Scale Assessment Reform," *American Educational Research Journal* 31, no. 2 (1994): 231–262; and Michael Young and Bokhee Yoon, *Estimating the Consistency and Accuracy of Classifications in a Standards-Referenced Assessment* (Los Angeles, CA: UCLA Center for Research on Evaluation, Standards, and Student Testing, 1998), 11–15, ERIC ED426067. Regarding the difficulty of portfolio evaluation, see Edward W. Wolfe and Timothy R. Miller, "Barriers to the Implementation of Portfolio Assessment in Secondary Education," *Applied Measurement in Education* 10, no. 3 (1997): 235–251. For a somewhat different view see William H. Thomas, Barbara A. Storms, Karen Sheingold, Joan Heller, Susan Paulukonis, Athena Nunes, and Jean Wing, *California Learning Assessment System: Portfolio Assessment Research and Development Project: Final Report* (ETS Center for Performance Assessment, CPA-1298, 1998), which focused on fourth and eighth grade language arts and mathematics. The quote is from Baker, "Researchers and Assessment," 474. On problems of identifying proficiency levels, see Barbara S. Plake and Ronald K. Hambleton, *A Standard Setting Method Designed for Complex Performance Assessments with Multiple Performance Categories: Categorical Assignments of Student Work* (Arlington, VA: National Science Foundation, 1998), ERIC, ED422371; and American College Testing Program, *Description of Writing Achievement Levels-Setting Process and Proposed Achievement Level Definitions: 1992 National Assessment of Educational Progress* (Iowa City: American College Testing Program, 1992), 4–17. On evaluating essays, see Clinton I. Chase, "Essay Test Scores and Reading Difficulty," *Journal of Educational Measurement* 20, no. 3 (Autumn 1983): 293–297. For a brief account of NAEP methods for scoring performance items, see Sheida White, Connie Smith, and Alan Vanneman, *How Does NAEP Ensure Consistency in Scoring?* (Washington, DC: National Center for Education Statistics, 2000), 1–6. On the writing skills of students, see Robert Harbison, "Put Pen to Paper More Often: Study Says 1992 Writing Report Card Finds That Writing Skills Are Improved, but Not Much," *Christian Science Monitor*, June 10, 1994, 1, which reported that "less than 2 percent of all students surveyed . . . can write a well-developed thesis paper." Also see Kenneth J. Cooper, "Students Weak in Essay Skills; Nationally, Three-Fourths Don't Meet Standard; Va. Schools Above Average, but D.C. Near Last," *Washington Post*, September 29, 1999, A03. And for a critical survey of writing assessment on state exams, see Hillocks, *Testing Trap*, chs. 2 and 12.

58 Craig D. Jerald, "The State of the States," in Gregory Chronister, ed., *Education Week: Quality Counts*, January 13, 2000, 62–65. Also see Dianne M. Piche, *Closing the Deal: A Preliminary Report on State Compliance with Final Assessment & Accountability Requirements under the Improving America's Schools Act of 1994* (Washington, DC: Citizens Commission on Civil Rights, 2001). On challenges, see David K. Cohen, "What Is the System in Systemic Reform?" *Educational Researcher* 24, no. 9 (December 1995): 11–17, 31.

59 Council of Chief State School Officers, *Key State Education Policies*, 44.

60 Diane Massell, Michael Kirst, and Margaret Hoppe, *Persistence and Change: Standards-Based Reform in Nine States* (Philadelphia, PA: Consortium for Policy

Research in Education, 1997), 1–7 and 15–41; Diego Ribadeneira, "Vermont Pioneers Portfolios," *Boston Globe*, December 2, 1990, A33; William Moloney, "Raising the Stakes in Maryland Schools: No State Has Set Such High Standards for Achievement," *Washington Post*, May 22, 1994, C8; "Prognosis on the Schools," *Washington Post*, December 17, 1995, C08 (on Maryland success); Joan Boycoff Baron, "Developing Performance Based Student Assessments: The Connecticut Experience," in *Performance-Based Student Assessment: Challenges and Possibilities, Ninety-Fifth Yearbook of the National Society for the Study of Education*, ed. Joan Boycoff Baron and Dennie Palmer Wolf (Chicago: University of Chicago Press, 1996), 166–191; and see her report *Exploring High and Improving Reading Achievement in Connecticut: Lessons from the States* (Washington, DC: National Education Goals Panel, 1999), ERIC, ED433506, s. 4. Also see Alex Medler, *Examples and Summaries of State Initiatives to Develop Goals, Standards and Outcomes* (Denver, CO: Education Commission of the States, 1994), 25–33, ERIC ED372472. On variation in standards, see Mark Musick, *Setting Education Standards High Enough* (Atlanta, GA: Southern Regional Education Board, 1997), ERIC, ED414309. On capacity-building strategies in various reform states, see Diane Massell, *State Strategies for Building Capacity in Education: Progress and Continuing Challenges* (Philadelphia, PA: Consortium for Policy Research in Education, 1998), 14–30, ERIC, ED426490. For an example of a state test during this period assessing multiple levels of achievement, see *FACT: Florida Comprehensive Assessment Test: State, District, and School Report of Results* (Tallahassee: Florida State Department of Education, 1999), ERIC, ED436587.

61 William Celis, "Kentucky Begins Drive to Revitalize Its Schools," *New York Times*, September 26, 1990, B8; Roger S. Pankratz, "The Legal and Legislative Battles," in *All Children Can Learn: Lessons from the Kentucky Reform Experience*, ed. Roger S. Pankratz and Joseph M. Petrosko (San Francisco, CA: Jossey-Bass, 2000), 11–28. Regarding passage and structure of reforms, also see Jack D. Foster, "The Role of Accountability in Kentucky's Education Reform Act of 1990," *Educational Leadership* 48, no. 5 (February 1991): 34–36; and Betty E. Steffy, "Top-Down–Bottom-Up: Systemic Change in Kentucky," *Educational Leadership* 51, no. 1 (September 1993): 42–44.

62 John P. Poggio, "Statewide Performance Assessment and School Accountability," in Pankratz and Petrosko, *All Children Can Learn*, 75–97.

63 Poggio, "Statewide Performance Assessment," 78–91; McDonnell, *Politics, Persuasion*, ch. 2; Mary Jordan, "Kentucky's Retooled Classrooms 'Erase the Board Clean,'" *Washington Post*, April 23, 1993; Kim Saylor and June Overton, "Kentucky Writing and Math Portfolios" (Paper presented at the National Conference on Creating the Quality School, 1993), ERIC, ED361382.

64 Daniel M. Koretz, Sheila Barron, Karen J. Mitchell, and Brian M. Stecher, *Perceived Effects of the Kentucky Instructional Results Information System (KIRIS)* (Santa Monica, CA: RAND, 1996), pt. 1 and 51–55. Also see Patricia J. Kannapel, "'I Don't Give a Hoot If Somebody Is Going to Pay Me $3600': Local School District Reactions to Kentucky's High Stakes Accountability Program" (Paper presented at the Annual Meeting of the American Educational Research Association, New York, April 1996), ERIC, ED397135. In his analysis of state writing assessments during the 1990s, George Hillocks found Kentucky's portfolio system to be the most popular among teachers; see Hillocks, *Testing Trap*, chs. 10 and 11. On the adoption of "reward and sanction" programs across the region, see Sid

Gaulden, "Get-Tough Education Plan Unveiled: School Accountability Act. The Bill Would Reward Schools and Districts for Good Performance, but Force Them to Face Consequences of Poor Performance," *Post and Courier* (Charleston, SC), February 9, 1996, 1; Lynn Cornett and Gail Gaines, *Accountability in the 1990s: Holding Schools Responsible for Student Achievement* (Atlanta, GA: Southern Regional Education Board, 1997), ERIC, ED406739; and Sid Gaulden, "Board of Education Visit: Governor Urges More Accountability," *Post and Courier* (Charleston, SC), September 11, 1997, 3. On problems in examining school-level test data from year to year see Robert L. Linn and Carolyn Haug, "Stability of School-Building Accountability Scores and Gains," *Educational Evaluation and Policy Analysis* 24, no. 1 (Spring 2002): 29–36; Neal Kingston, interview by author, March 30, 2020; Tom Guskey, interview by author, April 2, 2020.

65 Arthur A. Thacker, Lisa E. Koger, R. Gene Hoffman, and Milton E. Koger, *The Transition from KIRIS to CATS: Instruction, Communication, and Perceptions at 20 Kentucky Schools* (Alexandria, VA: Human Resources Research Association, 1999), 1–7; G. Williamson McDiarmid and Tom Corcoran, "Promoting the Professional Development of Teachers," in Pankratz and Petrosko, *All Children Can Learn*, 151; George K. Cunningham, "Learning from Kentucky's Failed Accountability System," in *Testing Student Learning, Evaluating Teaching Effectiveness*, ed. Williamson M. Evers and Herbert J. Walberg (Stanford, CA: Hoover Institution Press, 2004), 245–301. Also see Prichard Committee for Academic Excellence, *Gaining Ground*, 4–10. For a discussion of social background factors impacting student performance on KIRIS, see Thomas Guskey, "The Relationship between Socioeconomic Characteristics and School-Level Performance Assessment Results" (Paper presented at the Annual Meeting of the American Educational Research Association, Chicago, March 1997), ERIC, ED408300; and on school funding and test results, see Ann E. Flanagan and Sheila E. Murray, "A Decade of Reform: The Impact of School Reform in Kentucky," in *Helping Children Left Behind: State Aid and the Pursuit of Educational Equity*, ed. John Yinger (Cambridge, MA: MIT Press, 2004), 195–213.

66 Daniel Koretz, Brian Stecher, Stephen Klein, and Daniel McCaffrey, "The Vermont Portfolio Assessment Program: Findings and Implications," *Educational Measurement: Issues and Practice* 13, no. 3 (September 1994), 5.

67 Joseph Abruscato, "Early Results and Tentative Implications from the Vermont Portfolio Project," *Phi Delta Kappan* 74, no. 6 (February 1993): 474–477.

68 Koretz et al., "Vermont Portfolio," 5–16.

69 Daniel Koretz, *The Evolution of a Portfolio Program: The Impact and Quality of the Vermont Portfolio Program in Its Second Year (1992–93)* (Los Angeles, CA: UCLA National Center for Research on Evaluation, Standards, and Student Testing, 1994); Daniel Koretz, Daniel McCaffrey, Stephen Klein, Robert Bell, and Brian Stecher, *The Reliability of Scores from the 1992 Vermont Portfolio Assessment Program: Interim Report* (Santa Monica, CA: RAND, 1992).

70 McDonnell, *Politics, Persuasion*, 10–13.

71 Bill Honig and Francie Alexander in collaboration with Dennie Palmer Wolf, "Re-Writing the Tests: Lessons from the California State Assessment System," in Baron and Wolf, *Performance-Based Student Assessment*, 143–165.

72 McDonnell, *Politics, Persuasion*, ch. 4; Michael W. Kirst and Christopher Mazzeo, "The Rise, Fall and Rise of State Assessment in California, 1993–1996"

(Paper presented at the Annual Meeting of the American Educational Research Association, New York, April 8–12, 1996), ERIC, ED397133.

73 James Blair, "CLAS Test: What's All the Controversy About?" *Los Angeles Times*, June 20, 1994, WVB11; Jean Merl and Carl Ingram, "Wilson's Veto Halts Extension of CLAS Tests," *Los Angeles Times*, September 28, 1994, EVA1; Honig et al., "Re-Writing the Tests," 155–165; Edward Haertel, interview by author, March 24, 2020; Eva Baker, interview by author, April 3, 2020.

74 Thomas Timar, "The 'New Accountability' and School Governance in California," *Peabody Journal of Education* 78, no. 4 (2003): 177–200; Tina Nguyen, "Schools Defy State, Allow Exemptions on New Test," *Los Angeles Times*, March 22, 1998, A1.

75 McDonnell, *Politics, Persuasion*, 79–86.

76 Despite reports that some parents objected to "performance" or "authentic" test formats, Lorrie Shepard and Carribeth Bliem conducted a survey of parents in Denver area schools that found them to be favorably disposed to such questions when shown examples of them. See Lorrie A. Shepard and Carribeth L. Bliem, *Parent Opinions about Standardized Tests, Teacher's Information and Performance Assessments: A Case Study of the Effects of Alternative Assessment in Instruction, Student Learning and Accountability Practices* (CSE Technical Report 367, UCLA National Center for Research on Evaluation, Standards, and Student Testing, 1993). Eventually Wilson called for returning to a conventional, commercially based assessment system, see Richard Lee Colvin, "Third Time May Be the Charm for State Tests," *Los Angeles Times*, May 19, 1997, OCA3.

77 See, for instance, National Education Goals Panel, *Data Volume for the National Education Goals Report 1998* (Washington, DC: National Education Goals Panel, 1998).

78 Interstate comparisons could be positive or negative. For an example of the latter, see Sybil Fix, "S.C. Students Shortchanged: Scores Point to Underlying Problems," *Post and Courier* (Charleston, SC), September 26, 1999, 1; and for the former see Darragh Johnson, "Md. Kids Outscore Most in Math: Educators Attribute Students' Success to School Reforms," *Washington Post*, August 3, 2000, M01.

79 Stephen P. Klein, Laura S. Hamilton, Daniel F. McCaffrey, and Brian M. Stecher, "What Do Test Scores in Texas Tell Us?" *Education Policy Analysis Archives* 8, no. 49 (October 2000): 17. Effect sizes reportedly ranged from .31 to .49.

80 Richard Lee Colvin, "Texas Schools Gain Notice and Skepticism," *Los Angeles Times*, July 6, 1999, VYA1; Klein et al., 17; and Duke Helfand, "Researchers Cast Doubt on Texas School 'Miracle,'" *Los Angeles Times*, October 25, 2000, A1A. Also see Haney, "Myth of the Texas Miracle," s. 8.2 "Recapping the Myth," and other sources cited in note 47 above, along with Jennifer Booher-Jennings, "Below the Bubble: 'Educational Triage' and the Texas Accountability System," *American Educational Research Journal* 42, no. 2 (January 2005): 231–268. Linda McNeil also provided a compelling examination of how testing impacted instruction in Texas classrooms: see her book, *Contradictions of School Reform: Educational Costs of Standardized Testing* (New York: Routledge, 2000), pt. III. Tellingly, data reported by the NEGP in 1998 only included Texas among national leaders in achievement gains for fourth graders: see National Education Goals Panel, *National Education Goals Report*, 24–29. In its 1999 report, the NEGP concluded that for Texas "Between 1992 and 1998, there was no significant change in the

percentage of public school 4th graders who met the Goals Panel's performance standard in reading," and eighth grade performance was not among the higher states in the nation; see National Education Goals Panel, *Reading Achievement State by State, 1999* (Washington, DC: U.S. Government Printing Office, 1999), 100–101. On the economic impact, see David J. Deming, Sarah Cohodes, Jennifer Jennings, and Christopher Jencks, "School Accountability, Postsecondary Attainment, and Earnings," *Review of Economics and Statistics* 98, no. 5 (December 2014): 848–862 (quote is from the abstract).

81 For example, see Dennie Palmer Wolf and Sean F. Reardon, "Access to Excellence through New Forms of Student Assessment," in Baron and Wolf, *Performance-Based Student Assessment*, 1–31; Linda Darling-Hammond and Jacqueline Ancess, "Authentic Assessment and School Development," in Baron and Wolf, *Performance-Based Student Assessment*, 52–83; and Edmund W. Gordon and Carol Bonilla-Bowman, "Can Performance-Based Assessment Contribute to the Achievement of Educational Equity?" in Baron and Wolf, *Performance-Based Student Assessment*, 32–51.

82 Robert Linn and Eva Baker, "Can Performance-Based Student Assessments Be Psychometrically Sound?" in Baron and Wolf, *Performance-Based Student Assessment*, 98.

83 Linn and Baker, "Can Performance," 101. For discussion of these themes in the context of NAEP, see Edward H. Haertel and Ina V. S. Mullis, "The Evolution of the National Assessment of Educational Progress: Coherence with Best Practice," in Baron and Wolf, *Performance-Based Student Assessment*, 287–304.

84 Koretz and Hamilton, "Testing for Accountability," 535–536. On the limited coverage of some such tests, see Suzanne Lane, Carol S. Parke, and Clement Stone, *Consequences of the Maryland School Performance Assessment Program* (Washington, DC: U.S. Department of Education, 1999). On equity concerns in performance-based assessment, see Gordon and Bonilla-Bowman, "Can Performance," 32–51.

85 Vinovskis, *From A Nation at Risk*, 140–150; Associated Press, "U.S. Behind in Educational Goals," *Chicago Tribune*, December 3, 1999, L3; and Gail Russell Chaddock, "US 12th-Graders Miss the Mark," *Christian Science Monitor*, February 25, 1998, 1.

86 Laura S. Hamilton, Brian M. Stecher, and Stephen P. Klein, *Making Sense of Test-Based Accountability in Education* (Santa Monica, CA: RAND, 2002), 29; National Academy of Education Working Group on Standards, Assessment and Accountability, *Standards, Assessments, and Accountability: Education Policy White Paper* (Washington, D.C.: National Academy of Education, 2009), 1–4, https://files.eric.ed.gov/fulltext/ED531138.pdf. James Popham also expressed concern about instruction: W. James Popham, "Where Large Scale Educational Assessment Is Heading and Why It Shouldn't," *Educational Measurement: Issues and Practice* 18, no. 3 (Fall 1999): 13–17. On the need for more attention to instruction, see David K. Cohen and Deborah Loewenberg Ball, "Making Change: Instruction and Its Improvement," *Phi Delta Kappan* 83, no. 1 (September 2001): 73–77. Also see James P. Spillane, *Standards Deviation: How Schools Misunderstand Education Policy* (Cambridge, MA: Harvard University Press, 2004), chs. 1–3.

87 McDonnell, *Politics, Persuasion*, ch. 6. The quote is from Edward H. Haertel and Robert L. Linn, "Comparability," in Phillips, *Technical Issues*, 72.

88 On the continuing difficulty of identifying cut scores on NAEP, see Mark D. Reckase, Michael J. Feuer, and Edward H. Haertel, "The Controversy Over the National Assessment Governing Board Standards," *Brookings Papers on Education Policy*, no. 4 (2001): 231–265. On the inconsistencies in addressing standards at the school level, see Spillane, *Standards Deviation*, chs. 6, 7, and 8; and on the problem of failing schools see Jay Mathews, "State Testing Programs Face Special Challenges; Va. Officials Ponder How to Enforce Lofty Goals," *Washington Post*, April 25, 1999, C01.

Chapter 5   A Millennium Dawns

1 Paul Manna, "Leaving No Child Behind," in *Political Education: National Policy Comes of Age*, ed. Christopher T. Cross, rev. ed. (New York: Teachers College Press, 2010), 126–130.

2 Jesse H. Rhodes, *An Education in Politics: The Origin and Evolution of No Child Left Behind* (Ithaca, NY: Cornell University Press, 2012), ch. 5.

3 Rhodes, *Education in Politics*, 145–158; Maris A. Vinovskis, *From A Nation at Risk to No Child Left Behind: National Educational Goals and the Creation of Educational Policy* (New York: Teachers College Press, 2009), ch. 6.

4 William G. Howell, Paul E. Peterson, and Martin R. West, "What Americans Think about Their Schools: The 2007 Education Next—PEPG Survey," *Education Next* 7, no. 4 (2007), https://www.educationnext.org/what-americans-think -about-their-schools/. For a recent critique of NCLB and test-based accountability, see Diane Ravitch, "The Education Reform Movement Has Failed America: We Need Common Sense Solutions That Work," *Time Magazine*, February 1, 2020, https://time.com/5775795/education-reform-failed-america/.

5 David J. Hoff, "Not All Agree on Meaning of NCLB Proficiency," *Education Week*, April 17, 2007, https://www.edweek.org/policy-politics/not-all-agree-on -meaning-of-nclb-proficiency/2007/04. Bert D. Stoneberg, "Using NAEP to Confirm State Test Results in the No Child Left Behind Act," *Practical Assessment, Research and Evaluation* 12, no. 5 (2007), https://scholarworks.umass.edu /cgi/viewcontent.cgi?article=1172&context=pare. Also see Andrew D. Ho, "Discrepancies between Score Trends from NAEP and State Tests: A Scale-Invariant Perspective," *Educational Measurement: Issues and Practice* 26, no. 4 (Winter 2007): 11–20. On other problems, see Tim Walker, "Five Issues That Will Decide If the Era of No Child Left Behind Is Really Over," *NEA Today*, March 4, 2015, https://www.nea.org/advocating-for-change/new-from-nea/five-issues-will -decide-if-era-no-child-left-behind-really-over#:~:text=In%20its%20relentless%20 focus%20on,anyone%20looking%20for%20a%20scapegoat. For an example of continuing reflection in this arena, see Kurt F. Geisinger and Carina M. McCormick, "Adopting Cut Scores: Post-Standard-Setting Panel Considerations for Decision Makers," *Educational Measurement: Issues and Practice* 29, no. 1 (Spring 2010): 38–44.

6 Rhodes, *Education in Politics*, 174–178. For a sense of the critique that the Obama–Duncan accountability program faced, see Valerie Strauss, with Carol Corbett Burris and Kevin G. Welner, "Conversations with Obama, Duncan on Assessment," *Washington Post*, October 3, 2011, https://www.washingtonpost.com /blogs/answer-sheet/post/conversations-with-obama-duncan-on-assessment/2011 /10/02/gIQATtyYGL_blog.html. Also see Kimberly Scriven Berry and

Carolyn D. Herrington, "States and Their Struggles with NCLB: Does the Obama Blueprint Get It Right?" *Peabody Journal of Education* 86, no. 3 (2011): 272–290. On the limits of Obama's neoliberal orientation, see Gary Gerstle, *The Rise and Fall of the Neoliberal Order: America and the World in the Free Market Era* (New York: Oxford University Press, 2020), chs. 6 and 7.

7 U.S. Department of Education, "Every Student Succeeds Act (ESSA)," December 10, 2015, https://www.ed.gov/essa?src=rn; Leadership Conference Education Fund, "Accountability Provisions in the Every Student Succeeds Act," last updated April 20, 2016, http://civilrightsdocs.info/pdf/education/ESSA-Accountability -Fact-Sheet.pdf.

8 John Mintz, "George W. Bush: The Record in Texas," *Washington Post*, April 27, 2000, https://www.washingtonpost.com/archive/politics/2000/04/21/george-w -bush-the-record-in-texas/3fcc6109-7332-45a6-9658-de52abc4c4ed/; John Mintz, "Study Disputes Bush Claims on Texas Education Record," *Washington Post*, October 25, 2000, A19. Also see Ethan Bronner, "On the Record: Governor Bush and Education; Turnaround in Texas Schools Looks Good for Bush in 2000," *New York Times*, May 28, 1999, A1; and "School Miracles vs. Reality," *Los Angeles Times*, August 16, 2003, VCB18.

9 Both quotes are from Bronner, "On the Record," A1.

10 Manna, "Leaving No Child Behind," 127–128; Rhodes, *Education in Politics*, 138–145. For a contemporaneous perspective, see Dan Baiz, "On Federal Role in Education, Bush Walks a Fine Line," *Washington Post*, November 4, 1999, A2.

11 Vinovskis, *From A Nation at Risk*, 158–170; also see "President Bush Discusses No Child Left Behind," *White House Archives*, January 8, 2009, https://georgewbush -whitehouse.archives.gov/news/releases/2009/01/20090108-2.html.

12 Elizabeth H. DeBray, *Politics, Ideology, and Education: Federal Policy during the Clinton and Bush Administration* (New York: Teachers College Press, 2006), ch. 6; Manna, "Leaving No Child Behind," 127–141; also see Andrew Rudalevige, "No Child Left Behind: Forging a Congressional Compromise," in *No Child Left Behind? The Politics and Practice of School Accountability*, ed. Paul E. Peterson and Martin R. West (Washington, DC: Brookings Institution, 2003), 23–54.

13 Manna, "Leaving No Child Behind," 136–138; also see Darren Samuelsohn and Danny Vinik, "No Child Left Behind: The Oral History," *Politico*, September 23, 2015, https://www.politico.com/agenda/story/2015/09/no-child-left-behind -education-law-history-000241/. On setting standards, see Valarie Strauss, "Lawmakers Struggle to Define Failing Schools," *Washington Post*, August 28, 2001, A8.

14 Rhodes, *Education in Politics*, 148–157; Rudalevige, "No Child Left Behind," 23–54. On the position taken by the American Federation of Teachers, which was more positive than the National Education Association, see "NCLB: Its Problems, Its Promise" (AFT Teachers Policy Brief, no. 18, July 2004), 1–8. Regarding the response of civil rights groups, see Hugh B. Price, "President Bush's Education Initiative: A National Urban League Assessment," *Atlanta Daily World*, February 18, 2001, 8; and "National Coalition Calls Bush Education Bill Inadequate," *New Pittsburgh Courier*, January 12, 2002, 1.

15 On the congressional timetable and reactions, see Cross, *Political Education*, 132–143; Patrick J. McGuinn, *No Child Left Behind and the Transformation of Federal Education Policy, 1965–2005* (Lawrence: University Press of Kansas, 2006), 176; and DeBray, *Politics, Ideology, and Education*, ch. 8.

16 Thomas Toch, "Bush's Big Test," *Washington Monthly*, November 1, 2001, https://washingtonmonthly.com/2001/11/01/bushs-big-test/. Also see the slightly different version located at https://www.brookings.edu/author/thomas-toch/.

17 Vinovskis, *From A Nation at Risk*, 161–170; also see Alyson Klein, "No Child Left Behind: An Overview," *Education Week*, April 10, 2015, https://www.edweek.org /policy-politics/no-child-left-behind-an-overview/2015/04?override=web&s _kwcid=AL%216416%213%21156092717266%21b%21%21g%21%21&cmp=cpc-goog -ew-. dynamic%20ads&ccid=dynamic%20ads&ccag=nclb%20summary%20 dynamic&cckw=&cccv=dynamic%20 A.D.&gclid=CjwKCAiA8ov_BRAoEi- wAOZogwTdttx_t1_KZ-jpIopf6BOrpN_8od3vNRrZhRbXWfTI-v9yhrIPV jxoCZoYQAvD_BwE. For a critique of Reading First, see Michael Grunwald, "Billions for Inside Game on Reading," *Washington Post*, October 6, 2006, https://www.washingtonpost.com/archive/opinions/2006/10/01/billions-for -inside-game-on-reading/95faf84c-e82a-40a1-9831-1a167ff227b5/.

18 DeBray, *Politics, Ideology, and Education*, chs. 7 and 8; for a discussion of NCLB in the historical context of federal involvement in education policy, see Lee W. Anderson, "The No Child Left Behind Act and the Legacy of Federal Aid to Education," *Education Policy Analysis Archives* 13 (2005): 1–21. Also see Jack Jennings, *Presidents, Congress, and the Public Schools: The Politics of Education Reform* (Cambridge, MA: Harvard Education Press, 2015), ch. 6. Regarding critics, see Amy M. Azzam, Deborah Perkins-Gough, and Naomi Thiers, "NCLB: Taking Stock, Looking Forward," *Educational Leadership* 64, no. 3 (November 2006): 94–96; Stephanie Banchero, "Federal Judge Tosses Suit Challenging No Child Law," *Chicago Tribune*, November 24, 2005, W_A31; and Thomas S. Dee and Brian A. Jacob, "The Impact of No Child Left Behind on Students, Teachers, and Schools," *Brookings Papers on Economic Activity* 41, no. 2 (Fall 2010): 149–207. On concerns regarding NCLB within central city settings, see "Community Speaks Out on 'No Child Left Behind' Act," *Los Angeles Sentinel*, August 12, 2004, A10; and "No Child Left Behind Sets Up Schools to Fail," *Los Angeles Sentinel*, September 23, 2004, A13. Regarding the legislation's roots in state policy, see Lorraine M. McDonnell, "No Child Left Behind and the Federal Role in Education: Evolution or Revolution?" *Peabody Journal of Education* 80, no. 2 (2005): 19–38. Jack Jennings, interview by author, April 6, 2020.

19 Elizabeth Davidson, Randall Reback, Jonah Rockoff, and Heather L. Schwartz, "Fifty Ways to Leave a Child Behind: Idiosyncrasies and Discrepancies in States' Implementation of NCLB," *Educational Researcher* 44, no. 6 (August 2015): 347–358; Kerstin Carlson Le Floch, Felipe Martinez, Jennifer O'Day, Brian Stecher, James Taylor, and Andrea Cook, executive summary in *State and Local Implementation of the No Child Left Behind Act Volume III: Accountability under NCLB: Interim Report* (Washington, DC: U.S. Department of Education, 2007); and S. A. Reid, "New Law Priority for Black Educators," *Atlanta Journal— Constitution*, November 4, 2002, F5, on the support of the National Alliance of Black School Educators for the law. Also see Italia Ann-Terrone Negroni, "An Exploration of How School District Leaders Are Responding to the Connecticut Academic Achievement Test (CAPT)" (PhD diss., University of Connecticut, 2001), ch. 4; Jane Gordon, "Towns Are Rejecting No Child Left Behind," *New York Times*, December 21, 2003, CT1; Michael Dobbs, "More States Are Fighting 'No Child Left Behind' Law," *Washington Post*, February 19, 2004, A3; Richard Blumenthal, "Why Connecticut Sued the Federal Government over No Child

Left Behind," *Harvard Educational Review* 76, no. 4 (Winter 2006): 564–569; Alison Cowan, "At the Front of the Fight over No Child Left Behind: Connecticut Official Takes on Bush Law," *New York Times*, April 18, 2005, B5; Avi Salzman, "N.A.A.C.P. Is Bush Ally in School Suit Versus State," *New York Times*, February 1, 2006, B3; and Mark Walsh, "Court Upholds Dismissal of Conn.'s NCLB Suit," *Education Week*, July 14, 2010, https://www.edweek.org/education /court-upholds-dismissal-of-conn-s-nclb-suit/2010/07. On the new requirements for teachers, see Stephanie Banchero, "Aides Fail to Make Grade: Under Federal Law, Many Teaching Assistants Deemed Unqualified," *Chicago Tribune*, December 14, 2005, C1; and Stephanie Banchero, "State Relaxes Teacher Rules," *Chicago Tribune*, January 20, 2006, W_C1.

20 Debray, *Politics, Ideology, and Education*, ch. 9; Education Week Staff, "Adequate Yearly Progress," *Education Week*, September 10, 2004, https://www.edweek.org /policy-politics/adequate-yearly-progress/2004/09. Also see Susan Saulny, "State to State, Varied Ideas of 'Proficient,'" *New York Times,* January 19, 2005, 8; Mitchell Landsberg, "States' Graduation Rates Fail to Pass Muster, Report Says," *Los Angeles Times*, June 24, 2005, IEA17; Dewayne Matthews, "No Child Left Behind: The Challenge of Implementation," in *The Book of the States 2004* (Lexington, KY: Council of State Governments, 2004), 493–496; and Education Commission of the States, *No Child Left Behind Issue Brief: A Guide to Standards- Based Assessment* (Denver, CO: Education Commission of the States Communications Department, 2002), 1–6, ERIC, ED469726. For a range of perspectives, see Lisa Graham Keegan, Billie J. Orr, and Brian J. Jones, *Adequate Yearly Progress: Results, Not Process* (Thomas B. Fordham Foundation, 2002), 2–11, ERIC, ED474396; and Monty Neill, Lisa Guisbond, and Bob Schaeffer, *Failing Our Children: How "No Child Left Behind" Undermines Quality and Equity in Education* (Cambridge, MA: FairTest: The National Center for Fair & Open Testing, 2004), 1–6. On errors and rising demand for psychometric expertise, see Diana B. Henriques, "Rising Demands for Testing Push Limits of Its Accuracy," *New York Times*, September 2, 2003, 1; Karen W. Arenson, "Scaling Back Changes on Regents Standards," *New York Times*, October 14, 2003, B5, ProQuest Historical Newspapers—The New York Times with Index; Stephanie Banchero, "'Failing' Schools May Be Passing: Erroneous Data May Have Caused Wide Mislabeling," *Chicago Tribune*, December 10, 2003, NC3; and David Herszenhorn, "As Test-Taking Grows, Test-Makers Grow Rarer," *New York Times*, May 5, 2006, A1. Regarding the instability of school scores from one year to another, see Robert L. Linn and Carolyn Haug, "Stability of School-Building Accountability Scores and Gains," *Educational Evaluation and Policy Analysis* 24, no. 1 (Spring 2002): 29–36. And concerning improvements to AYP, see W. James Popham, "Transform Toxic AYP into a Beneficial Tool," *Phi Delta Kappan* 90, no. 8 (April 2009): 577–581.

21 Lorraine M. McDonnell, "Stability and Change in Title I Testing Policy," *RSF: The Russell Sage Foundation Journal of the Social Sciences* 1, no. 3 (December 2015): 178.

22 Kun Yuanand and Vi-Nhuan Le, *Estimating the Percentage of Students Who Were Tested on Cognitively Demanding Items through the State Achievement Tests* (Santa Monica, CA: RAND, 2012), 18–23, https://www.rand.org/content/dam/rand /pubs/working_papers/2012/RAND_WR967.pdf. The study was conducted as part of the Deeper Learning initiative at the William and Flora Hewlett

Foundation. States were selected through the use of "prior literature [which] suggested 17 states whose state achievement tests were more cognitively demanding and might have a higher probability of assessing deeper learning. Because statewide mathematics and English language arts tests are administered to students in grades 3–8 and in one high school grade level in most states, our analyses of the items focused on mathematics and English language arts tests at these grade levels in these 17 states" (pp. xi and xii). For additional information on Webb's categories of cognitive skills, see Norman L. Webb, "Issues Related to Judging the Alignment of Curriculum Standards and Assessments," *Applied Measurement in Education* 20, no. 1 (December 2007): 7–25. For a somewhat later evaluation of state-to-state differences in test scores, linked to international assessments, see Paul E. Peterson, Ludger Woessmann, Eric A. Hanushek, and Carlos X. Lastra-Anadón, *Globally Challenged: Are U. S. Students Ready to Compete? The Latest on Each State's International Standing in Math and Reading*, (Cambridge, MA: Taubman Center for State and Local Government, 2011), accessed May 8, 2020, http://hanushek.stanford.edu/sites/default/files /publications/Peterson%2BWoessmann%2BHanushek%2BLastra%202011%20 PEPG.pdf.

23 Yuanand and Le, *Estimating*, 45–54. On performance assessment at this time, see Rosann Tung, *Including Performance Assessments in Accountability Systems: A Review of Scale Up Efforts* (Center for Collaborative Education, January 2010), 42–49, https://files.eric.ed.gov/fulltext/ED509787.pdf.

24 For an overview of approaches to setting proficiency standards during this period, see Gregory J. Cizek, Michael B. Bunch, and Heather Koons, "Setting Performance Standards: Contemporary Methods," *Educational Measurement: Issues and Practice* 23, no. 4 (December 2004): 31–49; and Barbara S. Plake, "Standard Setters: Stand Up and Take a Stand!" *Educational Measurement: Issues and Practice* 27, no. 1 (June 2008): 3–9. On potential problems with standard setting see Ylan Q. Mui, "Standards Set for New Assessment Tests in Md," *Washington Post*, July 23, 2003, DMB6.

25 For the quote, see Kerstin Carlson Le Floch, Felipe Martinez, Jennifer O'Day, Brian Stecher, James Taylor, and Andrea Cook, *State and Local Implementation of the No Child Left Behind Act. Volume III—Accountability under NCLB: Interim Report* (Jessup, MD: Education Publications Center, U.S. Department of Education, 2007), xvii. Also see Duke Helfand and Doug Smith, "1,200 Schools in State Could Face Federal Penalties," *Los Angeles Times*, October 13, 2004, VCA1; "Left Far, Far Behind," *Los Angeles Times*, October 23, 2004, OCB14.

26 Bill Robinson, "800 S.C. Schools Might Fail to Meet Goals the First Year," *State* (Columbia, SC), February 9, 2003, D1; Amy M. Azzam, Deborah Perkins-Gough, and Naomi Thiers, "Special Report: The Impact of NCLB," *Educational Leadership* 64, no. 3 (November 2006): 94–96; David Hoff, "Schools Struggling to Meet Key Goal on Accountability: Number Failing to Make AYP Rises 28 Percent," *Education Week* 28, no. 16 (January 2009): 1, 14–15; Michele McNeil, "Proportion of Schools Falling Short on AYP Rises, Report Says," *Education Week*, April 28, 2011, https://www.edweek.org/policy-politics/proportion-of-schools-falling-short -on-ayp-rises-report-says/2011/04?cmp=clp-edweek&override=web. On reactions, see Sam Dillon, "Facing State Protests, U.S. Offers More Flexibility in Enforcing Education Law," *New York Times*, April 8, 2005, A22; and Robert L. Linn, "Toward a More Effective Definition of Adequate Yearly Progress," in *Holding*

NCLB Accountable: Achieving Accountability, Equity and School Reform, ed. Gail Sunderman (Thousand Oaks, CA: Corwin Press, 2008), 27–42. Discussion of a number of state responses to NCLB can be found in Sharon L. Nichols, Gene V. Glass, and David C. Berliner, "High-Stakes Testing and Student Achievement: Does Accountability Pressure Increase Student Learning?" *Education Policy Analysis Archives* 14 (2006), http://epaa.asu.edu/epaa/v14n1/. For cautions expressed at the outset of NCLB, see Robert L. Linn, "2003 (AERA) Presidential Address: Accountability: Responsibility and Reasonable Expectations," *Educational Researcher* 32, no. 7 (October 2003): 3–13. For statements in favor of NCLB, see Bill Evers and Herbert J. Walberg, "Why Not Put Schools to the Test?" *Christian Science Monitor*, July 12, 2004, 9; and Diane Ravitch, "Why We'll Mend It, Not End It," *Wall Street Journal*, April 25, 2005, A.14.

27 For an overview of these problems, and possible solutions, see Daniel Koretz, "Moving Beyond the Failure of Test-Based Accountability," *American Educator* (Winter 2017–2018): 22–26. Also see his chapter, titled "The Pending Reauthorization of NCLB: An Opportunity to Rethink the Basic Strategy," in Sunderman, *Holding NCLB Accountable*, 9–26. On the various ways that these factors influenced school leaders in a large urban district, see Jennifer L. Jennings, "School Choice or Schools' Choice? Managing in an Era of Accountability," *Sociology of Education* 83, no. 3 (July 2010): 227–247. For an illuminating exchange regarding another large urban district during this period, see Andrew Porter, Mitchell Chester, Daniel Koretz, and Theodore Hershberg, "Building a High-Quality Assessment and Accountability Program: The Philadelphia Example," *Brookings Papers on Education Policy*, no. 5 (2002): 285–337. Daniel Koretz, interview by author, February 27, 2020. An insightful compendium of critical viewpoints can be found in Wayne Au and Melissa Bollow Tempel, *Pencils Down: Rethinking High Stakes Testing and Accountability in Public Schools* (Milwaukee, WI: Rethinking Schools, 2012).

28 Laura S. Hamilton, Brian M. Stecher, Julie A. Marsh, Jennifer Sloan McCombs, Abby Robyn, Jennifer Lin Russell, Scott Naftel, and Heather Barney, *Accountability under No Child Left Behind: Experiences of Teachers and Administrators in Three States* (Santa Monica, CA: RAND, 2007), 133.

29 On the problem of alignment and ways to address it, see Andrew C. Porter, John Smithson, Rolf Blank, and Timothy Zeidner, "Alignment As a Teacher Variable," *Applied Measurement in Education* 20, no. 1 (December 2007): 27–51; also see Webb, "Issues," 7–21; Dennison S. Bhola, James C. Impara, and Chad W. Buckendahl, "Aligning Tests with States' Content Standards: Methods and Issues," *Educational Measurement: Issues and Practice* 16, no. 1 (Fall 2003): 21–29; James P. Spillane, *Standards Deviation: How Schools Misunderstand Education Policy* (Cambridge, MA: Harvard University Press, 2004), chs. 2, 6, 7, and 8; and Morgan S. Polikoff, "Instructional Alignment under No Child Left Behind," *American Journal of Education* 118 (May 2012): 341–368, who found moderate improvement in many states, but could not say whether student learning increased as a result. On subsequent narrowing of curricula and instructional practice, see Daniel Koretz, *Alignment, High Stakes, and the Inflation of Test Scores* (Los Angeles: UCLA National Center for Research on Evaluation, Standards, and Student Testing, 2005); and Hamilton et al., *Accountability*, 129–139. For an early account regarding these issues, see Michele Kurtz, "Teachers' Views Mixed on Testing," *Boston Globe*, March 5, 2003, B.5.

30 Jennifer L. Jennings and Jonathan Marc Bearak, "'Teaching to the Test' in the NCLB Era: How Test Predictability Affects Our Understanding of Student Performance," *Educational Researcher* 43, no. 8 (November 2014): 381–389.

31 For a general discussion of these problems, see Sharon L. Nichols and David Berliner, *Collateral Damage: How High Stakes Testing Corrupts America's Schools* (Cambridge, MA: Harvard Education Press, 2007), ch. 2. Also see Jennings, *Presidents, Congress*, ch. 6; and Amanda Walker Johnson, *Objectifying Measures: The Dominance of High Stakes Testing and the Politics of Schooling* (Philadelphia: Temple University Press, 2009), chs 1–4, which focuses on Texas. For a case study from a somewhat later period, see Dennis S. Davis and Angeli Willson, "Practices and Commitments of Test-Centric Literacy Instruction: Lessons from a Testing Transition," *Reading Research Quarterly* 50, no. 3 (July–August–September 2015): 357–379. Also see W. James Popham, "Educator Cheating on No Child Left Behind Tests," *Education Week*, April 18, 2006, https://www.edweek.org/teaching -learning/opinion-educator-cheating-on-no-child-left-behind-tests/2006/04; Craig D. Jerald, *Teach to the Test? Just Say No* (Washington, DC: Center for Comprehensive School Reform and Improvement, 2006), https://www .readingrockets.org/article/teach-test-just-say-no. Additionally, see Thomas S. Dee, Brian Jacob, and Nathaniel L. Schwartz, "The Effects of NCLB on School Resources and Practices," *Educational Evaluation and Policy Analysis* 35, no. 2 (June 2013): 252–279. Others argue that testing affects the content of lessons more than pedagogical approaches; see John B. Diamond, "Where the Rubber Meets the Road: Rethinking the Connection between High-Stakes Testing Policy and Classroom Instruction," *Sociology of Education* 80, no. 4 (October 2007): 285–313. And the status of the school could make a difference too; on this point see John B. Diamond and James P. Spillane, "High-Stakes Accountability in Urban Elementary Schools: Challenging or Reproducing Inequality?" *Teachers College Record* 106, no. 6 (June 2004): 1145–1176. For a personal account, see Janet L. Erskine, "It Changes How Teachers Teach: How Testing Is Corrupting Our Classrooms and Student Learning," *Multicultural Education* 21, no. 2 (Winter 2014): 38–40. Also see the discussion in Roberta Y. Schorr and William A. Firestone, "Conclusion," in *The Ambiguity of Teaching to the Test: Standards, Assessment, and Educational Reform*, ed. William A. Firestone, Roberta Y. Schorr, and Lora Frances Monfils (Mahwah, NJ: Lawrence Erlbaum, 2004), 159–168, which suggested that teaching to the test could take different forms depending upon the types of exam questions being addressed. Open-ended items prompted more varied classroom activities and perhaps deeper reflection, but still focused on specific topics. They also found that schools serving less affluent students devoted more time to test preparation.

32 Argun Saatcioglu, Thomas M. Skrtic, and Neal M. Kingston, "High-Stakes Accountability in Social and Political Context: Skill Gains and Losses in the No Child Left Behind Era," *Sociological Inquiry* 91, no. 1 (February 2021): 60–113.

33 Center on Education Policy, *From the Capital to the Classroom: Year 4 of the No Child Left Behind Act* (Washington, DC: Center on Education Policy, 2006), quoted in Gordon Cawelti, "The Side Effects of NCLB," *Educational Leadership* 64, No. 3 (November 2006): 64. Another study reported that "30% of elementary school principals surveyed said their schools have reduced the amount of time spent on social studies instruction, and 50% of principals in schools with large minorities reported decreased time for social studies instruction," reported in Susie Burroughs, Eric Groce, and Mary Lee Webeck, "Social Studies Education in

the Age of Testing and Accountability," *Educational Measurement: Issues and Practice* 24, no. 3 (September 2005): 14.

34 Jaekyung Lee, *Tracking Achievement Gaps and Assessing the Impact of NCLB on the Gaps: An In-Depth Look into National and State Reading and Math Outcome Trends* (Cambridge, MA: Civil Rights Project at Harvard University, 2006), 10–11, https://escholarship.org/uc/item/4db9154t; Jennifer Jennings and Heeju Sohn, "Measure for Measure: How Proficiency-Based Accountability Systems Affect Inequality in Academic Achievement," *Sociology of Education* 87, no. 2 (April 2014): 125–141; Daniel Koretz and Jennifer Jennings, "The Misunderstanding and Use of Data from Education Tests" (Paper commissioned by the Spencer Foundation for Working Group on Data Use, NYU Scholars, 2010), https://nyuscholars.nyu.edu/en/publications/the-misunderstanding-and-use-of-data-from-education-tests. Also see Douglas Lee Lauen and S. Michael Gaddis, "Accountability Pressure, Academic Standards, and Educational Triage," *Educational Evaluation and Policy Analysis* 38, no. 1 (March 2016): 127–147; and Sam Dillon, "Schools Cut Back Subjects to Push Reading and Math," *New York Times*, March 26, 2006, 1.

35 Jodi Cohen, Diane Rado, and Dernell Little, "Test Scores Don't Count the Neediest: Many Minorities, Late Enrollees Left Out of State Tallies," *Chicago Tribune*, December 16, 2004, W1.

36 W. James Popham, "Educator Cheating on No Child Left Behind Tests," *Education Week*, April 18, 2006, https://www.edweek.org/teaching-learning /opinion-educator-cheating-on-no-child-left-behind-tests/2006/04, quote on first page; Bobby Ann Slarnes, "Superstars, Cheating and Surprises," *Phi Delta Kappan* 93, no. 1 (September 2011): 70; Daniel Denvir, "Cheating Runs Rampant: No Child Left Behind Has Unleashed a Nationwide Epidemic of Cheating. Will Education Reformers Wake Up?" *Salon*, May 25, 2012, https://www.salon.com /2012/05/25/cheating_runs_rampant/; James R. Sadler, "No School Left Uncorrupted: How Cheating, High-Stakes Testing, and Declining Budgets Affected Student Achievement in Philadelphia," *CUREJ: College Undergraduate Research Electronic Journal*, (April 2013), http://repository.upenn.edu/curej/163; Allie Bidwell, "Atlanta Scandal Could Be the Tip of a 'Test Cheating Iceberg,'" *U.S. News*, April 2, 2015, https://www.usnews.com/news/articles/2015/04/02/11 -former-atlanta-educators-convicted-in-standardized-test-cheating-scandal; Jamie Brensilber, "Phila. Educators Plead Guilty to Charges for Cheating on Standardized Tests," *Daily Pennsylvanian*, March 3, 2016, https://www.thedp.com/article /2016/03/philadelphia-teachers-standardized-test-cheating; Alia Wong, "Why Would a Teacher Cheat?" *Atlantic*, April 27, 2016, https://www.theatlantic.com /education/archive/2016/04/why-teachers-cheat/480039/.

37 Jennifer L. Jennings and Douglas Lee Lauen, "Accountability, Inequality, and Achievement: The Effects of the No Child Left Behind Act on Multiple Measures of Student Learning," *RSF: The Russell Sage Foundation Journal of the Social Sciences* 2, no. 5 (September 2016): 220–241. Also see Jaekyung Lee and Todd Reeves, "Revisiting the Impact of NCLB High-Stakes School Accountability, Capacity, and Resources: State NAEP 1990–2009 Reading and Math Achievement Gaps and Trends," *Educational Evaluation and Policy Analysis* 34, no. 2 (June 2012): 209–231. For an earlier study that found NAEP scores to be "very strongly inversely related to the percentages of students at or above a state standard," see Henry Braun and Jiahe Qian, *Mapping State Standards to the*

NAEP Scale (Educational Testing Service, ETS RR-08-57, November 2008), 36; and Andrew Ho, "Discrepancies between Score Trends from NAEP and State Tests: A Scale-Invariant Perspective," *Educational Measurement: Issues and Practice* 26, no. 4 (Winter 2007): 11–20. Also see Rosalind Helderman and Ylan Q. Mui, "Comparing Schools' Progress Difficult," *Washington Post*, September 25, 2003, MDB1; Maria Glod, "'Dashboards' Provide Data on Schools: Reports Designed to Help Parents Rate Performance," *Washington Post*, January 14, 2008, BO2; and Sharon L. Nichols, Gene V. Glass, and David C. Berliner, "High-Stakes Testing and Student Achievement: Updated Analyses with NAEP Data," *Education Policy Analysis Archives* 20 (2012), http://epaa.asu.edu/ojs/article /view/1048. On Massachusetts and New York, see Achieve, "State Test Results Are Getting Closer to Student Achievement on NAEP," January 28, 2016, https://www.achieve.org/files/ProficiencyvsPrepared2.pdf.

38 On the importance of Campbell's Law, see Nichols and Berliner, *Collateral Damage*, ch. 7. Regarding the effect of social inequality, and specifically poverty, on test scores, see Selcuk R. Sirin, "Socioeconomic Status and Academic Achievement: A Meta-Analytic Review of Research," *Review of Educational Research* 75, no. 3 (Fall 2005): 417–453; and Sean F. Reardon, "School Segregation and Racial Academic Achievement Gaps," *RSF: The Russell Sage Foundation Journal of the Social Sciences* 2, no. 5 (September 2016): 34–57. Poverty may not affect *growth* in the same manner, however, as demonstrated in Douglas Lee Lauen and S. Michael Gaddis, "Exposure to Classroom Poverty and Test Score Achievement: Contextual Effects or Selection?" *American Journal of Sociology* 118, no. 4 (January 2013): 943–979. On "no excuses," see Frederick M. Hess and Michael J. Petrilli, "The Politics of No Child Left Behind: Will the Coalition Hold?" *Journal Of Education* 185, no. 3 (January 2004): 13–25; Anthony Cody, "John Thompson: No Excuses Reformers Find Plenty of Them for NCLB," *Education Week*, January 10, 2012, https://www.edweek.org/policy-politics/opinion-john-thompson-no -excuses-reformers-find-plenty-of-them-for-nclb/2012/01; and Valarie Strauss, "Enough with 'No Excuses' Rhetoric: Poverty Matters," *Washington Post*, September 29, 2012, https://www.washingtonpost.com/blogs/answer-sheet/post /the-bottom-line-on-no-excuses-and-poverty-in-school-reform/2012/09/29 /813683bc-08c1-11e2-afff-d6c7f20a83bf_blog.html.

39 Azzam et al., "Special Report," 94–96; Sam Dillon, "Most Public Schools May Miss Targets, Education Secretary Says," *New York Times*, March 9, 2011, https://www.nytimes.com/2011/03/10/education/10education.html?action =click&module=RelatedCoverage&pgtype=Article&region=Footer. On discipline problems in one state, see John B. Holbein and Helen F. Ladd, *Accountability Pressure and Non-Achievement Student Behaviors* (CALDER & American Institutes for Research, 2015), chs. 7 and 8, https://eric.ed.gov/?id =ED560678. Regarding district-level efforts, see V. Darleen Opfer, Gary T. Henry, and Andrew J. Mashburn, "The District Effect: Systemic Responses to High Stakes Accountability Policies in Six Southern States," *American Journal of Education* 114, no. 2 (February 2008): 299–332.

40 Steven Brint and Sue Teele, "Professionalism under Siege: Teachers' Views of the No Child Left Behind Act," in *No Child Left Behind and the Reduction of the Achievement Gap: Sociological Perspectives on Federal Educational Policy*, ed. Alan R. Sadovnik, Jennifer O'Day, George Bohrnstedt, and Katherine M. Borman (New York: Routledge, 2008), 135; Howard Blume, "Education Law Splits

Public, Educators," *Los Angeles Times*, June 20, 2007, OCB4. Also see Patrick C. Guggino and Steven Brint, "Does the No Child Left Behind Act Help or Hinder K-12 Education?" *Policy Matters: A Quarterly Publication of the University of California, Riverside* 3, no. 3 (Winter 2010): 1–8; Colleen Flaherty, "Educators Share How No Child Left Behind Has Affected Their Classroom," *Education Votes*, February 20, 2015, https://educationvotes.nea.org/2015/02/20/educators -share-how-no-child-left-behind-has-affected-their-classroom/; Tim Walker, "Five Issues That Will Decide If the Era of No Child Left Behind Is Really Over," *NEA News*, March 4, 2015, https://www.nea.org/advocating-for-change/new-from-nea /five-issues-will-decide-if-era-no-child-left-behind-really-over; Craig A. Mertler, "Teachers' Perceptions of the Influence of No Child Left Behind on Classroom Practices," *Current Issues in Education* 14, no. 1 (2011): 1–33. Also see David Hursh, "Assessing 'No Child Left Behind' and the Rise of Neoliberal Education Policies," *American Educational Research Journal* 44, no. 3 (September 2007): 493–518. On tests for students with disabilities, see Deb Albus, Sheryl S. Lazarus, Martha L. Thurlow, and Damien Cormier, *Characteristics of States' Alternate Assessments Based on Modified Academic Achievement Standards in 2008* (Synthesis Report 72) (Minneapolis: University of Minnesota, National Center on Educational Outcomes, September 2009), 3–14. Steven Brint, interview by author, March 19, 2020.

41 Jennifer Booher-Jennings, "Rationing Education in an Era of Accountability," *Phi Delta Kappan* 87, no. 10 (June 2006): 756–761; Derek Neal and Diane Whitmore Schanzenbach, "Left Behind by Design: Proficiency Counts and Test-Based Accountability" (NBER Working Paper 13293, August 2007), https://www.nber.org/papers/w13293; Lauen and Gaddis, "Accountability Pressure," 127–147; Suzanne E. Eckes and Julie Swando, "Special Education Subgroups under NCLB: Issues to Consider," *Teachers College Record* 111, no. 11 (November 2009): 2479–2504. Other researchers found less evidence of this effect later, see, for instance, Dale Ballou and Matthew G. Springer, "Has NCLB Encouraged Educational Triage? Accountability and the Distribution of Achievement Gains," *Education Finance and Policy* 12, no. 1 (Winter 2017): 77–106. On teacher quality, see Beatrice Birman, Kerstin Carlson Le Floch, Amy Klekotka, Meredith Ludwig, James Taylor, Kirk Walters, Andrew Wayne, Kwang-Suk Yoon, Georges Vernez, Michael S. Garet, and Jennifer O'Day, "Evaluating Teacher Quality under No Child Left Behind" (RAND Corporation Research Brief, 2007), https://www.rand.org/pubs/research_briefs/RB9287 .html; for somewhat different results in a single school system, see Karen J. DeAngelis, Bradford R. White, and Jennifer B. Presley, "The Changing Distribution of Teacher Qualifications across Schools: A Statewide Perspective Post-NCLB," *Education Policy Analysis Archives* 18, no. 28 (2010), http://epaa.asu.edu /ojs/article/view/722.

42 Nichols and Berliner, *Collateral Damage*, chs. 3 and 6; Ilana Seidel Horn, "Accountability as a Design for Teacher Learning: Sensemaking about Mathematics and Equity in the NCLB Era," *Urban Education* 53, no. 3 (March 2018): 382–408; Anna J. Markowitz, "Changes in School Engagement as a Function of No Child Left Behind: A Comparative Interrupted Time Series Analysis," *American Educational Research Journal* 55, no. 4 (August 2018): 721–760. For additional discussion of how teacher responses to testing requirements differed by the gender of students, see Jennifer Booher-Jennings, "Learning to Label:

Socialization, Gender, and the Hidden Curriculum of High-Stakes Testing,"
British Journal of Sociology of Education 29, no. 2 (March 2008): 149–160.

43 Brian A. Jacob, "Test-Based Accountability and Student Achievement: An
Investigation of Differential Performance on NAEP and State Assessments"
(NBER Working Papers 12817, National Bureau of Economic Research, 2007),
abstract.

44 Center on Educational Policy, *Answering the Question That Matters Most: Has
Student Achievement Increased Since No Child Left Behind?* (Washington, DC:
Center on Educational Policy, June 2007), 71. Also see Rebecca Holcombe,
Jennifer Jennings, and Daniel Koretz, "The Roots of Score Inflation: An Exami-
nation of Opportunities in Two States' Tests," in *Charting Reform, Achieving
Equity in a Diverse Nation*, ed. Gail L. Sunderman (Greenwich, CT: Information
Age Publishing, 2013), 163–189.

45 Robert Linn, Eva Baker, and Damian Betebenner, *Accountability Systems:
Implications of Requirements of the No Child Left Behind Act of 2001* (Los Angeles,
CA: UCLA National Center for Research on Evaluation, Standards, and Student
Testing, CSE-TR-567, 2002), 16, ERIC, ED467440.

46 For a lengthy discussion of how these questions played out in one group of
districts, see Valarie Strauss, "How Standardized Tests Are Affecting Public
Schools," *Washington Post*, May 18, 2012, https://www.washingtonpost.com/blogs
/answer-sheet/post/2012/05/17/gIQABH1NXU_blog.html. A useful summary of
these points, expressed in the views of educators, can be found in Richard J.
Murnane and John P. Papay, "Teachers' Views on No Child Left Behind: Support
for the Principles, Concerns about the Practices," *Journal of Economic Perspectives*
24, no. 3 (Summer 2010): 151–166.

47 Dee and Jacob, "Impact," abstract; Sam Dillon, "Young Students Post Solid Gains
in Federal Tests," *New York Times*, July 15, 2005, A1.

48 Researchers writing from a somewhat conservative viewpoint tended to emphasize
the positive impact of NCLB. See, for instance, Thomas Ahn and Jacob Vigdor,
"Were All Those Standardized Tests for Nothing? The Lessons of No Child Left
Behind" (Working Paper, American Enterprise Institute, May 2013), executive
summary. Support from civil rights advocates continued as well, such as that
expressed by Dianne Piché, "Basically a Good Model: NCLB Can Be Fixed,"
Education Next 7, no. 4 (Fall 2007): 57–59. For a somewhat different perspective,
see Cawelti, "Side Effects of NCLB," 64–68; and Daniel Koretz, "Moving Past No
Child Left Behind," *Science* 326, no. 5954 (November 6, 2009): 803–804.

49 On the correlation between NAEP and state test scores, see Center on Educational Policy, *Answering the Question*, 68. For some local reactions, see Jay
Mathews, "National School Testing Urged: Gaps between State, Federal Assessments Fuel Call for Change," *Washington Post*, September 3, 2006, A01. The only
positive and statistically significant one was for fourth grade reading, and that was
a moderate .364. The results discussed herein are from the so-called Main NAEP,
which was somewhat different from the Long-Term NAEP, in that it was
developed as a means of reporting state-level differences in achievement in 1990,
and was intended to evolve as curricular standards changed, and it reports results
by grade level (grades four, eight, and twelve). Long-Term NAEP was the original
national assessment and was intended to compare results over a longer period,
dating from the early 1970s. It reports results by age (nine, twelve, and seventeen
years). For a summary of Main NAEP results for grades four and eight, see

"NAEP Report Card: Mathematics," Nation's Report Card, accessed May 15, 2020, https://www.nationsreportcard.gov/mathematics?grade=4. For reading results, see the same report, available at https://www.nationsreportcard.gov/reading/?grade=4, accessed May 15, 2020. For Long-Term NAEP results, which show somewhat greater improvement for eighth graders (the same cohort that improved in fourth grade), see National Center for Educational Statistics, *The Condition of Education 2016*, ch. 3, "Elementary and Secondary Education, Assessment: Reading and Mathematics Score Trends," 2, accessed May 20, 2020, https://nces.ed.gov/programs/coe/pdf/coe_cnj.pdf. Long-Term NAEP reading scores for fourth and eighth graders also improved somewhat between 2004 and 2008, while they did not for twelfth graders. NAEP scores were also unchanged for the most part in history, geography, and civics, which had improved since 1994 but grew little after 2010, see https://www.nationsreportcard.gov/hgc_2014/#summary. Altogether, less than 20 percent of test takers were judged proficient in American history, and about a quarter in geography and civics; for many subgroups the results were lower still.

50 Results for achievement gaps can be found at "NAEP Report Card: Nation," Nation's Report Card, under "Student Group Scores and Score Gaps," accessed May 15, 2020, https://www.nationsreportcard.gov/mathematics/nation/groups/ (for mathematics) and https://www.nationsreportcard.gov/reading/nation/groups/ (for reading), grades four and eight results available for each. Results for twelfth grade students regarding achievement gaps for this period can be found at Kevin Mahnken, "Twelfth-Grade NAEP Scores Offer More Bad News for Reading, Stagnation in Math," *Newsfeed: The Big Picture*, October 28, 2020, https://www.the74million.org/twelfth-grade-naep-scores-offer-more-bad-news-for-reading-stagnation-in-math/. On the questionable character of achievement gains in the elementary grades, see Martin Carnoy, "Have State Accountability and High-Stakes Tests Influenced Student Progression Rates in High School?" *Educational Measurement: Issues and Practice* 24, no. 4 (Winter 2005): 19–31. Regarding local dimensions of the gap, see Avi Salzman, "No Child Left Behind? Hardly: Federal Law Forces a Hard Look at a Big Achievement Gap," *New York Times*, May 1, 2005, CT1.

51 See, for instance, Lisa Guisbond, Monty Neill, and Bob Schaeffer, "NCLB's Lost Decade for Educational Progress: What Can We Learn from This Policy Failure?" *Counterpoints* 451 (2013): 7–26; and an earlier FairTest statement, Neill et al., executive summary in *Failing Our Children*. On results in large urban districts, see Council of the Great City Schools, *Beating the Odds: Analysis of Student Performance on State Assessments, Results from the 2012–2013 School Year*, https://files.eric.ed.gov/fulltext/ED559565.pdf. Also see Mitchell Landsberg, "School Test Scores Rise, but Key Gaps Widen," *Los Angeles Times*, March 3, 2006, IEB3.

52 Ina V. S. Mullis, Michael O. Martin, Pierre Foy, and Alka Arora, *TIMSS 2011 International Results in Mathematics* (Chestnut Hill, MA: TIMSS & PIRLS International Study Center, 2012), ch. 1. For a discussion of how state results compared to international assessments, see Paul E. Peterson, Ludger Woessmann, Eric A. Hanushek, and Carlos X. Lastra-Anadón, *Globally Challenged: Are U.S. Students Ready to Compete?* (Cambridge, MA: Harvard University Program on Education Policy and Governance, PEPG 11-03, 2011), https://eric.ed.gov/?id=ED526954.

53 Ina V. S. Mullis, Michael O. Martin, Pierre Foy, and Alka Arora, *TIMSS 2011 International Results in Mathematics* (Chestnut Hill, MA: TIMSS & PIRLS International Study Center, 2012), chs. 7 and 2. On the effects of teacher mathematics training, see Heather C. Hill, Brian Rowan, and Deborah Loewenberg Ball, "Effects of Teachers' Mathematical Knowledge for Teaching on Student Achievement," *American Educational Research Journal* 42, no. 2 (Summer 2005): 371–406.

54 Mullis et al., *TIMSS 2011 International Results in Mathematics*, Ch. 5.

55 Organisation for Economic Co-operation and Development (OECD), *PISA 2012 Results in Focus: What 15-Year-Olds Know and What They Can Do with What They Know* (Paris: OECD, 2014), 5. For a critique of the 2012 PISA results, adjusting for the class composition of U.S. test takers, see Martin Carnoy and Richard Rothstein, *What Do International Tests Really Show about U.S. Student Performance?* (Economic Policy Institute, January 28, 2013), https://www.epi.org/publication/us-student-performance-testing/. For an answer to questions such as Carnoy and Rothstein's, see Ludger Woessmann, "The Importance of School Systems: Evidence from International Differences in Student Achievement," *Journal of Economic Perspectives* 30, no. 3 (Summer 2016): 3–31.

56 For a critique of PISA, see David F. Labaree, "Let's Measure What No One Teaches: PISA, NCLB, and the Shrinking Aims of Education," *Teachers College Record* 116, no. 9 (2014): 1–14. Also see Yong Zhao, "The Pisa Illusion," National Education Policy Center (NEPC), December 12, 2019, https://nepc.colorado.edu/blog/pisa-illusion.

57 For a critique of accountability-based incentives in education and other fields at this time, see Richard Rothstein, introduction to "Holding Accountability to Account: How Scholarship and Experience in Other Fields Inform Exploration of Performance Incentives in Education" (Working Paper 2008-04, National Center on Performance Incentives, February 2008).

58 Vinovskis, *From A Nation at Risk*, 206; Mike Kennedy, "Election '08," *American School & University* 81, no. 2 (October 2008): 18–23; Eleanor Chute, "Both Clinton and Obama Attack No Child Left Behind Act," *Pittsburgh Post-Gazette*, April 8, 2008, https://www.post-gazette.com/news/education/2008/04/09/Both-Clinton-and-Obama-attack-No-Child-Left-Behind-Act/stories/200804090213. On opposition to the law, see "Joint Organizational Statement on No Child Left Behind (NCLB) Act: List of 156 Signers Updated December 13, 2011," FairTest, October 21, 2004, https://www.fairtest.org/joint-organizational-statement-no-child-left-behin. The problems cited included "over-emphasizing standardized testing, narrowing curriculum and instruction to focus on test preparation rather than richer academic learning; over-identifying schools in need of improvement; using sanctions that do not help improve schools; inappropriately excluding low-scoring children in order to boost test results; and inadequate funding."

59 Sam Dillon, "Arne Duncan," *New York Times*, January 14, 2009, A20; Sam Dillon, "Education Standards Likely to See Toughening," *New York Times*, April 15, 2009, A12. Also see "Mr. Obama and No Child Left Behind," *New York Times*, March 18, 2010, A30. The quote is from testimony given to the U.S. Senate Committee on Health, Education, Labor, and Pensions on February 7, 2013, titled "No Child Left Behind: Early Lessons from State Flexibility Waivers," p. 12, https://files.eric.ed.gov/fulltext/ED572216.pdf.

60 Rhodes, *Education in Politics*, ch. 6; Patrick McGuinn, "Presidential Policymaking: Race to the Top, Executive Power, and the Obama Education Agenda," *Forum* 12, no. 1 (May 2014), https://www.degruyter.com/view/journals/for/12/1/article-p61.xml. For a somewhat detailed but relatively brief account of Race to the Top, see the United States Government Accountability Office, *Race to the Top: Reform Efforts Are Under Way and Information Sharing Could Be Improved* (Report to Congressional Committees, GAO-11-658, June 2011), which concluded that "the RTT grant competition prompted a robust national dialogue about comprehensive education reform and the role of competitive grants to support these reforms. It led some states to undertake new initiatives and others to accelerate their existing and planned educational reform efforts" (p. 26). On the National Education Association's other critics, see Stephan Sawchuk, "NEA at Odds with Obama Team Over 'Race to the Top' Criteria: Union's Complaints Could Foreshadow NCLB Replay," *Education Week*, September 2, 2009, 6; and Stacy Teicher Khadaroo, "Obama Refuses to Budge on Race to the Top Education Reforms," *Christian Science Monitor*, July 29, 2010, https://www.csmonitor.com/USA/Education/2010/0729/Obama-refuses-to-budge-on-Race-to-the-Top-education-reforms.

61 Michele McNeil and Alyson Klein, "Obama Offers Waivers from Key Provisions of NCLB," *Education Week*, September 27, 2011, https://www.edweek.org/policy-politics/obama-offers-waivers-from-key-provisions-of-nclb/2011/09. For concerns at the time, from the Right, see Martha Derthick and Andy Rotherham, "Obama's NCLB Waivers: Are They Necessary or Illegal?" *Education Next* 12, no. 2 (November 2011), https://www.educationnext.org/obamas-nclb-waivers-are-they-necessary-or-illegal/. For concerns on the Left, see Monty Neill, "Obama's NCLB Waivers: Do Flaws Outweigh Benefits?" *Washington Post*, September 26, 2011, https://www.washingtonpost.com/blogs/answer-sheet/post/obamas-nclb-waivers-do-flaws-outweigh-benefits/2011/09/25/gIQA5TgVxK_blog.html. Regarding impact in practical terms, see Winnie Hu, "10 States Are Given Waivers from Education Law," *New York Times*, February 10, 2012, A13. Also see Andrew Sault, Andrew McEachin, and Lance D. Fusarelli, "Waivering as Governance: Federalism during the Obama Administration," *Educational Researcher* 45, no. 6 (August–September 2016): 358–366.

62 The quote is from Morgan S. Polikoff, Andrew J. McEachin, Stephani L. Wrabel, and Matthew Duque, "The Waive of the Future? School Accountability in the Waiver Era," *Educational Researcher* 43, no. 1 (January–February 2014): 45; Jeremy Ayers and Isabel Owen, "No Child Left Behind Waivers: Promising Ideas from Second Round Applications," Center for American Progress, July 27, 2012, https://www.americanprogress.org/issues/education-k-12/reports/2012/07/27/11815/no-child-left-behind-waivers/. On the extent of this programmatic shift, see, for instance, U.S. Department of Education, "Obama Administration Approves NCLB Flexibility Request for Illinois: Total of 43 States, Washington, D.C. and Puerto Rico Now Approved for Waivers," press release, April 18, 2014, https://www.ed.gov/news/press-releases/obama-administration-approves-nclb-flexibility-request-illinois. On implications for next steps, see Elizabeth Mann Levesque, "The Long-Term Impact of NCLB Waivers on ESEA Renewal," Brown Center Chalkboard, December 10, 2015, https://www.brookings.edu/blog/brown-center-chalkboard/2015/12/10/the-long-term-impact-of-nclb-waivers-on-esea-renewal/. On the origins, support for, and opposition to the Common Core, see

Lorraine M. McDonnell and M. Stephen Weatherford, "Organized Interests and the Common Core," *Educational Researcher* 42, no. 9 (November 2013): 488–497; Lorraine M. McDonnell, "Educational Accountability and Policy Feedback," *Educational Policy* 27, no. 2 (March–April 2013): 170–189; Morgan S. Polikoff, Tenice Hardaway, Julie A. Marsh, and David N. Plank, "Who Is Opposed to Common Core and Why?" *Educational Researcher* 45, no. 4 (May 2016): 263–266; Michael A. Szolowicz, "Putting Political Spectacle to Work: Understanding Local Resistance to the Common Core," *Education Policy Analysis Archives* 24 (2016), https://epaa.asu.edu/index.php/epaa/article/view/2521; and Yinying Wang, "The Social Networks and Paradoxes of the Opt-Out Movement Amid the Common Core State Standards Implementation: The Case of New York," *Education Policy Analysis Archives* 25 (2017), https://epaa.asu.edu/index.php/epaa/article/view /2757. For complaints about weak state standards see Lydia Gensheimer, "Experts Push Lawmakers to Support States' Effort on Education Standards," *Congressional Quarterly Today*, April 29, 2009.

63 Sam Dillon, "After Criticism, the Administration Is Praised for Final Rules on Education Grants," *New York Times*, November 12, 2009, A20.

64 Henry I. Braun, *Using Student Progress to Evaluate Teachers: A Primer on Value-Added Models* (Policy Information Center, Educational Testing Service, 2005), 15; J. R. Lockwood, Daniel F. McCaffrey, Laura S. Hamilton, Brian Stecher, Vi-Nhuan Le, and Jose Felipe Martinez, "The Sensitivity of Value-Added Teacher Effect Estimates to Different Mathematics Achievement Measures," *Journal of Educational Measurement* 44, no. 1 (Spring 2007): 47–67; Daniel Koretz, "A Measured Approach: Value-Added Models Are a Promising Improvement, but No One Measure Can Evaluate Teacher Performance," *American Educator* 32, no. 3 (Fall 2008): 18–39; Steven Glazerman, Dan Goldhaber, Susanna Loeb, Stephen Raudenbush, Douglas Staiger, and Grover J. "Russ" Whitehurst, "Evaluating Teachers: The Important Role of Value-Added," Brown Center on Education Policy at Brookings, November 17, 2010, https://www .brookings.edu/research/evaluating-teachers-the-important-role-of-value-added/; National Research Council, *Getting Value Out of Value-Added: Report of a Workshop* (Washington, DC: National Academies Press, 2010), https://doi.org /10.17226/12820; Douglas N. Harris and Carolyn D. Herrington, "The Use of Teacher Value-Added Measures in Schools: New Evidence, Unanswered Questions, and Future Prospects," *Educational Researcher* 44, no. 2 (March 2015): 71–76; Audrey Amrein-Beardsley, Margarita Pivovarova, and Tray Geiger, "Value-Added Models: What the Experts Say," *Phi Delta Kappan* (October 1, 2016), https://kappanonline.org/value-added-models-what-the -experts-say/; Linda Darling-Hammond, "Can Value Added Add Value to Teacher Evaluation?" *Educational Researcher*. 44, no. 2 (March 2015): 132–137; Audrey Amrein-Beardsley and Kevin Close, "Teacher-Level Value-Added Models on Trial: Empirical and Pragmatic Issues of Concern across Five Court Cases," *Educational Policy* 35, no. 6 (2019).

65 Catherine Gewertz, "The Common Core Explained," *Education Week*, September 30, 2015, https://www.edweek.org/teaching-learning/the-common-core -explained/2015/09. Also see Libby Nelson, "Everything You Need to Know about the Common Core," *Vox*, May 13, 2015, https://www.vox.com/2014/10/7 /18088680/common-core; and "Common Core State Standards Initiative," Council of Chief State School Officers, 2020, http://www.corestandards.org/.

66 Valerie Strauss, "Obama's Real Education Legacy: Common Core, Testing, Charter Schools," *Washington Post*, October 21, 2016, https://www .washingtonpost.com/news/answer-sheet/wp/2016/10/21/obamas-real-education -legacy-common-core-testing-charter-schools/; David Whitman, "The Surprising Roots of the Common Core: How Conservatives Gave Rise to 'Obamacore,'" Brown Center on Education Policy, September 2015, https://www.brookings.edu /wp-content/uploads/2016/06/Surprising-Conservative-Roots-of-the-Common -Core_FINAL.pdf; Allie Bidwell, "The History of Common Core State Standards: What Some See As a Surprise Attack on States' Rights, Others Know As a Carefully Thought Out Education Reform," *U.S. News and World Report*, February 27, 2014, https://www.usnews.com/news/special-reports/articles/2014 /02/27/the-history-of-common-core-state-standards. Also see Ulrich Boser, Perpetual Baffour, and Steph Vela, *A Look at the Education Crisis: Tests, Standards, and the Future of American Education* (Washington, DC: Center for American Progress, 2016), 6–13, https://www.americanprogress.org/issues /education-k-12/reports/2016/01/26/129547/a-look-at-the-education-crisis/.

67 U.S. Department of Education, "Obama Administration Takes Action to Ensure Fewer and Better Tests for Students," press release, April 15, 2016, https://www.ed .gov/news/press-releases/obama-administration-takes-action-ensure-fewer-and -better-tests-students; Educational Testing Service (ETS), *The Road Ahead for State Assessments: What the Assessment Consortia Built, Why It Matters, and Emerging Options* (Princeton, NJ: Educational Testing Service, 2016), 3–6, 13, 17–29. On political controversy surrounding PARCC and the Common Core, see Janet D. Johnson and Brittany A. Richer, "'This is Against American Ideals': Rhode Island Teachers Respond to PARCC," *Teachers College Record*, October 14, 2015, https://www.tcrecord.org ID Number 18146, accessed November 6, 2022; "Adopt the PARCC Test: And Ignore the Political Noise," *Boston Globe*, October 19, 2015, A.8; and Patrick O'Donnell, "Ohio Dumps the PARCC Common Core Tests after Woeful First Year," *Cleveland Plain Dealer*, July 01, 2015, https://www.cleveland.com/metro/2015/06/ohio_dumps_the_parcc_common _core_tests_after_woeful_first_year.html#:~:text=Ohio%20dumps%20the%20 PARCC%20Common%20Core%20tests%20after%20woeful%20first%20year, -Updated%20Jan%2011&text=Ohio%20officially%20pulled%20out%20 of,just%20one%20year%20with%20PARCC. Regarding Smarter Balance, see Susan Tuz and Linda Conner Lambeck, "Controversy Abounds around Smarter Balance Assessment Consortium Tests," *Connecticut Post*, May 23, 2015, https:// www.ctpost.com/local/article/Controversy-abounds-around-Smarter-Balance -6283283.php.

68 Strauss, "Obama's Real Education Legacy"; Dana Goldstein, "After 10 Years of Hopes and Setbacks, What Happened to the Common Core?" *New York Times*, December 6, 2019, https://www.nytimes.com/2019/12/06/us/common-core.html; Will Ainsworth, "Opinion: Common Core Is a Failed, Obama-Era Relic That Must Come to a Quick and Immediate End," *Alabama Political Reporter*, March 22, 2019, https://www.alreporter.com/2019/03/22/opinion-common-core -is-a-failed-obama-era-relic-that-must-come-to-a-quick-and-immediate-end/; Valerie Strauss, "Leading Mathematician Debunks 'Value-Added,'" *Washington Post*, May 9, 2011, https://www.washingtonpost.com/blogs/answer-sheet/post /leading-mathematician-debunks-value-added/2011/05/08/AFb999UG_blog .html; Kevin Close and Audrey Amrein-Beardsley, "Learning from What Doesn't

Work in Teacher Evaluation," *Phi Delta Kappan* August 24, 2018, https://kappanonline.org/learning-from-what-doesnt-work-in-teacher-evaluation/; Jessica Levy, Martin Brunner, Ulrich Keller, and Antoine Fischbach, "Methodological Issues in Value-Added Modeling: An International Review from 26 Countries," *Educational Assessment, Evaluation and Accountability* 31 (2019): 257–287; Michael Winerip, "Evaluating New York Teachers, Perhaps the Numbers Do Lie," *New York Times*, March 6, 2011, https://www.nytimes.com/2011/03/07/education/07winerip.html; and Clarin Collins and Audrey Amrein-Beardsley, "Putting Growth and Value-Added Models on the Map: A National Overview," *Teachers College Record* 116 (2014): 1–32.

69 Kathryn P. Chapman, Lydia Ross, and Sherman Dorn, "Opting Out in the Empire State: A Geographic Analysis of Opting Out in New York, Spring 2015 & 2016," *Teachers College Record* 122, no. 2 (February 2020): 1–24; also see Oren Pizmony-Levy and Nancy Green Saraisky, executive summary in *Who Opts Out and Why? Results from a National Survey on Opting Out of Standardized Tests* (New York: Teachers College, Columbia University, 2016); Sarah Tully, "National Poll Shows Majority Oppose Common Core Standards," *EdSource*, August 2015, https://edsource.org/2015/national-poll-shows-most-oppose-common-core-standards/85212; Elizabeth A. Harris, "As New Testing Is Ushered In, Some Sit It Out," *New York Times*, March 2, 2015, A1; Elizabeth A. Harris, "20% of New York State Students Opted Out of Standardized Tests This Year," *New York Times*, August 12, 2015, https://www.nytimes.com/2015/08/13/nyregion/new-york-state-students-standardized-tests.html; Joanna Weiss, "Can the Tide Turn Against Testing?" *Boston Globe*, January 14, 2015, A11. On discussions about reauthorizing NCLB, see Christie Parsons and Lisa Mascaro, "Obama's Education Plan an Early Test of Civility," *Chicago Tribune*, February 8, 2011, D30. On earlier opt-out movements, see Carol DeMerle, "A Multi-State Political Process Analysis of the Anti-Testing Movement" (PhD diss., University of North Texas, 2006), ch. IV.

70 Julie Hirschfeld Davis, "President Obama Signs into Law a Rewrite of No Child Left Behind," *New York Times*, December 10, 2015, https://www.nytimes.com/2015/12/11/us/politics/president-obama-signs-into-law-a-rewrite-of-no-child-left-behind.html?action=click&module=RelatedCoverage&pgtype=Article&region=Footer; Alyson Klein, "The Every Student Succeeds Act: An ESSA Overview," *Education Week*, March 31, 2016, https://www.edweek.org/policy-politics/the-every-student-succeeds-act-an-essa-overview/2016/03; Debra L. Meibaum, *An Overview of the Every Student Succeeds Act* (Cayce, SC: Southeast Comprehensive Center of the American Institutes for Research, 2016), https://files.eric.ed.gov/fulltext/ED573536.pdf. On changing public opinion, see Adam Kernan-Schloss and Joshua P. Starr, "Testing Doesn't Measure Up for Americans: The 47th Annual PDK/Gallup Poll of the Public's Attitudes toward the Public Schools," *Phi Delta Kappan* 97, no. 1 (September 2015): K1–K3. Also see Leadership Conference on Civil and Human Rights, "Civil Rights Groups: 'We Oppose Anti-Testing Efforts,'" May 5, 2015, https://civilrights.org/2015/05/05/civil-rights-groups-we-oppose-anti-testing-efforts/. On deeper learning, see Linda Darling-Hammond, *Developing and Measuring Higher Order Skills: Models for State Performance Assessment Systems* (Washington, DC: Council of Chief State School Officers, 2017), 2–4.

71 Center for American Progress, "Release: With Test Season Approaching, Educators, Civil Rights, and Education Groups Launch a Testing Bill of Rights at

TestBetter.Org," press release, March 24, 2016, https://www.americanprogress.org
/press/release/2016/03/24/133751/release-with-test-season-approaching-educators
-civil-rights-and-education-groups-launch-a-testing-bill-of-rights-at-testbetter-org/.
As a point of comparison, see the *Code of Fair Testing Practices in Education
(Revised)* (Joint Committee on Testing Practices, Science Directorate, American
Psychological Association, 2004), https://www.apa.org/science/programs/testing
/fair-testing.pdf. On the problem of testing organizations complying with such
expectations, see William G. Harris, "The Challenges of Meeting the Standards:
A Perspective from the Test Publishing Community," *Educational Measurement:
Issues and Practice* 21, no. 3 (Fall 2006): 42–45; Lauress L. Wise, "Encouraging and
Supporting Compliance with Standards for Educational Tests," *Educational
Measurement: Issues and Practice* 21, no. 3 (Fall 2006): 51–53. For an insightful
summary of ESSA, see Daniel Koretz, *The Testing Charade: Pretending to Make
Schools Better* (Chicago: University of Chicago Press, 2017), 28–31.

72 Valerie Strauss, "Explaining Key Points of the New K-12 Education Law,"
Washington Post, January 21, 2016, https://www.washingtonpost.com/news
/answer-sheet/wp/2016/01/21/explaining-key-points-of-the-new-k-12-education
-law/; Valerie Strauss, "The Successor to No Child Left Behind Has, It Turns Out,
Big Problems of Its Own," *Washington Post*, December 7, 2015, https://www
.washingtonpost.com/news/answer-sheet/wp/2015/12/07/the-successor-to-no
-child-left-behind-has-it-turns-out-big-problems-of-its-own/. On making
improvements to accountability programs under ESSA, see Council of Chief State
School Officers, "Accountability Identification Is Only the Beginning: Monitoring and Evaluating Accountability Results and Implementation," 2018, https://eric
.ed.gov/?id=ED593496#:~:text=The%20passage%20of%20the%20
Every,development%20cycle%20for%20accountability%20systems.&text
=The%20correct%20identification%20of%20schools,deliver%20support%20
to%20local%20systems; Catherine Brown, Ulrich Boser, Scott Sargrad, and Max
Marchitello, *Implementing the Every Student Succeeds Act: Toward a Coherent,
Aligned Assessment System* (Washington, DC: Center for American Progress,
2016), https://www.americanprogress.org/issues/education-k-12/reports/2016/01
/29/130115/implementing-the-every-student-succeeds-act/; Linda Darling-
Hammond, Soung Bae, Channa M. Cook-Harvey, Livia Lam, Charmaine Mercer,
Anne Podolsky, and Elizabeth Leisy Stosich, *Pathways to New Accountability
through the Every Student Succeeds Act* (Palo Alto, CA: Learning Policy Institute,
2016), http://learningpolicyinstitute.org/our-work/publications-resources
/pathways-new-accountability-every-student-succeeds-act; and Channa M.
Cook-Harvey, Linda Darling-Hammond, Livia Lam, Charmaine Mercer, and
Martens Roc, *Equity and ESSA: Leveraging Educational Opportunity through the
Every Student Succeeds Act* (Palo Alto, CA: Learning Policy Institute, 2016), 1–5.
Regarding performance-based assessment, see Elizabeth Leisy Stosich, Jon Snyder,
and Katie Wilczak, "How Do States Integrate Performance Assessment in Their
Systems of Assessment?" *Education Policy Analysis Archives* 26, no. 13 (2018),
http://dx.doi.org/10.14507/epaa.26.2906. For a more critical perspective, see
Keisha Mcintosh Allen, Julius Davis, Renee L. Garraway, and Janeula M. Burt,
"Every Student Succeeds (Except for Black Males) Act," *Teachers College Record*
120, no. 3 (2018). On neoliberalism in Obama's approach to educational reform,
see David Hursh, "Explaining Obama: The Continuation of Free Market Policies

in Education and the Economy," *Journal of Inquiry & Action in Education* 4, no.1 (2011) https://digitalcommons.buffalostate.edu/jiae/vol4/iss1/2.

73 There was no shortage of criticism of NCLB at the time, much of which raised points discussed herein. See, for instance, Lily Eskelsen García and Otha Thornton, "'No Child Left Behind' Has Failed," *Washington Post*, February 13, 2015, https://www.washingtonpost.com/opinions/no-child-has-failed/2015/02/13/8d619026-b2f8-11e4-827f-93f454140e2b_story.html; Abby Jackson, "3 Big Ways No Child Left Behind Failed," *Business Insider*, March 25, 2015, https://www.businessinsider.com/heres-what-no-child-left-behind-got-wrong-2015-3; "No Child Left Behind Has Been Unsuccessful, Says Bipartisan Report," *Guardian*, August 9, 2016, https://www.theguardian.com/education/2016/aug/09/no-child-left-behind-bill-unsuccessful-report-us-schools; Neal McCluskey, "Has No Child Left Behind Worked?" (2015), accessed May 10, 2020, https://www.cato.org/testimony/has-no-child-left-behind-worked. Jack Jennings, interview by author, April 6, 2020.

74 Rhodes, *Education in Politics*, ch. 6 and conclusion. Also see Frederick M. Hess and Michael Q. McShane, "The Happy (and Not So Happy) Accidents of Bush–Obama School Reform," *Phi Delta Kappan* 100, no. 4 (December 2018–January 2019): 31–35. On polls, see Kernan-Schloss and Starr, "Testing."

75 Jaekyung Lee and Todd Reeves, "Revisiting the Impact of NCLB High-Stakes School Accountability, Capacity, and Resources: State NAEP 1990–2009 Reading and Math," *Educational Evaluation and Policy Analysis* 34, no. 2 (June 2012): 209–231; and Achieve, "State Test Results"; Andrew Ho, interview by author, February 27, 2020. On unresolved questions regarding test validity during the NCLB era, see Deborah L. Bandalos, Amanda E. Ferster, Susan L. Davis, and Karen M. Samulson, "Validity Arguments for High Stakes Testing and Accountability Systems," in *High-Stakes Testing in Education: Science and Practice in K-12 Settings*, ed. James A. Bovaird, Kurt F. Geisinger, and Chad W. Buckendakl (Washington, DC: American Psychological Association, 2012), 155–175.

76 For a clear example of this, see Daniel M. Koretz, Robert L. Linn, Stephen B. Dunbar, and Lorrie A. Shepard, "The Effects of High-Stakes Testing on Achievement: Preliminary Findings about Generalization across Tests" (Paper presented at the Annual Meetings of the American Educational Research Association, Chicago, April 3–7, 1991; and the National Council on Measurement in Education, Chicago, April 4–6, 1991), https://files.eric.ed.gov/fulltext/ED340730.pdf. Daniel Koretz, interview by author, February 27, 2020; Lorraine McDonnell, interview by author, September 8, 2020.

Conclusion

1 Lorraine M. McDonnell, introduction to *Politics, Persuasion, and Educational Testing* (Cambridge, MA: Harvard University Press, 2004); Lorraine M. McDonnell, "Assessment Policy as Persuasion and Regulation," *American Journal of Education* 102, no. 4 (August 1994): 394–420; Lorraine McDonnell, interview by author, September 8, 2020. For a classic example of the human capital argument, see Eric A. Hanushek, "Testing, Accountability, and the American Economy," *Annals of the American Academy of Social and Political Science* 683 (May 2019): 110–128.

2 On public opinion regarding tests and teachers, see Lorraine M. McDonnell, "Accountability As Seen through a Political Lens," in *Making Sense of Test-Based Accountability in Education*, ed. Laura S. Hamilton, Brian M. Stecher, and Stephen P. Klein (Santa Monica, CA: RAND, 2002), 109–111; Jay P. Heubert and Robert M. Hauser, *High Stakes: Testing for Tracking, Promotion, and Graduation* (Washington, DC: National Academies Press, 1999), 43–45, https://doi.org/10 .17226/6336.unions. Regarding control of education, see Rebecca Jacobsen and Andrew Saultz, "Trends: Who Should Control Education?" *Public Opinion Quarterly* 76, no. 2 (Summer 2012): 379–390. For a more recent perspective, see Flypaper, "(What) Do Americans Really Think about Education," Thomas B. Fordham Institute, October 29, 2014, available at https://fordhaminstitute.org /national/commentary/what-do-americans-really-think-about-education; and Frederick M. Hess and Michael Q. McShane, "The Happy (and Not So Happy) Accidents of Bush–Obama School Reform," *Phi Delta Kappan* 100, no. 4 (December 2018–January 2019): 31–35. On the new focus on outcomes, see Elizabeth Popp Berman, *Thinking like an Economist: How Efficiency Replaced Equality in U.S. Public Policy* (Princeton, NJ: Princeton University Press, 2022), chs. 3–5. For a discussion of how assessments can affect teacher perceptions of student ability, see Amanda Datnow, Bailey Choi, Vicki Park, and Elise St. John, "Teacher Talk about Student Ability and Achievement in the Era of Data-Driven Decision Making," *Teachers College Record* 120, no. 4 (2018): 1–34. And regarding the declining popularity of testing, see James D. Kirylo, "The Opt-Out Movement and the Power of Parents," *Phi Delta Kappan* 99, no. 8 (May 2018): 36–40.

3 An overview of this process is provided in Lorrie A. Shepard, "A Brief History of Accountability Testing, 1965–2007," in *The Future of Test-Based Educational Accountability*, ed. Katherine E. Ryan and Lorrie A Shepard (New York: Routledge, 2008), 25–46. Also see Maris A. Vinovskis, "History of Testing in the United States: PK–12 Education," *ANNALS of the American Academy of Political and Social Science* 683, no. 1 (May 2019): 22–37; and Robert L. Linn, "Assessments and Accountability," *Educational Researcher* 29, no. 2 (March 2000): 4–16.

4 On the relationship of housing values to school test scores, see Abbigail J. Chiodo, Rubén Hernández-Murillo, and Michael T. Owyang, "Nonlinear Effects of School Quality on House Prices," *Federal Reserve Bank of St. Louis Review* 92, no. 3 (May–June 2010): 185–204. Also see Quoctrung Bui and Conor Dougherty, "Good Schools, Affordable Homes: Finding Suburban Sweet Spots," *New York Times*, March 30, 2017, https://www.nytimes.com/interactive/2017/03/30/upshot /good-schools-affordable-homes-suburban-sweet-spots.html.

5 For a summary of developments regarding racial bias in standardized tests, see Christopher Jencks, "Racial Bias in Testing," in *The Black–White Test Score Gap*, ed. Christopher Jencks and Meredith Phillips (Washington, DC: Brookings Institution, 1998), 55–85. On measuring potential bias, see Brian E. Clauser and Kathleen M. Mazor, "Using Statistical Procedures to Identify Differentially Functioning Test Items," *Educational Measurement: Issues and Practice* 17, no. 1 (Spring 1998): 31–44. For a somewhat different perspective, see Kathleen Banks, "A Comprehensive Framework for Evaluating Hypotheses about Cultural Bias in Educational Testing," *Applied Measurement in Education* 19, no. 2 (2006): 115–132. For a general statement dismissing such concerns, see Robert T. Brown, Cecil R. Reynolds, and Jean S. Whitaker, "Bias in Mental Testing since *Bias in Mental Testing*," *School Psychology Quarterly* 14, no. 3 (1999): 208–238. On the industry

response to criticisms, reflected in the evolution of testing standards, see Wayne J. Camara and Suzanne Lane, "A Historical Perspective and Current Views on the Standards for Educational and Psychological Testing," *Educational Measurement: Issues and Practice* 25, no. 3 (Fall 2006): 35–41.

6 Christopher Jencks and Meredith Phillips, eds., "The Black–White Test Score Gap: An Introduction," in Jencks and Phillips, *Black–White Test*, 1–51. For a more recent discussion of psychological factors potentially affecting racial differences in tests scores, see James Soland, "Are Achievement Gap Estimates Biased by Differential Student Test Effort? Putting an Important Policy Metric to the Test," *Teachers College Record* 120, no. 12 (December 2018): 1–26.

7 For an overview of these developments, see Benjamin M. Superfine, *Equality in Education Law and Policy, 1954–2010* (New York: Cambridge University Press, 2013), ch. 5.

8 Superfine, *Equality in Education*; Shepard, "Brief History," 35–42.

9 FairTest, "Testing Our Children: Introduction," 1997, https://www.fairtest.org /testing-our-children-introduction. Also see Monty Neill, Lisa Guisbond, and Bob Schaeffer, *Failing Our Children: How "No Child Left Behind" Undermines Quality and Equity in Education and an Accountability Model That Supports School Improvement* (Cambridge, MA: FairTest, 2004). On alternative forms of assessment, see Robert L. Linn, "Educational Assessment: Expanded Expectations and Challenges," *Educational Evaluation and Policy Analysis* 15, no. 1 (Spring, 1993): 1–16.

10 Winnie Hu and Kyle Spencer, "Your 4-Year-Old Scored a 95? Better Luck Next Time," *New York Times*, September 25, 2013, https://www.nytimes.com/2013/09 /26/education/on-entrance-test-whose-days-appear-numbered-a-95-just-wasnt -good-enough.html.

11 Anemona Hartocollis, "The Nation: Grade Inflation; New Math: No One Is Below Average," *New York Times*, June 20, 1999, https://www.nytimes.com/1999 /06/20/weekinreview/the-nation-grade-inflation-new-math-no-one-is-below -average.html.

12 Daniel Koretz, *The Testing Charade: Pretending to Make Schools Better* (Chicago: University of Chicago Press, 2017), ch. 5; Lorraine MacDonnell, interview by author, September 8, 2020.

13 Koretz, *Testing Charade*, ch. 11; Robert L. Linn, *Test-Based Accountability* (Gordon Commission, Educational Testing Service, 2012), https://www.ets.org /Media/Research/pdf/linn_test_based_accountability.pdf; Daniel Koretz, interview by author, February 27, 2020. On validity questions concerning NAEP, see David Grissmer, *Estimating Effects of Non-Participation on State NAEP Scores Using Empirical Methods* (Palo Alto, CA: American Institutes for Research, 2007), 1–4; and for international comparisons, see Gary W. Phillips, *International Benchmarking: State and National Education Performance Standards* (Palo Alto, CA: American Institutes for Research, 2014), 1–14. For cautions regarding international comparisons, see Judith D. Singer, Henry I. Braun, and Naomi Chudowsky, eds., *International Education Assessments: Cautions, Conundrums, and Common Sense* (Washington, DC: National Academy of Education, 2018), 69–78. On public opinion, see Adam Kernan-Schloss and Joshua P. Starr, "Testing Doesn't Measure Up for Americans: The 47th Annual PDK/Gallup Poll of the Public's Attitudes toward the Public Schools," *Phi Delta Kappan* 97, no. 1 (September 2015): K1–K3.

14 John F. Jennings, *Why National Standards and Tests? Politics and the Quest for Better Schools* (Thousand Oaks, CA: Sage, 1998), chs. 1 and 2; Jesse H. Rhodes, *An Education in Politics: The Origins and Evolution of No Child Left Behind* (Ithaca, NY: Cornell University Press, 2012), chs. 3, 4, and 5; Christopher Cross, *Political Education: National Policy Comes of Age* (New York: Teachers College Press, 2010), chs. 6, 7, and 8.

15 Scott Baker, Anthony Myers, and Brittany Vasquez, "Desegregation, Accountability, and Equality: North Carolina and the Nation, 1971–2002," *Education Policy Analysis Archives* 22, no. 117 (December 2014): 1–28; Superfine, *Equality in Education*, ch. 5; Vinovskis, "History of Testing," 30. On the continuing controversy over high school exit exams, see Center on Education Policy, *State High School Exit Exams: A Challenging Year* (Washington, DC: Center on Education Policy, 2006), 1–6.

16 Maris A. Vinovskis, *From A Nation at Risk to No Child Left Behind: National Education Goals and the Creation of Federal Education Policy* (New York: Teachers College Press, 2009), chs. 3–6; Cross, *Political Education*, chs. 5 and 6 (with Paul Hanna).

17 Rhodes, *Education in Politics*, ch. 5; Patrick J. McGuinn, *No Child Left Behind and the Transformation of Federal Education Policy, 1965–2005* (Lawrence: University Press of Kansas, 2006), chs. 8 and 9.

18 Andrew Saultz, Andrew McEachin, and Lance D. Fusarelli, "Waivering as Governance: Federalism during the Obama Administration," *Educational Researcher* 45, no. 6 (August–September 2016): 358–366; "The Every Student Succeeds Act: Explained," *Education Week*, December 8, 2015, https://www .edweek.org/policy-politics/the-every-student-succeeds-act-explained/2015/12. For a statement in favor of standards-based reform in 2016, while acknowledging problems, see Ulrich Boser, Perpetual Baffour, and Steph Vela, *A Look at the Education Crisis: Tests, Standards, and the Future of American Education* (Washington, DC: Center for American Progress, 2016), 1–6. On neoliberalism, see Gary Gerstle, *The Rise and Fall of the Neoliberal Order: America and the World in the Free Market Era* (New York: Oxford University Press, 2022), pt. 2.

19 Erica L. Green, "Trump Orders Review of Education Policies to Strengthen Local Control," *New York Times*, April 26, 2017, https://www.nytimes.com/2017/04/26 /us/politics/trump-education-policy-review.html?auth=login-email&login =email.

20 Jack Schneider and Jennifer C. Berkshire, "How DeVos May Have Started a Counterrevolution in Education," *New York Times*, December 1, 2020, https:// www.nytimes.com/2020/12/01/opinion/betsy-devos-education.html.

21 Katherine Stewart, "DeVos and God's Plan for Schools," *New York Times*, December 13, 2016, A31; Erica L. Green, "States Surprised to Face Stickler on School Law," *New York Times*, July 8, 2017, A1; Erica L. Green, "Charter Schools in Surprise Political Fight as Trump and Democrats Turn Away," *New York Times*, February 25, 2020, https://www.nytimes.com/2020/02/25/us/politics/charter -schools-trump-devos-democrats.html?action=click&module =RelatedLinks&pgtype=Article.

22 Joseph Williams, "Why Some Black Leaders Aren't Down with Opting Out of Standardized Testing," Takepart, April 6, 2016, http://www.takepart.com/article /2016/04/06/black-leaders-not-down-with-opt-out-standardized-testing; Rann Miller, "The Anti-Black Intellectual Hierarchy Built by Standardized Testing

Needs to Come Down," RaceBaitr, January 21, 2020, https://racebaitr.com/2020
/01/21/the-anti-black-intellectual-hierarchy-built-by-standardized-testing-needs
-to-come-down/; "Civil Rights Groups: 'We Oppose Anti-Testing Efforts,'"
Leadership Conference on Civil and Human Rights, May 5, 2015, https://
civilrights.org/2015/05/05/civil-rights-groups-we-oppose-anti-testing-efforts/.

23 Lily Zheng, "We're Entering the Age of Corporate Social Justice," *Harvard
Business Review*, June 15, 2020, https://hbr.org/2020/06/were-entering-the-age-of
-corporate-social-justice; Porter Novelli, "73 Percent of Business Executives Agree
Companies Have More Responsibility Than Ever Before to Take Stands on Social
Justice Issues, According to Research by Porter Novella," Cision PR Newswire,
September 17, 2020, https://www.prnewswire.com/news-releases/73-percent-of
-business-executives-agree-companies-have-more-responsibility-than-ever-before
-to-take-stands-on-social-justice-issues-according-to-research-by-porter-novella
-301133383.html.

24 On the limited scale of this movement, even in New York where it is quite active,
see Kyle Spencer, "Some Parents Oppose Standardized Testing on Principle, but
Not in Practice," *New York Times*, April 13, 2015, https://www.nytimes.com/2015
/04/14/nyregion/despite-opposing-standardized-testing-many-new-york-parents
-and-students-opt-in.html.

25 Valerie Strauss, "Diane Ravitch to Obama: 'I Will Never Understand Why You
Decided to Align Your Education Policy with That of George W. Bush,'"
Washington Post, June 13, 2016, https://www.washingtonpost.com/news/answer
-sheet/wp/2016/06/13/diane-ravitch-to-obama-i-will-never-understand-why-you
-decided-to-align-your-education-policy-with-that-of-george-w-bush/. For
discussion of recent procedures regarding DIF, see Rebecca Zwick, *A Review of
ETS Differential Item Functioning Assessment Procedures: Flagging Rules,
Minimum Sample Size Requirements, and Criterion Refinement* (Princeton, NJ:
Educational Testing Service, Research Report ETS RR-12-08, May 2012), 22–25.

26 On setting proficiency levels, see Kurt F. Geisinger and Carina M. McCormick,
"Adopting Cut Scores: Post-Standard-Setting Panel Considerations for Decision
Makers," *Educational Measurement: Issues and Practice* 29, No. 1 (Spring 2010):
38–44.

27 Ibram X. Kendi, "Why the Academic Achievement Gap Is a Racist Idea," Black
Perspectives, October 20, 2016, https://www.aaihs.org/why-the-academic
-achievement-gap-is-a-racist-idea/. On confounding factors, see Nataliya Bragin-
sky, "Not an 'Achievement Gap,' a Racial Capitalist Chasm," LPE Project,
November 18, 2020, https://lpeproject.org/blog/not-an-achievement-gap-a-racial
-capitalist-chasm/. For a more somewhat balanced perspective, see Gloria
Ladson-Billings, "Pushing Past the Achievement Gap: An Essay on the Language
of Deficit," *Journal of Negro Education* 76, no. 3 (Summer 2007): 316–323.

28 Daniel Koretz, interview by author, February 27, 2020.

29 On the effect of background factors on tests, see National Academies of Sciences,
Engineering, and Medicine, *Monitoring Educational Equity* (Washington, DC:
National Academies Press, 2019), chs. 3, 4, and 5, https://doi.org/10.17226/25389.
Also see Jeanne M. Powers, Gustavo E. Fischman, and David C. Berliner,
"Making the Visible Invisible: Willful Ignorance of Poverty and Social Inequali-
ties in the Research–Policy Nexus," *Review of Research in Education* 40
(March 2016): 744–776; Ezekiel J. Dixon-Román, Howard T. Everson, and
John J. McArdle, "Race, Poverty and SAT Scores: Modeling the Influences of

Family Income on Black and White High School Students' SAT Performance," *Teachers College Record* 115, no. 4 (April 2013); Eric Grodsky, John Robert Warren, and Erika Felts, "Testing and Social Stratification in American Education," *Annual Review of Sociology* 34 (2008): 385–404; and Gerald W. Bracey, "Back to Coleman?" *Phi Delta Kappan* 80, no. 1 (September 1998): 88–89.

30 James J. Heckman, Jora Stixrud, and Sergio Urzua, "The Effects of Cognitive and Noncognitive Abilities on Labor Market Outcomes and Social Behavior," *Journal of Labor Economics* 24, no. 3 (2006): 411–482; Camille A. Farrington, David W. Johnson, Melissa Roderick, Elaine Allensworth, Jenny Nagaoka, Nicole Williams Beechum and Tasha Seneca Keyes, *Teaching Adolescents to Become Learners: The Role of Noncognitive Factors in Shaping School Performance: A Critical Literature Review* (Chicago: University of Chicago Consortium on Chicago School Research, 2012), ch. 9. Also see Gordon Cawelti, "The Side Effects of NCLB," *Educational Leadership* 64, no. 3 (November 2006): 64–68. On history instruction, see Tina L. Heafner and Paul G. Fitchett, "An Opportunity to Learn US History: What NAEP Data Suggest Regarding the Opportunity Gap," *High School Journal* 98, no. 3 (Spring 2015): 226–249.

31 On positives and negatives of the Bush–Obama reform years, see Hess and McShane, "Happy," 31–35.

32 On summer learning loss, see David M. Quinn and Morgan Polikoff, "Summer Learning Loss: What Is It, and What Can We Do about It?" Brookings, September 14, 2017, https://www.brookings.edu/research/summer-learning-loss-what-is -it-and-what-can-we-do-about-it/. For a somewhat different perspective, see Paul T. von Hippel, "Is Summer Learning Loss Real?" *Education Next* 19, no. 4 (Fall 2019), https://www.educationnext.org/is-summer-learning-loss-real-how-i -lost-faith-education-research-results/. On the effects of mobility on urban students, see Richard O. Welsh, "School Hopscotch: A Comprehensive Review of K-12 Student Mobility in the United States," *Review of Educational Research* 87, no. 3 (June 2017): 475–511.

33 Allison C. Atteberry and Andrew J. McEachin, "Not Where You Start, but How Much You Grow: An Addendum to the Coleman Report," *Educational Researcher* 49, no. 9 (December 2020): 678–685. On the beneficial impact of additional resources on test score performance in urban schools, see Christian Fischer, Barry Fishman, Abigail Jurist Levy, Arthur Eisenkraft, Christopher Dede, Frances Lawrenz, Yueming Jia, Janna Fuccillo Kook, Kim Frumin, and Ayana McCoy, "When Do Students in Low-SES Schools Perform Better-Than-Expected on a High-Stakes Test? Analyzing School, Teacher, Teaching, and Professional Development Characteristics," *Urban Education* 55, no. 1 (October 2016): 1–35.

34 Stephen Sireci, "Want to Understand Your Child's Test Scores? Here's What to Ignore," *Conversation*, September 29, 2016, https://theconversation.com/want-to -understand-your-childs-test-scores-heres-what-to-ignore-62155.

35 Richard F. Elmore, *School Reform from the Inside Out: Policy, Practice, and Performance* (Cambridge, MA: Harvard Education Press, 2004), chs. 1 and 2; Matthew Ronfeldt, Susanna Owens Farmer, Kiel McQueen and Jason A. Grissom, "Teacher Collaboration in Instructional Teams and Student Achievement," *American Educational Research Journal* 52, no. 3 (June 2015): 475–514; and Anthony S. Bryk, Penny Bender Sebring, Elaine Allensworth, Stuart Luppescu, and John Q. Easton, *Organizing Schools for Improvement: Lessons from Chicago* (Chicago: University of Chicago Press, 2010), ch. 4.

36   Linn, "Assessments and Accountability," 15. For a more fully elaborated discussion
     of these points, see Koretz, *Testing Charade*, ch. 13. On matrix sampling, see
     Ruth A. Childs and Andrew P. Jaciw, *Matrix Sampling of Test Items* (Washington,
     DC: ERIC Clearinghouse on Assessment and Evaluation, 2003), https://www
     .ericdigests.org/2005-1/matrix.htm; John Poggio, interview by author, Novem-
     ber 1, 2019; Vivekandan Kumar and David Boulanger, "Explainable Automated
     Essay Scoring: Deep Learning Really Has Pedagogical Value," *Frontiers in
     Education* 5 (2020), https://doi.org/10.3389/feduc.2020.572367. Also see John
     Gardner and Michael O'Leary, "Artificial Intelligence in Educational Assessment:
     'Breakthrough? Or Buncombe and Ballyhoo?'" *Journal of Computer Assisted
     Learning* 35, no. 5 (2021): 1207–1216.

37   Elmore, *School Reform*, ch. 1. On improvement science, see Anthony Bryk,
     introduction to *Improvement in Action: Advancing Quality in America's Schools*
     (Cambridge, MA: Harvard Education Press, 2020); and Anthony S. Bryk, Louis
     Gomez, Alicia Grunow, and Paul LeMahieu, *Learning to Improve: How America's
     Schools Can Get Better at Getting Better* (Cambridge, MA: Harvard Education
     Press, 2015), ch. 4. Regarding the recent use of performance assessment, see
     Elizabeth Leisy Stosich, Jon Snyder, and Katie Wilczak, "How Do States Integrate
     Performance Assessment in Their Systems of Assessment?" *Education Policy
     Analysis Archives* 26, no. 13 (2018), http://dx.doi.org/10.14507/epaa.26.2906. Also
     see Robert J. Mislevy, "Advances in Measurement and Cognition," *Annals of the
     American Academy of Political and Social Science* 683 (May 2019): 164–182; and
     Issac I. Bejar, Robert J. Mislevy, Andre Rupp, and Mo Zhang, "Automated
     Scoring with Validity in Mind," in *Handbook of Cognition and Assessment*,
     ed. Andre Rupp and Jacqueline Leighton (Hoboken, NJ: Wiley-Blackwell, 2016),
     226–246. For a critique of machine scoring, see Jim Webber, "Toward an Artful
     Critique of Reform: Responding to Standards, Assessment, and Machine
     Scoring," *College Composition and Communication* 69, no. 1 (September 2017):
     118–145.

38   For a discussion of how assessment can contribute to growth, see Eva L. Baker and
     Edmund W. Gordon, "From the Assessment OF Education to the Assessment
     FOR Education: Policy and Futures," *Teachers College Record* 116, no. 11 (Novem-
     ber 2014). Also see Edmund W. Gordon, "Toward Assessment in the Service of
     Learning," *Educational Measurement: Issues and Practice* 39, no. 3 (Fall 2020):
     72–78; Ethan Hutt and Morgan S. Polikoff have suggested that certain types of
     information could make accountability more productive and perhaps even
     democratic, and reports on growth may assist such endeavors; see their article
     "Toward a Framework for Public Accountability in Education Reform," *Educa-
     tional Researcher* 49, no. 7 (October 2020): 503–511. There are yet other approaches
     that have been suggested, including the creation of a professional inspectorate to
     periodically visit and assess the work of schools, as suggested in Richard Roth-
     stein, Rebecca Jacobson, and Tamara Wilder, *Grading Education: Getting
     Accountability Right* (New York: Teachers College Press, 2008); or the more
     localized and somewhat more comprehensive approach represented by the
     Massachusetts Consortium for Innovative Educational Assessment, which
     features various measures of school quality and performance assessments to
     produce informative profiles of schools (for more on this see https://www.mciea
     .org/). Yet another example is offered by the New York Performance Standards
     Consortium, which has existed for more than two decades, representing schools in

New York City, Rochester, and Ithaca (found at http://www.performance assessment.org/). These types of accountability systems likely would be considerably more costly than conventional testing regimes, even those with multiple assessments, and would entail the problems with performance assessment described earlier. It is an open question whether they would be politically acceptable for large swaths of the American public that has grown accustomed to test-based accountability, and tends to equate assessment objectivity with standardized tests of one sort or another. For considerably more positive accounts of such approaches, see Jack Schneider, *Beyond Test Scores: A Better Way to Measure School Quality* (Cambridge, MA: Harvard University Press, 2017), chs. 3–6; and Deborah Meier and Matthew Knoester, *Beyond Testing: Seven Assessments of Students and Schools More Effective Than Standardized Tests* (New York: Teachers College Press, 2017), ch. 10.

39 Elmore, *School Reform*, ch. 1. On the effect of the pandemic and a call for sensible assessment policy, see National Academy of Education, *Educational Assessments in the COVID-19 Era and Beyond* (Washington, DC: National Academy of Education, 2021). For a vision of positive assessment policies, see Daniel Koretz, "Moving Beyond the Failure of Test-Based Accountability," *American Educator* (Winter 2017–2018): 22–26.

Index

Abt Associates, 19

accountability: alternative or authentic assessment, 92, 93–97; alternatives in Vermont, 95–96; America 2000 and national tests, 81–83; analysis of impact, 31–32; bias in test items, 42–44; Chicago ITBS exit exam, 88; Clinton administration and Goals 2000, 84–86; Clinton national test proposal, 86–88; controversy in California, 96–97; and criterion-based tests and MCT, 22–25; critical reports, 71–73, 90–92; *Debra P. v. Turlington,* 47–50; declining public support for, 130–134; definition, 1; development of higher standards, 75–77; development of national standards, 83–84; dilemmas of NCLB, 109–114; early history of, 4–7; early lessons from, 37; education summit, 65–67; ESSA, 121–122; federal court cases, 46–47; Florida origins, 25–27; focus on racial achievement gap, 53–56; *GI Forum v. Texas Education Authority,* 50–52; growth across states, 29–31; G.W. Bush and, 97–98, 101–104; impact of NCLB, 114–117; implementing NCLB, 106–109, 200n22; Lake Wobegone controversy, 73–74; measurement driven instruction, 70; National Governors Association and, 63; NCLB legislation, 105–106; NIE debate, 32–36; Obama policies, 117–121;

origins in 1970s, 18–21; political origins, 1–4, 128–130; problems with, 7–11; prospects for change, 134–136; Ralph Tyler critique, 28; recent history, 11–15; reform in Southern states, 67–69; reforms in Kentucky, 95; review panels for tests, 45–46; shifting focus away from accountability, 70; shortcomings and future of, 15–17; Texas "miracle," 97–99

achievement: criterion-based tests for, 22–25; debates about, 32–36; fairness questions and, 41–46; falling test scores, 59–60; James Coleman and, 20; Lake Wobegone controversy, 73–74; measurement reform ideas, 134–136; minority groups and, 12–13; NAEP, 20; national politics and, 13–15; *Nation at Risk, A,* and, 13; NCLB and, 102, 107–108, 114–117; Obama policies and, 117–120; political focus, 2; problems in determining, 4, 7–11, 128; racial achievement gap, 53–56; raising standards for, 75–77, 79–81, 83–84, 86–87, 94–99; state tests and, 66–67; stereotype threat and, 52–53; test origins, 6–7

achievement gap, racial, 12, 14–16, 28, 39, 52–57, 80, 89, 90, 98–99, 102–103, 105, 111, 121, 123, 127, 169n76; civil rights groups and, 39; DoDEA schools, 55; ESSA and, 130; NCLB and, 16, 114–115; urban-suburban, 70

About the Author

JOHN L. RURY is a professor emeritus of education at the University of Kansas. His research has focused on historical facets of education policy, metropolitan development, and social inequality. He has long-standing interests in urban history, racial inequity, and human development, along with reform at all levels of the education system.